The
Weaver's Knot

The Weaver's Knot

THE CONTRADICTIONS OF CLASS
STRUGGLE AND FAMILY SOLIDARITY
IN WESTERN FRANCE, 1750–1914

TESSIE P. LIU

Cornell University Press Ithaca, New York

First published 1994 by Cornell University Press.

Library of Congress Cataloging-in-Publication Data
Liu, Tessie P., 1955–
    The weaver's knot :   the contradictions of class struggle and
family solidarity in Western France, 1750–1914   /   Tessie P. Liu.
       p.   cm.
    Includes bibliographical references and index.
    ISBN 0-8014-2738-X (alk. paper).   ISBN 0-8014-8019-1 (alk. paper :
pbk.)
       1. Textile industry—France—Cholet—History. 2. Rural
industries—France—Cholet—History. 3. Weavers—France—Cholet—
History. 4. Textile workers—France—Cholet—History. 5. Cholet
(France)—Rural conditions. I. Title.
HD9865.F73C484   1994
338.4'7677'0094418—dc20   93-43802

Printed in the United States of America

  ⊖ The paper in this book meets the minimum requirements of the
American National Standard for Information Sciences—Permanence
of Paper for Printed Library Materials, ANSI Z39.48-1984.

For the memory of Liu Kwang-Hwa

Contents

Preface

When threads break during the weaving process, weavers retie the strands rather than abandon the cloth. Invisible to the untrained eye, such a knot must hold the tension in the weave so that the entire cloth remains strong and taut. In this book, I examine the struggles of the men and women in a hand-weaving community in western France to maintain the fabric of their society in the face of industrial capitalism. The weaver's knot is both an emblem of the strength of class and family ties and a concrete image of its contradictions. This knot reminds us that the opposing pulls of competing solidarities are ever present in human relationships and are rarely, if ever, resolved. For nearly a hundred years, weavers in the Pays des Mauges forestalled the process of mechanization in their region. Ultimately, they lost their battle for independence as small producers, but their struggles force us to reinterpret the empirical and theoretical significance of rural small-scale production in the history of industrialization.

My fascination with this story of resistance and with the many hidden histories of failed struggles has weathered periods of self-doubt about motivations in social history and the naiveté of social historians. Post-structuralist theorists, emphasizing the constructed nature of human subjectivity and gender identities, have destabilized the simple concepts of agency and action social historians once took as unproblematic. I have learned much from this discussion, but I remain captured by the power of that first flash of insight when, as an undergraduate, I read Vico and Marx and realized that their common belief that human beings create themselves and make their own histories had concrete implications for historians.

Although notions of "interest" and "self" are ultimately fictions enacted in the midst of contingencies, such inventions are central to people's will to act, even if their bravery rests on uncertain foundations. Historians may discover how authenticity is constituted discursively. In that process, we can point to the exclusions and the elisions. But we can do little to change the belief in true identities that underlies cultural practice. The capacity to act, no matter how ironic or tragic the result, is a precious source of human dignity and hope. However misguided and whatever the unintended consequences, such actions have made our world.

The encouragement and ideas of many friends and colleagues sustained me during this long project. My greatest thanks go to Louise Tilly, who taught me the importance of asking open-ended questions and the value of careful empirical work. As mentors, both Louise and Charles Tilly have shaped my expectations about the nature of scholarly communities. The group of professors, graduate students, and visiting scholars gathered every Sunday evening for the Collective Action–Social History seminars on Hill Street in Ann Arbor gave me an enduring taste for sustained cross-disciplinary exchanges. At an early stage of my work, Charles Bright, Jane Burbank, Frederick Cooper, Susan Crowell, and Michael Geyer provided the familial supports, the intellectual stimulation, and above all the wonderful nourishment that sustained me. I thank Michael for listening to these ideas in their roughest forms. My friends Nancy Horn, Irina Livezeanu, Karen Mason, Rebecca Reed, Amy Saldinger, Diane Scherer, Elizabeth Wood, and Judith Wyman helped me learn gender analysis and feminist politics in the academy. Ann McKernan provided invaluable information on the linen industry and could be counted on to listen endlessly to talk of yarn counts and crop rotation. William Sewell and Geoff Eley encouraged my progress and challenged me to think more broadly in terms of theory. I thank Bill especially for his continuing support and guidance. Our continuing discussions over the years have helped me find a different voice.

Grants from the Social Science Research Council, the Georges Lurcy Foundation, and a Bourse Chateaubriand from the French government funded my early research. The American Council of Learned Societies and a summer grant from the University of Arizona Foundation provided funds for summer research and a year's leave for completing this manuscript. I thank John Merriman and Christopher Johnson for initiating me into the secrets of the French archival system and Judith Coffin and Whitney Walton for their comradery in the bleak days in Paris. In Angers, I owe special gratitude to Mademoiselle Poirier-Coutansais and her staff for graciously making their archives and their collection a second home for me. I thank Douglas W. Schwartz and the School of American Research for generously aiding the completion of this project.

At crucial moments in refining the arguments in this book, I benefited greatly from informal discussions about gender and power relations with Karen Anderson and Hermann Rebel. My other close friends and colleagues at the University of Arizona—John Campbell, Colette Hyman, Beverly Parker, Virginia Scharff, Laura Tabili, Douglas Weiner, and Donald Weinstein—supported me in my first clumsy attempts to balance research and writing with the demands of teaching. I thank my colleagues at Northwestern University, who read this work when it was largely completed, for their confidence and endorsement.

This book could not have been written without Kenneth Dauber. Without consulting him, I turned the project into a family enterprise. Ken's intellectual presence throughout the book is an essential part of its strength. I thank him for being smart and for his passion for ideas and rigor. But such lofty thanks do not do justice to the many hours of concrete labor, the cooking, cleaning, childcare, and time lost from his own work, that this project and our life together have exacted. Finally, I thank An-Lin for bringing laughter to her parents and for introducing Madeline, Babar, and Curious George to the other characters who populate our lives.

TESSIE P. LIU

Evanston, Illinois

The
Weaver's Knot

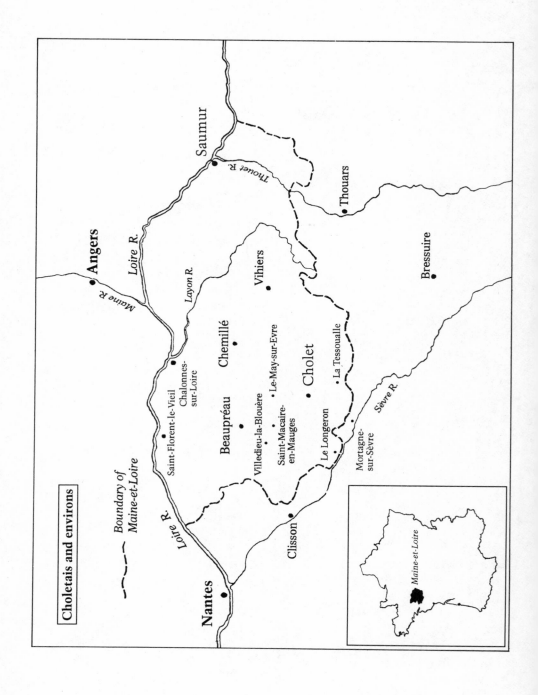

Choletais and environs

- - - Boundary of
Maine-et-Loire

Nantes

Angers

Saumur

Thouars

Bressuire

Loire R.

Maine R.

Layon R.

Thouet R.

Sèvre R.

Loire R.

Saint-Florent-le-Vieil

Chalonnes-
sur-Loire

Beaupréau

Chemillé

Vihiers

Villedieu-la-Blouère

Le-May-sur-Evre

Saint-Macaire-
en-Mauges

Cholet

La Tessoualle

Le Longeron

Mortagne-
sur-Sèvre

Clisson

Maine-et-Loire

I

Introduction

Industries and industrialization: these words conjure up smoke-stacks, factories, and mechanical power. We readily associate industries, one of the most profound social changes of the nineteenth century, with new mechanical inventions—gears and cranks, valves and pistons that work together to replicate human actions. And when we think of factories, we easily imagine them in overcrowded industrial cities populated by migrants from the countryside.

The subject of this book is industrialization. Yet the story I tell in the following pages focuses on the countryside, not the city, and examines the viability of hand labor and small-scale dispersed manufacturing in an economy increasingly dominated by factories and machine work. This story centers on the Pays des Mauges, a small region just south of the Loire valley in the old French province of Anjou. The Mauges is more formally the arrondissement of Cholet in the department of Maine-et-Loire. Cholet, the main commercial and administrative center, gives the region its modern name, the Choletais.

To French historians the Mauges is probably best known as the heart of the Vendée counterrevolutionary insurrection against the French Republic in 1793. The Mauges is also known, less notoriously, as an important center of light industries in western France. Dispersed rural manufacturing has a long history here. The tradition began with linen weaving for the Atlantic trade in the seventeenth and eighteenth centuries and continues today with clothing, shoes, electronic assembly, furniture making, and other forms of *confection* (ready-made consumer goods). The turbulent and contentious nature of this history, however, defies our normal associations with long and continued traditions.

In the eighteenth century the Mauges was the center of a flourishing international trade. But when local merchants, who had made their fortunes in this trade, tried in the early nineteenth century to mechanize and centralize the local textile industry, their efforts failed dismally. By 1850, threatened by a decade of continued unrest during which officials in Cholet regularly called in the army to protect property and to keep the peace, industrialists had withdrawn from cloth production. Through their collective resistance, handloom weavers brought the first phase of mechanization in this region to an abrupt end.

In the second half of the nineteenth century, cottage industries flourished despite a second and more successful move toward mechanization of textiles that began slowly in the 1860s and 1870s. Although handloom weavers mobilized in opposition, this time their ranks were fractured by divisive politics. Their inability to stop the mechanization did not, however, mean the demise of small-scale production. By the early twentieth century, the Choletais was one of two centers of linen production in France still known for its handmade products. At the same time, a different form of dispersed labor-intensive manufacturing had moved into the region, creating a new specialization in finished goods for urban consumer markets. Homework in shoemaking and in the garment trade became the new basis for a manufacturing economy and the source of the region's contemporary prosperity. At present, though the Choletais is one of the most important centers of the fashionable garment and shoe industry in France, the home of an impressive array of prestigious *prêt-à-porter* firms, its industrial landscape continues to be pastoral with small workshops and factories at rural crossroads and in small burgs. For much of the twentieth century, the majority of the manufacturing population worked in home workshops where familial ties dominated work roles.[1]

Regional histories like this are rare in the documented economic histories of modern European society. The dominant tendency, quite naturally, has been to focus on the most dramatic aspects of economic change in this era: the growth of factories and large-scale manufacturing. Conversely, studies of the countryside during industrialization focus primarily on agriculture. The assumption, even with the recent historiographic interest in the rural origins of industrial development, is that rural industries inevitably died out with

1. See Guy Minguet, *Naissance de l'Anjou industriel: Entreprise et société locale à Angers et dans le Choletais* (Paris: Éditions l'Harmattan, 1985).

the triumph of the factory system. With this demise and the departure of the manufacturing population, the countryside became exclusively agricultural. The continued presence of rural manufacturing in the Mauges throughout the period of industrialization, its relatively stable population (there was no rural exodus in the second half of the nineteenth century as in other regions of France[2]), and its prosperous family-based commercial farms distinguish this area from others whose histories are used to characterize French development.

The obscurity of regions like the Mauges in social and economic history should be one reason for our interest. Too often, historians and social scientists are drawn to spectacular successes and to equally spectacular failures. The Mauges, languishing on the periphery of industrial development, adapting to changes in the broader national and international economy and yet never fully escaping its marginal status, offers us important lessons as well.

But it is not only the gap in our existing knowledge that compels our attention. More important, the concepts and analytical vocabulary we must develop to understand this particular pattern of transformation challenge our received notions about the nature of social change and industrialization. The central puzzle I wish to unravel is the complex and changing relationship between dispersed and centralized ways of organizing production before and after mechanization.

But how does one incorporate experiences like those of the Choletais into the general history of European industrialization? Since the early 1970s, monographic studies like this one have emerged as an important part of the rewriting of this history. In this period, economic history has been thoroughly transformed under the impact of social history. Once, historians had a simple story to tell about the modern transformation of the European economy, one that focused on the twin revolutions in agriculture and manufacturing and the growth of cities. Although it was always clear that these transitions were not frictionless, scholars were confident nonetheless of their linear trajectory. Research in recent decades has chipped away at this master narrative. The addition of new characters (most notably, women workers), new subplots (like changes in the work process and workplace culture), and the challenges to basic categories (such as the notion of skill, the role of entrepreneurship, the historical constitution of markets) have strained the old plot. At present, the history of

2. See Abel Châtelain, "Évolution des densités de population en Anjou (1806–1936)," *Revue de géographie de Lyon* 31 (1956): 43–60.

industrialization is no longer one coherent story but a tale with multiple variants. Still, even as this new scholarship opens the way for innovative interpretations, in many cases the old habits of storytelling die hard. With some notable exceptions, researchers have been content with empirical modifications of the old accounts, leaving intact the underlying interpretative frameworks.[3]

In this and the following chapter, which serve as an introduction both to the region and to the central questions and interpretative frameworks of this book, I explain why, despite the expressed intention of prominent research projects (most notably the proto-industrialization debate), small-scale production as a subject has remained elusive and marginal to our basic understanding of industrialization. My analysis in these two chapters focuses on the failure of scholars to fully challenge the narrative explanation—that is, the logic that renders the events coherent and continuous—implicit in the "old" picture of industrialization they sought to revise. The result is that the persisting narrative logic of industrialization reins in the possibilities for new analysis. Even as small-scale production strains to become its own story, the mismatch between the intended subject and our received forms of narrative prevents that story from being told. The effect affirms the prejudice that the proper subject of studies of industrial society is the development of the factory system.

The Role of Small-Scale Production in French Economic History

Although the Mauges may seem unusual among case studies of French industrialization, a generation ago economic historians considered this pattern of development to be typical of what ailed the French economy during the nineteenth century.[4] Like the descriptions of the Choletais during the nineteenth century, descriptions of

3. For further elaborations of this argument, see Jonathan Zeitlin, "Les voies multiples de l'industrialisation," Le mouvement social 133 (October–December 1985): 27.

4. The literature on French industrialization in the nineteenth century is vast. For recent syntheses, consult Christian Le Bas, Histoire sociale des faits économiques: La France au XIXe siècle (Lyon: Presses universitaires de Lyon, 1984), and Patrick Fridenson and André Straus, Le capitalisme français XIXe–XXe siècle: Blocage et dynamisme d'une croissance (Paris: Fayard, 1987). Older studies remain helpful; see, for example, Claude Fohlen, "The Industrial Revolution in France 1700–1914," in The Emergence of Industrial Societies, vol. 4 pt. 1 of The Fontana Economic History of Europe, ed. Carlo M. Cippolla (London: Fontana, 1973), pp. 7–75, and Rondo E. Cameron, ed., Essays in French Economic History (Homewood, Ill.: Richard Irwin, 1970).

the French economy stressed the endurance of a preindustrial order. France remained rural. Urban growth was slow. In agriculture and manufacturing, production units were often small, relying on labor-using rather than labor-saving technology and employing primarily family members.

What puzzled scholars of this generation most was the pace of structural change. In the eighteenth century France was a strong mercantile nation, one of the commanding powers of Europe. Comparisons of wealth, population, and productive capacities which grew inevitably out of the political rivalries between France and the island nation across the channel often gave advantage to the French and not to the English. All the preconditions for modern industrial development existed in France, but it was England that took the commanding lead. By the early nineteenth century France lagged behind in technological innovations, and as the century progressed it fell farther behind.[5]

As economic historians refined their tools for measuring national economic performance after the Second World War, the puzzle of French development was given a more precise contour. In the 1950s and early 1960s, the notion of an industrial "take-off"—a measurable accleration of economic growth leading to sustained high growth rates—had replaced older descriptive metaphors such as "Industrial Revolution."[6] Measured against the "take-off" model, the French economy performed poorly. Carefully constructed time series charting the growth of the French economy during the nineteenth century did not reveal significant periods of accelerated growth. Rather, French economic growth made steady but slow progress throughout.[7]

5. François Crouzet, *De la superiorité de l'Angleterre sur la France: L'économie et l'imaginaire, XVIIIe–XXe siècle* (Paris: Perrin, 1985). For early statements of this thesis, consult J. H. Clapham, *Economic Development of France and Germany, 1815–1914,* 4th ed. (Cambridge: Cambridge University Press, 1968), and S. B. Clough, "Retardative Factors in French Economic Development in the Nineteenth and Twentieth Centuries," *Journal of Economic History* 6, Supplement (1946): 91–102. An extensive bibliography on this subject can be found in Richard Roehl, "French Industrialization: A Reconsideration," *Explorations in Economic History* 13 (1976): 233–81.

6. The notion of "take-off toward sustained growth" was popularized by Walt W. Rostow in *The Stages of Economic Growth: A Non-Communist Manifesto* (Cambridge: Cambridge University Press, 1960).

7. See especially Jean Marczewski, "The Take-off and French Experience," in *The Economics of Take-off into Sustained Growth,* ed. W. W. Rostow (London: Macmillan, 1963). Also consult Maurice Lévy-Leboyer, "La croissance économique en France au XIXe siècle," *Annales: Économies, sociétés, civilisations* 23 (1968): 788–807, "Les processus d'industrialisation: Le cas de l'Angleterre et de la France," *Revue historique* 239 (1968): 281–98, and "La décélération de l'économie française dans la seconde moitié du XIXe siècle," *Revue d'histoire économique et sociale* 49 (1971): 485–507. François Crouzet makes similar points

Whereas England and Germany experienced periods of rapid economic growth and structural change in their industrial revolutions, many scholars wondered whether French industries and agriculture changed at all.

In the intellectual and political climate of the growth-oriented 1950s and 1960s, what mattered was not whether the French economy changed or how it changed, or even what could be learned from sustained but slow economic growth. The important challenge was to identify the factors that prevented the French economy from achieving rapid and sustained high growth rates (with a greater emphasis on "rapid" and "high" than on "sustained"). Moreover, if the newly constituted "Western powers" were exporting industrialization and its attendant well-being to the rest of the developing world, how could they explain this troublesome pattern in their own midst? With a view toward correcting future development, many scholars searched the nature of French society, mentality, and institutions for "retardative factors."[8] Most lines of inquiry inevitably returned to interpretations of the importance of small-scale and labor-intensive production. The discussion, however, quickly became mired in tautologies, as small-scale production became the concrete manifestation of structural difficulties in the French economy as well as their

---

in "Essai de construction d'un indice annuel de la production industrielle française au XIXe siècle," *Annales: Économies, sociétés, civilisations* 25 (1970): 56–99, and "French Economic Growth Reconsidered," *History* 59 (1974): 167–79. For a more recent synthesis, see Maurice Lévy-Leboyer and François Bourguignon, *The French Economy in the Nineteenth Century: An Essay in Econometric Analysis*, trans. Jesse Bryant and Virginie Pérotin (Cambridge: Cambridge University Press, 1990).

8. For a general discussion of the institutional obstacles to rapid industrial growth in France, see Shepard B. Clough, *France: A History of National Economics, 1789–1939* (New York: Octagon Books, 1939). See also Tom Kemp, "Structural Factors in the Retardation of French Economic Growth," *Kyklos* 15 (1962): 325–50, and *Economic Forces in French History* (London: Dobson, 1971). Rondo E. Cameron has studied the role of banks and banking institutions in French industrial development; see *France and the Economic Development of Europe, 1800–1914* (Princeton: Princeton University Press, 1967), and "France, 1800–1867," in *Banking in the Early Stages of Industrialization*, ed. Cameron et al. (New York: Oxford University Press, 1967). David S. Landes has written extensively assessing the role of entrepreneurship in French economic development; see "French Entrepreneurship and Industrial Growth in the Nineteenth Century," *Journal of Economic History* 9 (1949): 45–61, "French Business and the Businessman: A Social and Cultural Analysis," in *Modern France: Problems of the Third and Fourth Republics*, ed. E. M. Earle (New York: Russel and Russel, 1951), and "New Model Entrepreneurship in France and Problems of Historical Explanation," *Explorations in Economic History* 1 (1963): 56–75. For studies on agriculture and its relation to industrial development in France, see Robert Forster, "Obstacles to Agricultural Growth in 18th-Century France," *American Historical Review* 75 (1970): 1600–1615, Colin Heywood, "The Role of the Peasantry in French Industrialization, 1815–1880," *Economic History Review* 34 (August 1981): 359–76, and Peter McPhee, "A Reconsideration of the 'Peasantry' of Nineteenth-Century France," *Peasant Studies* 9 (Fall 1981): 5–25.

cause. The existing framework of analysis could not yield the requisite insights because its notions of economic efficiency and the nature of historical change had already marginalized small-scale production, and these categories remained unchallenged.[9]

In the 1970s and 1980s, new studies of French industrialization criticized the consensus of the 1950s and 1960s. Of these new interpretations, the work of Patrick O'Brien and Caglar Keyder was the most important and influential challenge to the retardation thesis.[10] Constructing new indices to compare English and French economic performance in the nineteenth century, they found that if one examines the distribution of income, the value added per worker, the product mix, and the total value of industrial and agricultural output, the English advantage based on efficiency and higher productivity appears less significant. They argued that "retardation" was merely a problem created by an inappropriate measure: using the rate at which new technology diffuses through an economy as the measure of market efficiency. Accordingly, O'Brien and Keyder revised the existing conception of economic development by arguing that there are many efficient uses of technology and resources depending on different market conditions. Thus the pattern of French industrialization was not

9. The historiography on the industrial revolution in England has come full circle. In the past decade, scholars have emphasized that economic growth, industrial transformation, and demographic patterns in the classic period of the English industrial revolution were gradual and marked by continuities with the past rather than sharp breaks. N. F. R. Crafts's influential quantitative analysis of national trends in *British Economic Growth during the Industrial Revolution* (Oxford: Oxford University Press, 1985) has confirmed this gradualist perspective. Ironically, assessments of British economic performance have begun to resemble the scholarship on France, raising similar problems of interpretation. For example, as Maxine Berg and Pat Hudson point out, when Crafts blames the dominance of "traditional sectors" for the overall poor performance of British manufacturing, he relies on an artificial divide between "traditional" and "modern" which equates innovation with factories and assumes that small-scale, labor-intensive manufacturing was unaffected by mechanization. In "Rehabilitating the Industrial Revolution," *Economic History Review* 45 (1992): 24–50, Berg and Hudson argue for the dynamic relation between small-scale production and factory-based mass production and the need to study economic change by regions and by industry to fully appreciate the extent of discontinuities. See also Jeffrey G. Williamson, "Why Was British Economic Growth So Slow during the Industrial Revolution," *Journal of Economic History* 44 (1984): 689–712, and Joel Mokyr, "Has the Industrial Revolution Been Crowded Out? Some Reflections on Crafts and Williamson," *Explorations in Economic History* 24 (1987): 293–319.

10. Patrick O'Brien and Caglar Keyder, *Economic Growth in Britain and France, 1780–1940: Two Paths to the Twentieth Century* (London: Allen and Unwin, 1978). For a critique of O'Brien and Keyder, see N. F. R. Crafts, "Economic Growth in France and Britain, 1830–1910: A Review of the Evidence," *Journal of Economic History* 44 (March 1984): 49–67. For other scholarship of the period which tries to establish a new basis for understanding the patterns of French economic development, consult Roehl, "French Industrialization," and Alan S. Milward and S. B. Saul, *The Development of Continental Europe, 1850–1914* (Cambridge: Harvard University Press, 1977).

anomalous: it was a healthy adaptation to a competitive market. While the English controlled the world market with mass production and large-scale operations in industry and agriculture, the French aimed for luxury handicrafts and fine foods and dominated markets in these products. It was hardly justifiable to characterize one production strategy as progress and the other as stagnation, when each represented a different market orientation.

Rather than millstones dragging down economic progress, small workshops, family firms, and family farms became the pillars of French industrial civilization. This conclusion flatters the French self-image and no doubt reinforces the cultural mythologies that distinguish Latins from Anglo-Saxons. Although future work in French economic history, including this book, will build on O'Brien and Keyder, especially their emphasis on market differentiation and specialization in explaining the variety of productive forms in modern economies, their general account of small-scale production remains partial. Actual divisions between centralized and dispersed production and between labor-saving and labor-using technologies are more complex. O'Brien and Keyder consider only small-scale production for high-priced luxury goods. They ignore the fact that there exists in all industrial economies a "sweated" alternative to the factory system, in which the availability of cheap labor discourages entrepreneurs from investing in labor-saving technology and in more centralized forms of production.[11] In this sector, dispersed production and small units mean outwork. Homeworkers perform repetitive tasks within an elaborate division of labor controlled by subcontractors. Typically, these conditions foster abusive work conditions and excessively low wages. Higher productivity is literally sweated out of human labor by employers prolonging the workday by forcing down the piece rates. This latter form of small-scale production more accurately characterizes rural manufacturing in the Pays des Mauges, particularly in the last decades of the nineteenth century, than does O'Brien and Keyder's description of small-scale manufacturing.

In overlooking the importance of cheap goods mass-produced in small workshops and homes, O'Brien and Keyder end up endorsing a romanticized vision of the economic advantages of small-scale pro-

11. On the logic of the sweated alternative, see Duncan Bythell, *The Sweated Trades: Outwork in the Nineteenth Century* (London: Batsford Academic, 1978). On the continued reliance on hand labor and human power in industrial production, see Raphael Samuel, "Workshop of the World: Steam Power and Hand Technology in Mid-Victorian Britain," *History Workshop* 3 (1977): 6–72.

duction. By considering only cases where this specialization brought optimal results, they ignore the extensive and persisting regional disparities in wealth and prosperity in France and the many structural vulnerabilities associated with small-scale production.[12]

At the outset, then, I face several conceptual tangles. Against those who view the continuation of small-scale production as either symptom or source of French economic difficulties, O'Brien and Keyder assert that the persistence of small-scale production signified a healthy and desirable adaptation to market conditions. But in fact this positive assessment is not uniformly valid. In many regions where small-scale production continued, like the one I study here, this organization of production was a sign of poverty and long-term emiseration. Although emphasis on the positive side of adaptation is rhetorically important to the academic arguments in which these authors are engaged, O'Brien and Keyder's assessment of small-scale production is structured by the terms of the argument they seek to refute: they have argued for its mirror opposite. Consequently, we still lack an appropriate analytical framework. Clearly, the problem needs to be reviewed from a different perspective. I take up this alternative in Chapter 2. In particular, I assess current theories that champion the merits of small-scale production, most prominently the work of Charles F. Sabel and Jonathan Zeitlin.[13] Before I turn to this task, however, it is instructive to begin by considering why, after many decades of study and debate, small-scale production remains an elusive subject.

In researching small-scale production, one quickly realizes the difficulty of discussing the phenomenon objectively—simply as one way to organize production among a range of possibilities. The dis-

---

12. French geographer Albert Demangeon has shown in his classic *Géographie économique et humaine de la France* (Paris: A. Colin, 1948) that structural inequalities were built into the geography of production in France. Heavy industries clearly concentrated in the Seine, Rhine, and Rhône basins. Light industries and agriculture characterized other river basins such as the Loire, Cher, Indre, Garonne, Dordogne, and Charente. Jean-Claude Toutain, taking a different approach to the problem, has documented the persistence of income disparities between the regions of the northeast and those of the south and west; see "The Uneven Growth of Regional Incomes in France from 1840 to 1970," in *Disparities in Economic Development since the Industrial Revolution*, ed. Paul Bairoch and Maurice Lévy-Leboyer (London: Macmillan, 1981). On contemporary problems of uneven development within Western Europe, consult Allan M. Williams, *The Western European Economy: A Geography of Post-War Development* (London: Hutchinson, 1987), and Lloyd Rodwin and Hidehiko Sazabami, eds., *Industrial Change and Regional Economic Transformation: The Experience of Western Europe* (London: Harper Collins Academic, 1991).

13. Charles F. Sabel and Jonathan Zeitlin, "Historical Alternatives to Mass Production," *Past and Present* 108 (August 1985): 133–76.

cussion soon turns into a moral and political debate over the merits of industrial society itself. This is because small-scale production has not existed as its own historical subject: it has been a symbol in another debate. As the "other" to industrial development—that which industrial society is not—the phenomenon takes its definition from researchers' views of industrialization itself. Those who champion industrialization identify machine labor and factory organization as rational and efficient. For them, economic prosperity depends on industrial production. They thus interpret small-scale production as a sign of backwardness or resistance to change. By contrast, those who oppose the industrial world often see small-scale production, particularly in a rural setting, as an alternative to industrial society—a more humane way to order economic life.[14] Accordingly, they greet the persistence of small-scale producers in an industrial age as a sign of people rejecting the values of industrial society and forging a better way of life.

Given such basic attitudes, it should not be surprising that the social and economic realities of this form of manufacturing elude both positions. Seeing the impoverished and seamier side of small-scale production leads us to demand a more dynamic explanation for these variations, since it would be hard to argue that certain small-scale producers actively chose the sweated alternative. The existence of a market niche does not unproblematically call forth producers to fill it. We need to understand how some small-scale producers were driven, over time and in particular struggles, to adopt self-exploitation as a strategy in the broader context of mechanization and shifts in markets.

The Pays des Mauges as a Backward and Traditional Region

The methodological problems just discussed have a special relevance for French rural history and specifically for the local history of

14. An influential exponent of this latter view is E. F. Schumacher; see *Small Is Beautiful* (London: Blond and Briggs, 1973). For a more in-depth discussion of the intellectual roots of developmental alternatives based on small-scale production, see Gavin Kitching, *Development and Underdevelopment in Historical Perspective: Populism, Nationalism, and Industrialization* (London: Methuen, 1982). In part, I intend to show some of the fallacies of the populist analysis of small-scale production, especially in its assessment of small-scale property and social justice. For a critique of populist developmental policies, see T. J. Byres, "Of Neo-Populist Pipedreams: Daedalus in the Third World and the Myth of the Urban Bias" *Journal of Peasant Studies* 6 (1979): 210–44.

the Pays des Mauges. Just as the debate on the merits of industrial society has overshadowed the study of small-scale production, so the political battles of republican France since 1789 have obscured the analysis of economic, social, and political development in the Choletais.

French historical geographers, and historians of French rural society after them, have long divided their native agricultural landscape into units called *pays*. Each region is identified by distinct field and settlement patterns. These characteristics have come to stand for eternal qualities linked to the land and its people. Indeed, the divergent zones are said to represent distinct agrarian civilizations. They exemplify ways of cultivation, patterns of landholding, and some would even add social relationships and mentalities which grew out of the endowments of nature and human workings of the soil.

For Vidal de la Blache, founder of the French school of human geography, the agrarian way of life rooted in the customs and history of each *pays* gave it a distinct personality.[15] The provinces of Maine and Anjou, for example, which together composed the departments Maine-et-Loire, Mayenne, and Sarthe, formed a "marche frontière," a dividing line that separated the West from the Paris region. But more than a physical division, this frontier marked the boundary between personalities. The Pays des Mauges is a border zone. The contrast between the particular characteristics of the Mauges and those of its neighboring *pays* belonging to the Val de Loire, the Touraine, and the Beauce has dominated interpretations of the personality of the Mauges. Just as assessments of the region's economy demonstrate in microcosm the general discussion of the problems of small-scale production in France, attempts to identify a regional character for the Mauges typify the general debate on progress and backwardness in the countryside. The Pays des Mauges is considered the archetype of traditionalism in France.[16]

Geologically, the Mauges lies entirely within the eastern boundary of the primary massif of Armorica, which defines the physical boundary of western France. To the north, the Mauges is bounded by the clear and broad sweep of the majestic Loire. The Layon river, a small tributary of the Loire, forms the eastern boundary of the region. These northern and eastern limits are marked by very different geo-

15. Paul Vidal de la Blache, *Tableau de la géographie de la France* (Paris: Hachette, 1903).
16. For an excellent introduction to French historical geography, consult the essays in Hugh D. Clout, ed., *Themes in the Historical Geography of France* (New York: Academic Press, 1977).

logical and agricultural formations. Across the Layon lie the open fields, rolling plains, and rich vineyards of the Saumurois. To the north are the bountiful orchards, nurseries, and vineyards of Angers and the Loire valley. By contrast, the western and southern boundaries of the Mauges are not as distinct. The physical landscape blends indistinguishably into the hinterlands of Nantes to the west and into the hills of Haute-Poitou to the south.

As one moves south from the Loire valley, beyond Saint-Florent-le-Vieil crowning the bluffs overlooking the Loire, the terrain of the Mauges progressively takes on the rugged character of the Armorican massif. Here and there in this hilly terrain, the schist and granite subsoil of the massif protrudes through the thin layers of topsoil. At a first glance, the Mauges appears very agricultural, but clearly it is not one of the rich farming regions of France. The poverty of the region's agriculture is even more pronounced in comparison with the richer lands of the Loire valley and the wheat fields of the Beauce.

Before the liming revolution in the mid-nineteenth century, this nitrogen-poor topsoil barely yielded enough rye to feed the local population. Much of the arable land has since been converted into pasture and used to cultivate fodder. Specialization in livestock farming was part of the extensive transformation of agriculture in the second half of the nineteenth century. But, despite such developments, the physical landscape of the Mauges has changed little.

The Mauges still bears traces of wooded hedges and fences that made up the field pattern so closely identified with the Armorican massif of western France—the *bocage*. Physically, the bocage is a rural landscape with small parcels of cultivated fields and pastures enclosed by rows of hedges and trees planted on high banks of earth. Peasants of the bocage live in small hamlets or single farmsteads surrounded by the lands they cultivate. This pattern is distinctly different from the open-field system and nucleated village settlements of the Loire valley and the Beauce. This rural landscape was known for its isolation. Until the mid-nineteenth century, it was almost inaccessible from the outside. Few major roads passed through the bocage. The small dirt roads that wove through the countryside were so deeply rutted that most of the year they were impassable by carriage. Thus it was said that, to the occasional traveler to these parts, at a distance the hedges gave the appearance of dense foliage, creating an illusion of a vast forest sprinkled with isolated clearings.

If the West of France had a distinct regional identity, it was clearly linked to the bocage. It was, however, politics that ultimately gave the bocage its special meaning. The special character of the Pays des Mauges dates from the Revolution of 1789 and specifically from the role of the bocage country in the counterrevolutionary insurrection of 1793, the Vendée. The legacy of the counterrevolution has left an indelible imprint on the image of the region, just as the political geography of insurrection has given special meaning to bocage landscape.

The great rebellion against the Republic in 1793 erupted almost simultaneously in several locations in the West. But, in the strict geography of the rebellion, there was an important difference between the areas north and south of the Loire. North, in lower Normandy and the Maine, the rebellion took the form of sporadic guerrilla warfare known as the *chouannerie*. The southern uprisings originated in western Poitou, parts of Brittany and southern Anjou. In these areas, the rebellion was led by the Catholic and Royal army and took the form of an organized counterrevolution. The bocage of Poitou and southern Anjou was its stronghold. In these areas the rebellion was sustained by popular support, and the peasant population provided recruits for the royalist army. By contrast, the plains and river valleys of the Loire and the Sèvre Nantaise favored the Revolution and remained republican. The different political affiliations of the bocage and plains persisted throughout the nineteenth century. Since 1793, it is said, the bocage has remained in the conservative camp.

The political geographer André Siegfried's influential study of western France, *Tableau politique de la France de l'Ouest*, placed great significance on the contrast between plain and bocage. For Siegfried, the West of France was distinct from modern France. Democratic influences, he wrote, perished "at the threshold of the Armorican massif." The bocage country south of the Loire was like an untamed recluse "behind its live hedges and big trees," characterized by "a regime of large landed property that has maintained a feudal hierarchy across a century of democracy [and by] an all-powerful clergy listened to and venerated as [on] the very day of the great insurrection. In this Vendée, whose name remains a symbol of the resisting ancien régime, the past is not dead as elsewhere. When one enters into the mystery of the bocage, one does not merely pass from one region to another. One also leaves the present to discover the political atmosphere of past epochs."

In his view, not only was the bocage landscape a remnant of the past; it was as if the hedges themselves had shielded this society from outside influences, allowing it to continue as it had been on the eve of the Vendée insurrection. While other regions evolved, Siegfried implied, the provinces of the interior West remained "the ultimate fortress of counterrevolutionary spirit."[17]

It is important to note that Siegfried did not explicitly document the type of continuity he claimed existed in the West. "Changelessness" and "isolation" in this text signify nothing more than antirepublican sentiments. Siegfried equated change with progress, and progress meant republicanism. Although it is true that the bocage has consistently voted to the right, Siegfried read changelessness into this electoral pattern.

The inaccuracy of Siegfried's political portrait, the methodological problems in his research and explanations, have been amply demonstrated by other historians of western France.[18] Nor was Siegfried the first to characterize the inner bocage as a society stubbornly adhering to its unenlightened backwardness.[19] This portrait is important precisely because it is broadly shared. *Tableau politique de la France de l'Ouest* clearly demonstrates how political debates have shaped the perception of social and economic change in the French countryside. In fact, we can trace the intellectual roots of important misinterpretations of French rural development back to myths of progress and backwardness originating in the revolution and counterrevolution. For the purpose of this book, however, the problem goes beyond recognizing that political divisions have structured the perceptions of change and changelessness in the countryside, and that these categories may have blinded us to changes that have occurred. The greatest impediment to understanding the society within the bocage is Siegfried's notion of how societies change.[20]

Siegfried's political geography is fundamentally static, but the picture is not completely immobile. A notion of change is implicit even when he claimed that "the region is in some sense impenetrable to

17. André Siegfried, *Tableau politique de la France de l'Ouest sous la Troisième République* (Paris: A. Colin, 1913), pp. 9–11.

18. See Paul Bois, *Paysans de l'Ouest* (Le Mans: Imprimerie M. Vilaire, 1960), esp. chap. one.

19. The authorship of this vision may well be attributed to Jules Michelet; see *Histoire de la Révolution française*, 7 vols. (Paris: Chamerot, 1847–1853).

20. We should not, however, completely dismiss this important tome as a study imbued with the author's political prejudices. The work is still a useful survey of the geography of party affiliation and voting records in the early Third Republic. It offers us important insights into the material basis of political power and influence. Siegfried showed an intuitive sensitivity to detail, particularly in distinguishing the shades of differences between types of conservatism in western France.

outside infiltration."[21] The transformation, however, is unidirectional, characterized as progress acting on a passive or resistant regional entity. In other words, for Siegfried the only source of change comes from the outside: society within the bocage has no internal dynamism; it is inherently incapable of innovation.

Siegfried's views on social change were made more explicit in his preface to the 1944 edition of Roger Thabault's classic *Mon village: Ascension d'un peuple*. In it, Siegfried enthusiastically endorsed Thabault's account of how political and social change came to Thabault's home village in the bocage. As Thabault wrote in his own introduction, "I have tried to show how the exchange economy, which step by step replaced the closed economy in which the people of my country existed in 1850, convinced first the town dwellers and later the peasants of the value of symbols: how the habit of travel, the rise in the standard of living, and social change all broadened their horizon."[22] For Thabault, literacy and appreciation for schooling were the culmination of a long process in his native village, Mazières-en-Gâtine, in the department of Deux-Sèvres. The process began with the commercialization of agriculture. In his own words, commercial agriculture "opened" the "closed" local economy as roads, railroads, and money economy brought an end to isolation. Changes in material conditions facilitated changing attitudes. They brought a new language and a new culture, distinct from local ways, reflecting the world of metropolitan French culture.

This view of social change in the bocage has been extremely influential. Eugen Weber, for example, acknowledges Thabault's formative influence on his own understanding of French peasant society. In *Peasants into Frenchmen* we find echoes of Thabault's influence in Weber's summary of the modernization of rural France:

> Roads, railroads, schools, markets, military service, and the circulation of money, goods, and printed matter . . . swept away old commitments, instilled a national view of things. We are talking about the process of acculturation: the civilization of the French by urban France, the disintegration of local cultures by modernity and their absorption into the dominant civilization of Paris and the schools. Left largely to their own

21. Siegfried, *Tableau politique*, p. 9.
22. Roger Thabault, *Education and Change in a Village Community: Mazières-en-Gâtine, 1848–1914*, trans. Peter Tregear (New York: Schocken Books, 1971), pp. 5–6.

devices until their promotion to citizenship, the unassimilated rural
masses had to be integrated in that dominant culture as they had been
integrated into an administrative entity. What happened was akin to
colonization.[23]

According to Weber's view of change in the French countryside, the
formative impulse for an industrial and urban capitalist society came
from urban culture and urban-based commerce: more significant, rural society did not participate. Rather, economic development, along
with political and cultural integration and new national identity,
were brought to the "poor and backward" countryside. Once contact
was established, the transformative powers of urban society were formidable. They refashioned production and social life in the image of
the "colonizers."

Suffice it to say that the West of France was never as isolated as
these accounts would have us believe. Recent scholarship in economic history has stressed the importance of the countryside in the
growth of modern mass production. In the sixteenth and seventeenth
centuries, an Atlantic world was built on the exchange of sugar and
tobacco from the New World for finished goods, woolens and linens,
wheat and wines from Europe, and slaves from Africa. Throughout
the European continent, a wide network of export-oriented industries
furnished the Atlantic trade. Linen-producing areas like Silesia, Saxony, Flanders, Brittany, and Maine-Anjou were important centers of
this international textile trade. Obscure regions like the Mauges produced for the capitalist world market.

The problem is not just that accounts of rural transformation like
those presented by Weber, Thabault, and Siegfried ignore the importance of rural industries. One could easily incorporate rural industries and international trade into these accounts and yet still not
correct the problem. Such revised accounts simply indicate that integration had occurred earlier than commonly believed, when it is
the logic and the process of rural transformation that is at issue.

Weber's choice of imagery—that the modernization process is akin
to colonization—is particularly revealing. As in classic colonialist
discourse, it is the colonizers who are active, while the colonized are
passive recipients who are sometimes sympathetically portrayed as
victims. This division between active and passive guarantees that

23. Eugen Weber, *Peasants into Frenchmen: The Modernization of Rural France, 1870–
1914* (Stanford: Stanford University Press, 1976), p. 486.

the subject of the history is the colonizer and not the colonized.[24] Similarly, Weber's characterization of the transformation of the countryside does not really allow us to focus on the dynamics of rural society, despite the many pages of picturesque and eloquent portrayal of rural culture. The real subjects of his inquiry are the transformative forces—roads, money economy, the metropole—and not the pliant and amorphous object of transformation. Thus, for much the same reasons that small-scale production has remained elusive despite decades of research and debates, the dynamics of rural society are obscured by these studies of change in the countryside.

As is not surprising, this vision of a changeless countryside (except when subjected to outside forces) is often embraced by rural populations themselves, though for very different reasons. Just as the Vendée wars created a lasting image for outsiders, an image of the region as conservative and isolated from the rest of France, the same event has forged a different yet fundamentally similar identity which the people of the Mauges claim as their own. For many Maugeois, the special mentality and character of their *pays* was formed in this historical moment.[25] In the Choletais today, the revived memory of the Vendée reconstructs an interpretation of the past to service the present. The political battles of the past no longer have the significance they once had, but the region's special historical identity is often called on to explain and dignify current economic developments. The legacy of the Vendée is invoked to champion small-scale production over large-scale industries. This view is perhaps best expressed by Maurice Ligot, a deputy for the Choletais who for a decade had served as deputy mayor and then mayor of Cholet:

> If one surveys the economic history of the Choletais, one comes away with two phenomena: continuous conversion and diversification. Our mentality has been created by this economic history. . . . The Revolution is the other important element which has forged the mentality of the Choletais. The Great War in the Choletais is not [the war of] '14 to '18, but 1793. . . . The people of the Mauges did not accept these changes [of the Revolution of 1789] because they wanted to live in the community of their family, village, and region according to their own authority without obligation to account to the state. But the battle was

24. For an elaboration of this argument, see Albert Memmi, *The Colonizers and Colonized* (Boston: Beacon Press, 1967).

25. Jean-Clément Martin, "La Vendée, région-mémoire," in *Les lieux de mémoire: La République,* ed. Pierre Nora (Paris: Gallimard, 1984), pp. 595–617, and *La Vendée de la mémoire (1800–1980)* (Paris: Seuil, 1989).

lost. The people felt oppressed, vanquished, and isolated, as if they were insulated: we were alone in the middle of France and our only resource was to struggle alone. Our riches: they are our men and families. The most gifted are those who have the entrepreneurial spirit and who create employment for others. And this spirit of enterprise born of "insularity" and this will to independence characterize the Choletais.[26]

Notice that Ligot invokes the same images to explain his region which Siegfried used nearly seven decades earlier. But in the eyes of the mayor, the region's isolation and separation from the rest of France had nurtured an independent spirit, a sense of ingenuity to which he attributes the present economic successes in the Choletais. As mayor and deputy of the modern Cholet, Ligot is eager to draw the attention of the rest of France to "le modèle choletais": "[With its] bocage country [and] green prairies, the Choletais offers its calm and enchanting landscape to hikers [who have] come to seek peace and serenity away from the tumult of urban life and to the businessmen [who have] come to participate in the economic dynamism of the region. Here is the Choletais: region of the rural factory. Refusing the duality of city and countryside, on the contrary, the region has known the harmony of these elements, [which] confer onto the Pays des Mauges all its originality."[27]

Reminiscent of many populist notions, Ligot claims that rural industries in the Choletais, or "les usines à la campagne," represent an ecological and harmonious alternative to urban congestion and heavy industries.[28] Unlike other regions, production in the Choletais, he claims, is based on the harmonious integration of agriculture and manufacturing. To what we can attribute this unique balance? Ligot would say that it must be attributed to the attachment of local people to traditional values: "Those who seek to understand this history will discover in it the permanence of an ethic and social practice: attachment to family, to work, to spiritual values, but also a will to undertake, to participate, in the development and the prosperity of their native soil and to maintain its autonomy. Progress far from accompanied by the decline in tradition has been strongly rooted in the mentality of the men [sic] of the region."[29]

26. "Interview avec Maurice Ligot, Député-Maire de Cholet et ancien Ministre," *Hommes et activités: Le Choletais,* 1981, pp. 8–9.
27. Ibid., p. 6.
28. This view of economic development in the Choletais is endorsed by recent academic studies that accept at face value the assertions of social solidarity; see Minguet, *Naissance de l'Anjou industriel.*
29. "Interview avec Ligot," p. 3.

This description of the regional economy is more than a manifestation of local pride. Ligot's musings are important because they retell the local history of the nineteenth century. His is a modern mythology of the region's past.

This is the story he tells: After the "Great War," the vanquished population of the bocage lived in isolation, sheltered from the forces that had transformed the rest of France. They were protected not only from industrialization and urban growth but from class conflict and revolutionary ideologies as well. Exempt from the political battles that engulfed the rest of France, the Pays des Mauges was peaceful during the nineteenth century, quietly adapting but essentially remaining the same because the people held on to the same values that had sparked their opposition in 1793.

More important than what this history asserts is what it denies. The very claim that local society was harmonious and based on common values masks the bitter history of the nineteenth century. Administrative and police archives give a very different picture—one virtually lost to living memory. Contemporary reports and newspapers record the long and recurring battles between weavers, manufacturers, and merchants. They document the ruthless slashing of piece rates and the progressive impoverishment of handloom weavers. New forms of rural industry grew in a restructured labor market. Adaptation was the result not of peaceful change and consent but of struggles and defeats.

Social Change and Regional History

It is not my purpose to pass judgment on the accuracy of Ligot's representation of the past. As an outsider, I cannot presume to share the same perspective and emotional bond to a past that is not my own. Yet, as I hope to have shown in the previous discussion, Ligot's reasoning is not unique; there is a more general interpretation of the nineteenth century at stake. Ligot and other advocates of "le modèle choletais" on the one side and Siegfried and Weber on the other constitute mirror opposites, but both replicate the kind of reasoning that obscures the changing and dynamic history of small-scale production. Just as Siegfried repeats the old republican accusations, stressing the dominance of a powerful aristocracy who conspired against a democratic revolution and who, even in defeat, refused to forsake the privileges of the former regime, Ligot replicates the old royalist defense: that the Vendée was a unified and spontaneous upsurge sparked by outrage and motivated by loyalty to church and king. For different political reasons, both sides assert a common vision of the bocage as a changeless society. In addition, both positions share a view of bocage society as different and exceptional. The intellectual analogue to this deeply ingrained sense of regional exceptionalism is a rejection of a broader analytical language, and hence a search for "essences" that capture the distinct character of the region. Consequently, attempts to understand political, economic, cultural, and social developments in the Mauges have been caught in binary thinking.

By contrast, in their studies of the social origins of the Vendée counterrevolution, both Charles Tilly and Paul Bois have demonstrated, for Maine-et-Loire and Sarthe, respectively, that the penetration of mercantile capital into rural production was an important component in the factional politics. [30] Profits from the Atlantic trade created new economic interests and new political allegiances. This new wealth set merchants in competition with farmers for land. Conflicting interests and new alliances ultimately built the barriers along which factions and opposing parties formed.

By emphasizing the role of local conflicts, these historians challenged both traditional royalist and republican accounts of the counterrevolution. They sought to understand how bocage society had been transformed by market relations and political integration into the monarchical state, but they did not judge whether the change was good or bad, whether the Mauges should have accepted or rejected the Revolution; these were the pivotal issues of the traditional accounts of counterrevolution. Tilly and Bois argued instead that one needs to understand how bocage society changed in order to understand the local conflicts which led to the mobilization against the Republic. So, when we return to study the events in which the regional identity of the Pays des Mauges was born, we do not find a static society wishing to remain unchanged; instead we find a changing society in which changes had engendered conflicting interests and new alliances. In this sense, the counterrevolution was an episode in a larger historical process.

Similarly, I seek to establish the transformation of social and economic relationships in this remote region of western France as part of a general history of economic and social change in the nineteenth century. My goal is to uncover the history of small-scale production in this region to shed new light on the general process of European

---

30. Charles Tilly, *The Vendée* (Cambridge: Harvard University Press, 1964); Bois, *Paysans de l'Ouest.*

industrialization. Such an examination leads us, I believe, to rethink the traditional center from the periphery. In a sense, my aim is to "normalize" our assessment of regions like the Choletais, to begin to consider the pattern of development here as one of the typical ways that manufacturing is organized in an industrial society. To do so, we must revise the very logic of industrial development.

2

Rural Industries and the
Evolution of Capitalist Production

It may seem that recovering the importance of small-scale production for the history of industrialization means making it a subject in its own right. The dangers of this course, given the discussion in Chapter 1, should be clear. In claiming a distinct status for small-scale production, one risks giving the phenomenon a misplaced solidity, compensating for its former invisibility by becoming overly concerned with establishing its boundaries and demonstrating its internal order and coherence. In the late nineteenth century, for example, when scholars of the German Historical Economic school turned their attention to small-scale production, they characterized it as a distinct "social mode of production" with its own historical trajectory and internal dynamics.[1] Such arguments lead the discussion back into the type of oppositional thinking that initially marginalized the topic. The various forms of small-scale production we can observe over time are not stages in the evolution of a particular mode of production or social formation. The same can be said of the factory system. Both are momentary configurations in a process that we can broadly identify as the development of capitalist relations of production.

We can more effectively account for the variety of ways economic life is organized by adopting more historically contingent explanations. Such an approach requires that we look less for systemic answers (in the sense of searching for a generative logic) and more

1. See Dieter Lindenlaub, *Richtungskaempfe im Verein für Sozialpolitik* (Wiesbaden: F. Stein, 1967). For an interesting perspective on this project, see Joel S. Kahn, "Towards a History of the Critique of Economism: the 19th-Century German Origins of the Ethnographer's Dilemma," *Man* 25 (1990): 230–49.

toward modeling the dialectics of strategy and human action.[2] A case study of the Pays des Mauges demonstrates the advantages and possibilities of this orientation.

My search for a new way to characterize the process of industrialization begins with a debate among European economic historians over the rural origins of the factory system: the literature on proto-industrialization is a significant attempt to situate small-scale production historically and in active relation to large-scale industries.[3] Ultimately, I argue, the explanations offered by proto-industrialization theory fail to dislodge us from the standard view of industrialization. In both its assumptions and main hypothesis, it replicates the perspective on industrialization it initially intended to criticize. Despite these failings, however, it is still worthwhile for us to consider its arguments carefully. The alternative I outline inverts some basic assumptions of the proto-industrialization hypothesis, so the theory provides an important point of departure.

Proto-industrialization and De-industrialization

Since the early 1970s, all studies of rural industries have had to engage the lively scholarly debate on proto-industrialization. The expansion of small-scale production into the European countryside between the sixteenth and eighteenth centuries was well known to the economic historians of the early twentieth century. Russian scholar Evgenii Tarlé and French scholar Henri Sée wrote extensively on the subject.[4] In the early 1970s, Franklin Mendels proposed a pathbreaking reinterpretation of this phenomenon. Based on his own research on demographic and economic patterns of Flanders in the eighteenth century, and building on the earlier work of Rudolph Braun, Eric

2. See Pierre Bourdieu, *Outline for a Theory of Practice,* trans. Richard Nice (Cambridge: Cambridge University Press, 1977).

3. For a review of the positive contributions of research on proto-industrialization despite the evident shortcomings of the original hypothesis, see Jean H. Quataert, "A New View of Industrialization: 'Protoindustry' or the Role of Small-Scale, Labor-Intensive Manufacture in the Capitalist Environment," *International Labor and Working-Class History* 33 (Spring 1988): 3–22. For a critique of Quataert's argument, see Charles F. Sabel, "Protoindustry and the Problem of Capitalism as a Concept: Response to Jean H. Quataert," *International Labor and Working-Class History* 33 (Spring 1988): 30–37.

4. Evgenii Tarlé, *L'industrie dans les campagnes en France à la fin de l'Ancien Régime* (Paris: Édouard Cornéley, 1910); and Henri Sée, "Remarques sur le caractère de l'industrie rurale en France et les causes de son extension au XVIIIe siècle," *Revue historique* 142 (1923): 47–53, *L'évolution commerciale et industrielle de la France sous l'Ancien Régime* (Paris: Marcel Giard, 1925), and many other writings.

Jones, Herbert Kisch, and Joan Thirsk,[5] Mendels suggested that this export-oriented cottage industry might be a preparatory stage for industrialization.[6] Rural outwork, he argued, created the preconditions for "economic take-off" in the early nineteenth century. Mendels called the expansion of export-oriented cottage industry in the countryside "proto-industrialization."

An important aspect of Mendels's hypothesis is the suggestion of a systemic and causal role for rural handicrafts in the development of the factory system. Proto-industrialization helped to form an entrepreneurial class, creating skills and concentration of capital. The demographic process involved—declining age of marriage, population growth—also helped to create a rural proletariat out of marginal subsistence farmers. The rise of a population no longer self-sufficient in food solidified the differentiation between manufacturing and agriculture by creating new markets for specialists in agriculture.[7]

When Mendels compared the experiences of different European regions, however, he noted that some proto-industrial regions became important centers for factory-based manufacturing while many others did not fare as well. Mendels thus tried to conceive of industrialization as an open-ended, not a determinate, process: in some regions, proto-industrialization led to successful industrialization; in others, where a factory system was not successful, this failure led to a "de-industrialization" of the proto-industrial countryside. In fact, vast areas of the European continent de-industrialized. The West of France and Silesia are two notable examples. According to this typology, the Pays des Mauges also de-industrialized.

5. Rudolf Braun, *Industrialisierung und Volksleben* (Zurich: Rentschm, 1960), "Early Industrialization and Demographic Change in the Canton of Zurich," in *Historical Studies of Changing Fertility*, ed. Charles Tilly (Princeton: Princeton University Press, 1978), "The Impact of Cottage Industry on an Agricultural Population," in *The Rise of Capitalism*, ed. David S. Landes (New York: Macmillan, 1966), and "The Rise of a Rural Class of Industrial Entrepreneurs," *Cahiers d'histoire mondiale* 10 (1967): 551–66; Eric L. Jones, "The Agricultural Origins of Industry," *Past and Present* 40 (1968): 58–71; Herbert Kisch, "The Textile Industries in Silesia and the Rhineland: A Comparative Study in Industrialization," *Journal of Economic History* 19 (1959): 541–63, "Prussian Mercantilism and the Rise of the Krefeld Silk Industry: Variations on an Eighteenth-Century Theme," *Transactions of the American Philosophical Society*, n.s. 58, 7 (1968), "From Monopoly to Laissez-faire: The Early Growth of the Wupper Valley Textile Trades," *Journal of European Economic History* 1 (1972): 298–407; Joan Thirsk, "Industries in the Countryside," in *Essays in the Economic and Social History of Tudor and Stuart England*, ed. F. J. Fisher (Cambridge: Cambridge University Press, 1961): 70–88.

6. Franklin F. Mendels, "Proto-industrialization: The First Phase in the Industrialization Process," *Journal of Economic History* 32 (1972): 241–61.

7. Ibid., pp. 244–45.

This recasting of our thinking about industrialization has certain advantages. It suggests that the transition to a factory system was by no means problem-free. Specifically, many regions now considered the backwaters of the European economy were actually casualties of structural changes in production and shifts in investment patterns during industrialization. The processes that created large-scale mechanized industries in some regions produced economic blight in others. This connection between de-industrialization and under-development promised a new synthesis in development theory. The proto-industrialization hypothesis made it possible to focus on local production and investment decisions as the source of uneven development and imbalanced growth, as opposed to the surplus extraction and unequal terms of trade suggested by dependency theory.[8]

The proto-industrialization hypothesis has stimulated many new directions for inquiry and research projects. These studies have made their most important contribution in drawing the connections be-

8. By dependency theory, I mean specifically the works of André Gunder Frank, *Capitalism and Underdevelopment in Latin America: Historical Studies of Chile and Brazil* (New York: Monthly Review Press, 1969); and Immanuel Wallerstein, *The Modern World-System: Capitalist Agriculture and the Origins of the European World Economy in the 16th Century* (New York: Academic Press, 1974), and *The Modern World-System: Mercantilism and the Consolidation of the European World Economy, 1600–1750* (New York: Academic Press, 1980). Unlike those of the Latin American Structuralist School who also addressed the problems of dependency, these two authors have had much greater intellectual impact in the Western European–North American academic world. For an interesting political assessment of political differences among dependency theorists, see Fernando Henrique Cardoso, "The Consumption of Dependency Theory in the United States," *Latin American Research Review* 12 (1977): 7–24, and Tulio Halperin-Donghi, "Dependency Theory and Latin American Historiography," *Latin American Research Review* 17 (1982): 115–30.

Dependency theory has drawn most criticism for the "surplus expropriation chain" by which it explains underdevelopment. Without denying that the metropolis has extracted and continues to extract vital surpluses from the periphery, and recognizing the detrimental effect of the process on the peripheral societies, one can still question whether this extraction is essential for capitalist development. Robert Brenner points out in "The Origins of Capitalist Development: A Critique of Neo-Smithian Marxism," *New Left Review* 104 (July–August 1977): 25–92, that the concept of the surplus expropriation chain fundamentally misconstrues the nature of capitalist production. Unlike other modes of production, Brenner argues, capitalism has internal methods for generating surplus based on production itself. These methods are built into the nature of production based on labor power as a commodity. Surpluses are generated by intensifying production and increasing the productivity of labor with machinery. Thus Brenner claims that the metropolitan core developed by increasing the efficiency of the factors of production (and increasing the level of exploitation at home) rather than relying on emptying the periphery. In "Agrarian Class Structure and Economic Development in Pre-Industrial Europe," *Past and Present* 70 (February 1976): 30–75, Brenner argues that social struggles over production, that is, class struggle, are at the heart of the process of capitalist development and underdevelopment. What is often characterized as underdevelopment is actually the result of successful resistance to the commodification of la-

tween demographic patterns and capitalist development.[9] We now have a better understanding of the relationship between population pressures and the expansion of rural industries. We also understand that there is an important demographic component in the rise of a rural proletariat.[10]

In recent years, however, proto-industrialization as a theory, as opposed to a set of suggestive research questions, has been criticized from numerous perspectives.[11] Some critics claim the theory tries to explain too much;[12] others claim it explains nothing new at all.[13] Many researchers working on specific regions or specific industries complain that the definitions and typologies do not suit their case.[14]

---

bor. I have found this emphasis on the logic of production and localized social struggles particularly helpful for explaining the pattern of economic and social relationships in regions like the Pays des Mauges.

9. Franklin F. Mendels, *Industrialization and Population Pressure in Eighteenth-Century Flanders* (New York: Arno Press, 1981). For a different perspective, see Wally Seccombe, "Marxism and Demography," *New Left Review* 13 (1983): 22–47.

10. David Levine, *Family Formation in the Age of Nascent Capitalism* (New York: Academic Press, 1977), and Charles Tilly, "The Demographic Origins of the European Proletariat," in *Proletarianization and Family History*, ed. David Levine (Orlando: Academic Press, 1984). For more extensive synthesis, see David Levine, *Reproducing Families: the Political Economy of English Population History* (Cambridge: Cambridge University Press, 1987).

11. In their introduction to *Manufacture in Town and Country before the Factory* (Cambridge: Cambridge University Press, 1983), Maxine Berg, Pat Hudson, and Michael Sonenscher argue that the proto-industrialization model is too linear. In its emphasis on putting-out systems (*verlagsystem*), the recent literature has obscured the importance and variety of social organizations under the *kaufsystem*.

12. D. C. Coleman, "Proto-industrialization: A Concept Too Many," *Economic History Review*, 2d series, 36 (August 1983): 435–48. For a similar critique, see also Leslie A. Clarkson, *Proto-industrialization: The First Phase of Industrialization* (Houndmills, Basingstoke, Hampshire: Macmillan, 1985).

13. Pat Hudson, in "Proto-industrialization: The Case of the West Riding Wool Textile Industry in the 18th and early 19th centuries," *History Workshop Journal* 12 (Autumn 1981): 34–61, expresses her doubts that the proto-industrial perspective could shed light on the process of transition to capitalist production. In a more recent overview, Hudson points out that the deficiencies of the theory have not held back innovative research on rural industries. On balance, interest in proto-industrialization has advanced our knowlege of rural industries and industrialization; see Hudson, "The Regional Perspective," in *Regions and Industries: A Perspective on the Industrial Revolution in Britain* (Cambridge: Cambridge University Press, 1989).

14. The proto-industrialization framework does not fit many regions. For a view of the range of differences, see Hudson, "Proto-industrialization," and her contribution on West Riding and J. K. L. Thomson's on Languedoc in *Manufacture in Town and Country before the Factory*. See also Christopher H. Johnson, "Proto-industrialization and De-industrialization in Languedoc: Lodève and Its Region, 1700–1870," paper presented at the "Proto-industrialization: Theory and Reality" conference, Bad Homburg, 1981. Gay L. Gullickson's studies of the Pays de Caux in Normandy add the important dimension of women's work and gender analysis to the proto-industrialization discussions. See "Agriculture and Cottage Industry: Redefining the Causes of Proto-Industrialization," *Journal of Economic History* 43 (December 1983): 831–50, "Proto-Industrialization, Demographic Behavior, and the Sexual Division of Labor in Auffay, France, 1750–1850," *Peasant Studies* 9 (Winter 1982):

A systematic and thorough critique of the proto-industrialization hypothesis is in fact extremely difficult, in large measure because of the history of the hypothesis itself.

For Mendels, the phenomenon was always closely tied to demographic pressures on subsistence agriculture and tightly bound to his original Flemish case study. His later clarification of his earlier work insisted more explicitly on the functional relation among cottage industry, demography, and the emergence of a distinct industrial sector on which his initial hypothesis relied. As a result, Mendels further restricted his definitions of proto-industry and de-industrialization.[15] Accordingly only those household economies that combine seasonal manufacture for export markets with subsistence agriculture and small-scale landholding should be called proto-industrial. Moreover, de-industrialization is not just any crisis in rural manufacturing; it is specifically the process in which the countryside, after losing its proto-industrial population through outmigration, comes to specialize in commercial agriculture. Thus the de-industrialization of the countryside is functionally linked to industrialization and the growth of cities. In a classic Parsonian model of development and change, Mendels argued that, as the capitalist economy became more complex (moving away from its pre-industrial/proto-industrial roots), cities differentiated from the countryside, each acquiring its own specialization.[16]

According to these more stringent definitions, the Pays des Mauges in fact neither had proto-industry nor de-industrialized. In the eighteenth century, weaving and agriculture were distinct occupations. Rural manufacturing continued in the countryside after Cholet's unsuccessful bid at mechanizing and centralizing textile production in

---

106–18, "The Sexual Division of Labor in Cottage Industry and Agriculture in the Pays de Caux, Auffay, 1750–1850," *French Historical Studies* 12 (Fall 1981): 177–99, and *The Spinners and Weavers of Auffay: Rural Industry and the Sexual Division of Labor in a French Village, 1750–1850* (Cambridge: Cambridge University Press, 1986).

15. Franklin F. Mendels, "General Report, Eighth International Economic History Congress, Section A.2: Proto-industrialization: Theory and Reality," Budapest, August, 1982. Myron Gutman and René Leboutte have argued that the proto-industrialization hypothesis can be vindicated by showing it to be a special case of a more general class of developments, provided that proto-industry is "disruptively novel"; see "Rethinking Proto-industrialization and the Family," *Journal of Interdisciplinary History* 14 (Winter 1984): 267–310.

16. Franklin F. Mendels, "Agriculture and Peasant Industry in Eighteenth-Century Flanders," in *European Peasants and Their Markets*, ed. William N. Parker and Eric L. Jones (Princeton: Princeton University Press, 1975), and the "Seasons and Regions in Agriculture and Industry during the Process of Industrialization," in *Region und Industrialisierung*, ed. Sidney Pollard (Göttingen: Vandenhoeck and Ruprecht, 1980). For an excellent study of de-industrialization defined as industrial decline, see Donald Reid, *The Miners of Decazeville: A Genealogy of Deindustrialization* (Cambridge: Harvard University Press, 1985).

the middle of the nineteenth century. But the popularity of Mendels's hypothesis has led researchers to broaden its application to rural industries around the globe, in radically different cultures and periods than those of early industrial Europe. This process, stimulated in part by the broader interpretation of Mendels's work proposed by Richard and Charles Tilly, has added new dimensions to the research problems centered around the proto-industrial phenomenon.[17] The most ambitious of this work, by the German scholars Peter Kriedte, Hans Medick, and Jurgen Schlumbohm, has altered the theoretical orientation of the proto-industrialization hypothesis in significant ways.

Kriedte, Medick, and Schlumbohm have more liberal definitions than those Mendels stipulates. In their stimulating *Industrialization before Industrialization*, the three authors point out that conceiving of proto-industries as a transitional mode of production offers a new perspective on the origins of capitalist relations of production. They thus hope to reinvigorate the Marxist debate on the transition from feudalism to capitalism.[18] In addition to studies on production and general population trends, Kriedte et al. also encourage research on the social and cultural aspects of proto-industrial societies in order to clarify the breakdown of feudal social relationships and the rise of new types of social relationships within families and village communities. Medick's contributions on the proto-industrial family (adding a Chayanovian dimension) and his studies of "plebeian" customs and rituals (reminiscent of E. P. Thompson) have been the most influential in this respect.[19] Finally, these scholars note the importance of

17. Charles Tilly and Richard Tilly, "An Agenda for Economic History in the 1970's," *Journal of Economic History* 31 (1971): 184–98.

18. Peter Kriedte, Hans Medick, and Jurgen Schlumbohm, *Industrialization before Industrialization*, trans. Beate Schempp (New York: Cambridge University Press, 1981). Specifically, they address the Maurice Dobb–Paul Sweezy debate on the decline of feudalism and the origins of capitalist relations of production. Rodney Hilton has edited and introduced a volume of the essays in this debate: *The Transition from Feudalism to Capitalism* (London: New Left Books, 1976). Robert Brenner's "Agrarian Class Structure and Economic Development in Pre-Industrial Europe" is especially helpful in explaining how Kriedte, Medick, and Schlumbohm hoped to transform the transition debate. To survey the critical assessment of the Brenner thesis, consult T. H. Ashton and C. H. E. Philipon, eds. *The Brenner Debates* (Cambridge: Cambridge University Press, 1985).

19. Hans Medick, "The Proto-industrial Family Economy: The Structural Function of Household and Family during the Transition from Peasant Society to Industrial Capitalism," *Social History* 3 (October 1976): 291–315. See also Kriedte, Medick, and Schlumbohm, *Industrialization before Industrialization*, chap. 2. For an English translation of the works of A. V. Chayanov, see Daniel Thorner, Basile Kerbaly, and R. E. F. Smith, ed., *A. V. Chayanov on the Theory of Peasant Economy* (Homewood, Ill.: Richard D. Irwin, published for the American Economics Association, 1966). Chayanov's theories on peasant households were revived and made popular among intellectuals and especially developmental economists

the proto-industrialization hypothesis for demonstrating that theories of uneven development apply to Europe as well. Citing both Gunnar Myrdal and dependency theorists, they point out that even in Europe, the "core," a capitalist organization of production and commerce created poverty at the same time it generated prosperity. Proto-industrialization in Europe must be understood within the context of the expanding capitalist world system. Like Mendels, they underscore that capitalist development and underdevelopment must be viewed as a single process. In *Industrialization before Industrialization*, Kriedte, Medick, and Schlumbohm thus present a comprehensive plan for studying the origins and development of capitalism from global economy to the most intimate family relationships.

This dizzying and encyclopedic inclusion is both inspiring and perplexing. On the one hand, we must admire the scope of their interests and learn from this imaginative attempt at a richly textured "total history." On the other, one senses that too many different theoretical perspectives have been grafted together without careful consideration of the contradictions between them. Beginning with Mendels's functionalist linear typologies and explanations, they add the vocabulary of the historical school of German national economics and combine these diverse elements to address a Marxist problematic. It is not the variety of theoretical perspectives that causes difficulty, though, but their differing assumptions. Functionalist theories, the German school of national economy from which the authors draw evidence, and to some degree Chayanov's theory of peasant economy, have their intellectual roots in theories of social solidarity, whereas Marxist theories build on a conflictual understanding of society and social change. Because the authors do not discuss the tensions between these perspectives, they risk doing violence to one or the other.

On closer reading, it is evident that Kriedte et al. implicitly settle for a functionalist linear model.[20] Like most scholars working on this

---

and sociologists in Western Europe and North America by the works of Teodor Shanin, "The Nature and Logic of the Peasant Economy," *Journal of Peasant Studies* 1 (1973–74): 65–80, 186–206, and *The Awkward Class: Political Sociology of the Peasantry in a Developing Society, Russia 1910–1925* (Oxford: Oxford University Press, 1972). For a critical examination of Chayanov's categories in the Russian context, see Mark Harrison, "Chayanov and the Economics of the Russian Peasantry," *Journal of Peasant Studies* 2 (1975): 389–417. See also Medick's fascinating "Village Spinning Bees: Sexual Culture and Free Time among Rural Youth in Early Modern Germany," in *Interest and Emotion: Essays on the Study of Family and Kinship*, ed. Hans Medick and David Sabean (Cambridge: Cambridge University Press, 1984). For notions of plebian culture, see E. P. Thompson, "Patrician Society, Plebian Culture," *Journal of Social History* 7 (1974): 382–405.

20. In his more recent work Medick argues for a more dialectical and contextual approach. In his study of the linen industry in Württemberg, Medick shows that weavers' ability to

subject, they concentrate primarily on either the origins of proto-industries or the path from proto-industries to industries. Despite their programmatic statements, their research efforts and theoretical interests continue to focus on the rise of the factory system and on "successful" transitions. Once again, industrialization takes center stage and small-scale production is relegated to a marginal status.

This move toward the conventional narrative of industrial development is subtle but important to pinpoint. The problem is clearest, and most damaging, in Schlumbohm's examination of the transition to industrial capitalism, "Relations of Production—Productive Forces—Crisis in Proto-industrialization." Schlumbohm begins with an important observation: the existing literature on the emergence of capitalism has not systematically analyzed the reasons why capital, which had long been present in the form of merchants' and usurers' capital, penetrated into the sphere of production. Contrary to many authors who treat this question as if capital had an inherent interest in production, Schlumbohm points out that, in fact, capital's only inherent interest is in profit. The important question that follows from this insight is thus, why does interest in profit bring merchant capital into the sphere of production? In other words, one can ask, what is particular about the relationship between merchants and small-scale direct producers that pushes the former into the production process?

Schlumbohm, however, poses his question in a slightly different way. He asks, "How and under what conditions did an interest in the *maximization of profit* bring about the penetration of capital into the sphere of production?"[21] This slight variation is crucial to Schlumbohm's conception of the relationship between merchants and small producers. By positing a secure structural position from which merchants could sally forth in search of even greater profits, Schlumbohm reduces the possible outcomes to two: either merchants and direct producers maintain their positions, or merchants succeed in appropriating the surplus theretofore retained by direct producers. Reasoning that direct producers would not readily give up this surplus and their independence, Schlumbohm concentrates on specifying the conditions under which small producers must acquiesce.

---

maintain control of rural manufacturing in the eighteenth century paved the way for the region's specialization in highly skilled, artisanal, precision industries; "Privilegiertes Handelskapital und Kleine Industrie," *Archiv für Sozialgeschichte* 23 (1983): 587–607.

21. Kriedte, Medick, and Schlumbohm, *Industrialization before Industrialization*, p. 103, emphasis added.

Without a doubt these observations offer important insights into the dynamics of proletarianization. Yet this analysis fails to address a third possibility: that merchants might lose their claim on profits altogether, and that small-scale producers might successfully resist the encroachment of merchant capital. In other words, Schlumbohm's model for transitions toward capitalist relations of production takes the proletarian status of small producers for granted. Merchants may well have struggled, not for greater profits, but for any profit at all.

It is precisely at this point that Schlumbohm overdetermines his theory of transition and falls back into teleological thinking. The tendency to move toward capitalist relations of production is taken as a given rather than as a problematic, contested process that could fail as well as succeed. Even though Schlumbohm takes great care to highlight the battles waged by small producers to preserve their autonomy, their struggles take on a tragic tone. In the examples he presents, the forces of capital always win. Such accounts inspire admiration for the pain and courage of those who struggled and lost but do not encourage us to see them as other than preordained by the master historical script to lose.

The failure to fully integrate an analysis of struggles at the point of production into the causal account of proto-industrialization, industrialization, and de-industrialization is an important missed opportunity. This is all the more disappointing because in earlier chapters Kriedte et al. promise a more dialectical approach, one that emphasizes the struggles between capital and labor in the development of capitalist relations of production. Although the authors endorse Robert Brenner's criticism of dependency theorists for ignoring the formative role of class struggles,[22] they do not in fact put this insight into practice.

Brenner's suggestion that underdevelopment might be better understood as the failure of capitalists to transform existing noncapitalist relations of production (or, put another way, his assertion that underdevelopment is successful resistance) is consistent with the expressed aims of the proto-industrialization hypothesis and with Mendels's perception that industrialization is an open-ended process. Brenner provides the crucial, yet missing, positive scenario for understanding de-industrialization by showing that the phenomenon is theoretically more interesting than merely an example of a failed transition: industrialization itself must be analyzed from the per-

22. Brenner, "Origins of Capitalist Development."

spective of its "failures" as well as its "successes." Moreover, this argument adds a crucial dimension for breaking out of a linear, unidirectional view of industrial capitalist growth by explicitly articulating that capitalist development itself is contingent on the outcomes of class struggles.

Capitalist Class Formation and the Politics of Production

At this important point in the argument—on the question of capitalist class formation and specifically on stacking the analysis in favor of capitalist relations of production—the proto-industrialization thesis in effect reverts back to the standard narrative of industrial development as blind destiny. Yet it is also clear that Schlumbohm posed the essential questions: How did capitalist relations of production arise? How did merchants who did not invest in production become industrial capitalist producers? How did small producers who owned the means of production and had the means to market and profit from their labor become proletarians who must sell their labor? These questions serve as my point of departure for an alternative analysis, one that begins by taking Brenner's suggestion seriously. Analyzing these struggles at the point of production as a process of class formation is the central explanatory framework I use to account for the pattern of economic development in the Choletais.

But what precisely do we mean by "class struggle," and why do these struggles have transformative powers? That class struggle is the motor of historical development is such a truism within the Marxist canon that few scholars stop to examine in detail the concrete meanings of such an assertion. For example, although Brenner enjoins us to take class struggles seriously, his analyses of such conflicts are surprisingly vague, abstracted from the muscles and sinews of actual conflicts. Moreover, the literature on class formation tends to take a fairly unproblematic view of the development of the forces of production. Since the "objective conditions" of capitalist production are not in themselves in question, studies of class formation tend to privilege questions of class consciousness.[23] In this book, in contrast, I refer to

23. For an insightful overview of this literature, but one that replicates the distinctions between the "objective conditions" of production and class experience, see Ira Katznelson, "Working-Class Formation: Constructing Cases and Comparisons," in *Working-Class Formation: Nineteenth-Century Patterns in Western Europe and the United States,* ed.

capitalist class formation in the much more basic sense of the social formation of capitalist and proletarians, conceived as roles or identities developed in struggles over the production process. The subset of conflicts on which I focus are battles over control, struggles that have been called the "politics of production."[24]

The question is, why do these conflicts exist, and what is at stake? If we follow Schlumbohm's reasoning, beyond the token resistance of small producers defending their hold over production, such struggles are not significant if one assumes that capitalists eventually win. Yet this assessment, I believe, represents an anachronistic reading of capitalist power relations back into a noncapitalist arrangement. It is a misreading of the power relationships between merchants and small producers. In fact, as I document in Chapter 3, the relations are the inverse of what we might expect. Under conditions of open access to markets and competitive bidding, it is the merchant who was vulnerable to the actions of small-scale producers because under such conditions the merchant has no secure role in the production process. The merchant is extraneous because small-scale producers engage in marketing and also provide the capital and labor required for production. In an important sense, these producers are both workers and entrepreneurs.

Fundamentally, merchants are vulnerable because they do not engage in production. Operating in the realm of circulation, the merchant's profit is based on the difference between the market price and the price he has paid to the actual producer. The survival of the merchant relies on the existence of surplus. Without this profit the entire exchange would be futile. By contrast, petty producers do not operate with a similar structural need for profit beyond the reproduction cost of labor and materials. Like capitalist producers, independent commodity producers are constrained by the conditions of the market. They both have to meet the prevailing prices and suit the market demand. But within the production unit, production decisions are not dictated by the necessity for surplus beyond reproduction costs, that

---

Katznelson and Aristide R. Zolberg (Princeton: Princeton University Press, 1986). Alain Cottereau's essay in *Working-Class Formation*, "The Distinctiveness of Working-Class Cultures in France, 1848–1900," develops a perspective on class formation similar to my own. Specifically, he focuses on struggles for control of production processes which rely on disciplinary strategies other than mechanization.

24. For a general discussion of the politics of production, see Paul Thompson, *The Nature of Work: An Introduction to Debates on the Labor Process* (London: Macmillan, 1983), and Michael Burawoy, *The Politics of Production: Factory Regimes under Capitalism and Socialism* (London: Verso, 1985).

is, above the cost of replenishing supplies and reproducing the workforce. Because their survival is not defined by a structural need for profit, independent commodity producers at the same level of technology can and will sell at a market price lower than the price at which capitalist producers must cease production for lack of return. In a situation of open access to markets, small producers easily underbid merchants, forcing them to diminish their profits. Moreover, to preserve their autonomy when their independence is threatened, petty producers often reduce their level of consumption or work longer hours in order to reduce their prices to meet the competition. The ability of independent commodity producers to resist the centralizing efforts of manufacturers, even the efforts of putters-out to control production, lies with the very logic of their internal organization.[25] Thus, merchants were not merely drawn into production by opportunities to maximize profits, as Schlumbohm contends. Rather, they were often forced to struggle with small producers over control of the production process in order to secure any profits at all.[26]

Power, Action, and Identities

Inverting Schlumbohm's assumptions about the relative power of merchants and small producers is the first analytical move in building an alternative narrative of mechanization, one that explains the particular configurations of production arrangements observed in the region. But the solution is not to see small producers as inevitable

25. My description of the logic of the relationship between production and reproduction in petty commodity-producing households relies on the work of Harriet Friedmann: "Household Production and National Economy: Concepts for the Analysis of Agrarian Formations," *Journal of Peasant Studies* 7 (January 1980): 158–84, and "World Market, State, and Family Farm: Social Basis of Household Production in the Era of Wage Labor," *Comparative Studies of Society and History* 20 (October 1978): 545–86. See also Carol A. Smith, "Forms of Production in Practice: Fresh Approaches to Simple Commodity Production," *Journal of Peasant Studies* 11 (July 1984): 201–21, Jacques M. Chevalier, "There Is Nothing Simple about Simple Commodity Production," *Journal of Peasant Studies* 10 (July 1983): 153–86, and Gavin Smith, "Reflections on the Social Relations of Simple Commodity Production," *Journal of Peasant Studies* 13 (October 1985): 99–108. For a critique of this literature, see William Roseberry, *Anthropologies and Histories: Essays in Culture, History, and Political Economy* (New Brunswick: Rutgers University Press, 1989).

26. For a similar perspective on the origins of the putting-out system, see Stephen Marglin, "What Do Bosses Do? The Origins and Functions of Hierarchy in Capitalist Production," in *The Division of Labor: The Labor Process and Class Struggle in Modern Capitalism*, ed. André Gorz (London: Harvester Press, 1978), pp. 13–54. For an interesting critique of Marglin, see David S. Landes, "What Do Bosses Really Do?" *Journal of Economic History* 46 (September 1986): 585–623.

victors, not least because they were ultimately defeated. Rather, we need to see the continuing struggles over position and advantage as crucial to outcomes, not just as symptomatic of larger-scale structural shifts. The ingenious (often valiant, but at times tragic) ways handloom weavers subverted mercantile incursions into the production process forced merchants to devise new strategies. In turn, the struggles of merchants first to insert themselves into the production process, and then to exert control (against the continued resistance of handloom weavers), transformed the organization of production in unexpected ways, leading the process of capitalist development into unpredicted turns.

In such a context, power relations do not look like fixed hierarchies according to which one can determine a priori which party will be advantaged in a particular interaction. Rather, power is unstable and contingent on factors whose efficacy cannot be specified in the abstract. A feature of a context may or may not serve as a resource, depending on the relative position of the actors involved and the range of possibilities present. Resources may be as diverse as faraway markets or a particular configuration of intimate relations.

For example, in the Choletais during the eighteenth century, weavers' source of independence and their ability to circumvent merchants was based on their access to yarn and cloth markets. By the mid-nineteenth century, after merchant/industrialists succeeded in creating dependence, weavers relied on their relations to each other. Solidarity and strength in numbers limited the range of entrepreneurial strategies. But when mechanized weaving finally triumphed at the end of the nineteenth century, a victory aided by political rifts within the weaving community, handloom weavers turned to the financial support of other family members to sustain them in their trade. After other avenues of resistance were exhausted, handloom weavers drew on their positions as fathers and heads of households. They were able to advance their own goals by defining the collective interest of the household in terms of their own survival as small producers. Ultimately, these actions created a fully proletarianized workforce. Handloom weavers' resistance to proletarian status reduced other members of their households to working for wages. The irony of this victory exposes the importance of exploring how intimate relations are implicated in the process of capitalist class formation, a subject to which I return later in this chapter.

The underlying dynamics of these conflicts suggest the value of linking the concept of "identity" to the shifting quality of resources and positions. In the standard history of industrialization, identities derive from positions in fixed structures: merchants and small producers in the period before industrialization, owners and workers afterward. By contrast, by "identities" I mean the range of relations and possibilities for action in which actors are embedded. In such a conception, identities both shape struggles and are struggled over. Thus, in delimiting the range of activities available to small producers, merchants were redefining positions in the production process. In doing so, they were remaking identities, their own and those of small producers. If the ground of contention in the process of class formation is identity as I have defined it, then class struggle centers on opening up opportunities for oneself while closing down the options of others. The resilience of small producers is rooted in the heterogeneity of human identities. Like merchants, handloom weavers lived within multiple sets of social relationships. The complexity of social ties enabled action along many different dimensions, presenting the possibility of calling on other aspects of identity as resources for action.

However elusive power may be, enduring changes do emerge from such struggles. Production roles and identities can be transformed with lasting effect. By emphasizing a "positional" conception of power, I mean to direct the analysis toward how actors maneuver for advantage. Assuming that control requires constant attention prevents us, in studying these social processes, from taking hierarchy for granted. It forces us in each instance to specify how dominance was achieved.[27] When applied to explaining the pattern of economic organization in the Choletais, this perspective on action decenters the significance of machines and technological innovation by resituating technology in a broader politics of production. Specifically, mechanization becomes one strategy for control among others.

Technology and Social Struggles

Classically, economists argue that entrepreneurs introduce new technology and centralize production in order to benefit from the greater efficiency of machines and gains from economies of scale. Al-

27. For a similar conception of power and social action, see William H. Sewell Jr., "A Theory of Structure: Duality, Agency, and Transformation," *American Journal of Sociology* 98 (July 1992): 1–29. See also Joan W. Scott, *Gender and the Politics of History* (New York: Columbia University Press, 1988), pp. 5–8.

though these advantages certainly exist, efficiency arguments err in assuming that entrepreneurs are always free to realize them, that is, that they always have full control of the production process and thus are free to shape it to maximize profit. In a region like the Choletais, where gaining control is the central problem, the successful introduction of labor-saving machinery has a very different significance: it marks a social triumph. More generally, I am suggesting that the state of productive technology at any one moment reflects the distribution of local power and control over the production process. As Michael J. Piore and Charles F. Sabel have succinctly put it, "Machines are as much a mirror as the motor of social development."[28]

For merchants in the Choletais, machines served as a resource in their struggles against small producers. Machines cemented a position of dominance once it was achieved. The ability to introduce labor-saving machinery and the timing of these actions, however, depended on the success of prior engagements. For example, mechanizing spinning was feasible only after the collapse of the international linen trade and local civil war had idled most handloom weavers. Merchants took this opportunity to introduce cotton, the supply for which they could monopolize, in order to make weavers dependent on them for markets and yarn.

A similar story can be told about the mechanization of weaving. In the middle of the nineteenth century, the collective mobilization of weavers defending their place in the production process forced merchant/mill owners to rethink their ability to challenge the strength of small producers. When industrial spinners finally introduced power-looms (three decades after most industrial textile centers in France), they did so at a moment when handloom weavers were weakened by shortages in the international market for raw materials. In both instances, merchants and industrialists took advantage of conjunctural openings. They let the seemingly anonymous actions of distant markets create the social conditions necessary to advance their economic goals. That these actors had to wait for opportunities to present themselves rather than forcing the social world to conform to their design testifies to the strength of the opposition.

Achieving control was critical for other production strategies as well, most notably those strategies that led to the introduction of new forms of dispersed, labor-intensive manufacturing—the "sweated" alternatives to the factory system. The partisan nature of

28. Michael J. Piore and Charles F. Sabel, *The Second Industrial Divide: Possibilities for Prosperity* (New York: Basic Books, 1984), p. 5.

academic disputes over the role of the small-scale producers in industrial society makes it difficult to conceive of a common analysis that
bridges the gulf between luxury trades and the exploitative sweated
alternatives to factory-based mass production. The work of Sabel and
Jonathan Zeitlin, building on ideas put forward in the study by Piore
and Sabel cited earlier, indirectly suggests such a link.[29] Although
their intent is to highlight the positive contributions of small-scale
production to mass production (emphasizing such advantages as the
capacity to innovate and remain responsive to the demands of markets), the limiting conditions imposed on their arguments in favor of
"flexible specialization" suggests their awareness of the proximity of
sweated alternatives.[30]

Before turning to this subject, I need first to explain more generally
why small-scale production finds a place in industrial economies. In
his work on "technological dualism," Piore argues that risk-averting
strategies are crucial to explanations of the development of dual
structures in industrial economies. Since demand fluctuates over
time, if producers were to invest in the machinery, labor, and plant
space necessary to meet the greatest demand, they would risk idling
fixed capital when demand dropped off. Price competition, Piore con-
cludes, pushes producers to "separate out a relatively stable and predictable component of demand (where production can utilize the
most advanced division of labor) from the fluctuating component of
demand, which can be met profitably only with less specialized
resources."[31]

Technical dualism is thus a response to flux and instability in demand. Those firms with sufficient capital try to shelter themselves
against this uncertainty by capturing the most constant element of
the demand. They invest their capital in specialized machinery and a
full-time labor force, on which the firm spends time and money for
training in expectation of long-term employment. In this process,

29. Charles F. Sabel and Jonathan Zeitlin, "Historical Alternatives to Mass Production," *Past and Present* 108 (August 1985): 133–76.

30. For a critique of "flexible specialization," see Ash Amin, "Flexible Specialization and Small Firms in Italy: Myths and Realities," *Antipodes* 21 (1989): 13–34. See also Anna Cento Bull, "Proto-industrialization, Small-Scale Capital Accumulation, and Diffused Entrepreneurship: The Case of the Brianza in Lombardy," *Social History* 14 (May 1989): 177–200.

31. Michael J. Piore, "Dualism as a Response to Flux and Uncertainty," and "Technological Foundations of Dualism and Discontinuity," in *Dualism and Discontinuities in Industrialized Societies*, ed. Suzanne Berger and Piore (Cambridge: Cambridge University Press, 1980), p. 8. Given the direction of his later work, no doubt he would qualify his original claim that such strategies represented the most efficient use of capital resources. Still, the logic of his argument remains important for explaining the market rationale for persistence of small-scale production in this region.

these firms drive down costs by fully capturing the efficiency advantages of mass production, while forcing other producers into the fringes of the market, where they specialize in filling the fluctuating and uncertain components of demand.

From the point of view of the market and consumers, technical dualism represents an optimal response to the inevitable fluctuations in an industrial society: the constant, predictable component of demand is met at the lowest possible price, while the capacity exists to meet fluctuations as well. From the point of view of firms and workers, however, the picture is not so sanguine. Firms operating in the periphery of the product market either have lost out in competition with producers who dominate the core demand and thus are forced to take smaller orders at irregular intervals or are actually working under subcontracts from the core manufacturers. Firms working on the margins of the product market tend to minimize their own risk by not investing in costly machinery and plant space and by making the workforce absorb the uncertainties of the market in the form of frequent unemployment and constantly changing wage rates. These are the producers who favor small workshops and homework, hand labor, and a flexible labor force of workers who can be easily hired, trained, and fired at the end of the season or contract. Moreover, since these producers cannot benefit from the economies of scale realized with machine production, greater profits and higher productivity can be had only by sweating both out of the workforce by pushing down wage rates and prolonging work hours.

In the Choletais, a crucial dimension of struggles among merchants, between merchants and producers, and later between industrialists and small producers was over absorbing the risks associated with market fluctuations. Once well positioned, merchants and industrialists tried to shelter themselves from the hazards of market competition by passing on to weaker, dependent actors the costs and insecurities. Production strategies that led to sweating were designed to accomplish this end. The consequences of this strategy for the organization of production are most visible in my analysis of the sweated alternative to the factory system in Chapters 6, 7, and 9. In these chapters I discuss the divisions of labor and product markets between dispersed labor-intensive production and centralized machine-aided production in textiles and the new garment and shoe trades. To serve their own risk-averting strategies, highly mechanized capitalist producers forced small producers of all types into marginal sectors of the product market. In more hidden ways, however, this logic, which I call the "logic of sweating," was present in all the relations of production and exchange examined in this book.

Piore, Sabel, and Zeitlin point out that the advantages of flexible specialization can be realized only when small producers are able to minimize competition between firms and share the risks involved in innovations and market fluctuations. In doing so, they are in effect arguing that flexible specialization can work only when there are mechanisms in place that defend against the logic of sweating. The artisanal forerunners of the small innovative firms studied by Sabel and Zeitlin were able to shape the kind of technology they adopted and the internal division of labor because of their control over production and markets.

This emphasis on harmonious social relationships, on cooperation and paternalism, is significant in its contrast to conditions in the Choletais. There, the political collapse of the handloom weavers' resistance in the late nineteenth century created the economic conditions for sweated work. Sabel and Zeitlin's limiting conditions did not hold, and small-scale producers were forced to take up the uncertain component of demand. Placing the findings of Sabel, Zeitlin, and Piore in the context of the Choletais suggests that the two poles of small-scale production—flexibility in the pursuit of greater surplus and labor-intensive production at the margins of industrial markets—are different outcomes of struggles for control over the production process and security within product markets.

Gender and Class Formation

The pervasiveness of sweating as a production strategy in the Choletais should lead us to ask, how were these relations of dominance and dependence created and reproduced socially? I have already discussed the creation and maintenance of these power relations in marketplace struggles, but it is important to note that a similar logic operated in weaving households as well. Such power relations are most pronounced, and most consequential for my argument, in the construction of family solidarity around the identity and status of the male head of the household. In recognizing these parallels, I break down the usual distinction between public and private realms of behavior. Such divides become artificial when family ties can serve as resources for market-based struggles, just as market position can at times privilege some family members in domestic struggles. Concretely, this analytical move helps to account for how one form of small-scale production endured and why a new type of dispersed, labor-intensive manufacturing was introduced. More generally, the analysis adds a feminist perspective on the process of capitalist class formation by answering why the new sweated trades employed most female workers.[32]

That small producers and proletarianized outworkers lived side by side in the same family offers an important lesson for conceptualizing the relationships between gender and class formation. The proletarianization of women reveals much about the tensions and norms in these families. The transformations within weaving households suggest that gender constitutes a class divide within small-producer households. Admittedly this is an unusual use of the concept "class." This conception, however, enhances and is consistent with the ways I have specified the relation between class formation and economic development.[33] The thornier problem of understanding patriarchal power and its relation to capitalism can be deferred for closer scrutiny in Chapter 9.

Clearly, everyone labored in weaving households. I invoke class to denote the differential relations to ownership and concepts of skill which define the primary activities of the household. Male and female identities and work roles in weaving households were defined in relation to the primary activity of the household, cloth making. The identity of the household was linked to an internal hierarchy of skill, itself linked to responsibility and adeptness at weaving and ancillary activities. These gender and skill distinctions are consequential because they constitute the fissures along which we can examine the process of proletarianization within families. Under stress, handloom weavers continued to weave, carrying on the fight, while other family members, defined as less crucial to the social identity of the household, were forced to look elsewhere for additional income. By contrast, an abandonment of weaving for another occupation by the head

---

32. For an incisive critical overview of this literature, see Jill Rubery, "Structured Labor Markets, Worker Organization, and Low Pay," *Cambridge Journal of Economics* 2 (1978): 17–36; see also Peter B. Doeringer and Michael Piore, *Internal Labor Markets and Manpower Analysis* (Lexington, Mass.: D.C. Heath, 1971), and R. C. Edwards, M. Reich, and D. M. Gordon, eds., *Labor Market Segmentation* (Lexington, Mass.: D.C. Heath, 1975).

33. For a similar analysis of household relations, see Annette Kuhn, "Structures of Patriarchy and Capital in the Family," *Feminism and Materialism*, ed. Annette Kuhn and Ann-Marie Wolpe (London: Routledge and Kegan Paul, 1978). See also the article by Kate Young, "Modes of Appropriation and the Sexual Division of Labor: A Case Study from Oaxaca, Mexico," in the same volume, and Harriet Friedmann, "Patriarchal Commodity Production," *Social Analysis* 20 (December 1986): 47–55.

of the household signaled both social and economic defeat. The wages of wives and daughters thus supported a male-defined notion of their common social identity.

This analysis discourages us from treating the households as a single entity that reacts to external pressures, such as proletarianization, as an undifferentiated whole. As the work of Gay Gullickson, for example, has shown, analytically disaggregating activities within households and distinguishing the labor of males and females are essential if one is to account for the existence of proto-industries in such rich agricultural regions as Normandy.[34] More generally, Belinda Bozzoli has observed that proletarianization often follows a gendered logic. Injecting Brenner's analysis of the relationship between class struggle and economic development with feminist concerns, Bozzoli distinguishes two forms of conflict: struggle within the household (what Bozzoli calls the "domestic system") and struggle between the domestic sphere and the capitalist one. Arguing against the typical Marxist tendency to give primacy to production over reproduction, Bozzoli stresses that the outcomes of domestic struggles are significant. They may in fact "condition and shape the *very form taken by capitalism in that society.*"[35]

Certainly, the dynamics within weaving families in the Choletais provide a case in point. The outcomes of such domestic struggles did shape the subsequent economic development of the region, by restructuring the local labor market and generating a supply of female workers with few other alternatives. The availability of this group of workers attracted the new types of sweated industry to the area.[36]

Attention to family dynamics exposes the particular nature of capitalist class formation in the Pays des Mauges. The hundred-year struggle of handloom weavers to maintain control over the production process was, in a sense, successful. Although handloom weavers ceded over time a great deal of entrepreneurial control over weaving,

34. See note 14.

35. Belinda Bozzoli, "Marxism, Feminism and South African Studies," *Journal of Southern African Studies* 9 (April 1983): 139–71, 147.

36. Jane Humphries and Jill Rubery adopt a similar approach in "The Reconstitution of the Supply Side of the Labour Market: The Relative Autonomy of Social Reproduction," *Cambridge Journal of Economics* 8 (December 1984): 331–46. Jill Rubery and Frank Wilkinson's "Outwork and Segmented Labor Markets," in *The Dynamics of Labor Market Segmentation,* ed. Wilkinson (New York: Academic Press, 1981), pp. 115–32, makes an important contribution toward conceptualizing the relationship between homework and labor markets. See also Christine Craig, Jill Rubery, Roger Tarling, and Frank Wilkinson, *Labor Market Structure, Industrial Organization, and Low Pay* (Cambridge: Cambridge University Press, 1982).

and although they eventually became impoverished dependent producers, they remained the organizers of transformative processes mediating yarn and cloth. In the end, their status as dependent producers served the interest of industrialists. Still, small producers in the Mauges were not themselves fully proletarianized. The actual process of proletarianization occurred within weaving households and was rooted in the cultural assumptions underlying how weavers perceived themselves as craftsmen and how they subsequently defended their trade.

Proto-industrial Theory Reexamined

Ironically, once we attribute a causal role to actual struggles and acknowledge that the progress of capitalist relations of production is contingent on the outcomes of such engagements, the proto-industrialization hypothesis itself threatens to unravel. Once we grant that noncapitalist relations of production and marketing in rural manufacturing (even among those organized for export) favored small producers over merchants and that mercantile control was an uphill battle with many risks and frustrations, it is more difficult to sustain the argument that rural industries were a preparatory stage for capitalist industrialization. When accounting for the risks and costs of centralizing production, one must also include the social cost of transforming the social relations of production. In a region where small-scale producers are a well-entrenched population, such struggles may present insurmountable odds or, at least, raise the costs of such actions beyond what capitalist entrepreneurs can reasonably sustain. By contrast, it is easier to build large-scale factories that integrate many phases of production in areas with no previous history of manufacturing. In Alsace, for example, Swiss banking capital, an influx of migrant workers, and cheap water power together fueled the highly integrated and mechanized luxury cotton industry which was the pride of the high-quality French textile mills before 1870.

The rapid success of Alsace sets a sharp contrast to areas in the West of France, except perhaps in Rouen, where a long history of rural manufacturing and dispersed entrepreneurship led to sluggish patterns of industrialization. In addition to the well-organized opposition from deeply entrenched groups of small-scale producers, in older manufacturing districts each individual entrepreneur faced myriads of others in the same sector of production all trying to accomplish the same objective. Given this reasoning, it is quite possible that successful transitions from proto-industries to factory-based mass production were rather exceptional cases and that de-industrialization (defined as failed attempts at industrialization) was the more typical scenario. If the latter is true, then case studies that focus directly on the dynamics of regional economies in which industrialization was stalled by successful resistance, such as the developments in the Choletais, have an even more important story to tell about the difficulties of this transition and what happens subsequently to these regional economies.

Thus, at the center of my alternative narrative of industrialization is struggle: over roles in production, access to profits, connections to markets, and the requirements of family solidarity in changing circumstances. Factors such as technology and market segmentation are elements in these conflicts, not determinants. I begin by uncoupling the close association between machines and market efficiency in order to link the choice of production techniques to social struggles. The pattern of economic development in the Choletais can be explained as the outcome of local struggles between merchants and small producers for control of the production process. More generally, labor-saving automatic machinery is a resource for capitalist control of production. Industrial technology instantiates a system of control and power relations; it is the materialization of a social victory. Both small producers and would-be capitalists fought over these victories, knew triumph and defeat, and struggled for the right to define their future relations.

I have argued that in examining these struggles we are studying the process of capitalist class formation. I want to stress, as we enter the narrative itself, that I do no mean class as an endpoint. Instead, the key is to focus on formation, on the relation between action and changing structure. It is this which makes local struggle so important in explaining the pattern of regional society and development, and in particular in understanding why the Choletais appears developed or underdeveloped relative to other areas. It is also this which makes it necessary to rewrite the history of industrialization, to introduce new contingencies and new uncertainties.

3

The Putting-Out Wilderness:
The Vulnerability of Merchants
in the Marketplace

In describing the manufacturing economy of ancien régime France, historians have typically invoked two stereotypes. In the cities, urban guilds jealously guarded their privileges and guaranteed monopolies to the detriment of commerce and technical advancement. In the countryside, in contrast, production and commerce flowed freely under the control of merchants who had successfully escaped the shackles of the urban corporate economy. Recent scholarship has questioned this simple view of the urban guild economy.[1] Historians have demonstrated, at least in several regional studies, that merchant guilds effectively used guild structures to expand and stabilize their positions as capitalist entrepreneurs.[2]

Similarly, but from a very different vantage point, this chapter challenges the stereotypical view of rural manufacturing by questioning the freedom of merchants to control production in the countryside.[3] Although a world without guild regulations did free entrepre-

1. See the special issue of the *Annales* devoted to the guilds: "Corps et communautés d'Ancien Régime," *Annales: Économies, sociétés, civilisations* 43 (March–April 1988), especially the introduction by Jacques Revel and articles by Jochen Hoock, "Réunion de métiers et marché régional: Les marchands réunis de la ville de Rouen au début du XVIIIe siècle," Simona Cerutti, "Du corps au métier: La corporation des tailleurs à Turin entre le XVIIe et le XVIIIe siècle," and Gail Bossenga, "La Révolution française et les corporations: Trois exemples lillois." Of equal interest are the revisionist articles on guilds published in a forum titled "Three Views on Guilds," *French Historical Studies* 15 (Fall 1988), especially the introduction by Cissie Fairchilds and articles by Gail Bossenga, "Protecting Merchants: Guilds and Commercial Capitalism in Eighteenth-Century France," and Liana Vardi, "The Abolition of Guilds during the French Revolution."
2. See Gail Bossenga, *The Politics of Privilege: Old Regime and Revolution in Lille* (New York: Cambridge University Press, 1991), chap. 7, and "Protecting Merchants."
3. The phrase "putting-out wilderness" in my chapter title comes from William M. Reddy, *The Rise of Market Culture: The Textile Trades and French Society, 1750–1900* (Cambridge: Cambridge University Press, 1984).

neurship of all sorts, I argue that this freedom did not necessarily favor capitalist relations of production. By focusing on struggles between merchants and rural small producers over control of the production process, I show that, far from benefiting from the openness of rural markets and freedom from guild regulations, merchants desperately tried to restrict access to markets. Ironically, their efforts brought merchants into conflict with the royal administration, which repeatedly accused them of monopolistic actions and obstructing the free flow of commerce.

My aim is to invert the standard assumptions about the power relations between merchants and rural small producers. The fundamental problem for merchants in the unregulated countryside, I argue, was their vulnerability to small-scale producers. In the linen economy of the region, with an indigenous source for raw materials, few merchants had access to the dependent workforce necessary to be successful putters-out. In the eighteenth century, in the Choletais, merchants faced great obstacles in imposing dependence on independent small-scale producers.

Struggles over raw materials demonstrate the difficulties merchants faced. The first effective putting-out system in the region did not exist until after the French linen market collapsed in the late eighteenth century and merchants sank their capital into mechanizing and centralizing the spinning of cotton. By controlling the local supply of cotton yarn, these merchant/mill owners had the tools necessary to control cloth production as putters-out.

This chapter, then, is the first building block for an argument carried through in the following two chapters which develops an alternative to the proto-industrialization hypothesis—one that highlights the causal significance of struggles in a contentious production process and emphasizes that the labels "development" and "underdevelopment" are simply shorthand ways of describing who gains control of that process.

Cholet in the International Export Economy

The town of Cholet was an unlikely regional market center for export manufacturing. Cholet in 1700 was an obscure bourg on the banks of the Moyne river with a small population of five or six hundred. Lost in the bocage south of the Loire valley, located about 50 kilometers southwest of Angers and 50 kilometers southeast of Nantes, the town was served by neither major roads nor navigable waterways. The rise of Cholet from obscurity was clearly linked to the growth and expansion of an international export market in linens.

Local historians attribute the origins of the export-oriented textile trade to aristocratic initiatives, but which of the two families that held the fiefdom during the seventeenth century (the Colberts or the De Broons) should be credited with the foresight is much debated.[4] The spinning and weaving of natural fibers such as flax and wool into cloth was likely a very ancient craft among the rural population. Like the tailors, blacksmiths, and clog makers of the countryside, rural weavers practiced their trade for a local clientele. By the late seventeenth century, however, linen production had taken on an entirely different character. The new linen producers specialized in varieties of finer cloths, especially the fine linen kerchiefs for which the region was developing its reputation. The rural population around the town of Cholet was brought into the net of an international export trade.

The eighteenth century was the high point of the French Atlantic economy. During the century, the volume of finished goods, agricultural commodities, and slaves crossing the Atlantic grew exponentially. During the shipping season, vessels loaded with manufactured goods like textiles, guns, leather goods, crystals, and glass, and agricultural products such as wines, wheat, cured meats, and preserves regularly departed the ports of Nantes, Saint-Malo, and Bordeaux headed for the French sugar islands of Saint-Domingue and Guadeloupe. Many fleets, especially those leaving Nantes, sailed first to the west coast of Africa. After using some of their cargo to trade for slaves, the ships traversed the Atlantic with their goods and human cargo. At the other end, colonists waited anxiously for the goods necessary to maintain their European lifestyles and the slaves to work their plantations. Discharging their cargo in the islands for a handsome profit, the same ships were reloaded with sugar, coffee, and indigo for European consumers and producers.[5]

4. See Auguste-Amaury Gellusseau, *Histoire de Cholet et de son industrie* (Cholet: Éd. Fillion, 1862), and Victor Dauphin, "Le textile dans les Mauges avant 1789," *Bulletin de la Société des sciences, lettres, et beaux-arts de Cholet et de sa région,* 1954; pp. 27–28 are devoted to this debate.

5. Most of the monographic literature on French port commerce focuses on individual port cities. On Bordeaux, consult Paul Butel, *Les négociants bordelaises: L'Europe et les îles au XVIIIe siècle* (Paris: Aubier, 1974). For Nantes, consult Paul Jeulin, *L'évolution du port de Nantes, organisation et trafic depuis les origines* (Paris: Presses universitaires de France, 1929); Gaston Martin, *Nantes au XVIIIe siècle: L'ère des négriers 1714–1774* (Paris: L. Durance, 1928); and Jean Meyer, *L'armement nantais dans la deuxième moitié du XVIIIe siècle* (Paris, S.E.V.P.E.N., 1969), and "Le commerce négrier nantais (1774–1792)," *Annales: Économies, sociétés, civilisations* 15 (January–February 1960): 120–29.

Atlantic commerce created a dense network of trade and manufacturing that reached deep into the interior of the Continent from the port cities. Producers of cloth and yarn sold mostly in town markets near their homes. Cloth traveled through established channels of local markets and regional fairs to reach the merchant houses and ship suppliers in Bordeaux, Nantes, Marseilles, and Saint-Malo. The vast flow of goods tied these small-scale producers to Africans and to those who labored and leisured across the Atlantic. These lives were sewn together through the vicissitudes of international trade.

Compared to other textile centers in western France, Cholet was a latecomer to the Atlantic trade. In the sixteenth century, Brittany and the Maine already exported their linens and woolens to Spain and the Spanish Americas. Export-oriented manufacturing did not develop in southern Anjou until the late seventeenth century. Despite a late beginning, Cholet's linen achieved rapid success and prospered with the good fortunes of the French colonial trade. By 1788, textiles from the West constituted 38 percent of all exports from Bordeaux. Brittany alone supplied linens valued at 2.8 million livres tournois, close to one-fifth of all textiles exported. Linen exports from Laval, another ancient center of linen production of the Maine, was valued at 1.1 million livres tournois, and Cholet exported 1.2 million livres, representing respectively 7.8 and 8.5 percent of the total export from Bordeaux.[6] By the mid-eighteenth century, Cholet had become a bustling commercial center with its own linen market attracting merchants and ship suppliers from Normandy, the Midi, and the port cities of the Atlantic and Mediterranean.

Several times a year, via caravans of packmules, wholesale merchants (*négociants*) from Cholet carted the cloth they purchased to Beaucaire and Bordeaux, the great international cloth fairs of the Midi, and to the lesser fairs in the Limousin, Poitou, and Auvergne. On their journeys they also frequented important cities on the cloth routes: Lyon, Toulouse, Agen, and Montpellier. On the return trip, they carried dyes, dyed yarns, and wine.[7] Over time, Cholet's merchants established connections with merchant houses in other regions. These associations led to joint ventures, partnerships, and sometimes families linked by marriage. These alliances became important sources for capital to fund the ventures of Cholet's future manufacturing elite.

6. Butel, *Négociants bordelaises*, p. 103.
7. Elie Chamard, *Vingt siècles de l'histoire de Cholet* (Cholet: Farré et fils, 1970), pp. 68–69 and *La Maison Richard Frères* (Cholet: L'imprimerie Vételé, 1959).

Other merchants in Cholet invested directly in the Atlantic trade
by purchasing local goods to provision their own trading ships. Some
even journeyed to the New World and settled some of their family
there.[8] The Mesnards, one such merchant family, were said to have
supplied ships leaving the ports of Granville and Nantes. Local leg-
ends recount that the Mesnards sailed to the coast of west Africa,
trading cloth and fishing for cod.[9]

Wholesale merchants were by far the wealthiest merchants in the
region's textile trade.[10] They built opulent residences in the Saint-
Pierre section of Cholet and filled their houses and gardens with ex-
otic goods and plants rarely seen in the region. As specialists with
crucial connections to external markets, the négociants were powerful figures who dictated the terms to all producers and smaller merchants. This group gained both political and economic strength as
the international trade flourished. For subsequent generations, mercantile fortunes financed the families' upward mobility. Some négociant families retired to country estates, enobled their names, and
purchased royal offices for their sons.

Below the handful of négociants in Cholet, the mercantile community was both vast and diverse. There were, of course, itinerant merchants and peddlers who roamed the countryside buying up and
reselling bits of yarn and cloth. More important, however, were the
linen drapers (called *fabricants*) who bought up raw materials to put
out to weavers and later sold cloths to wholesale merchants. The differences in wealth between wholesale merchants and linen drapers
were enormous. The fortune of a wealthy négociant could easily be
twenty or thirty time that of an average fabricant.[11] Linen drapers
were often indistinguishable from handloom weavers, and at times
they were even poorer.[12]

8. François Dornic, *L'industrie textile dans le Maine et ses débouchés internationaux* (Le
Mans: Éditions Pierre Bellon, 1955), p. 80.
9. Chamard, *Histoire de Cholet,* pp. 63, 68.
10. For example, Chamard reports that one merchant's widow, Veuve Beritault de la Che-
snaie, left an estate valued at 80,000 livres in unsold cloth and furniture, grain, and wine
valued at 15,000 livres. Chamard does not indicate the extend of landed property. See Chamard, *Histoire de Cholet,* p. 69.
11. Comparing the average wealth of négociants and fabricants using the inventories of
personal and real property for assessing estate taxes (the registries of the *mutations après
décès*) for deaths registered between 1820 and 1824 from the Bureau of Cholet, Serge Chassagne reported that the average wealth of négociants was 118,905 francs, compared to 4,447
francs for fabricants; Chassagne, "La diffusion rurale de l'industrie cotonnière en France
(1750–1850)," *Revue du Nord* 240 (January–March 1979): 111.
12. In his study of the fortunes of former combatants of the Vendée war, Claude Petitfrère
has concluded from pension claims and surveys of the death inventories drawn for the mu-

In the Mauges weaving was not a supplement to agricultural incomes, as it was in other regions. Rural weavers were almost completely severed from the land. They might have owned a garden plot, a small house, and if fortunate a cow, but their primary income was from manufacturing.[13] They were likely recruited from among the land-poor and landless rural population created by the enclosure movement led by aristocratic landowners between the fifteenth and seventeenth centuries. In the process of consolidating former common lands into large tenant farms, nucleated villages were progressively destroyed.[14] Peasants displaced by enclosure eked out a living on tiny plots, clustered around the remnants of villages. No longer able to subsist on their land, they increasingly relied on wasteland for pasturing their meager livestock and gathering firewood and fuel. The clearing of wastelands for arable agriculture throughout the eighteenth and nineteenth centuries further impoverished this land-poor population. Because weaving required only a short apprenticeship and looms were relatively inexpensive, weaving represented a viable economic alternative.

Weavers lived in small hamlets of several weaving families or in the bourgs of many parishes. Weaving houses were readily recognizable by their cellars. Half under ground and half above, these cellars with half-moon windows to admit daylight were the weaver's work-

tations après décès that the terms "fabricant" and "tisserand" are poor predictors of actual wealth. For example, Louis Rochard, a fabricant who was wounded during the Vendée wars, claimed that he lost 2,500 francs in movable property, merchandise, and weaving implements through fire and pillage. Similarly Jacques Griffon of Cholet, who was listed as a tisserand on his marriage certificate, but listed as a fabricant on the mutations après décès, left an equally modest 3,000 francs in property, merchandise, and weaving implements. By contrast, many tisserands were richer than fabricants. Joseph Lemoine, for example, claimed that during the Vendée wars he lost two houses and two shops to fire and pillage. Combining property value, furnishings, and merchandise, Lemoine claimed a loss of 9,300 francs. The mutations après décès of weaver François Griffon of Roussay listed 10,039 francs in community property with his wife and 7,300 francs in immovable property; Claude Petitfrère, Les Vendéens d'Anjou: Analyse des structures militaires, sociales, et mentales (Paris: Bibliothèque nationale, 1981), pp. 349–50. These weavers were, of course, exceptional. According to Chassagne, "Diffusion rurale," the average wealth of weavers in the district of Cholet from the mutations après décès was 500 francs. We can conclude, however, that although fabricants were generally wealthier than tisserands, the range for both groups varied enormously and there was no clear-cut division between them. In fact, it was possible for weavers to be wealthier than fabricants.

13. Richard H. Andrews, Les paysans des Mauges au XVIIIe siècle (Tours: Arrault, 1935), p. 37; Charles Tilly, The Vendée (Cambridge: Harvard University Press, 1964), p. 136.

14. Louis Merle, Le métairie et l'évolution de la gâtine poitevine de la fin du moyen âge à la Révolution (Paris: S.E.V.P.E.N., 1958). For similar processes in the nineteenth century, see G. Vergneau, "La mise en valeur du domaine de Bouzillé (commune de Mélay, Maine-et-Loire): Contribution à l'étude de la métairie dans le bocage vendéen," Actes de 97e congrès national des sociétés savantes, Nantes, 1972, pp. 153–68.

shops. The typical cellar workshop was large enough to hold several looms. The cellars were kept cool and humid. Their floors were made of packed dirt and the walls were whitewashed with lime. The dampness was essential for good linen but terrible for the weavers' health. Living quarters above the cellar consisted of one single room of 20 to 25 square meters, large enough only for a stove, beds, table, and cupboard. A small loft under the rafters served as extra storage and for sleeping.[15]

The vast majority of weaving households owned their own looms. Most households had more than one loom with more than one family member weaving at a time. The weaving equipment itself was simple and inexpensive. The common handloom consisted of four upright posts bound together by cross ties. Heddles, composed of many pieces of twine with loops at the center of each through which the warp threads passed in front, hung from pulleys at the top of the loom and connected to treddles underneath the frame. Most of the cloths produced in the region were plain weaves for which two heddles and two treddles sufficed.[16]

Weaving was a family enterprise. Every member of a weaving household was engaged in some aspect of cloth production. The tasks were divided by sex and age. Weaving was officially a male occupation, the profession of the head of the household. Women and children were assigned auxiliary tasks: preparing the warp threads, mounting the loom, winding the weft threads onto bobbins for the shuttle. The actual division of tasks, however, probably varied depending on the status of the weaving household.

Some weaving households were headed by independent entrepreneurs. They purchased the yarns, owned all the implements necessary to make cloth, and sold the cloth in local markets. Other weaving households depended on petty traders from whom they either purchased yarn and or sold their cloth. In these cases, the household owned the yarn, cloth, and implements but did not go to local town markets. The bought and sold to local intermediaries. Finally, some weaving households worked on commission at an agreed price, receiving work from fabricants who provided the yarn and specified the quantity and variety of cloth desired. In these cases, the household provided the implements but owned neither the yarn nor the fi-

15. Louis Renard, "Les maisons d'habitation des tisserands," *Bulletin de la Société des sciences, lettres, et beaux-arts de Cholet,* 1890.
16. Ibid.

nal product.[17] These three different relations to the product and to markets were not rigid distinctions, though. An independent weaver entrepreneur could act as an intermediary for other weaving families in their cluster of houses as well as sell his own cloth. A weaver might work on commission on one occasion or season and sell directly on the cloth market in the next season.

If the household purchased its own yarn, most of the ancillary activities were performed within the household. These tasks included winding the weft (horizontal) threads for the shuttle and winding warp (vertical) threads onto the yarn beam of the loom. Weft threads were wound onto a bobbin which was placed in a hollow in the weaver's shuttle. These threads ran off freely as the shuttle was passed from side to side during the weaving of the cloth.[18] In these households, women not only wound the weft onto bobbins but also operated the warping frames (an *ourdissoir* and a *dévidoir*) and were called *ourdisseuses* and *dévideuses*. If the household worked on commission from a linen draper, the warp was generally mounted in the fabricant's shop, and the weaver received the warp, heddles, and reeds from the fabricant. In these cases, winding weft bobbins was left to the weaving household.

Typically, weavers worked long days, rising at dawn or before, descending to their cellars to weave, and taking breaks only for meals. Their productivity, their income, and hence their standard of living depended on the kind of cloth they wove. In 1790, kerchiefs sold for 10 to 72 livres a dozen. A piece of *siamoise* (a blend of cotton and linen) 20 aunes in length was valued at between 80 and 120 livres, and grosses toiles sold for 20 and 30 livres for 20 aunes.[19] The standard handloom production was 4–5 meters for a full working day. At this rate, each weaver produced about four dozen kerchiefs a week, or spent 4–5 days producing a bolt of cloth of 20 aunes.[20] Arthur Young estimates for the same period that weavers' income in Anjou averaged 30–35 sous a day.[21] Compared to the prices of cloths, these weaving incomes appear too low. Because of the variety of productive arrangements, there must have been a wide range in weavers' stan-

17. Andrews, *Paysans des Mauges*, pp. 149–50.

18. A. J. Warden, *The Linen Trade: Ancient and Modern* (London: Longman, 1864), pp. 702–3.

19. Archives départementales de Maine-et-Loire (hereafter A.D. M-et-L) 1L546: Tableau de la fabrique des toiles, Bureau de marque de Vihiers, 1790. An *aune* measures approximately 1.18 meters. See Ronald E. Zupko, *French Weights and Measures before the Revolution: A Dictionary of Provincial and Local Units* (Bloomington: Indiana University Press, 1978).

20. Dauphin, "Textile dans les Mauges," p. 36.

21. Arthur Young, *Voyages en France en 1787, 1788, 1789*, trans. (into French) Henri Sée (Paris: Armand Colin, 1932), 3:981. By convention 1 sou = 5 centimes, 20 sous = 1 livre.

dards of living. Even at the low end of the scale, however, weavers earned a decent living for their toil.

The Organization of Linen Production

The coordinating centers of local manufacturing were the market-places. The output of all the different phases of the production process, from combed flax to finished cloth, came together in the various yarn and cloth markets that dotted the region. Yet trying to deduce a simple description of the structure of manufacturing from those who were present at the markets is a difficult task. The structure of this manufacturing network—its division of labor and social relations of production—was complex. In fact, most historians' attempts to comprehend rural manufacturing in this era have failed to capture its most interesting characteristic: the fluidity of its structures and the indistinctness of production roles.

For example, the central cloth market in the region was held in Cholet every Saturday. The cloth market preceded the yarn market held on the same grounds, located next to the cattle market. Market days animated the usually quiet town life. On these days, vendors of all sorts—spinners, weavers, and various types of intermediaries and hawkers—arrived early, sometimes before dawn, to vie for the best places to display their wares.

At the crossroads, constantly jostled by people, animals, and bolts of cloth passing by, buyers surveyed the range of goods, inspected the numerous samples, and mentally calculated prices and future demand. Among the buyers at the cloth market were resident wholesale cloth merchants, itinerant peddlers of all varieties of goods, bleachers, and not infrequently agents representing merchant houses and cloth wholesalers from faraway cities. In the midst of this confusion, commerce flowed at a rapid pace. Purchasing in this tumble of shouting and haggling required a good eye for detail and familiarity with the work process so as to judge the quality at a glance and guard against fraud.

Among the parties selling, we find rural weavers who came to town with the accumulated product of weeks or months of labor. Sometimes these weavers also sold their neighbors' goods on commission; at other times they sold only their own. Other sellers included intermediaries who sold cloth produced by weavers to whom they had provided the spun yarn, and hawkers and itinerant peddlers who roamed the countryside buying up cloth to sell for a small profit at local fairs.

Cholet's yarn market took place on Saturdays after the closing of the cloth market.[22] Yarn markets were notoriously chaotic, and this one was no exception. At these markets, yarn was sold by weight and priced according to the fineness of the strand and its quality. Yarn prices varied enormously, from 1–2 livres a pound (approximately 50 grams) for yarn used to make coarse cloths, to 3–19 livres a pound for kerchief quality, to 4–30 livres a pound for luxury linens depending again on fineness and quality.[23]

As weavers and merchants went from booth to booth testing and twisting the yarn, they faced great difficulty in matching the various packets of yarn of different counts and different qualities to achieve an even quality in the final cloth. The quality of their cloths, indeed their reputations and livelihoods, depended on the quality of the yarn.[24] Although yarn reckoning was standardized, there were no controls over which counts of yarn spinners brought to market. Even more serious, yarn was constantly in short supply, because it often required as many as ten spinners to supply enough yarn for one full-time weaver.[25] This further aggravated the loose coordination be-

22. Although Cholet's yarn market was significant, Beaupréau, Montrevault, Montlimart, and other small towns all had active yarn markets. The most important yarn market in the region was in Chalonnes, which was known to carry the best yarns, as well as the best flax, in the region. Many producers and linen drapers from Cholet would travel nearly 35 kilometers to Chalonnes, on horseback and sometimes even on foot, even though yarn was readily available in their own town. See Andrews, *Paysans des Mauges*, pp. 148, 151, and Gellusseau, *Histoire de Cholet*, p. 96.

23. A.D. M-et-L 1L546: Tableau de la fabrique des toiles, Bureau de marque de Vihiers, 1790. From our limited knowledge of yarn prices, it is difficult to determine how spinners fared in this production process. It is generally believed that spinning was not a lucrative trade. Arthur Young (*Voyages en France*, 3:981) reported that spinners in Anjou on the average made 8–9 sous a day on the eve of the French Revolution, that is, 40–45 centimes. These figures are consistent with other reports on spinning wages in the West, but at the lower end of the scale. In Normandy, for example, spinners received from 9 to as much as 20 sous a day. Gay L. Gullickson, *The Spinners and Weavers of Auffay: Rural Industry and the Sexual Division of Labor in the French Village, 1750–1850* (Cambridge: Cambridge University Press, 1986), p. 72. Equally, spinners may have been much better remunerated than these reports suggest.

24. Andrews, *Paysans des Mauges*, p. 148.

25. Two types of spinning instruments were employed in the eighteenth century. Some women used a simple distaff and spindle, others used a distaff with a spinning wheel. The distaff was a stick about a meter long, on the top of which the wad of combed fibers was stuck. The spinner held the distaff under her left arm and drew a continuous strand of flax from it with her left hand. She then passed the strand from her left hand to her right, where she twisted it between her forefinger and thumb. The yarn then passed onto the spindle, which dangled from her right hand. As the strand of yarn lengthened, the spindle dropped slowly to the floor. When it reached the floor, the spinner wound the yarn onto the spindle and the process began again. With a spinning wheel, the spinner turned the wheel with her right hand and pulled the combed flax from the distaff with her right hand. As she turned the wheel, it rotated one or two small bobbins that drew out the flax from her left hand. The key

tween quality, supply, and demand. Needless to say, competition for yarn was keen.

The identities of sellers and buyers at the yarn market were as diverse as in the cloth market. Spinners in the Choletais were primarily farm women from the interior of the bocage, an area dominated by subsistence farming where flax was typically not cultivated.[26] Some spinners purchased combed flax from flax markets in the Loire valley or purchased the materials from itinerant peddlers who frequented the flax markets of the region. Others spun flax provided to them by putters-out, who purchased the flax and retained ownership of it in order to possess the yarn which they would, in turn, sell at yarn markets or put out to weavers.[27] Sellers included farm women selling the product of their own labor and that of female members of their household, yarn merchants who owned the raw materials and put out their materials to spinners, and peddlers of all goods. Among the purchasers were weavers intent on turning yarn into cloth and merchants. The merchants included putters-out, itinerant peddlers, and bleachers who might resell the yarn after bleaching or put out their yarn to weavers.

Looking at the variety of people present at both markets, how should we describe the social organization of linen production in this region? Traditionally, historians of rural manufacturing have tried to make sense of the bewildering organizational complexities and the varieties of property and work arrangements in these markets by sorting out patterns, conceding all the while that there were as many exceptions as there were regularities. Evgenii Tarlé's famous study in

---

to spinning was to hold the fiber with an even tension in relation to the speed with which one turned the wheel and drew out the raw fiber. If the tension was too loose, the spun yarn would be too thick; when it was woven, the fabric would be heavy and coarse. If the tension was too tight, the yarn would be too thin and would break in the weaving process. Variations in the tensions would result in uneven yarn, which would not produce an even woven fabric. Flax spinning, particularly producing a fine and even thread, was a special skill. Many women acquired this skill in early adolescence and practiced it all their lives. For further details on hand-spinning techniques, see Gullickson, *Spinners and Weavers of Auffay,* pp. 70–71, and Ivy Pinchbeck, *Women Workers and the Industrial Revolution* (London: Virago Press, 1981), p. 129.

26. Although the crop was cultivated throughout the Mauges, the finest flax was grown in the northern Mauges, in the Loire valley along the banks of the Loire between Chalonnes-sur-Loire and Saint-Florent-le-Vieil. The very best was cultivated on the large islands in the Loire river: Chalonnes, Menard, Montjean, and Mesnil. Peasant proprietors grew flax as a cash crop, planting it intensively on their small holdings and rotating the crop with wheat, which was sometimes seeded with clover. Summer flax, sown from mid-April to mid-May, was the preferred variety; Andrews, *Paysans des Mauges,* pp. 117–20.

27. See Chapter 8 for a more extensive discussion of the role of spinners in the agricultural economy.

the early twentieth century identified four distinct types, which he arranged in ascending complexity: the first was characterized by a direct relationship between producer and consumer without intermediaries; the second by an exchange through an intermediary, a simple merchant who buys from the producer and sells to the consumer; the third by the merchant providing the materials to the producers; and the last by the merchant providing not only materials but also the tools and implements.

Political economists and economic historians of the early twentieth century and theorists of rural manufacturing, many of whom independently came to observations similar to those of Tarlé, took this ordering to its logical conclusion. They argued that it represented a evolutionary movement toward greater specialization and interdependence. Recently, historians interested in the debate on proto-industrialization have revived these turn-of-the-century studies and accepted this evolutionary scheme as further corroboration of the inherent tendency of rural dispersed manufacturing to evolve toward factory production. There is, however, little direct evidence to support the evolutionary interpretation. Among the documents Tarlé examined, there were few opportunities to observe the same region over a long duration. Moreover, in many districts, as in Cholet, several types of rural manufacturing existed at the same time. To argue that one type was on the rise and another on the wane is to appeal to a set of criteria imposed from the outside.[28] The compulsion to impose order onto the messiness of rural production fosters a false clarity. This attempt fails to capture the fluidity of the situation. Not only is confusion a more accurate depiction of rural manufacturing and commerce, but accepting its messiness brings us closer to understanding the tension within the system and the logic and dynamics of its transformation.

The Fluidity of Roles in the Production Process

The fluidity of identities in the production process was especially marked by the vocabulary of rural manufacturing. Despite the problems of his typology, Tarlé's careful reading and reporting of the documents offer us an important clue. In each of the manufacturing

28. For a similar discussion of the difficulties of classifying relations of production in manufacturing, see Philippe Guignet, *Mines, manufactures et ouvriers du Valenciennois au XVIIIe siècle* (New York: Arno Press, 1977), pp. 42–47, 211–15.

regions he examined, Tarlé took great care to define and contextualize the term "fabricant" in all the multiple usages he encountered. By current convention, most historians of French rural manufacturing understand the term to indicate a go-between or subcontractor, someone, usually a merchant, who puts out to producers but is not personally engaged in production.

The dictionary definition, however, reveals an ambiguity that more closely approximates the actual usages in the documents Tarlé examined. According to Littré's dictionary of the French language, a fabricant is "celui qui fabrique" as well as "celui qui fait fabriquer": someone who works as well as someone who has work done. In a capitalist context, these two roles are located on opposite sides of a deep divide we call class. That "fabricant" could be used to denote both meanings should caution us against an anachronistic reading of capitalist class formation. It suggests that the line between producing and having something produced was crossed easily. In the world of rural manufacturing, producing and selling did not correspond to distinct social identities: they were not well-differentiated roles. The same person could engage in both sets of activities. I follow the common understanding of a fabricant as a putter-out, but it is important to be alive to the ambiguities embedded in this term.

Concretely, there was often little difference between prosperous independent weavers, small-scale traders, and intermediaries. A weaver could easily become a petty merchant or a small-time linen draper simply by accepting a commission from several fellow weavers to buy yarn or sell their products and then taking a cut of the profits for performing these services. The distinction between "celui qui fabrique" and "celui qui fait fabriquer" might have been a temporary one or have been blurred in one individual. Whether it was worthwhile to make the temporary passage into a permanent one was an open question. As William M. Reddy argues, neither entrepreneurship nor labor "as an abstract factor of production played [any] role in the day to day practice of the French textile trade in the ancien régime.[29]

The situation Reddy identifies is a sharp contrast with a fully developed capitalist economy, in which "capitalist" and "worker" are clearly defined roles, reciprocally constituted and distinct. When we speak of entrepreneurs, we commonly refer those people who own capital and direct the manufacturing process but do not actually engage in production. For this purpose, they hire labor. Thus the exis-

29. Reddy, *Rise of Market Culture,* p. 19.

tence of the capitalist entrepreneur also assumes the existence of people who sell their labor, people we call proletarians or wage workers. The power of the entrepreneur, possessing the tools, materials, and the finished product, contrasts sharply with the position of the worker, who, owning none of the means to establish his or her own independence, must trade labor for cash.

We recognize in these two figures, the early nineteenth-century merchant/factory master and the wage-earning factory operative, the archetypes defining industrial capitalist social relations of production. These relations are themselves products of historical change. Accordingly, the fundamental task for comprehending the rise of a capitalist organization of production is to study the formation of the categories "capitalist" and "worker"—how these social groups emerged.

In the eighteenth-century French countryside, as Reddy points out, the processes producing this deep division had not yet occurred: "If anyone exercised entrepreneurship, it was the laborer; he was in control of production, and he bore the main financial risks associated with that control. . . . In fact, the textile laborers of the eighteenth century were active in the defense of their interests as *entrepreneurs.*"[30] By emphasizing the entrepreneurial activities of the laborer/direct producer, Reddy supports my contention that we need not view eighteenth-century small producers as proletarians. At least in the Choletais, many small producers are more accurately described as "petty commodity producers," following the terminology of development economists. Later I explore the fuller social ramifications of this designation. For now, it is sufficient to point out that "petty commodity producers" are producers who own the means of production, purchase their materials on the open market, and sell their products on the open market. Thus, as Reddy points out, these weavers combined the roles of producer and merchant.

This combination was troublesome for merchants, except for those who specialized in long-distance trade. With open access to buying and marketing, those who did not engage in production, especially petty traders, were vulnerable. Because they engaged only in the circulation of goods, merchants and petty traders could not expect consistent profit. At one end, they depended on producers for their supply and could not effectively control the cost of the product to them; at the other, they could not effectively control market prices. Moreover, traders and peddlers were powerless to stop direct producers from

30. Ibid., p. 10, emphasis added.

"underbidding" them, that is, from selling to wholesale merchants at the same price they sold to traders and peddlers. The very livelihoods of these local merchants were vulnerable to the actions of direct producers.

Traders and merchants could remedy their vulnerability by putting out. In this way they could regularize their relationship to producers, control the supply of goods, and sometimes press down production costs by forcing down the rates paid for cloth. But, as is evident from the previous discussion, putting-out as a solution meant changing the social relations of production. As long as spinners and weavers had access to markets for raw materials and for their products and could provide their own working capital, such changes were unlikely. With access to markets and working capital, small-scale producers could easily bypass the putter-out.

In the countryside, possibilities for merchants, petty traders, and other intermediaries to insert themselves between the various stages of manufacturing and selling abounded. Yet this ease was the source of the problem for establishing capitalist relations of production. In a situation of open access to markets, there were too many entrepreneurs. Clearly the situation favored the entrepreneur who controlled production and marketing: the direct producer.

This description of rural manufacturing casts the question of capitalist class formation in the countryside in a new light. It suggests that we can fruitfully view capitalist class formation as a series of struggles over entrepreneurship. The very process by which merchants became capitalist entrepreneurs was also the process by which independent producers became proletarians. In other words, merchants could exercise capitalist entrepreneurship only by seizing entrepreneurship away from the direct producer. It is clear why merchants wanted to control production, but how did spinners and weavers lose the means of their independence? If the direct producer owned the raw materials and working capital, provided labor, directed production, and engaged in marketing, how did he or she lose control? How did these same tasks, except for providing labor power, become the reserve of the merchant/capitalist?

Capitalist Class Formation: City and Countryside

Before turning to the aforementioned questions, let us contrast the rural situation with urban trades. A long-standing tradition in French history encourages us to view city and countryside as distinct. The traditional economic history of this period focuses on the differences between economies dominated by guilds and those free of corporate regulations. Yet a new look at urban manufacturing might convince us otherwise. Despite the most visible differences, the underlying processes of class formation were very similar.[31]

The countryside was by no means exempt from regulation. Cholet's burgeoning commerce expanded so rapidly in the early part of the eighteenth century that the inspector of manufacturing under the intendant of Tours suggested the need to bring the region's activities under state supervision and quality control. In 1748 a royal patent to produce cloth under the seal of Cholet was granted to (actually, forced onto) the manufacturing district.[32] The patent letter specified the fiber content, production procedures, and the exact dimensions of the finished cloths and kerchiefs. It also established royal inspection offices (the *bureaux de marque et visite*). Sworn guardians (*gardes jurés*)—elected by their fellow merchants, fabricants, and weavers for a year term—checked and measured each piece of cloth before it received the requisite certification, the marque or stamp of the fabrique. Only then could the cloth be put on the market. The bureau collected a fee for this service but also levied fines for irregular or shoddy work. Disputes over violations were referred to the local royal judge of manufacturing. One-half of the fees and fines belonged to the guardians and officials appointed by the crown, one-half belonged to the central caisse de commerce in Paris, a general fund for stimulating trade and industry. In addition to their other duties, the officials of the bureau policed the markets. They made sure that the designated days and hours of yarn and cloth markets were observed.[33]

These rules were different from guild statutes in one important respect: the lettre de patent regulated the product, not *who* could participate in which phase of production and marketing. This marks a significant difference in the constitution of distinct identities in the

31. For a similar argument, see Paul M. Hohenberg and Lynn Hollen Lees, *The Making of Urban Europe, 1000–1950* (Cambridge: Harvard University Press, 1985).

32. Local producers were initially ambivalent about this new set of regulations on commerce. That it was a mechanism for the state to tax production was evident to all. Although many complained that the cost of the marque added to the price of the cloth, most merchants, spinners, weavers, and bleachers accepted the seal with some reluctance.

33. For a discussion of the offices of inspection, see Harold T. Parker, *The Bureau of Commerce in 1781 and Its Policies with Respect to French Industry* (Durham, N.C.: Carolina Academic Press, 1979), pp. 39–40.

production process. By creating monopolies, guilds statutes intended, in a sense, to freeze production roles by limiting activities according to guild membership. Yet the frequency with which guilds sued both each other and individuals over rights in different phases of production and marketing indicates that the boundaries marking off distinct monopolies and production roles were often violated.

For example, throughout the seventeenth century the two merchant guilds and three producer guilds of Le Mans' famed woolen industry (which was also under the administration of the généralité of Tours) litigated continuously over which guilds were permitted to engage in particular practices. The substance of the disputes is familiar to any student of the guild system. In a period of expanding commerce and international trade, the merchant guilds in Le Mans tried to prohibit one of the producer guilds from purchasing or selling any cloth other than that permitted by the guild's charter. One weavers' guild tried to limit the variety of cloths produced by the other. Especially contested were rights to produce muslins and camlets of various weights and qualities that were especially popular with consumers. The two merchant guilds also fought over the right to trade internationally and to sell goods made elsewhere.

Although the language of these disputes referred back to original charters (dating in these cases to Henri IV), clearly the court cases were initiated out of contemporary concerns regarding competition among producers and sellers in the market. None of the guilds involved produced the exact cloths the original charters specified. All had changed their produced the exact cloths the original charters specified. All had changed their products with changes in fashion. The guilds' attempts to impose restrictions and limitations were attempts to reinforce their market positions or to beat back a new threat. The battles between the guilds were finally resolved from above in 1697 and 1700 by decrees forcibly uniting the guilds into two: one guild for merchants, another for producers.[34]

Uniting the squabbling guilds did not eliminate further conflicts, however. As the famous case of Guillaume Véron against the Communauté des marchands merciers et drapiers in 1712 shows, conflicts also occurred over the boundaries of who could produce and who could sell, indicating that problems akin to those of rural merchants also plagued the cities. Véron was a master weaver in Le Mans who invented a new device (a mill) for the washing, degreasing, and fulling

---

34. Dornic, *L'industrie textile dans le Maine,* pp. 14–16.

of étamine (a fine muslin made from wool) which gave the cloth a particular finish and luster popular with merchants everywhere. Véron's trade became so popular that demand for his prepared cloth exceeded his ability to weave, so he took in the cloth of other producers to finish. This expansion in his activities attracted the attention of the merchant guilds. In 1695, Véron was invited to join the merchant guild. In the reorganization of the guilds in 1697, he was caught in the middle. In the realignment, the producers guild claimed the exclusive right to wash, degrease, and finish fabrics. Véron, as a member of the merchant guild, was in violation of these rules. His equipment and cloth were seized. The affair was resolved in 1699, when a royal edict reaffirmed the guild statutes of 1697 but granted Véron the right to enjoy the benefits of his invention and to continue his commerce as both producer and merchant.

This double identity in a world divided into merchant guilds and producer guilds was a troublesome anomaly. In 1712, Véron appealed to the royal courts for the right to pass on the 1699 edict to his children. His request brought forth vociferous opposition. Véron combined production and selling. His business hired 400 people. He was the quintessential capitalist entrepreneur in a world where such entrepreneurship was difficult to practice and in fact required a special dispensation.[35]

Despite the opposition, Véron won his request. But his success did not mean that the royal administration generally supported capitalist entrepreneurship. Certainly many enterprising merchants with similar ambitions were frustrated in their attempts.[36] Yet, as Gail Bossenga points out, guild regulations themselves enabled merchants to dominate all facets of trade. With examples from Lille, Paris, Lyon, and Orléans, Bossenga shows that cloth merchants manipulated guild regulations to secure their monopoly over the flow of goods onto the market and their exclusive access to rapidly expanding international markets. For example, in eighteenth-century Lille, négociants had initially tried to circumvent urban producer guilds by commissioning weavers in the countryside to make cloth. But when rural manufacturing grew, urban merchants found that suppliers had

35. Ibid., pp. 19–29.
36. For example, in 1751 the Lille town council denied merchant Gilles-François Vanhoenacker's request to produce a new kind of woolen cloth made by urban workers outside the guild of wool weavers. The council claimed, much as in the case of Véron, that "it has never been permitted in Lille for négociants to have workers working directly under and for them. This is a right that has always belonged to the masters of the guild. Sieur Vanhoenacker is proposing an innovation without precedent." See Bossenga, "Protecting Merchants," p. 695.

become competitors. When independent brokers threatened to cast off their dependence on urban finishing processes and export markets, négociants in Lille resorted to their legal privileges and corporate organization to retain their exclusive control. Through local commercial courts and the Chamber of Commerce, the merchants had independent brokerage outlawed.[37]

In light of these anecdotes from the world of guilds, one might conclude, ironically, that the difficulties of establishing capitalist relations of production in the countryside were due to the absence of guilds. Because guilds regulated identities and production roles—that is, who had rights over which activities—merchants could use the prohibitions against producers to ensure forms of dependence. Producers fought back with legal means, but the power and influence of merchants were precisely articulated in their control over the courts. The absence of restrictions on production roles in the countryside meant that struggles over capitalist entrepreneurship took the form of direct confrontation in markets. Behind these marketplace struggles, we also see the royal administration playing a role in defining entrepreneurship.

Struggles over Entrepreneurship: The Yarn Market

Within the rural production system, the most intense competition pitted weavers against petty merchants. A look at the production process and the value added at each stage, using a report containing the costs of production for a putter-out in the linen trade in Rouen, indicates why this was the case.[38] The cost of yarn and flax together represented about two-thirds of the final price of the cloth. The combed flax, which was sold in the markets for spinning, represented about 26 percent and 38 percent of the final sale price of fine-grade cloth and coarse cloth, respectively.[39] The cost of spinning fine yarn

37. Ibid., pp. 698–702.
38. Archives nationales (hereafter A.N.) F12 1569: Renseignements sur les toiles de lin connues dans le commerce sous le nom de "toiles de Caux," Rouen, 1807.
39. Of all the different subprocesses in linen production, flax cultivation provided the greatest return on investment. Flax was a profitable crop for farmers: on the average, the returns on investment, including land, seeds, and labor, was as high as 100 percent. Compared to the market price of wheat in the same area, which on the average yielded 30 percent return on investment, flax was a favored crop. Given these figures, it is understandable why

amounted to 39 percent of the final sale price of cloth and 27 percent of the final sale price for coarser cloths. The cost of spun yarn was thus about 66 percent of the final price of the cloth. Weavers who worked for putters-out received another 15–20 percent of the price of the cloth (depending on its quality), leaving the putter-out with slightly less than 10 percent of the price of the cloth as profit.[40]

It was this 10 percent of the price that produced the potential for conflict. Weavers who remained independent of putters-out could capture this increment for themselves, adding half again to their compensation for weaving a piece of cloth. Although the capital outlay for the materials needed for weaving represented a sizable portion of final price of the cloth, and taking cloth to market represented some effort, there was a strong incentive for weavers to find ways to manage these difficulties and remain independent of putters-out. Posed in another way, weavers weighed the increase in their returns against the incoveniences of going to market and buying yarn. Was it worth one-third of the weavers' profit to become dependent on putters-out?

Such incentives make the constant tension over the organization and access to markets in this productive system understandable. The competition was especially fierce in the yarn markets because controlling the yarn supply was essential to any putting-out strategy. Conversely, preserving open access to a source of yarn was crucial to maintaining the independence of the small-scale producer.[41] Interestingly, these conflicts over the rules of yarn and cloth markets did not develop as open struggles between producers and merchants but came to light in confrontations between merchants and the local royal administration.[42]

Although both weavers and merchants complained about the erratic nature of the yarn supply and the general problems of securing

---

farm households that cultivated flax did not spin. A second crop of linen or hemp was far more lucrative than spinning. See Oscar Leclerc-Thouin, *L'agriculture de l'Ouest de la France* (Paris: Bouchard-Huzard, 1843), pp. 317–23.

40. Philippe Guignet reports similar findings for the Valenciennois. According to a report in 1758, the cost for spun yarn to make medium-quality fine linen (batiste) amounted to 72 percent of the sale price of the cloth. The cost of labor for weaving was 15 percent of the final price, leaving the putter-out with about 13 percent profit. A report from the prefect of the Nord in 1789 indicated a similar distribution of costs for yarn and labor and similar profits, see Guignet, *Mines, manufactures*, pp. 38–39.

41. For an examination of parallel issues in the English guild system, see Heather Swanson, "The Illusion of Economic Structure: Craft Guilds in Late Medieval English Towns," *Past and Present* 121 (November 1988): 29–48.

42. For examples of competition in other yarn markets in France, see Reddy, *Rise of Market Culture*, pp. 31–32, and Guignet, *Mines, manufactures*, pp. 126–38.

adequate provisions, it was generally weavers who were the most adamant that the rules of the marketplace be strictly enforced. For example, in 1779 the "fabricants" (meaning, in this case, producers) in Cholet petitioned the king to request new vigilance in maintaining inspection standards and to enforce the rules and hours of the yarn market.[43] Shoddy cloths and kerchiefs were ruining Cholet's reputation, the petitioners asserted. Starched and glued to disguise defective weaves, these cloths dissolved into threads after the first washing. Yet these inferior grades have been allowed onto the markets and sold with the marque of the region. Next, the petitioners demanded the enforcement of the prohibitions against selling yarn during and before the cloth market. Moreover, they wished the yarn market to begin only after cloths had been sold. The reason was simple, and it reflected the fiscal concerns of small-scale producers engaged in both buying materials and selling the final product. When required to purchase yarn before they had sold their cloth, weavers incurred an extra financial burden: they needed to bring cash. Given the price of yarn, an additional cash outlay of such proportions greatly burdened weavers.

A petition in 1786 to the seneschal of the marquisat of Beaupréau articulated more fully the worries of these producers.[44] Again the demand was for a more rigorous enforcement of market hours. The designated time for the opening of the Beaupréau yarn market was Monday morning. But competition was so keen that unofficial transactions began earlier and earlier, pushing the activities into the predawn hours. Not only did the dimness hide all sorts of fraud in yarn weights and quality, but the early hours also meant that weavers lost two days of work time just to provision their looms. They spent an extra day to get to the market before it was emptied of yarn. Traveling at night, weavers feared theft and injury on the deserted an rutted roads between the dense hedges of the countryside.

It was not simply the difficulties of shopping by candlelight which pushed weavers to complain. Most of all, they feared exclusion: "In addition to these great inconveniences, producers are forced to watch helplessly as they are squeezed out of the markets by merchants [*les marchands revendeurs*] who buy up all the yarn indiscriminately, without regard to quality. [These merchants] get preferred treatment from the sellers [because they buy in bulk], setting the sellers against

43. A.D. M.-et-L. C16 Manufactures des toiles, Petition of 15 May 1779.
44. A.D. Indre-et-Loire C129: Appel des fabricants de Beaupréau, Cholet, et les paroisses environnantes, 1786.

those who value the quality of their product and consequently are forced to pay dearly for their right to select."[45] Unlike small-scale producers who had to spend time weaving, putters-out could specialize in shopping for yarn. Merchants were apparently winning the struggle to gain control over the yarn supply. The *marchands revendeurs* might well have edged out the small producers if it had not been for the actions of the state. These disputes over the yarn supply were critical to the ability of weavers to maintain access to their raw materials, and hence to secure their independence.

The petitioners to the inspector of manufacturing were assured a sympathetic ear. For example, when the inspector outlined in a letter addressed the inspector general in Paris the need to bring yarn markets under tighter regulation, he spoke of rampant abuses: "There are places where the sale of yarn takes place the night before the opening of the market; in other places, it takes place before daybreak. These *régateurs* and *monopoliseurs* find it easy to seize all the raw materials without the police, even the most vigilant, being able to stop them. In this manner, the fabricants [producers] find the markets emptied and must then go to the same *régateur* and pay a high price for the materials they need."[46]

When Huet de Vaudour uses the terms "régateurs" and "monopoliseurs" to refer to merchants, he tells us unambiguously how he views their actions. The "abuses" named by the inspector, however, were essential parts of the putting-out process. Successful putting-out required merchants to buy up as much yarn as possible to deprive direct producers of independent access to raw materials. Direct producers were then forced to either buy from or work for merchants. When Huet de Vaudour complained against these actions, he was opposing the putting-out system itself.

We find another expression of hostility toward the actions of putters-out in an incident in the district of Laval (in the jurisdiction of the généralité of Tours) involving an unlucky weaver, Pierre Duguet, who was caught buying yarn before the designated hour. Showing a surprising degree of severity against this poor weaver, who by the testimony of his curé was a hard-working small producer, Huet de Vaudour advised that no clemency be shown in this case because of the principles involved. Although Duguet was not a putter-out, Huet

45. Ibid.
46. A.N. F12 1428: Manufactures des toiles, linons, etc., généralité de Tours, 11 November 1786.

de Vaudour wanted to make him an example as a warning to all who violated the rules of the market:

> The excessive dryness of the season and the past six months have destroyed this year's harvest of raw materials in our généralité. The current troublesome situation with the scarcity of linen and yarn requires the most vigilant maintenance of order. In order to sustain and advantage the fabrique of Laval, raw materials must be sold in the designated and established public markets and not clandestinely to merchants and other intermediaries who practice no other occupation than running about the countryside, going from one person who spins or will accept spinning, making off with the best yarns and leaving only the rejects to provision the public markets. Often so much material is carried off that the markets are deprived of the assortments of yarn necessary to the fabrique. This anarchy empowers merchants and intermediaries to lay down the law to [dictate the terms to] producers. [They] profit from the shortages to set exorbitant prices to resell the yarn or ship the yarn to other regions to provision other manufacturers.[47]

Duguet was fined the exorbitant amount of 100 livres, which amounted to the cost of yarn for a bolt of cloth. As is evident from his own words, Huet de Vaudour was primarily concerned with the orderly functioning of the market, although he was clearly aware of the power merchants gained from avoiding the regimen of the marketplace. He was not explicitly concerned about putting-out as such. But, as we see in a dispute over whether Cholet needed to build a cloth hall, observance of the rules of the marketplace meant discouraging the actions of putters-out.

The proposal to build a cloth hall in Cholet was first initiated by the producers of Cholet in 1778. They petitioned the seigneur of Cholet, the Count of Rougé, to build such a hall because of the inconveniences of the open air markets. Not only were their goods exposed to the elements, but the location of the market right next to the cattle market brought complaints from both sellers and buyers of being crushed and crowded by passing animals.[48] In 1783, however, when Huet de Vaudour visited Cholet to consult with the merchants and producers of the city regarding the project, the inspector of manufacturing was disappointed to learn that both merchants and producers rejected the idea when they learned that the hall would be

---

47. A.N. F12 1428: Lettre de Huet de Vaudour, inspecteur de manfacture à M. Montaran, intendant de commerce, 30 June 1785.

48. A.N. F12 1231: Foires et marchés, Mémoire du comte de Rougé, seigneur de Cholet, 1778.

paid for by a surcharge on the existing marque fees. Without funds from the royal administration or the généralité, which were clearly not available, the project had to be abandoned. Disappointed by this result, Huet de Vaudour chastised the local population for their short-sightedness. For the inspector of manufacturing, the cloth hall would have corrected what he considered rampant abuses of market rules. "These producers," the inspector complained, "are not sufficiently clear about their true interests and the general interest of the commerce of the city. It is only by the exact observance of the rules . . . that they can hope to improve their fabrique. The true way to sell their merchandise to those who offer the best price is by establishing the greatest competition in selling their cloths publicly in cloth halls where all the buyers, whether from the region or from far away, can come freely." The situation in Cholet, the inspector argued, had gotten out of hand. Increasingly, cloth was sold and bought outside the marketplace. That commerce was carried on in private homes, in the inns, on the road to market—in fact everywhere *except* the market-place—was attributable to the lack of a central cloth hall. Huet de Vaudour especially fretted over the fact that several of the wealthiest merchants who dominated the trade obliged weavers to sell directly to them. Weavers went from one merchant house to another peddling their wares. Particularly troubling were the changing power relations between producers and merchants. As the inspector astutely pointed out, "The fear of inconveniencing these merchants and that their cloths might be refused forces producers to acquiesce to the merchants' opinions and mind set. The producers are dragged into supporting the interests of these merchants who seek only to capture [for themselves] the entire commerce in Cholet. . . . For these negative reasons, [these merchants] easily influenced the assembled producers by exhorting them to accept the merchants' view."[49]

Once again, Huet de Vaudour charged merchants with monopolistic practices and undermining the common good. In this accusation, the inspector of manufacturing revealed his own principle of fair trade and the public good. Officials in the administrative and policing bureaucracies of the intendant of Tours and the intendant of commerce and manufacturing shared a vision of the importance of orderliness, a vision based on the conviction that the free exchange of

49. A.N. F12 1231: Foires et marchés, Report of the inspector of manufacturing, généralité de Tours, Huet de Vaudour to the intendant of commerce, 31 March 1783.

high-quality goods was essential in encouraging manufacturing.[50] Enforcing the rules of the marketplace was not simply a sign of a rule-obsessed bureaucratic mentality. By upholding the rules that guaranteed competition and open access (synonymous with order), the administration understood itself to be promoting social well-being. "Disorderly" merchants should be stopped, Huet de Vaudour argued, because they violated the principle of the marketplace: free and open exchange.

Of course, order is in the eye of the beholder. The royal administration's faith in the "visible hand" endorsed the world as it was seen by the small-scale independent producer. The many petitions from weavers to the king and the inspector of manufacturing indicate that small-scale producers had a vested interest in enforcing the rules of the marketplace. Putters-out could plausibly claim, though, that they brought orderliness to the production process by streamlining the phases of production under one entrepreneur's control, rather than letting the haphazard and chaotic conditions of the marketplace coordinate manufacturing.

Certainly, this view is closer to our contemporary conceptions of efficient production. But if we focus on power relations in the struggle over entrepreneurship, the charge that putters-out were would-be monopolizers was also accurate. In reality, putters-out could not exercise entrepreneurship by promoting competition; they could only achieve their goals by monopolizing raw materials. This meant circumventing open markets: buying up the yarn before it reached the market, and forcing weavers to sell to or take commissions from them exclusively. Contrary to the image historians have long accepted uncritically, that the regulatory state obstructed commerce with its endless tomes of obsolete rules, bureaucrats in the royal administration championed open markets and free competition. Their support of these market ideals impeded the development of capitalist entrepreneurship, but not of commerce in general.

Two Conceptions of Markets

Historian Steven Kaplan has suggested a useful distinction between "marketplace" and "market principle" which helps us make

---

50. For a general discussion of the ideological orientation of the intendants of commerce, see Parker, *Bureau of Commerce*.

sense of administrative policies and their relation to merchants. The ambiguity of the phrase "freedom of commerce" is less pronounced when we realize that there were two competing notions of markets at stake, with more or less concrete conceptions of exchange. As Kaplan notes, "The market principle signified a system of relations in which prices were determined by the impersonal forces of supply and demand, regardless of the site of the transaction, and in which these prices allocated resources, income, and outputs. Predicated upon a global scheme of endless self-adjustment, the market principle demanded an untrammeled freedom of action for commerce." Although the market principle required no determinate locus of exchange, "the marketplace demanded physical concentration of goods and actors at a fixed place. The market principle required freedom from control and constraint, whereas the marketplace imposed surveillance and regulation. . . . The market principle was fundamentally private in ethos and operation, the marketplace quintessentially public."[51]

The police adhered to the notion of the market as a place—a physical location, a designated site. For Huet de Vaudour, transactions between négociants and weavers outside the marketplace were suspect because they were covert, whereas marketplace exchanges were open and exposed to public scrutiny. The very foundation of the regulatory apparatus rested on binding markets to specific locations. Defined as a principle, the market was not subject to easy administrative control: "It was at once everywhere and nowhere."[52] As a place, the market permitted and encouraged policing.

These two different conceptions of markets were not simply rationalizations of bureaucratic logic or, conversely, of rebellion against control. These ideas about markets reflected different positions within social relations of production and exchange. The battles in the eighteenth century were over which sets of relations should prevail. We should thus understand statements defining freedom of commerce and trade in strategic terms. For small producers who feared exclusion, the well-policed market and strict observance of market rules meant open access to raw materials and customers. This access guaranteed their livelihood and independence. Merchants clamored against regulation of the marketplace because existing rules favored small producers and hence reinforced the merchants' fundamental

51. Steven A. Kaplan, *Provisioning Paris: Merchants and Millers in the Grain and Flour Trade during the Eighteenth Century* (Ithaca: Cornell University Press, 1984), pp. 25, 27.
52. Ibid., p. 27.

vulnerability. Certainly merchants claimed that they wanted open markets. But they meant access to distant markets. Closer to home, they wanted security, not competition. They wanted to ensure their own position in relation to small producers by monopolizing resources and securing their control over the production process. Merchants' arguments for laissez-faire were attacks on state interference on behalf of small producers.

Merchants Fight Back

As commerce continued to flourish in the region, merchants increasingly strained against the rules of the regulatory apparatus. By the middle of the 1780s, they were ready to strike back. They began to subvert the system of regulations both overtly and covertly. Like other merchants in France, some local merchants called on new philosophies of free trade to support their position. The most effective means of subversion, however, was avoidance. As Huet de Vaudour had recognized earlier, many merchants under his jurisdiction were simply bypassing the inspection and stamping procedures. They dealt with weavers or linen drapers directly, had their cloths finished by bleachers, and shipped merchandise off to distant destinations without ever passing through the bureau de marque and the scrutiny of the gardes jurés. Some merchants used fake marques. Others were so brazen as to not bother with the entire procedure at all.

Disturbed by these trends, Huet de Vaudour stepped up the enforcement process by ordering random searches of bleach works, seizing unmarqued cloths and kerchiefs, and levying heavy fines against the bleachers and cloth owners. The inspector of manufacturing proceeded with the greatest confidence that severe punishment of infractions would deter the violators. But on one such raid in September 1784 in the district of Cholet, the accused bleachers, financed by powerful merchants, took the offensive and challenged these procedures in court. As Huet de Vaudour realized too late, the subsequent battle between the bureau de marque and bleachers threatened to bring down the entire regulatory apparatus.

The incident began on 17 September, when the gardes jurés from the bureau de marque made surprise inspections of several bleach works in Cholet and found unmarqued kerchiefs and cloths hidden among other marqued pieces. These kerchiefs and cloths were seized. Several days later, appearing before the royal judge of manufacturing, these bleachers were found in violation of the 1748 lettre de patente. The merchandise was not returned to them and each bleacher was fined 100 livres.[53]

Of course, the merchants who actually owned the contraband cloths were upset by the seizures. In a larger sense, though, they had succeeded in provoking a confrontation. As Huet de Vaudour noted in his report to Montaran, intendant of manufacturing in Paris, it was the merchants (whom the inspector called "republicans") who incited producers to evade the regulations. Weavers and bleachers themselves were apt to obey the rules, but they were under pressure from merchants (on whom they were becoming dependent) who wanted ever cheaper merchandise regardless of quality. Huet de Vaudour urged greater vigilance to stop this "liberté indéfinie."[54]

In the subsequent days, most of the unpleasantness over the seizure was directed against the gardes jurés personally. The gardes complained that bleachers, merchants, and linen drapers throughout the town taunted them with threats of vengeance. They felt unjustly treated as criminals and thieves when they were only carrying out their duty. The situation worsened considerably when on 29 November the bleachers, with the support of the richest négociants (such as Pierre Lecoq and Crespin), brought a court case against the gardes jurés. Already afraid to carry out their duties because of the threats, the gardes jurés found the prospects of the court case utterly debilitating.[55]

It took Huet de Vaudour little time to understand what was at stake. As the inspector of manufacturing recognized, there was slight chance that royal courts would find fault with the actions of the gardes jurés. The bleachers' defense was weak. They claimed that the unmarqued cloths were not substandard according to the patente of 1748, and that the cloths' sole defect was the lack of a stamp. Against the charge that they purposely evaded the regulatory apparatus, they claimed that the unmarqued cloths had accidentally slipped by the

53. A.N. F12 1406: Extraits des procès-verbaux de saisie sur Messieurs Pierre Michel Louis Blain, Michel Brosseau, Mathurin Matignon, Jean Onillion, Jean Bouchet, Jean Chauveau, Joseph Marie, et Madame Perrine Bollard (Veuve Pierre Guibert), blanchisseurs de la paroisse de Saint-Pierre de Cholet, 17 September 1784; and Mémoire . . . blanchisseurs de toile et toilerie de la fabrique de Cholet et . . . autres négociants de la même ville, 1784.

54. A.N. F12 1406: Lettre de Huet de Vaudour à M. de Montaran, intendant de commerce 29 September 1784.

55. A.N. F12 1406: Lettre de Huet de Vaudour, inspecteur de manufacture à M. de Montaran, intendant de commerce, 30 October and 4 December 1784; and Mémoire des blanchisseurs, 1784.

bureau because of the bureau's own disorganization. Finally, the bleachers pleaded for a lighter fine because of their poverty.[56]

The threat to the regulatory system was therefore not that the bleachers might win their cause; rather merchants had found a way to sap the regulatory apparatus from within. The gardes jurés were, for the most part, simple weavers elected to the function for a year. Most were illiterate. By threatening court cases against them, making them personally liable for any deviation from the strict letter of the law, the merchants intended to intimidate the gardes into submission, so that they would be persuaded to the wisdom of overlooking certain irregularities rather than expose themselves to court action. The bleachers' court action, though weak, sufficed to convey the message. Certainly, this point was evident to the inspector: in an uncharacteristic move, Huet de Vaudour recommended clemency, in the form of a lighter fine, in exchange for the bleachers dropping their case.[57]

Huet de Vaudour showed himself to be an able political actor. He knew when to cut his losses. Yet it certainly did not escape the merchants that the regulatory system had suffered a stinging defeat. In the following year, Pierre Urban Lecoq, the négociant who had financed the bleachers' court case, attacked the regulatory system more openly. Lecoq engineered his own election in 1785 as an inspector for the bureau de marque. Once part of the bureau, he set about trying to persuade others of its obsolescence. In March, Lecoq convinced the gardes jurés to not pay the marque for their own cloths, claiming this right as compensation for their efforts on behalf of the trade and for their time lost from weaving. Posed as compensation, the gardes' actions made sense. But Lecoq had succeeded in getting members of the bureau de marque to disregard the bureau's own regulations. The gardes were quickly fined, and Lecoq, along with several other merchant inspectors, was removed from office.[58]

It was unlikely that these mercantile actions could have changed the principles of the regulatory system; it was not the merchants' goal to engage in a debate about economic principles. But as a strategy to subvert the effective functioning of the system the merchants'

56. A.N. F12 1406: Lettre de Huet de Vaudour, inspecteur de manufacture à M. de Montaran, intendant de commerce, 25 December 1784; and Mémoire des blanchisseurs, 1784.

57. A.N. F12 1406: Lettre de Huet de Vaudour, inspecteur de manufacture à M. de Montaran, intendant de commerce, 12 December 1784.

58. A.N. F12 842: Lettre de Huet de Vaudour à M. de Montaran, 8 April 1785; procès-verbal contre les gardes jurés, 16 March 1785, Cholet; and Suppression des inspecteurs marchands, Cholet, 7 July 1785.

actions probably did have an effect. We will, however, never know just how effective they might have been. Within a few years, the Revolution swept away the entire regulatory apparatus. Postrevolutionary regimes were friendlier to the merchants' notion of freedom of commerce. With the end of the regulatory system, small producers lost an important advocate for their notion of market competition based on open access to markets for all.

4

Winning Control over Entrepreneurship: Merchants and the New Cotton Regime

In 1806, a decade after the official peace which put to rest the Vendée rebellion against the French Republic, the prefect of Maine-et-Loire reported on the continuing hardships in his department. Writing to his superiors, he noted: "The public spirit is good. The emperor is nowhere more loved, more cherished, more admired than he is here; but we lack [the] men and manpower [for a timely recovery]. The agricultural lands are not what they should be. Almost everywhere cultivation rests on the backs of women. The misfortunes of the Vendée have left some profound traces. Everywhere one looks, one sees ruins and charred remains. The man who rebuilds his house cannot at the same time tend to his plow and workshop."[1] Indeed, the Revolution and the civil war that ensued devastated the region. The demographic and economic dislocations were felt decades after. For the economy, the greatest casualty was the linen industry, which never recovered its former prosperity.

Despite the slow pace of recovery, those watching for hopeful signs placed their faith in the fledgling cotton industry. In his 1806 report, the prefect saw great promise in the attitudes and actions of the region's mercantile and manufacturing elite, most of whom had switched from linens to cottons. He wrote: "I will not close this letter, Monseigneur, without mentioning my praises for the initiatives of Messieurs Cesbron, the mayor of Chemillé and Tharreau, his brother-in-law, the mayor of Cholet. . . . These excellent citizens have used their fortunes to revitalize manufacture, and with each day bring it and agriculture to a new stage of mechanization. [They do

1. A.D. M-et-L 1M: Situation politique et morale, year 14 (1806).

this] to help their fellow citizens to forget, with each tear, the subject that used to divide them."[2]

Michel Tristan Cesbron was certainly the maverick entrepreneur of the Choletais's new cotton manufacture. By 1806, Cesbron, with his longtime partner from Bordeaux, David Verdonnet, had already established an impressive manufacturing center specializing in cottons in the parish of Saint-Pierre in Chemillé. This manufacturing center grouped together a spinning complex, a laundry with bleach houses and bleach greens, and additional buildings for finishing and sizing cloth. In 1808, Cesbron reported that he put out cotton yarn to three hundred weaving households and employed eight to nine hundred weavers, skein winders, spinners, and finishers.[3] Indeed, Cesbron himself was well aware that his manufacturing complex was the showcase of the region's future.

The prefect's praise for Cesbron revealed his own hopes for the future: that progress, industry, and prosperity would bring an embattled society to a new consensus. In retrospect, this faith in a new society revived around cotton production proved to be accurate, at least in the short run. The most visible signs of dynamic change in the following decades came in the form of factories and the introduction of labor-saving machinery, marking the first phase of mechanized production in the region.

Local historians have long associated the vitality of the early history of Cholet's industrialization with the vigor of its textile entrepreneurs. They attributed Cholet's recovery from civil war to the business acumen of this group. This is how Auguste-Amaury Gellusseau, a medical doctor and amateur historian from a prominent merchant family in Cholet, characterized the source of Cholet's spirit of renewal in 1862: "We have taken secret pleasures in discovering the depths of the fortunes of the industrial city of Cholet, and in finding, among the frightful ruins which would seem to eternalize misery, the wherewithal to sire riches."[4] By self-representation and with the endorsement of the central political regime, the capitalist entrepreneur became the hero of the age.

"One is born a merchant as one is born a poet," Gellusseau wrote.[5] Success in commerce, he maintained, was a testament of a God-given character. For Gellusseau, the cotton manufacturers of the Choletais

2. Ibid.
3. A.D. M-et-L 67M5: État et situation des établissements de tissage de coton dans la commune de Chemillé, 1809.
4. Auguste-Amaury Gellusseau, *Histoire de Cholet et de son industrie,* vol. 2 (Cholet: Édition Fillion, 1862), p. 369.
5. Ibid.

were men of talent and hard work. More than mere products of the new society, they were the bearers of technical change. For local historians, just as for the prefect of Maine-et-Loire, these entrepreneurs were agents of economic and social transformation, an active force in creating the new society.

For their role in rebuilding a devastated economy, the first industrialists of the Choletais deserved the recognition of their fellow citizens. One can acknowledge their contributions and, at the same time, appreciate the irony of their achievement. Although the turmoils of revolution and counterrevolution wreaked havoc on the livelihood of the region's population, these same upheavals strengthened the economic power of men like Michel Cesbron. The collapse of the eighteenth-century linen economy freed merchants and linen drapers from the undermining actions of small-scale producers. Only under these circumstances could these merchants become capitalist entrepreneurs and innovators in production. Even so, the actual process of mechanization and centralizing control in the cotton industry was clearly a response to the difficulties merchants had experienced earlier in the linen industry. Against the self-proclaimed heroism of entrepreneurial genius, in this chapter I reinterpret mechanization and centralized control as a strategy in the local politics of production. Let us lay the foundation for this analysis of the rebirth of the region's textile industry in the early nineteenth century by examining in greater detail the decline of linens.

The Collapse of the Linen Trade

Crisis struck the linen market in 1788, ending nearly a century of prosperity for the Choletais. With each succeeding year in the eighteenth century, weavers in the Mauges produced more cloths and kerchiefs. In 1787 and 1788, cloth sales amounted to 3.4 million livres tournois, the highest sales on record. Thereafter, commerce dropped off precipitously. In 1789 cloth sales dropped to 2.5 million livres, and to 1.2 million livres in 1790.[6] Local officials blamed the crisis of 1788 on competition resulting from the Anglo-French free trade treaty of 1786. Early in 1789, Huet de Vaudour, inspector of manufacturing for the généralité of Tours reported;

> The merchants of Cholet are complaining that their commerce is falling, and that they are losing their markets because of the ill effects of

6. Charles Tilly, *The Vendée* (Cambridge: Harvard University Press, 1964), p. 216 and appendix C.

the commercial treaty with England. Their warehouses are full of textile merchandise, and they are not able to move them. Business is so bad that they do not dare to trust any merchant, whether from this kingdom or overseas. They have suffered bankruptcies and losses of more than 600,000 livres since last year, and as a result several of Cholet's houses have themselves failed and have gone out of business.[7]

He further elaborated on these problems in his report at the year's end: "The French, Spanish, and Anglo-American colonies are hardly buying from Cholet any more; within this kingdom, trade has been very moderate. People attribute the problem to the shortage of cash and the unhappy events of the times; since bread and every other necessity are very expensive, everyone is economizing."[8]

To make matters worse, in the early days of the Revolution the loss of Saint-Domingue dealt a heavy blow to the port economies of coastal France and its productive hinterlands. Three-quarters of French colonial commerce in the eighteenth century was conducted with Saint-Domingue, the "jewel of the Caribbean." The linen-producing regions of western France, including Brittany, Normandy, the Maine, and Anjou, were hit hard. During the Revolution, French linen exports to markets in the West Indies and the Spanish Americas were stopped almost completely. When the French Antilles fell into the orbit of American traders, the prospects for a speedy recovery for western France seemed dim.[9]

In 1790 statistical reports on poverty prepared for the Comité de mendicité of the National Assembly revealed the human toll of the manufacturing crisis. Many textile communes listed a quarter to a third of their population as needy, substantially higher than in non-weaving districts. Communal officers in Chemillé claimed that 33 percent of its population needed public assistance. Cholet and Saint-Macaire both reported 24 percent destitute, and Le May, 23 percent. In the same year, the inspector of Vihiers complained: "Often these poor fellows have no bread at home when they come to the market, and the hard times they have selling their goods puts them in an ill-humor, and makes them reply angrily." After two years of poor commerce, many weavers were reduced to begging. They wandered around the homes of fabricants and merchants and other well-off in-

7. A.D. Indre-et-Loire C135, quoted in Tilly, *Vendée*, p. 217.
8. A.D. Indre-et-Loire C134, quoted in Tilly, *Vendée*, p. 217.
9. See François Crouzet, "Wars, Blockades, and Economic Change in Europe, 1792–1815," *Journal of Economic History* 24 (December 1964): 569–74.

habitants of the commune. Communal administrators set up public works projects, such as road construction, to try to alleviate the crisis, but the problem reached disquieting proportions as the needs of the breadless exceeded the resources available. Time and again anger and frustration over grain movements and bread supplies brought weavers and other poor people into conflict with communal officers, many of whom were cloth merchants and well-off fabricants.[10]

This misery was compounded by the counterrevolution, which further devastated the local economy. The demographic and economic dislocations of the civil war were daunting.[11] Between 1792 and 1802, the department of Maine-et-Loire lost 20 percent of its population. The population of Cholet fell by 38 percent. A quarter of the housing was destroyed. Disruptions of the grain trade in the region compounded the food shortages created by crop destruction and the general neglect of agriculture. Throughout the first years of the Empire, the subprefect of the arrondissement of Beaupréau, the subprefecture incorporating all the Mauges, reported that vagabonds and brigands continued to menace the rural population. These "brigands," however, were often bands of children roaming the countryside stealing food.

The determination to rebuild was strong. Even before the flames of civil war had completely died, the inhabitants of this small commercial town had drifted back to Cholet to claim their residences, to rebuild from rubble, and to begin commerce anew. Indeed in the year VI (1798) at the first exposition of the products of French industry, held on the grounds of the Champs de Mars in Paris, the jury noted its great pleasure at finding kerchiefs and cloths produced by the Onze associés in Cholet and by the citizen Jacquier of Mayenne among the works exhibited.[12] While the mood was hopeful, production levels were still slow to reach their prerevolutionary levels. In 1810, for example, the fabrique of Laval produced 18,000 pieces of linen, as against 36,000 pieces in 1789.[13] In the Choletais, 110,000 dozen kerchiefs were produced in 1810, overtaking the 105,000 dozen produced in 1789 and nearly matching the 134,000 dozen made in 1788. But in subsequent years, the linen trade fared poorly. Kerchief production

10. Tilly, *Vendée*, pp. 218–20.
11. For a survey of the extent of the damage for the entire Vendée militaire, see Reynald Secher, *Le génocide franco-français: La Vendée-Vengé* (Paris: Presses universitaires de France, 1986).
12. François Dornic, *L'industrie textile dans le Maine et ses débouchés internationaux* (Le Mans: Édition Pierre-Bellon, 1955), p. 284.
13. Crouzet, "Wars, Blockades," pp. 571–72.

dropped to 36,000 dozen in the first half-year of 1811, against 55,000 dozen during the same period in 1810. In 1812, kerchief production declined again to about 40,000 dozen for the entire year. The production of linen cloths fared even worse. The standard pure linen cloth had almost entirely disappeared.[14]

Estimates of the number of handlooms in operation are extremely unreliable. In 1810 the mayor of Cholet estimated that there were 7,000 active linen looms in the district, compared to 23,000–24,000 in 1790. In 1811 the mayor reported between 4,000 and 6,000 linen looms in operation, and he estimated only 4,000 in 1812.[15] The accuracy of these statistics may be dubious, but it clear that the mayor wanted to indicate that linen weaving occupied only a quarter to a third of its former importance.

So, though linen manufacture had resumed, its future was uncertain. Cholet continued to produce its kerchiefs, but far fewer linens than before. During the early years of the war with England, French producers continued to export through Barcelona, Lisbon, Hamburg, Copenhagen, and Trieste, mostly trading under American and other neutral flags. After 1807, however, England tightened its blockade of enemy ports, prohibiting even this indirect trade. In the same period, the British conquered the last of the French overseas possessions. Finally in 1808, when the Spanish colonies sided with the Spanish insurgents against Napoleon, the Iberian market too fell under English economic hegemony.[16]

The revolutionary era thus closed off access to the trading networks on which the vitality of the linen industry rested. Other Continental producers, such as the linen districts of Westphalia, Saxony, and Silesia, fared well until 1806/7, but then they too suffered the same fate.[17]

The Rise of the Cotton Industry: The First Attempt at Industrialization

The difficulties of the linen sector were not shared by all branches of the textile industry. The Anglo-French antagonisms, Napoleonic

14. A.D. M-et-L 67M5: État et situation de la fabrique et manufacture de toiles et autres tissus de chanvre et lin 1810, 1811, 1812; Tilly, *Vendée*, appendix C.
15. A.D. M-et-L 67M5: Fabrique de Cholet, report of the mayor of Cholet, 1811; État et situation de la fabrique et manufacture de toiles et autres tissus de chanvre et lin, 1810.
16. Crouzet, "Wars, Blockades," pp. 570–88.
17. Ibid., p. 572.

tariffs, and the English blockade were boons to the Continental cotton industry. French economic historians now agree that the period between 1792 and 1815 was an important watershed for French industrial development. During the last years of the Directory and the first years of the Empire, the French cotton industry blossomed.[18]

Until this time, the cotton industry had concentrated primarily on finishing and decorating cloth. Emulating the printed cottons from India that first appeared in Europe in the late sixteenth century, this trade was appropriately known as *indiennage* and its producers called *indienneurs*. The radiant colors, refined textures, and lively designs of Indian calico and muslin prints outshone the European woolen and linen monotones. By the middle of the seventeenth century, the passion for *toiles peintes* and chintz had grown to such a fervor among the European upper classes that the new fashion was called the "Indian craze."

This commercial success attracted European imitators. During the eighteenth century, artists and artisans experimented with designs, dyes, coloring, and printing techniques in attempts to perfect a passable indigenous product. Initially, textile printing was concentrated primarily in port cities such as London, Antwerp, Amsterdam, Hamburg, Nantes, Le Havre, and Marseille, where merchants with access to cloths from India diverted capital into printing. As skills developed, however, European printers set up their own workshops throughout the continent. By the mid-eighteenth century, several European indienneurs had achieved great acclaim. Among them were Christoff-Philipp Oberkampf, with his works in Jouy outside Versailles, Johann Heinrich von Scheule of Augsburg, Johann Joseph Leitenberg of Levin (Bohemia), and Sir Robert Peel of Manchester. Other famous printers worked in Geneva, Zurich, and Neuchâtel.[19]

With the exception of several notable British and Swiss textile printers, few European indienneurs manufactured cloth. They either purchased domestically produced cloth or imported their cottons from India. Oberkampf, for example, purchased siamoise for cheaper-grade prints and relied on Indian pure cotton cloths for the high-quality, luxury prints. Oberkampf purchased calicos and guineas produced in Coromandel and sennas and baffetas from Bengal through

18. See Louis Bergeron, *L'épisode napoléonien: Aspects intérieurs 1799–1815* (Paris: Éditions du Seuil, 1972), pp. 194–202.

19. Stanley D. Chapman and Serge Chassagne, *European Textile Printers in the Eighteenth Century: A Study of Peel and Oberkampf* (London: Heineman, 1981), pp. 3–21.

the London East India company. In the 1780s, when Manchester produced a bleached calico acceptable to his standards, Oberkampf imported British textiles.[20]

During the first phases of the Revolution, French textile printers continued to import their cloths. Even though the Revolution had severed many of their commercial links, they were still able to obtain fine Indian calicos, although at great expense. By 1802, however, the new policy on custom duties had seriously affected supplies. The Decree of 24 frimaire XI (1802) increased duties on white fabrics tenfold. The next year, a new tariff designed to help French weavers compete with Indian imports imposed a uniform duty. The duty on woven cotton goods was doubled in 1805, and finally the decree of 22 September 1806 prohibited all imports.

These tariff barriers prompted textile printers to produce their own cloths. In 1805, Oberkampf began to prepare the Chantemerle estate in Essonnes for the construction of a spinning mill and cloth manufacture to supply his own printing works. The Chantemerle complex began operation in 1810.[21] This pattern was typical of many textile printers. Koechlin and Schlumbergers of Mulhouse began to invest in production in the first years of the Empire. Others, like the speculator Richard (known also as Richard-Lenoir) in Paris, took advantage of the thirst for cottons by investing in spinning and weaving. For a brief decade, Richard and his partners coordinated, with their mills and factories in Paris and the Norman countryside, the most extensive cotton manufacture in France.[22] Elsewhere in the county, many linen and woolen districts converted to cotton. Textile printers' need for domestic and Continental sources for cloth was at the root of the growth of cotton manufacturing in France. The Choletais was swept into this wave.

Responding to an inquiry on the conditions of the cotton trades in France after the prohibition of English goods, the mayors of Cholet and Chemillé both reported that cotton manufacture had expanded at an astonishing rate, to the neglect of the linen trade. By the end of the first decade of the century, the region was already producing an array of new cloths, consisting of calicos and baffetas for which textile printers paid a premium price, fine light cottons such as bazins and gauzes, and cambrics and nanking cotton for kerchiefs. As is ev-

20. Ibid., pp. 147–61.
21. Ibid., pp. 162–70.
22. Serge Chassagne, "La diffusion rurale de l'industrie cotonnière en France (1750–1850)" *Revue du Nord* 61 (January–March 1979): 97–114.

ident from their names, the new products imitated Indian and other Asian cottons.[23]

Cotton was not new to the region, however. One might think that the dissolution of restrictions on production and commerce with the Revolution would have had an important effect on the economic life of the region. But neither the removal of internal trade barriers nor the abolition of production controls, like those imposed by the bureaux de marque of Cholet, Vihiers, and Maulévriers, seemed to have a profound impact.[24] The disappearance of production controls did mean that local producers were no longer officially prohibited from using cotton. But these official bans had not prevented local production of cotton yarn and cloth containing cotton. In 1758, for example, Hérault, a merchant in Cholet, introduced to the fabrique brightly dyed cotton yarns he imported from Normandy and the Midi. These yarns were woven into the border designs of Cholet's kerchiefs. Cotton spinning was introduced on a small scale in the late eighteenth century. Cotton yarn (for the weft) was used in conjunction with linen (for the warp) to produce siamoise. Although it was not one of the cloths included in the royal patent, the inspectors apparently accepted the innovation without opposition. So, though the restrictions existed, they do not appear to have been such an onerous burden that their abolition liberated production. Thus the only novelty after the Revolution was cloth made of pure cotton.[25]

It is likely that the impetus to switch to cotton on a large scale came first from outsiders. As Doctor Gellusseau tells us, several merchant houses from Normandy and the Midi that had established themselves in the Mauges before the Revolution hastened back with the first signs of peace. In the eighteenth century, Farel frères and Cambon from Montpellier, Verdier from Nimes, and Vallée jeune and Desmaret et Pinel frères from Rouen supplied the fabrique with brightly colored cotton yarns in scarlets, blues, and violets. After the Revolution, Verdier, Vallée jeune, Desmaret, and Pinel were not content with merely selling yarn; they began to put out their yarn to weavers in the Mauges. Because of the great surge in demand for cottons and the troubles of the linen market, these businesses prospered. Local merchants, fearful of being excluded, were quick to follow their

23. A.D. M-et-L 67M5: État et situation des établissements de tissage de coton dans la commune de Chemillé, 1809; État et situation des établissements de tissage de coton dans la commune de Cholet, 1809.

24. See Tilly, *Vendée*, p. 202.

25. Gellusseau, *Histoire de Cholet*, p. 94.

lead. Gellusseau, always a booster for local entrepreneurial talent, noted somewhat defensively that "these cottons, as beautiful and rich as they were, would have remained dead material [in the hands of the merchants from Rouen], if, after the disaster of the war, the men who escaped the events of the revolution had not rediscovered their industrial genius, their talent for manufacture, and embraced cotton to their bosoms."[26]

Manufacturing the new cloths did not exhaust the entrepreneurial interests of Cholet's merchants. The commercial elite of Cholet were also greatly excited and curious about the new techniques and machines from England. A wealthy marchand-fabricant, Rousselot, introduced mule jennies to Cholet. Rousselot was clearly a mechanical buff. He had made his considerable fortune, assessed to be close to a half-million livres, by introducing the fly shuttle. Gellusseau told how Rousselot had been so proud of the new implement that he displayed the first bolt of cloth, which he himself had insisted on weaving. Having heard of the marvels of the Crompton spinning machine, Rousselot attended the 1806 Paris Exposition to examine it. Impressed, he acquired several mules (not the latest models) through a firm in Liège. Along with his machines, Rousselot hired several English workers to take to Cholet to mount the machines properly and to instruct local workers. Before his return to Cholet, Rousselot, who had little knowledge of spinning processes, attended the Conservatoire des arts et métiers to learn how to spin and to be instructed in the workings of his new machine.[27]

On his return, Rousselot and his brother-in-law, Bonnet, began spinning cotton and putting out the yarn to weavers. After seeing the results, other marchand-fabricants quickly followed. Within a few years, Louis-Toussaint Richard and his father Jean, Michel Cesbron and his brother Charles Cesbron-Lavau, the Turpault brothers, and the Brémond brothers had all extended their economic interests to spinning and producing cotton.[28]

Of the early spinning mills, we have the most detailed information on Michel Cesbron's establishment in Chemillé. Many considered Cesbron's mill the industrial showpiece of the region. Recall from an earlier description that by 1806 Cesbron's manufacturing center already included a spinning mill, laundry and bleach houses, bleach greens, and other finishing facilities. In 1808 he employed eight to

26. Ibid., pp. 369–70.
27. Ibid., pp. 389–92.
28. Ibid., pp. 393–94.

nine hundred workers, including three hundred handloom weaving households to whom he put out his yarn.[29]

In 1809, Michel Cesbron applied to the central government for a loan of 50,000 francs for expansion of his plant. In the same year, an inspection of his manufacturing center assessed its entire worth at 208,000 francs. His holdings included two large buildings: a four-story structure housing the spinning mill, assessed at 45,000 francs, and a second building for the bleach works, assessed at 36,000 francs. The treadmill, watermill, and other equipment powering the spinning plant were valued at 4,000 francs. The land occupied by his manufacturing center was valued at 15,000 francs.

The land and buildings together accounted for just under half the value of the manufacturing center. The other half consisted of the productive equipment. Cesbron's mill grouped together ten carding machines, thirteen water frames, and ten mule jennies. The mill had a spinning capacity of up to three thousand spindles, though not all the spindles were used in every season. The spinning machines were valued at 36,000 francs and bleaching, dying, and finishing equipment at 8,700 francs; finally, Cesbron possessed 7,800 francs in handlooms, heddles, and reeds which were dispersed and kept in the weaving households with whom he had putting-out relations. On average, cotton looms were valued at 55 francs each. Cesbron provided looms to about half the weaving families working under his commission.[30]

Under Cesbron's tutelage, Chemillé was fast becoming the most important center for cottons in the region. In addition to calicos and baffetas, Chemillé also produced fancier and finer light cottons. In contrast to Chemillé, where linen was hardly produced at all, Cholet and its dependent countryside still produced primarily linen kerchiefs, although cotton was growing in importance. Producing almost no calicos, Cholet manufactured siamoise and baffetas, both used for printed textiles. Within the region, Chemillé took the innovative lead.[31]

Louis-Toussaint Richard built his business in much the same way Cesbron did. In 1807, Richard and his father Jean were fabricants in

29. A.D. M-et-L 67M5: État et situation des établissements de tissage de coton dans la commune de Chemillé, 1809.

30. A.D. M-et-L 66M3: Commission ad hoc à l'effet de reconnaître et estimer la valeur foncière et immobilière de la manufacture du sieur Cesbron, 1809, 1817.

31. Compare the total number of linen and cotton cloths produced in Cholet and Chemillé, A.D. M-et-L 67M5: État et situation des fabriques et manufactures de toiles et autres tissus de chanvre, et de lin, Cholet et Chemillé 1812; État et situation des fabriques et manufactures de coton, Cholet et Chemillé, 1812.

the cotton trade. The agreement signed between father and son on the father's retirement indicates that the family business owned little productive equipment besides a few heddles and some finishing equipment. In the first decade of the century, Louis-Toussaint acquired land in the town of Cholet. By 1815 he had set up his manufacturing center, which housed a spinning mill, bleaching facilities, and a shop and equipment for finishing cloth in six contiguous buildings with several interior courtyards and bleach greens. An insurance report in 1830 offers the only detailed description of the center's productive capacity. Forty mule jennies with a total capacity of 9,500 spindles operated in the Richard mill. A treadmill run by a team of eight horses powered the spinning and carding machines. Based on the presence of machines to prepare warp and weft threads, heddles, and reeds, we can infer that Richard put out yarn to handloom weavers. The Richards were reputed to be among the most important fabricants in town (although we have no written public record of the number of weavers working under their commission). They specialized in calicos, fustians, and cotton kerchiefs. In addition, they sold cotton yarn."[32]

By 1815, Cholet and Chemillé had begun to resemble other small factory towns in the countryside, with large brick mills looming over the rural landscape. In the period between the Revolution and the end of the First Empire, a generation of industrial capitalists had matured. This generation of men, mostly born in the 1770s, had roots in the eighteenth-century economy. They and their fathers had made their fortunes in the linen trade, as cloth merchants who had also ventured into putting-out (hence their frequent designation as marchand-fabricants). In the early nineteenth century, having survived the collapse of the linen industry during the revolutionary turmoils, they reestablished themselves as cloth merchants by riding the wave of the new demand for cotton.

Winning Control over Entrepreneurship with Cotton

My description of the efforts of entrepreneurs has so far featured the excitement of the new technology they introduced and the physical novelty of their spinning mills, as has the local history of the re-

32. Elie Chamard, *La Maison Richard Frères* (Cholet: L'imprimerie Vételé, 1959), pp. 9–13.

gion. I have traced the transformation of these fabricants into industrial capitalists using the explanations they themselves provided. After the Revolution and counterrevolution, they sought out new opportunities presented by the fervent demand for cotton and by the technological innovations available. It is possible, however, to tell this story from a different vantage point, and to argue that these entrepreneurs' interest in securing a commanding role in a putting-out system outweighed their simple fascination with the new spinning technology. To make this argument, let us now take a second and more critical look at the effects of the revolutionary turmoils on these linen merchants and drapers. This time, my focus is on a fundamental transformation that is often obscured by the spectacle of factories and technological change: the successful establishment of a putting-out system. In particular, I stress the direct link between entrepreneurs' interest in mechanizing spinning and their success as cotton merchants and putters-out. I ask, why did merchants have to invest capital in land, buildings, machines, and ultimately steam engines, just to ensure themselves a place as putters-out?

Marchand-fabricants became the giants of the Choletais cotton trade because they controlled spinning, finishing, and marketing. As industrial spinners they assured their role as fabricants, by securing a supply of yarn to put out to handloom weavers. As bleachers and finishers, they added the final touches to the cloth before selling it as merchants. They were thus directly involved in both producing the raw material for cloth and marketing it, precisely the points of vulnerability for earlier merchants and fabricants.

These merchant sons were positioned well to take advantage of the opportunities presented them in the early nineteenth century. In assets and commercial activities, they were different from the wealthiest négociants of Cholet, who were wholesale merchants dealing exclusively in long-distance trade in linens and cottons. It was the négociants of Cholet who invested in and provisioned their own cargo ships in the Atlantic trade. By contrast, marchand-fabricants were poorer than négociants, they owned less property, and they were themselves dependent on the négociants' business connections. Interestingly, many of the wealthiest négociant families retired from commerce during the revolutionary turmoils.[33] More important for

---

33. A.D. M-et-L 3M57: Listes des électeurs, 1812, 1820, 1830. Many prominent négociants of the eighteenth century and their sons who were too young to be retired from business were listed as "propriétaires" on the registries of the listes des électeurs during the early nineteenth century.

post-Revolution Choletais, marchand-fabricants like Cesbron and Richard married into these négociant families and benefited from their many business connections. For example, the Richard family was connected through marriages to the Gellusseaus and the Retailleaus (a prominent merchant family in the eighteenth century). The Cesbrons were connected to the Ménards and the Tharreaus.[34]

In addition to these connections, the first generation of industrial capitalists drew on their experience as local merchants who had tried putting-out in the eighteenth century. These marchand-fabricants were probably the most successful among the multitude of putters-out, but they knew firsthand the frustrations of the system. They understood that fabricants in the linen trade operated at a disadvantage and that their profits were constantly threatened by small-scale owner-producers. Most critical, marchand-fabricants like Cesbron, Richard, and Bonnet had the assets and connections to redress their vulnerability as merchants, whereas poorer putters-out did not.

By the early nineteenth century, merchants had succeeded in establishing an effective putting-out system under their control. Entrepreneurship was no longer securely in the hands of the small producers. Local markets that had earlier secured for petty producers their claims in manufacturing and commerce were no longer important centers for coordinating production. In the process of switching over to cottons, most small traders and other intermediaries lost out as well. No matter how ineffective this coordination might have been from moment to moment, the cloth halls and the yarn and flax markets had provided some equality of access in the linen era. In their place, cloth merchants and mill owners like Cesbron, Richard, and others took over the coordination that had once been centered in the marketplace.

In terms of power in the market, merchants in Cholet benefited enormously from the economic turmoils of the revolutionary era. The collapse of the linen trade and the loss of the important linen markets gave merchants, who could take advantage of the growing demand for cotton, the leverage to force unemployed and often desperate spinners and handloom weavers to accept either raw cotton or cotton yarn to work on commission. Moreover, the dismantling of the regulatory agencies of the French crown left the putters-out with greater freedom to pursue their aims. No longer pursued by royal inspectors like Huet de Vaudour for their monopolistic actions, mer-

34. Chamard, *La Maison Richard Frères,* and *Histoire de Cholet,* pp. 135–38.

chants were free to assert the dominance of the market principle over the standard of open access to marketplaces.

What made this shift so important was that cotton was not an indigenous fiber. Because cotton was not grown in the region, it was possible to control the source of raw materials, a tactic virtually impossible with linen. Merchants with long-distance connections, especially to port cities like Le Havre or Nantes, enjoyed an added edge. With contacts in place, they were in strong positions to buy the cotton, either in the raw or as yarn, necessary to begin a putting-out industry.

The Politics of Labor-Saving Machines

The collapse of the linen market and the ability of merchants to monopolize sources for raw cotton, though critical in shutting off alternatives for obstreperous small producers, do not explain why cotton spinning was so quickly centralized and mechanized in the region. Switching to a nonindigenous fiber weighed the struggle in favor of merchants, but the possibility of defeating small-scale producers still existed only as a potential. New developments in spinning technology, and competition from merchants from other regions who also enjoyed advantages vis-à-vis sources for cotton, threatened the monopoly of merchants in Cholet. These factors pushed local merchants toward capital investment in machinery and large mills. Merchants found it necessary to invest in mechanizing spinning to control the putting-out system.

Nothing intrinsic to cotton as a fiber discouraged its spinning by small-scale producers. In fact, when cotton spinning was first introduced to the region, entrepreneurship was quite diffuse. In 1806 the mayor of Cholet reported that the number of entrepreneurs processing cotton had multiplied at an astounding rate "in every bourg and bourgade of the fabriques of Cholet, Chemillé, Beaupréau, Vihiers, Mortagne, Jallais, and some hundred hamlets in the region."[35] There were so many that the mayor refused to count them. The only one worth mentioning, he claimed, was Michel Cesbron's mill. No doubt, Tharreau was trying to build the reputation of his brother-in-law.

According to Tharreau, the most popular methods for spinning cotton were the new spinning jennies and the old-fashioned spindles and

35. A.D. M-et-L 67M5: État des filatures de coton, fabrique de Cholet, 1806.

wheels. No one method dominated. The demand was such that all methods for spinning proliferated at the same time. In his report, Tharreau noted that the number of jennies in the region had grown from between six and seven hundred in 1804 to about a thousand in 1806. Each jenny provided full-time employment for four women, the mayor reported. Thus there were approximately four thousand women making their living from the jennies alone. As for the number of hand spinners, Tharreau did not even venture an estimate.[36]

Spinning jennies enhanced the viability and productivity of small producers. As William Reddy has noted, the origin of the jenny tells us much about its popularity with small producers.[37] It is hardly surprising that James Hargreaves was a weaver. Like all handloom weavers, Hargreaves was well aware of the bottlenecks in production resulting from the constant shortage of yarn. In tinkering to improve the productivity of spinning, he produced a simple device (which imitated and multiplied the actions of the spinner's hand) that was cheap to produce and easy to operate. Light and portable, jennies used human power but greatly improved its productivity. The first jennies carried twelve spindles, but within several years sixty spindles became the average. Hargreaves's invention was instantly popular because it was easily adapted into the worklife of petty commodity producers. Weavers and small traders could easily set up jennies in their shops. True to the social conditions of its invention, weavers were better able to control their yarn supply and small traders could use jenny yarn to launch themselves as putters-out. This invention reinforced the dispersed nature of entrepreneurship.[38]

For merchants aspiring to gain and maintain control over the burgeoning cotton trade, the spinning jenny presented a difficult problem. Jennies threatened to allow independent weavers even greater control over the entire production process, by solving their yarn supply problem with very small capital investments. From the perspective of merchants and putters-out at the beginning of the nineteenth century, the situation in the cotton trades threatened to replicate the dispersed organization of linen. The problem, once again, was too many entrepreneurs.

36. Ibid.
37. William M. Reddy, *The Rise of Market Culture: The Textile Trades and French Society, 1750–1900* (Cambridge: Cambridge University Press, 1984), p. 49.
38. Stanley D. Chapman, *The Early Factory Masters: The Transition to the Factory System in the Midlands Textile Trades* (Newton Abbot, Devon: David and Charles, 1967), pp. 53, 60; R. L. Hills, "Hargreaves, Arkwright, and Crompton: Why Three Inventors?" *Textile History* 10 (1979): 114–26.

Not only did merchants face new groups of small-scale entrepreneurs, they faced competition from merchants in other regions who also tried to profit from the crisis of the linen industry. As we have already seen, when peace resumed merchants from Normandy flocked to the Choletais with raw cotton and cotton yarns, looking for spinners and weavers. This external source for materials, especially raw cotton, even if sold only in small packets threatened the effective control of merchants.

In this context, the implications of Richard Arkwright's water frame and Samuel Crompton's mule jenny for the politics of production became all important. Arkwright's water frame worked on a very different principle than the jenny. Arkwright's spinning machine used the principle of rollers and flyers derived from the earlier patents of Lewis Paul and John Wyatt. Instead of drawing out the fiber with clamps, the roving is passed through a series of weighted rollers to draw out the fiber, then twisted and wound onto a bobbin. The water frame did not produce a better yarn than Hargreaves's jenny, and neither system surpassed the quality and versatility of hand-spun. Jenny yarn was weak and could only be used for weft, and Arkwright's machine produced coarse counts suitable only for warp. The sole advantage of the water frame, and the feature that made it preferable to merchants and would-be industrialists, was its scale of operation. Whereas the jenny was designed to augment the productivity of human power by use of a crank, Arkwright attached the water frame to far more powerful sources of energy. In 1768 he set up his first spinning frame driven by horsepower. Three years later, he purchased property in Cromford and set up the first fully automated spinning mill driven by water power. These innovations announced the era of the fully automated factory with its vast possibilities of increased productivity.

The value of Arkwright's invention was its effect on the politics of production, not its ability to spin a better thread. The water frame and the fully automated spinning mill were critical factors in the struggle between small-scale producers and producers with considerably more capital. Arkwright's system required a large capital investment in land, factory building, power source, and machines. To realize the full advantage of the water frame, one had to automate the preparatory processes as well. Thus Arkwright's spinning frame also required machines for carding, drawing and roving. Needless to say, the system was extremely costly to build and operate—far beyond the means of small producers, and expensive even for those with much greater resources. The advantage of mill spinning was that it concentrated a great deal of yarn in the hands of the mill owner. This advantage, I argue, was critical to merchants, like Cesbron or Richard, who attempted to translate their superior capital resources into a dominant position in the crucial raw material for cloth.

There is some evidence to suggest that Arkwright was himself aware of the implications in his design for the politics of production. The Science Museum in London built a replica of Arkwright's 1769 patent machine which could be operated by visitors turning a hand-crank. This possibility indicates that Arkwright's spinning frame could have been built in small units, placed in cottages, and turned by hand. It could have been used, like the jenny, as a domestic spinning machine. R. L. Hills speculates that Arkwright or his partners saw this potential as a threat to their patent, much as Hargreaves lost control over the jenny design because of its multiple replications. Thus their solution was to limit the licenses to units of a thousand spindles, making their machines, economically feasible only when used in water-powered mills.[39]

Over the long run, of course, the economies of scale realized with automated spinning drove production costs down, and mill-spun yarn could be obtained more cheaply than hand-spun and jenny-spun. The limitations of the water frame were overcome by Samuel Crompton's mule jenny, which combined the best features of Hargreaves's jenny and Arkwright's roller frame. The mule could spin both warp and weft threads and spin a higher count (a finer thread) than Hargreaves's jenny.[40] The technical superiority of the mule complemented the capacity of the water frame. In the spinning mills of the Choletais, we find both mule jennies and water frames.

The advantages of mechanized spinning for the capitalist entrepreneur were thus twofold. First, the scale of production assured a steady supply of yarn at a time when weavers found it difficult to find an alternative but equally steady source of raw cotton or yarn. Second, yarn that entrepreneurs' spun themselves could at least potentially undercut the cost of hand-spun yarn or yarn obtained from another source, giving capitalists room to offer favorable piece rates to weavers and yet still make a profit. Both scale and price were important in establishing the leverage that capitalist entrepreneurs enjoyed in these relations of production.

39. Hills, "Hargreaves, Arkwright, and Crompton," p. 123.
40. Chapman Early Factory Masters, pp. 58, 69–70. See Also Hills, "Hargreaves, Arkwright, and Crompton."

The crucial struggle in the fabrique during the early nineteenth century, as in the eighteenth century, was over cotton yarn. Whoever controlled the yarn supply could control cloth production. Initially, merchants were not necessarily at an advantage: weavers had alternative sources for yarn, through technologies that diffused the capacity to produce yarn and from competing merchants in Rouen and elsewhere. Altering the position of merchant entrepreneurs in the production process depended on mule jennies and water frames. The technical superiority of these machines gave merchants with accumulated capital a way to exercise control over yarn supply, and thus entrepreneurship, which was not available to them previously. Their success as industrial spinners was necessary to their success as putters-out. Only tight control over these subcontracting relations prevented the rise of open markets for cotton yarn in the region.

Capitalist Transformations of the Social Relations of Production

Capitalist entrepreneurial control of spinning was most evident in the changes in spinning as an occupation. Industrialization thoroughly transformed the trade. Hand spinning had been a female-dominated operation. Many women were independent producers and entrepreneurs, controlling marketing and production. Notably, the new industrial spinners, the mule operatives, were adult men. The mills hired men and women in equal proportions, but the sexual segregation of work was designed so as not to replicate the organization of rural hand spinning. Thus men became spinners, mechanics, and foremen. Women were hired as piecers, carders, bobbin minders, and skein winders. Male mule spinners constituted a new elite, but proletarianized, workforce. Their wages were comparable to weaving incomes and in time surpassed them, as weaving incomes declined. Female mill workers earned about half of what mule operatives earned and about a quarter of a foreman's wage.[41]

In the first decades of the nineteenth century, dispersed hand spinning and centralized machine spinning continued side by side. We

41. There are only scattered references to the composition of the workforce and wage rates in local spinning mills: A.D. M-et-L 67M2: Statistique industrielle du département de Maine-et-Loire, arrondissement de Beaupréau, 1841; Archives municipales de Cholet, V2 dossier 4: Souscription et secours aux ouvriers inoccupés par suite de l'incendie de filature de M. Deschamps, 1863.

have only the vaguest suggestion of unemployment among farm women, and even then not until the 1830s. It is likely that women continued to spin weft yarns and very fine counts of cotton by hand, but mostly they spun linen. Although the recovery of linen was slow, and the market was certainly not as dynamic as for cotton, farm women continued to find some work. Mechanization of cotton spinning enabled merchant capitalists to bypass and eventually to displace female spinners. In their place, merchant capitalists created a new male wage-earning elite.

Despite their success in controlling the yarn supply, industrialists did not completely proletarianize handloom weavers. Handloom weavers remained petty producers. What industrialists succeeded in creating was dependence. In defeating the weavers' abilities to act as entrepreneurs in their own right, capitalist entrepreneurs subordinated handloom weavers within subcontracting arrangements. In essence, handloom weavers became dependent producers. Within the putting-out system, weavers remained the coordinators of cloth production, organizing the work process and the labor force (represented by the unpaid labor of the weavers' family). Weavers no longer owned the materials or the final product, but they retained ownership of the tools of transformation. The mill owner/putters-out could not dispense with the weavers' knowledge of cloth making, because they had not introduced machines to perform the actual weaving.

Despite the change in status, cotton weaving provided a good income. Cotton was easier than linen to master. The fiber was more pliable and lighter, so productivity was higher and the apprenticeship period shorter. Until the 1830s, cotton cloths paid well. During the Napoleonic era, cotton weavers earned nearly three times more than linen weavers. Daily income for an adult weaver in linens hovered around 20–25 sous (1.0–1.25 francs) while cotton incomes were as high as 3 francs a day.[42] Moreover, more family members could weave cottons. Young children could begin to weave cottons before they had attained the skill and strength to weave linens.[43]

Through the early decades of the nineteenth century, the number of cotton weavers grew steadily. In 1811 the mayor of Cholet put the number of handlooms at ten to twelve thousand, with five thousand looms working cottons, one thousand looms making flannels, and four to six thousand linen looms. By 1814 the weaving population

42. A.D. M-et-L 67M2: Letter from the mayor of Chemillé to subprefect of Beaupréau, 14 February 1832.
43. Private communication, Anne McKernan.

had attained its prerevolutionary level, about twenty thousand weavers and twenty-five or thirty thousand women and children engaged in ancillary activities. In 1837 the next report on the size of the weaving population indicated a stability in numbers: a population of fifty thousand including weavers, bobbin winders, and skein winders. The report estimated twenty-five thousand handlooms.[44] The latter two estimates do not differentiate between linen and cotton, but by other indications we know that the division probably favored cotton. There were five or six hundred cotton weavers in Cholet itself. The estimates of rural cotton weavers differed dramatically, from ten to fifteen to eighteen thousand.[45]

As dependent producers, cotton weavers had lost a large measure of their autonomy to combine production and marketing. But as long as incomes remained high, they did not feel the full effects of their loss. They drew monetary benefits as they ceded their entrepreneurial roles.

A Look Ahead: The Origins of Backward Development

Cotton manufacture flourished in the Choletais through the first three decades of the nineteenth century. During the Restoration, the pace of mechanization in spinning increased. In 1824, Mathurin Bonnet, Bonnet's son and Rousselot's nephew, set up a very large cotton and woolens mill on the banks of the Sèvre river in the commune of Le Longeron. Powered by water and later steam, this mill had a spinning capacity of 13,000 spindles for cotton and 700 spindles for wool. The next year, Nicolas Deschamps and Henri Journet established an important spinning mill in Cholet with a spinning capacity of 9,200 spindles.[46] In this era, many established mill owners updated their existing facilities. For example, Charles Cesbron-Lavau installed the first steam engine in Cholet in 1825. Later, in 1840, the Richard brothers updated their old mill with steam power and additional spinning machines.

44. A.D. M-et-L 67M5: Notice sur la fabrique de Cholet, 25 August 1814; 67M2: Letter from subprefect of Beaupréau to prefect of Maine-et-Loire, 24 May 1837.
45. These estimates come from strike reports: A.D. M-et-L 71M1.
46. P. A. Millet de la Turtaudière, *Indicateur de Maine-et-Loire* (Angers: Cosnier et Lachèse, 1865), pp. 68–69; A.D. M-et-L 67M2: Letter from subprefect of Beaupréau to prefect of Maine-et-Loire, 24 May 1837.

The prosperity of these years did not, however, prepare these industrialist for the crisis to come. In the changing international and domestic markets from the 1830s on, new competition in yarn and cloth prices profoundly shook the economic prospects of the fabrique. In 1829, as an omen of things to come, Michel Cesbron was forced into bankruptcy. The records from his court hearing indicate that Cesbron had been heavily in debt for years. Not only had he borrowed from the state to cover his losses, he had also borrowed close to the net worth of his manufacturing plant from a wealthy widow in Angers. How he spent these loans is particularly revealing about his confidence in the future of the fabrique. Cesbron spent much of this money trying to extricate himself and his children from the regional cotton trade. A large portion of the borrowed sum was lost by his son in an attempt to obtain a lucrative tobacco monopoly in Spain (the details of this venture, and why it went sour, remain obscure). More indicative of his confidence, perhaps, is that he managed to establish for his sons lucrative positions in merchant houses and advantaged marriages outside of the region, in Paris and Cateau-Cambrésis (in the Nord).[47]

In a broader sense, Cesbron's financial difficulties suggest the uneasy nature of the solution wealthy merchants devised to the problem of defeating small-producer entrepreneurship. Mechanization, though yielding for the first time an assured supply of yarn, was an extremely expensive path to go down. Although the yarn produced by the mills was undoubtedly "cheaper" than hand-spun yarn, its cheapness was achieved by tying down enormous amounts of capital. With weavers still able to bargain over the terms of the putting-out relationship, if not its existence, merchants must have wondered whether the advantages they secured were worth the uncertainties they faced.

47. Serge Chassagne, "Industrialisation et désindustrialisation dans les campagnes françaises: Quelques réflexions à partir du textile," *Revue du Nord* 63 (January–March 1981): 43.

5

Cooperation and Collectivity:
Weavers Mobilize to Retake Control

In the fall of 1851, the subprefect of the arrondissement of Beaupréau reported that the oldest and richest merchant houses in Cholet, along with the industrial mill owners, had renounced their role in the production of cotton cloths.[1] This momentous decision marked the end of an era. The optimism and vitality that characterized the Napoleonic period and the Restoration had dissipated into suspicion and fear. The decision to abandon cloth production seemed to seal the fate of the region as a residual industrial area. From the mid-nineteenth century onward, the Choletais was known more for its small-scale industries than as an industrial center.

   In this chapter I examine the events that led to this crucial decision, concentrating on the social unrest and protracted conflicts between handloom weavers, middlemen, and mill owners which plagued the region between 1840 and 1850. The decision to abandon cloth production was a direct response to this unrest. The disputes centered on piece rates and whether merchant/mill owners and other putters-out were willing to abide by minimum rates established through collective negotiations. Although the disagreements, which often escalated into armed struggle, were over payment, the disputes were also another phase of the struggle between merchants and small producers over control of the production process. In effect, when the most important mill owners decided to abandon cloth production, handloom weavers won a battle against proletarianization. The survival of dispersed, small-scale manufacturing resulted from weavers successfully defending their place in the production process.

---

1. A.D. M-et-L 67M3: "Situation du commerce pendant le 2e semestre de 1851," Report of the subprefect of Beaupréau, 9 February 1852.

The Tarif

For mill owners and middlemen, the troubles began in October 1840.[2] On the seventh of the month, while making his noon rounds, the commissaire de police of Cholet was startled to find a hundred weavers assembled on the grounds of the cattle market. When he inquired about the purpose of this gathering, one weaver told this story:

> Last Monday, many of our comrades went to turn in work to Monsieur Ricou. The merchant warned them that it was necessary to cut the piece rate in order to sustain competition with his confrères, who pay less than he for the same quality. Our comrades responded that they would rather turn in their cards and stop work, if he wanted to cut rates and reduce their pay. Well, Monsieur Ricou, seeing that he might lose some fifteen of his best weavers, said to them, "There doesn't have to be a reduction. If I cut rates, it is only to put myself on par with my confrères, who pay seven and a half centimes less per meter for the same pieces you produce. I will give you my rates, if my confrères would do the same for their workers. Better still, if they were of the same opinion, we could give you several centimes more, and we would not sell less."

The crowd had gathered, the weaver explained, to wait for their delegation to return with news of how other merchants received Ricou's proposition. "They are charged with a mission on which rests our lives or our deaths." He continued: "What would become of us if they reduce us again? Do they want us to die of hunger? Or turn us into thieves? We don't want to insult anyone, but we want to discuss our interest with the merchants who have had us work for such a long time at prices which no longer feed us. All the while that they profit from our misery, they grow rich and buy property everywhere—they, who had nothing when they started."

This weaver recounted his plight without exaggeration. Perhaps weavers were not on the verge of starvation, but piece rates had dropped precipitously for nearly a decade. During the protective regime of the First Empire, an able cotton weaver could earn 3 francs and even 3.50 francs a day producing calicos and other cottons used for printing. Between the First Empire and 1830, prices dropped dramatically. Whereas a fine-grade cotton sold for 4.25 francs an aune in

2. The narrative in this section is reconstructed from A.D. M-et-L 71M1: Letters from commissaire de police de Cholet to prefect of Maine-et-Loire, 9 and 16 October 1840.

1806, and 2.60 francs in 1816, by 1829 the same cloth might be selling for as low as 80 centimes an aune.[3] With the general decline in cotton prices, piece rates fell. Handloom weavers earned, on the average, between 25 and 30 sous a day, and in the worse years of economic crisis as little as 12–15 sous.[4] Each sou was worth about 5 centimes, so weavers' incomes had fallen to as low as 60–75 centimes a day from five times that.

Knowing the accuracy of the weavers' lament, and aware of the grave consequences Ricou's proposition could bring, the commissaire de police rushed off to consult with the deputy mayor. As the day wore on, the size of the assembly doubled and tripled as more weavers joined in to hear the news. The town, however, remained quiet all day. Near nightfall the deputy mayor asked the crowd to disperse. Except for one altercation at a cabaret, they obliged quietly. By eight in the evening, everything had returned to normal. There were no further rallies during the night.

The next morning, more weavers had heard the news of Ricou's proposition. This time, six hundred weavers gathered to hear what the négociants had decided. Near four o'clock in the afternoon, the merchants left the city hall, and shortly after the premier adjoint called in the weavers' delegation to communicate to them the results of the deliberations. With one glance at the offer, the delegates could see trouble. They feared bodily harm if they appeared before their exasperated comrades with such feeble results. But the city officials assured them that they could remain in the city hall under the protection of the law. With the commissaire de police at his side, the local magistrate himself descended the steps of the Hotel de Ville and, after a short preamble, he read the tarif (the list of piece rates) to the waiting crowd.

After a moment of silence, the voices rose in protest. "This is not Ricou's tarif! The Ricou tarif is what we want and we will not budge until we get it." The premier adjoint rushed in to explain that "the tarif reflects the actual state of commerce." In his most soothing and

---

3. Maurice Lévy-Leboyer, *Les banques européennes et l'industrialisation internationale dans la première moitié du XIX siècle* (Paris: Presses universitaires de France, 1964), p. 82.
4. A.D. M-et-L 71M1: Letter from prefect of Maine-et-Loire to minister of interior, 31 October 1841; 67M2: Letter from the mayor of Chemillé to the subprefect of Beaupréau, 14 February 1832; "Situation commerciale de l'arrondissement de Beaupréau pendant le second semestre de 1834," 28 August 1834. This pattern was not atypical. Handloom weaver Charles Nioret reports that cotton weavers in Rouen earned 38.50 francs a week in 1815 and 7.52 francs a week in 1835, that is, a drop from 5.50–6.40 francs a day (depending on whether they worked six or seven days in a week), to 1–1.25 francs a day; see Lévy-Leboyer, *Banques européennes*, p. 82, n. 76.

polite voice, he pleaded with the weavers to disperse. He would not want to see force applied, he told them.

But the weavers could not be dissuaded. "Better to die today by the bayonet than to die of hunger and misery," they shouted indignantly. The magistrate also tried to calm the crowd, but seeing the determination of the group, he gave the signal for the gendarmerie and the troupe de ligne to march against them. On seeing the soldiers, the weavers fled the Hôtel de Ville and sought refuge in the quartier Rambourg, the center of the weaving community. As they retreated, the commissaire de police thought he heard threats and plots whispered from ear to ear: "Demain matin la soupe sera mangée chez Richard, et le soir, le feu mis à ses établissements." ("Tomorrow morning soup will be served at Richard's; at night, the place will be torched.") Assembling the gendarmerie and the troupe de ligne, the commissaire de police and the premier adjoint pursued the weavers into their neighborhood. Arriving at the quartier, the premier adjoint called his troops to a halt. Then, with two hundred armed men facing six hundred unarmed weavers, he asked the weavers to return to their houses voluntarily before there was bloodshed.

At this moment, the commissaire de police mingled into the crowd. In their midst, one weaver approached and addressed him:

> Monsieur le commissaire de police, you know me to be an honest man who has served his *pays* and who is incapable of doing harm in his native city. . . . Hé bien, I must tell you that these men who have assembled here today will disperse immediately if Monsieur Libaud and Monsieur Sauvestre would accept the tarif of Monsieur Ricou. Up to now I have done what I could to quiet my comrades, but I can do no more. They are at wits' end, and [if] Messieurs Libaud and Sauvestre refuse the tarif proposed to them, they will be the cause of a great disaster. Maybe tomorrow, there will be ten thousand workers from the countryside in Cholet. So see what you can do to persuade these messieurs that they should decide in favor of the unhappy workers who only demand what is just, or have them shot without pity, for they have decided not to go home until they are granted what they demand.

This weaver's intervention made a difference. He proposed a peaceful resolution to the problem. Moreover, he laid the problem on the shoulders of two identifiable individuals. Given that it was far easier for the town officials to deal with these two men than to cope with a faceless and disgruntled crowd, the suggestion had an immediate effect. As the commissaire de police later noted in his report, this weaver was a man he held in great esteem. His reasonable words left an impression. When the adjoint learned of the weavers' determination, he summoned the two merchants. Informed of the weavers' exigency and the disaster their refusal would bring, Libaud and Sauvestre were given little choice but to consent. They authorized the city administration to announce on their behalf that they were willing to accept the tarif of Monsieur Ricou.

Overjoyed by the news, the weavers' delegates ran back to Rambourg district shouting "Le tarif à Ricou est adopté!" Arriving at the quartier where six hundred weavers still waited, the commissaire de police announced officially that the tarif of Ricou had been accepted and that they must now disperse immediately. On hearing the news, the weavers cheered, "Vive le Roi. Vive Ricou, qui nous donne notre vie à gagner." ("Long live the king. Long live Ricou, who gives us back our livelihood.") Within an hour, the streets and cabarets were deserted and the weavers had gone home. The next afternoon, not ten thousand, but two or three hundred weavers arrived from the countryside. Contented with the news, they turned back and left without incident.

By 9 October, calm had returned to Cholet, but the city administration still fretted. The ninth and tenth were days of the annual fair of Saint-Denis. Cholet was teeming with visitors, but the weavers remained at their looms. On Sunday, the eleventh, the commissaire de police was worried again. Since weavers did not work this day and had time to socialize, to reflect and discuss, there was time for their mistrusts and suspicions to seize hold. A small group of weavers wandered aimlessly at the Hôtel de Ville as the merchants inside gathered to draw up the official tarif. The commissaire feared that the weavers were searching for any object on which to vent their rage.

Sunday's tension was brought to a head when the commissaire de police learned that rural weavers were preparing to come to Cholet the next day. On hearing this news, the adjoint convened the municipal council with the commanders of the garde nationale and the troupe de ligne in attendance. They deliberated how to resolve the crisis at hand. How were they to repress the disorder that might break out with even greater force than in the days before? Their solutions focused on the more effective use of force. They decided that the troupe de ligne would occupy all the vantage points in the city to prevent the weavers of one quartier from contacting and congregating with those of another. The troops would also occupy all points of entry to rebuff the mobs of weavers coming in from the countryside.

The most difficult question to resolve was how best to deal with
the garde nationale. Clearly, the city officials feared armed insurrection. The president of the municipal council summarized the dilemma. Since weavers were well represented in the armed civil
militia, especially in those companies from weaving districts, there
was a serious question whether the garde would defend "public
safety" or whether would they "defect" to the side of the weavers.
The majority agreed that the weapons held by the garde nationale
should be collected and stored in a central arsenal. On this matter,
those with opposing opinions were quickly silenced when they heard
that rural weavers intended to march on Cholet. Nevertheless, there
were complications. Some council members expressed concern that
such actions were in themselves provocative. Others pointed out that
the garde nationale had always been reliable in maintaining civic order. They had carried out their duties with devotion and zeal. Their
actions in the past had earned the well-merited respect of city authorities and all the citizenry. Thus the question was how to reiterate this
recognition and still reclaim the arms for security purposes.

After much deliberation, it was finally resolved that the garde nationale would be called on company by company to defend the city
hall. At the end of their shift, each company would deposit their arms
in the Hôtel de Ville. In this way, the garde themselves would keep
watch over the arms and the arms would remain securely in the central arsenal.[5] Before this plan could be carried out, however, the royal
prosecutor and the subprefect in Beaupréau had to be summoned.
These two officials hastened to Cholet during the night. The next
morning they issued the order.

But as the commissaire de police had feared, the plan was all too
transparent to the weavers. The decree excited rumors, and further
attempts to quiet these suspicions only escalated the doubts. Some
weavers who were garde members went in groups to remind the merchants not to renege on their deal. Without brandishing arms, they
verbally suggested the very scenarios the merchants and manufacturers had feared.

During the early morning on the twelfth, the troops surveyed the
town and took up their positions. By noon, all the vantage points
were occupied. Perhaps because the weavers expected to rally, or perhaps out of simple curiosity, they left their neighborhoods to watch
the events around town. Their presence made officials nervous. They
were tracked so closely by the troops patrolling the town that most

5. Archives municipales de Cholet, JA Dossier 6(1): "Extrait du régistre du Conseil municipal de la commune de Cholet," 12 October 1840.

weavers quickly returned home. A handful of weavers, however, persisted. Several tried to persuade masons to join them in protest. These weavers were quickly arrested before their words had any effect.

In the meantime, weavers in the countryside were gathering in their parish squares, readying to march on Cholet. By mid-afternoon, the weavers from Vézins arrived at Cholet. The gendarmerie were able to stop most of them on the road just before the town, but some thirty weavers evaded the guards and slipped into town by crossing fields and hiding in hedge rows. Once in Cholet, however, the weavers from Vézins took refuge in a cabaret.[6] As it turned out, this slight disturbance was the only incident of the day. Despite the rumored invasion by rural weavers, and the murmured threats, the day passed without major confrontations. By eleven in the evening, the troops had left their watch and only the garde nationale remained posted in front of the city hall.

On the commissaire's morning rounds the next day, most weavers were at work. They expressed their intention to remain in their workshops but reminded the commissaire of the importance of the tarif. By the thirteenth, the troops had relinquished their positions around town. Although at mid-day the calm was disturbed by several gardes from La Tessoualle who announced that weavers from their commune were marching en masse to Cholet, as with the day before the gendarmerie turned back most of the group at the gate. Those who managed to get into town were quickly arrested.

The next days passed without new outbreaks. When the general tarif was published and posted on 16 October, the weavers were content with the result. They got what they were promised and busied themselves on their looms to make up for lost time. There "is no longer fear that the tranquility will be troubled again, at least not so soon," wrote the commissaire in concluding his report on the day's events.

The weavers won a resounding victory this October. They prevented the piece rates from falling, and they achieved this for all cotton weavers. Some weavers worked for higher rates as a result of the general tarif. The weavers' actions demonstrated the power of collectivity. Their strength derived not from absolute numbers but from the effectiveness of their extensive network. Urban weavers were able to mobilize rural weavers on call. Again and again in the deliberations, the threat that weavers in the countryside would march on Cholet turned the negotiations to the weavers' advantage.

6. A.D. M-et-L 71M1: Letter from commandant de la compagnie de Maine-et-Loire to prefect of Maine-et-Loire, 13 October 1840.

If weavers had only threatened violence and disorder, they might have been brutally repressed. This possibility did not occur because the commissaire de police and the rest of the town administration saw the legitimacy of the weavers' claims. Without the commissaire's intervention on the eighth, when he listened to and was persuaded by one weaver, the encounter between the gendarmerie and weavers might have turned violent. Without the commissaire acting as an intermediary and relaying weaver' demands after the weavers' own negotiations failed, there would have been no tarif.

Demanding uniform rates was an act of collective self-protection. The tarif represented more than pure economic gain; it was an important step in the self-organization of weavers. Weavers were challenging and changing the power relations in the putting-out system.[7] As I discussed in Chapters 3 and 4, the social relations of production in the putting-out system required that producers who received contracts be dependent on merchants who were both their suppliers and their buyers. Such relations rested on the power of merchants and the dependence of producers. In the Choletais, this dependence was imposed on weavers at a high cost to merchants. Merchants did profit from the collapse of the linen market. But most were not able to fully capture the benefits of cotton production without investing a great deal of capital into spinning mills in order to ensure their control over the supply of yarn.

Once merchants established dependence, as putters-out they effectively dictated the terms of the relationship to their own economic advantage. Although the initial outlay for yarn was substantial, especially in the case of industrial spinners, the risks associated with market fluctuations in cloth prices could be passed on to weavers in the form of fluctuating piece rates. It was weavers who had to absorb the insecurities of the market, not the putter-out. When weavers used their collective strength to set piece rates, then, they were challenging the power relations on which the putting-out arrangement rested. By refusing to accept the burden of market uncertainties, they challenged the core of the merchants' risk-averting strategy, thus forcing them to endanger their profits.

In a sense, weavers won the tarif because some merchants wanted the same thing. At root, the conflict in October originated within the

7. For a discussion of the social relationships and strategies built around tarif negociations, see Alain Cottereau, "The Distinctiveness of Working-Class Cultures in France, 1848–1900," in *Working-Class Formation,* ed. Ira Katznelson and Aristide R. Zolberg (Princeton: Princeton University Press, 1986).

ranks of those who put out to weavers. The conflict revealed a division of interest between those who purchased yarn to put out to weavers and mill owners whose factories produced the yarn they then put out. In the changing international market, new strategies became available to putters-out who had not invested in spinning mills. Once it was possible to import cheaper English yarn, as local merchants began to do in the 1830s, these putters-out challenged the dominant position of industrial spinners in the putting-out system. The availability of yarn from the international market created new opportunities for entrepreneurship and diluted the advantages of local industrialists.[8]

It was evident to all that Ricou, the merchant who encouraged weavers to demand uniform rates, acted out of self-interest. As the commissaire de police reported to the prefect on the day the new tarif was posted, Ricou and other merchants had wanted to equalize rates for some time because they wanted to reduce the competition among putters-out. Yet, if equalizing rates was designed to prevent bidding up the piece rate, then it is an unlikely explanation for Ricou's actions. Ricou's plan raised the rates rather than lowered them. The commissaire suspected other motives. We have almost no information about Ricou, but it is evident that he was not a mill owner or a member of the important, well-established fabricant families who were related by marriage or through partnerships to the industrial spinners. The commissaire speculated that Ricou obtained his materials at a cheaper price. It is likely that he imported his yarn. Yarn at the international market price was very likely cheaper than the yarn produced by local mill owners.[9]

---

8. The first indication that the Choletais was importing yarn came in a report responding to a ministerial inquiry from the minister of commerce and manufacture in 1831: A.D. M-et-L 67M2: "Réponse aux questions proposées par le ministre du commerce et de la manufacture," drafted by the subprefect of Beaupréau, 23 August 1831; see also the interchange between the Chambre consultative des arts et métiers de Cholet and the Ministère de l'agriculture et du commerce on protection from English competiton: A.D. M-et-L 67M2: Extrait du registre des délibérations de la Chambre consultative des arts et manufacture [sic] de Cholet, séance de 4 October 1839; Letter from sécretaire d'état de l'agriculture et du commerce to the Chambre consultative des arts et métiers de Cholet, 25 October 1839; Letter from Chambre consultative of Cholet to Ministre de l'agriculture et du commerce, 25 December 1939; Letter from mayor of Cholet to prefect of Maine-et-Loire, 21 February 1840; Letter from the Ministre de l'agriculture et du commerce to prefect of Maine-et-Loire, 22 May 1840.

9. More precise information will be needed to compute actual differences in production costs between various French manufacturers in different regions and English spinning mills. In general, French production costs were higher, see Lévy-Leboyer, *Banques européennes*, pp. 85–92.

If this was the case, Ricou paid higher rates because he had to attract weavers away from more established industrial spinners. Realizing, after he had sufficient weavers, that he was in a sense
overpaying, he initially took measures to correct the situation. But
assuming that Ricou operated at close margins, lowering his rates
risked losing his weavers, who would react angrily to the betrayal.
By encouraging weavers to demand higher prices for the cost of
transforming yarn to cloth, perhaps Ricou was trying to reestablish
his competitive position while cutting into the overall profits of
the mill owners and others who had higher operating expenses.
If he could not change his prices for fear of losing his weavers, he
could force down the profits of his competitors, thus securing his
own position.

This strategy helped Ricou in the short run, but in the long run it
exposed the entire fabrique to difficulties that were not evident until
later in the decade. When local weavers took up Ricou's suggestion,
they set a precedent for collectively negotiating rates which proved to
be a practice difficult to defeat. Ricou's plan endangered the flexibility he and other fabricants had previously enjoyed. It was a perilous
strategy in a market where price competition was stiff. Raising the
cost of labor at a time when calico prices were declining precipitously
ultimately forced local producers out of the market as labor costs ate
into profits.

The incident exposed the vulnerability of industrialization in the
region. From the perspective of mill owners, small merchants with
little capital to invest drew benefits from the success of mill owners
in creating the conditions for a putting-out system. It was mill owners' capital, and the productivity of their mills, that created the dependence of weavers on mill owners as suppliers and buyers. Small
merchants drew benefits from these conditions by living off the margins of these relations. Yet these small merchants could also threaten
industrial profits, as the case of Ricou demonstrated, by forcing up
labor costs. Once again, we see the precariousness of mechanization and industrial production in a region where entrepreneurship is
diffuse.

Round Two

By December 1840, market conditions had diluted the economic
gains achieved in October. Many weavers were idled because the cost
of cloth had risen by 5 percent as a result of the rate increase and de-

mand had dropped off.[10] Weavers seemed to accept this condition. Early in 1841, however, the demand for cloth revived. Moreover, the season was more prosperous than it had been for the past several years. Almost on the anniversary of the events in 1840, cotton weavers were active again.

On the 4 October 1841, the mayor of Cholet reported that weavers were restless and for several days had clamored individually for an increase in piece rates. A group of forty or fifty weavers argued vigorously for a collective march on fabricants' houses to demand an increase. While patrolling the town, the justice of the peace and the lieutenant of the gendarmerie overheard an old weaver explain to younger man that the next day rural weavers would arrive and their rally would be more complete.[11]

Because the mayor expected trouble, on the fifth the subprefect hastened to Cholet with the royal prosecutor and the examining magistrate, followed by the mounted police. Their presence aggravated the tension in Cholet, but no formal rallies were held on that day. Rain drove Cholet's weavers into the cabarets. The anticipated arrival of rural weavers never materialized. Talks between weavers and fabricants continued with no end in sight.[12]

On the next day, as the deliberations continued in the Hotel de Ville, weavers organized marches throughout the town. To show their determination, they paraded an unfinished warp through the streets. On reaching place Travot, the central square, amid hooting and hollering, the crowd passed the unfinished warp above their heads and threw it into the center. Then they set it ablaze.

The message was clear. Warps in the putting-out system belonged to the putters-out. The act warned fabricants and mill owners that their property, and not just their warp threads, was vulnerable to the same flames. But no further incidents followed. By nightfall, the crowd dispersed easily as the gendarmerie cleared the central square. Despite the high-pitched emotions of the day, there were only thirteen arrests and no bloodshed.[13]

10. A.D. M-et-L 67M2: "Rapport sur la situation du commerce de l'arrondissement de Beaupréau pendant le deuxième semestre de l'année 1840," drafted by the subprefect of Beaupréau, 24 January 1841.

11. A.D. M-et-L 71M1: Letter from the mayor of Cholet to the subprefect of Beaupréau, 4 October 1841.

12. A.D. M-et-L 71M1: Letter from subprefect of Beaupréau to the prefect of Maine-et-Loire, 5 October 1841.

13. A.N. BB18 1396 (2571): Grève à Cholet; see also William M. Reddy, *The Rise of Market Culture: The Textile Trades and French Society, 1750–1900* (Cambridge: Cambridge University Press, 1984), pp. 200–201.

The following two days were calm. The weavers' delegation had warned that there would be a general work stoppage if they did not receive their increase by 12 October. On the ninth, weavers resumed their work. Even the thirteenth passed without incident. On that day, some fabricants paid an increase, but their actions were by no means uniform. Some paid an extra 5 centimes per meter while others paid only 2 centimes.[14] Over the next days, other fabricants paid increases, but some remained intransigent. Not only were the increases unevenly distributed, a portion of the weaving population gained nothing at all. Nevertheless, on the whole weavers had won another victory, even if they had only preserved the gains from 1840.

As Caternault, the mayor, was quick to report to the prefect of Maine-et-Loire, weavers achieved their goal by intimidation: "The fabricants [who] had not wanted to pay the increase before the fourth, fifth, and sixth of this month, despite the repeated and urgent appeals of their workers, have done so hastily after the disturbances. This [act] impressed on the weavers that their increase was gotten by the fear they instilled in the fabricants." Amplifying these observations, Caternault laid the foundation of his argument that the town needed greater security measures. "The source of the anxiety . . . exists not only in Cholet. The 120 [surrounding] communes which depend on the fabrique of Cholet have workers under the sway of similar forces. Each of the times that the workers of our city were incensed, they have called to their aid the workers of these communes. Many have responded to their call." Adding that the municipal authorities did not have the means to prevent the more than 30,000 weavers in the countryside from entering Cholet, the mayor enumerated his requests. He wanted troops permanently garrisoned in Cholet. To expedite administrative action, he wanted the seat of subprefecture as well the courts transferred to Cholet from Beaupréau. To improve the means of surveillance, he wanted to increase the police force.[15]

Caternault was himself a fabricant and mill owner. The fears he reported were his own. When the prefect, in turn, reported to the minister of interior, he did not pass on Caternault's requests. The prefect, more detached from the situation, did not share the mayor's sense of alarm. The prefect's goal was to communicate to the minister of interior the perfect execution of administrative and judicial duties by

14. A.D. M-et-L 71M1: Letter from mayor of Cholet to prefect of Maine-et-Loire, 23 October 1841. The letter reports 10 centimes a day. I arrived at the increase of 2 centimes per meter by assuming an average productivity of 5 meters per day.
15. Ibid.

himself and his subordinates. He emphasized the skill the local bureaucrats showed in resolving the tumultuous events of the past month without bloodshed. The disorderly conduct of the weavers, the prefect noted, had its roots in their great misery. Moreover, he showed sympathy for their plight: "For the workers of the city especially, the price of work is really insufficient for the needs of the family; this numerous class of weavers becomes more miserable from day to day and this misery, as the fabricants recognize themselves, makes them easily susceptible to provocation and, soon perhaps, to bad political influences." Adopting a more understanding position toward the weavers' behavior than the municipal authorities, the prefect believed that the problem stemmed from Cholet's place in the national market. Not only had Cholet lost many of its export markets, its domestic markets were endangered as well: "The internal markets are considerably limited because of the quantity of similar products leaving the factories of Rouen, of Saint-Quentin, of Mulhouse and delivered to market at low prices, [products which] until now only the fabrique of Cholet had supplied." Yet competition alone did not reduce Cholet to its present state, the prefect noted. The fault lay equally with how fabricants and mill owners had chosen to deal with their competitors: "This industrial rivalry, against which it must be said that the fabricants of Cholet have not made sufficient efforts to sustain, either by improving their operations or varying their products to suit consumer taste, has resulted in the necessity to cut production costs, reductions which are borne almost exclusively by labor."[16]

The Market Strategies of Cholet's Industrialists

The prefect had seen through the essence of the market strategy of Cholet's putters-out. To appreciate Cholet's strategy and its subsequent problems, we need to situate Cholet's producers in the broader context of other regional cotton industries in France.[17] In the heyday of the cotton boom during the Continental Blockade, most textile regions in France produced a great variety of cotton cloths. After 1815 regions were forced into competition with each other. By the 1830s

16. A.D. M-et-L 71M1: Letter from prefect of Maine-et-Loire to the minister of interior, 31 October 1841.

17. The following review of the French textile industry is taken from Lévy-Leboyer, *Banques européennes,* pp. 66–93.

the French cotton market was stratified and divided between east and west. Alsace, in the east, specialized in the luxury markets—the ginghams and richly colored and finely printed cottons—while Normandy, in the west, specialized in the more common grades known as *rouenerie*. The finest light cottons, the chiffons, organdies, and nainsooks, were the specialties of Tartare. Saint-Quentin produced percales and muslins. These divisions and specializations, especially between east and west, were the result of Alsace taking the commanding lead in cotton production and other regions adjusting when they no longer could compete.

The pattern and pace of industrialization in Alsace was characterized by rich capital resources and a fully integrated structure of production. Alsatian producers integrated backward from the finished product. The early industrialists were textile printers who specialized in the luxury end of the market. During the early days of the First Empire, they built large spinning mills and a decade later introduced powerlooms. In the 1830s, Alsatian producers significantly expanded their calico production. Already after 1823, textile mills in the east produced more calicos than they printed. For example, in 1827, Haut-Rhin consumed 330,000 pieces of calico and dumped 220,000 pieces in the Parisian market at 20–22 francs a piece, priced at half the price of calicos produced in Normandy. Benefiting from the technical efficiency and economies of scale, Alsatian calicos flooded the French market. In 1834 about 55 percent of the calicos printed in Rouen came from Mulhouse.

The effects rippled through each tier of the product market. All producers were obliged to reduce prices. When Mulhouse gave Rouen competition, Rouen brought down the prices of intermediary calicos and switched to cheaper grades. Within this stratified product market, Cholet manufactured the cheapest range of calicos. Facing competition from Normandy, Cholet was forced to reduce its prices even further.

The ability to take a commanding position within stratified produce markets was linked directly to the regional pattern of mechanization and centralization. Alsace was a relatively new center for cloth production. From the beginning, entrepreneurial control was firmly held by the industrial textile printers. Industrial producers did not face rivalry from other small producers or from an extensive handicraft population. With abundant sources of water power and capital, Alsatian industrialists quickly dominated the French cotton markets by realizing the benefits of the economies of scale gained from mechanized spinning and weaving. Normandy, like the rest of western France, mechanized in a piecemeal fashion. Because it was an older manufacturing region with a long history of dispersed production, spinning, weaving, finishing, and printing were divided among numerous entrepreneurs, both large and small. Integrated firms in the Alsatian mode were rare. Norman cloth producers followed one of two strategies. Some of the larger firms in Rouen mechanized weaving in the 1830s in response to the Alsatian threat. Other firms, much more typical of the responses of Cholet's producers, tried to make do by cutting their prices and switching to a cheaper product. Thus in the 1830s we see the emergence of dual structures in cotton manufacturing. On the one hand, we find fully mechanized spinning and weaving mills. On the other, the Norman countryside supported an enormous population of hand producers.

All Cholet's producers took the labor-intensive route. In the heyday of the cotton boom, and even during the Restoration, specializing in the cheaper grades of calicos when prices were relatively high worked to the advantage of fabricants. It assured them a place in the product market without extensive capital investment. For decades, the fabricants had the best of two worlds. They could control the supply of yarn and control the product; at the same time, they passed the risks of the market onto the actual producers. It was profit making without bearing the uncertainties of competition. Even when fabricants in the Choletais competed with industrialized producers who had lowered their production costs by introducing powerlooms, as long as these fabricants could pass on the cost of lowering prices, they did not have to mechanize to remain competitive. The key to Cholet's survival in the cotton markets rested on whether the fabricants could continue to pass on the burden of declining cloth prices to handloom weavers. In a period of declining prices, this strategy locked them into conflict with weavers as a matter of survival.

The prefect of Maine-et-Loire clearly saw the injustice in this strategy and sympathized with the weavers' anger, even if he did not approve of the forms of its expression. Yet a solution to the weavers' anger, even if he did not approve of the forms of its expression. Yet a solution to the weavers' difficulties was not easy to find, and the prefect offered none. The subprefect of the arrondissement shared the prefect's general analysis of the problem. Writing to the prefect a month after the events in October 1841, he could think of few remedies to better the weavers' situation. His predictions were grim: soon, "no further struggles will be possible against Rouen and

Alsace. Sooner or later, Cholet must renounce the manufacture of cotton cloths if it does not abandon its old routines; yet adopting new methods will leave too many workers unemployed."[18] In short, it seemed that whichever direction the fabrique took, handloom weavers faced unemployment. In the face of these dire prospects, the subprefect could only suggest that the government try to establish charity workshops, so that the weavers would at least see that the government had not forgotten their misery.

Round Three

Much as the subprefect had foreseen, three years later, in 1844, the fabrique of Cholet renounced calico production. The context was another wave of weaver protests over declining prices. By this time, the rhythm of protest was well established. On 2 July, the chief of the gendarmerie reported brooding discontent among weavers over diminished rates imposed by the fabricants. On the third, six hundred weavers rallied in the night. The next day, more weavers gathered, including many from the countryside. On the same day, Maison Richard rescinded its new lower rates and agreed to pay the former higher rates. Other fabricants followed suit. In response to the weaver's demand, the 1840 tarif was reinstated. Throughout the days the gendarmerie had been ready for action, but the deliberations went smoothly. There had been no need for armed intervention.[19]

In August, however, the mayor of Cholet, who as we recall was a fabricant, reported renewed discontent. Weavers were meeting to discuss a plan of action. "The weavers got the tarif they demanded in their last rally," complained the mayor to the prefect, "but what has happened [as a result]? Only that they resent that the rate schedule is most favorable for precisely those cloths which have nearly no demand. . . . One must not lose sight of [the fact that] four years ago we still made calicos in the widths we called ¾ and wider and we no longer make them today. We attribute the loss for Cholet in large part to the unrest. Another article, the 'façon cambray,' has also disap-

18. A.D. M-et-L 71M1: Letter from subprefect of Beaupréau to prefect of Maine-et-Loire, 4 November 1841.
19. A.D. M-et-L 71M1: Letter from chef de gendarmerie de Maine-et-Loire to prefect of Maine-et-Loire, 2 July 1844; Letter from subprefect of Beaupréau to prefect of Maine-et-Loire, 2 July 1844; Letter from chef de gendarmerie de Maine-et-Loire to prefect of Maine-et-Loire, 4 July 1844; Letter from subprefect of Beaupréau to prefect of Maine-et-Loire, 4 July 1844; see also A.N. BB18 1423 (8756) 1844.

peared from Cholet. Rouen has succeeded in producing it for a lower price."[20] It was precisely this kind of unself-reflective stance of the mill owners and fabricants that had turned the sympathy of the prefect toward the weavers. Even though mill owners like Caternault were unwilling to acknowledge their role in the economic troubles of the fabrique, by the mid-1840s the increases pushed through by weavers were showing their effects.

In the competition against Normandy, every extra centime and half-centime was significant. The range in the cheap end of the calico market was narrow. As in the Choletais, the piece rate for cottons in Normandy followed the same downward spiral. Cloths that paid 1.10 francs per meter in 1818 and 1.25 francs per meter in 1824 paid only 36–40 centimes per meter in 1834. In 1842 calicos in Rouen sold for the unbelievably low price of 34 francs for a bolt of cloth 35 aunes in length (approximately 41.3 meters). In Alsace, the average calico sold for 60 francs. After printing, Alsatian bolts sold for 120 francs but could sell for as much as 710 francs for the finest quality cloth and print. Rouen produced a cheaper grade of calico aimed at an intermediate market and sold at moderate prices. Merchants there brought down the price primarily by economizing on labor costs. Historian Maurice Lévy-Leboyer calculates that, on the average, labor costs constituted only 16 percent of cloth prices.[21] This meant that the calico produced in Rouen, which sold for 34 francs a piece (97 centimes per aune), paid a piece rate of approximately 15.5 centimes per aune (13.2 centimes per meter). Cholet's rates were higher. In 1842 the rate was probably around 18 centimes per meter, approximately 36 percent higher than in Rouen.[22] These calculations suggest why weavers and fabricants struggled so intensely over several centimes. For both sides, survival was at stake.

The weavers' successes in 1840, 1841, 1842, and 1844 were making it difficult for the fabricants to profit from the putting-out system, at least in the calico markets. The fabricants faced several alternatives: they could try to force down the piece rate; they could invest in powerlooms to benefit from the economies of scale and higher productivity; they could switch products; or they could leave production. Whichever option they chose, they had to contend with weavers as a collective force. Here we see the results of what Ricou had un-

---

20. A.D. M-et-L 71M1: Letter from mayor of Cholet to prefect of Maine-et-Loire, 6 August 1844.

21. Lévy-Leboyer, *Banques européennes*, pp. 69–70, nn. 17–18.

22. Rate calculated from 1846 tarif; see A.N. BB18 1445 (2457): 1846 tarif.

leashed—the principle of collective negotiations. Weavers used their solidarity to reclaim some of the power they lost individually to fabricants in the putting-out system. Whereas in 1840 and 1841 there were merchants and fabricants who benefited from the uniform tarif or who could see the justice behind the weavers' demands, by 1844 they gave in because of their anxieties and fears. Rumors constantly circulated around Cholet. Many even suspected that the weavers were plotting insurrection.

On 2 August 1844, for example, Cholet's mayor wrote to the prefect that he had been informed by a nameless source that one night during the last assembly of weavers in July, five to six hundred weavers met in the fields next to the Grolleau woods just outside town.[23] The weavers had called on other weavers from neighboring communes and together they debated how to respond to one of the principal manufacturers of Cholet. Although the mayor did not indicate the manufacturer, it was most likely Richard. Recall that during the July protests Richard had agreed after many initial refusals to adhere to the older and higher rates. Perhaps this was the story behind Richard's consent.

During this secret nocturnal meeting, the mayor continued, some weavers wanted to see a lynching, but most opposed such an action. Others were determined to burn Richard's property to the ground. Apparently the latter proposal won greater approval. In the middle of the night, the mayor's informant told him, a group of men, guided by one weaver while another carried a torch, forced open a small door and infiltrated the manufacturer's establishment. The mayor tried to verify the story with the commissaire de police, who knew nothing of the incident. Nonetheless, the mayor wrote, the story had a disquieting effect. All Cholet would feel more secure with a greater number of troops, he wrote—as if weavers were not residents and citizens of the city.[24] Several days later, the mayor sent another letter of urgent appeal:

"I continue to stress that the means of repression are too weak. I think, Monsieur le Préfet, that we share my conviction on this subject. A permanent superior administrative and judiciary authority must be installed in our city to clamp down on the ill will among the agitators. But in the meantime and [regarding] more pressing matters, I am con-

23. A.D. M-et-L 71M1: Letter from mayor of Cholet to prefect of Maine-et-Loire, 2 August 1844.
24. Ibid.

vinced that a greater military force is indispensible to silence the agitators. I entreat you, Monsieur le Préfet, to adopt these expedient measures to calm the fervent unease."[25]

Cholet did not become the seat of the subprefecture until 1859. The prefect, though clearly not altogether in agreement with the mayor, still took seriously the fears of the fabricants, mill owners, and city authorities. Throughout the decade, the central administration always came through promptly to aid Cholet's elite citizens. Their constant requests for more protection thus did not reflect neglect on the part of the prefecture; it was a testament of fear. In 1846, when weavers demanded and achieved the reinstatement of the tarif of 1842, the urgent letters and requests sent between Cholet and Angers, and Cholet and Beaupréau, now had a familiar sound. The same sequence of events was to be played out again in 1849, when finally the largest mill owners in town decided that they had had enough.

Climax

On 16 September 1849, the mayor of Cholet reported to the prefect in Angers that, since the day before, rumors had circulated through the city that cotton weavers intended to call a demonstration for Monday the seventeenth.[26] These murmurs of discontent came in a period of rising demand for cotton cloths. Weavers anticipated full employment in the coming busy season. The piece rates paid to weavers, however, had not risen with the higher market prices and with the anticipated recovery of demand after the economic crisis of 1847 and 1848.[27] The city administration was alarmed, especially because the troops garrisoned in Cholet had received their orders to leave in a week's time and no other regiment had been assigned to take their place. From the experience of the unrest in the late summers and autumns of 1840, 1841, 1844, and most recently 1846, the mayor warned the prefect that the garde nationale of Cholet could not be relied on to keep public order during these troubled times. As in all the previous reports, the mayor stressed the need for a permanent gar-

25. A.D. M-et-L 71M1: Letter from mayor of Cholet to prefect of Maine-et-Loire, 6 August 1844.
26. A.D. M-et-L 71M1: Letter from mayor of Cholet to prefect of Maine-et-Loire, 16 September 1849.
27. A.D. M-et-L 67M3: "Rapport sur la situation du commerce dans l'arrondissement de Beaupréau, 1er semestre de 1849."

rison of government troops in Cholet. The next day, the seventeenth, several hundred weavers rallied in place Travot. They declared their intention to demand a 5 centimes per meter increase on the piece rates established in 1846. Most looms in Cholet stood idle that day. Weavers roamed the streets in groups of twos and threes. The general atmosphere, however, was calm.[28]

The following days passed in tense uncertainty. The city administrators, the prefect, and the subprefect wanted to ensure a peaceful settlement, but at the same time they prepared to use violence to counter violence. None of the groups involved in the dispute was preparing for the unknown. In a sense, the weavers, fabricants, merchant-industrialists, the city's administrators and police all knew the possible scenarios. The grievances were familiar. The unwillingness of either side to compromise, the high stakes, and the possible violence were equally familiar. Frustration and anger compounded the ill will and mistrust between the groups.

On the afternoon of the twenty-second, accompanied by Monsieur Durfort de Civrac, an influential local aristocrat who was the appointed deputy of the prefect, the mayor and his adjoint finally succeeded in bringing together the representatives from the two sides in order to facilitate an agreement.[29] In chambers of the municipal council, the prefect's deputy assured a group of fifteen weavers of the administration's neutrality and of his good will in facilitating an agreement between weavers and fabricants. He advised the group to lower their demands if they wanted to win concessions from the other side. The weavers responded cordially but stressed that their comrades had set absolute conditions. They would not rescind their demand for 5 centimes. The representatives could not promise that negotiations were possible.

Turning next to the fabricants assembled by the mayor in the other wing of the Hôtel de Ville, Durfort expressed the wishes of the department's administration for a peaceful settlement of the affair. Addressing the underlying problems first, Durfort stressed that over the past decade or so the fabrique had fallen behind. Their outmoded ways, he chided, had exposed the city to these periodic crises. While Durfort shared the fabricants' contention that the uniform tarif had been detrimental because the cost of labor had been fixed without regard to the conditions of commerce, he underscored the need for

28. A.D. M-et-L 71M1: Report of the chef de gendarmerie to prefect of Maine-et-Loire, 17 September 1849.
29. Events of 22 September reconstructed from A.D. M-et-L 71M1: Report of special consul to the prefect, Durfort de Civrac, to prefect of Maine-et-Loire, 30 September 1849.

greater charity and better rapport between weavers and fabricants. Because of the fabricants' intransigence, Durfort pointed out, "rebellion has become the supreme arbiter for settling wage issues." He urged them to share with the weavers the benefits of a good season in order to justify their demand for sacrifices in the poor seasons.

The fabricants, however, were too preoccupied to contemplate Durfort's advice. Foremost in their minds was their personal safety and that of their property. After long deliberations, they conceded a raise of 2 centimes per meter instead of the 5 centimes the weavers demanded. This concession, however, did not differ from their initial response when weavers first demanded an increase.

When presented with this proposal, the weavers' representatives felt disposed to accept the compromise for the sake of social peace, but they doubted whether their fellow weavers, whose patience was stretched near breaking point, would accept less than half of what they demanded. The subsequent negotiations brought the two groups no closer to an acceptable compromise. The meeting ended in deadlock.

Outside the Hôtel de Ville, a crowd had gathered during the deliberations. At seven in the evening the weavers' delegation reported their news to a jeering and suspicious crowd. No sooner had Durfort de Civrac appeared to warn the crowd that any attempt to disrupt the public peace would bring the relentless repression of the authorities, then the crowd took matters into their own hands. Shouts thundered through place Travot and echoed in the adjoining streets: "Le tarif ou la mort!" ("The tarif or death!")

Drenched by the rain that had fallen all afternoon, by early evening the crowd slowly began to dissipate. But around half past nine, just as the crowd calmed and quiet was almost restored, the movement took a different turn. Suddenly, a group of women broke from the crowd and headed down the main street toward the house of Richard. Five or six hundred weavers followed.

Taken by surprise, Durfort tried to gather his troops. In the midst of the confusion, the city's administration could not raise the garde nationale. Finally, assembling a mounted contingent and arming the fire brigade, the mayor, the prefect's deputy, the commissaire de police, and an assortment of other officials rushed to cordon off the procession headed toward Maison Richard.

Despite exhortations from the assembled officials not to give in to these demands, Richard signed the tarif under duress. Satisfied, the weavers, their families, and sympathizers marched to the houses of Lambert and Grasset. On seeing this menacing crowd, these two négociants immediately opened their doors and granted what was asked of them. As the group pushed against the gates of the fourth négociant, Besnard, the mayor, with his troops poised to take action, warned the crowd that the illegality of their actions would bring them a prison sentence. "Prison! Well it's prison we want . . . ," a voice in the crowd retorted. "There, we would be fed. There, we won't die of hunger. Another voice asked the mayor, "Why do you want to harm us? We have done no harm to anybody, not even to the négociants who treat us so harshly. We will not resort to violence but we will stay here until they give us what we have the right to demand. You know as well as we do that we have no other choice." But the mayor turned a deaf ear. At his command, his armed men charged at the crowd. The weavers dispersed immediately, and twenty were arrested.

Calm was restored by early morning. The next day, weavers returned to their looms. There were no further confrontations in the following days. Neither did negotiations continue. On Saturday, the market day and the day to turn in work, fabricants paid only the 2-centime increase. Weavers grumbled but did not call for a new showdown. Although the atmosphere in town was thick with resentment, the subprefect reported, the weavers remained at work. Yet sullen agitation stirred beneath the tenuous calm. By the end of the first week in October, only a handful of fabricants had actually paid the increase. The panic and fear provoked by events on 22 and 23 September had set off its own dynamic. Toward the end of September, the subprefect suspected that urban weavers were meeting regularly with weavers in the countryside in secret. As yet, he explained in his report, there had been no new disturbances, but local authorities were ready to intervene and to guard the town against the rural population. Despite the calm, the subprefect asked for a permanent garrison of government soldiers in town. Otherwise, he warned, Cholet would never be secure.[30]

At the same time, the municipal council, under the auspices of the prefect of the department, passed measures to reorganize the garde nationale. Protests against the mayor's illegal arming of the fire brigade were simply ignored.[31] Instead, the municipal council debated

30. A.D. M-et-L 71M1: Letters from subprefect of Beaupréau to prefect of Maine-et-Loire, 28 September and 9 October 1849.

31. Archives municipales de Cholet, JA Dossier 6(1): Letters from subprefect of Beaupréau to mayor of Cholet, 9 and 22 October 1849; 6(4): "Sapeurs Pompiers 1849"; A.D. M-et-L 71M1: Letters from mayor of Cholet to subprefect of Beaupréau, 23 and 25 October 1849.

how to disarm weavers without compromising security and without arousing suspicion and provoking a new outbreak. By prefectural decree, the weapons that had previously been left under the care of each garde nationale individually were recalled and deposited in a central arsenal under the guard of the captain of the fire brigade, who, not surprisingly, was a son of a fabricant.

The political delicacy of these operations must not be underestimated. Although the initial incident and weavers' protest did not have specific political overtones, the question of maintaining the peace and squashing violence put the new political authorities in a difficult and contradictory position. The February revolution had attained its legitimacy by proclaiming universal suffrage. The government had relied on the support of the garde nationale. The West had been very quiet in 1848. But, as one of the last bastions of Bourbon royalism, the regions' attachment to republicanism was always suspect. By disarming the garde nationale in order to disarm weavers, local authorities must have worried whether they made themselves vulnerable to an armed legitimist attack.

More important for the economic future of Cholet, the events of the twenty-second touched off panic among the prominent merchant-industrialists. They discussed whether it would be safer for their investments, their property, and their persons to leave cotton production altogether. Over the decade, the level of violence had escalated. In 1840 weavers congregated and marched to show their collective strength. There were verbal abuses, many rumors, and veiled threats. The next year, weavers threatened property symbolically, by publicly burning an unfinished warp. But now, in September 1849, the weavers cried "Le tarif ou la mort!" and for the first time physically threatened mill owners and merchants at their own doors. By mid-decade, many producers had already renounced calico production, which had been one of the staple cloths of the region since the introduction of cotton. With all these factors weighing on them, the subprefect reported in 1852, the oldest and richest merchant houses in the region had abandoned weaving in the last trimester of 1851: "The richest [merchant] houses almost without exception have withdrawn from manufacturing because of the successive strikes, the violence, and threats to which they have so frequently been subjected." Cloth production was now concentrated in the hands of rural fabricants. Handloom weavers continued to find work, although they had to make do with less income. The rural fabricants had so little capital, the subprefect complained, that they would not be able to advance the industry of the region. Furthermore, they could not guarantee weavers regular employment and regular incomes because they had to work so close to seasonal demand.[32]

Throughout this conflict-ridden decade, there had been no bloodshed and only a few arrests. Although the city's administration worried endlessly over the arms held by the garde nationale, at no time were these weapons actually used against fabricants or mill owners or any city official. And despite the numerous times Richard's establishment was threatened by fire, in 1850 it remained intact. There had been no damage to the property. Yet the older established manufacturing houses and spinning mill owners abandoned cloth production, at least for the time being. Clearly the threats and intimidations were effective.

Regional Industrialization in National Perspective

From the perspective of long-term developments, the 1840s marked a significant turning point. Although Cholet had never been one of the most important textile centers, until the 1830s the region had kept pace with the technical innovations in the field. Its pattern of mechanization did not differ significantly from other textile regions making the same transition from handicraft production. It is only in retrospect, knowing the subsequent history of the region, that we look for signs of stagnation in the first half of the nineteenth century. Serge Chassagne has pointed out that economic historians have often labeled the actions of entrepreneurs in "residual" industrial regions as backward without careful comparison and sufficient evidence.[33] With these cautions in mind, let us take another look at the actions of industrialists in Cholet and Chemillé and compare them with cotton producers in the rest of France.

It is easy to paint a portrait of backwardness and retarded development. For example, if we compare the spinning capacity of various manufacturing regions in France during the First Empire, the Choletais makes a poor showing. Around 1810, Cholet reported a total spinning capacity of 25,000 spindles, whereas Rouen reported

32. A.D. M-et-L 67M3: "Situation du commerce pendant le 2e trimestre de 1851," 9 February 1852.
33. Serge Chassagne, "Industrialisation et désindustrialisation dans les campagnes françaises: Quelques réflexions à partir du textile," *Revue du Nord* 63 (January–March 1981): 35–57.

350,000, Lille 200,000, and Paris 250,000 spindles.[34] If this comparative statistic were taken as a reflection of the relative importance of the manufacturing region, then Cholet falls behind even lower Normandy, which reported a spinning capacity of 50,000 spindles. Turning to individual mills, the Cesbron mill in 1809 had a spinning capacity of 3,000 spindles. If we compare Cesbron to Richard-Lenoir, whose various spinning mills contained a total of 109,000 spindles and whose two mills in Paris totaled close to 27,000 spindles, Cesbron looks quite mediocre.[35]

Yet Richard-Lenoir was clearly exceptional. In 1812 his factories controlled 10 percent of the national capacity in cotton spinning. The 1806 national inquiry on cotton production known as the Enquête Champagny, offers a more accurate picture of typical mill sizes in France in this era. According to the Champagny inquiry, nearly half (525 of 1,027) the shops operating mules jennies and water frames in France and the conquered territories were located in the department of Seine-Inferieure, which included Rouen and most of its dependent region. These 525 shops operated a total of 297,900 spindles (87,940 on water frames and 209,960 on mule jennies), averaging 567 spindles per shop. Only twenty-one of the shops operated more than a thousand spindles. Together these larger shops accounted for 79,040 spindles. On average, the larger mills in Seine-Inférieure had a spinning capacity of 3,763 spindles per shop. The remaining 504 shops with less than a thousand spindles averaged 434 spindles per shop, and these smaller establishments accounted for 73.4 percent of the region's capacity.[36] When compared with the productive capacity for mills in what was at this time the largest cotton-producing region in France, Cesbron's shows up well. Cesbron's operation ranked among the larger mills of western France, with a productive capacity well above the typical mill of Normandy.

In terms of the productivity of his spinning equipment, Cesbron's mule jennies operated close to the national norm. In 1808, Cesbron reported that each mule jenny in his mill produced an average 2.5–3.2 kilograms of calico weight yarn per day.[37] Cesbron's mule jennies

34. Lévy-Leboyer, *Banques européennes*, p. 59.

35. Serge Chassagne, "La diffusion rurale de l'industrie cotonnière en France (1750–1850)," *Revue du Nord* 61 (January–March 1979): 106.

36. Reddy, *Rise of Market Culture*, p. 76. See also Serge Chassagne, "L'enquête dite de Champagny, sur la situation de l'industrie cotonnière française au début de l'Empire (1805–1806)," *Revue d'histoire économique et sociale* 54 (1976): 361–62.

37. A.D. M-et-L 67M5: État et situation des établissements de filature de coton dans la commune de Chemillé, 1808.

ranged from 100 to 300 spindles per machine. By William Reddy's calculations, a productivity of 3.5 kilograms of calico weight yarn per day from a mule jenny with 240 spindles was not uncommon under the Empire. According to Achille Penot, a social reformer from Mulhouse, Alsatian mills in 1816 and 1817 had difficulty producing more than 3 kilograms per day of No. 32 yarn (an average calico weight) on a mule with 240 spindles.[38]

These comparisons suggest that the relatively small size and population of the Choletais are responsible for its failure to appear as an important manufacturing region. However, the size of its textile industry reflected neither its technological capacity nor its organization. When we look at the important mills in the region, they compare well with the large mills in the most extensive cotton-manufacturing regions. In terms of equipment and productivity, mills in the Choletais were not backward. Mill owners in the region introduced mule jennies at the same time they appeared in other parts of France. The mules operated with the same degree of efficiency.

This correspondence in the First Empire continued through the Restoration and the July Monarchy. In 1826 the average number of spindles (for cotton) per firm in Normandy was 3,500; in the Lille-Roubaix region, 3,300; in Alsace and Saint-Quentin, 8,800 and 8,000, respectively.[39] These numbers reflect an average of all mills in these regions; if we took the average of the few mills in the Choletais— 9,500 spindles for Richard, 13,000 spindles for Bonnet-Allion, and 9,200 for Deschamps—it would be closer to the average for Alsace and Saint-Quentin than for Normandy. In 1826 the average Roubaix cotton firm had a spinning capacity of 4,000 spindles on thirty mules. The largest Roubaix cotton firm had 13,000 spindles. Only two or three of the forty mills used steam power.[40] Compared to the average firm in Roubaix, Richard's mill in 1830, with its 9,500 spindles on forty mules powered by a team of horses, cannot be considered backward. In addition, except for the Richard mill, all the other mills in the region were powered by steam in combination with other forms of mechanical power.

Finally, the productivity and efficiency of mule spinning in the Mauges was comparable to that of other regions. I have estimated that, in 1841, Bonnet-Allion's mills produced 10.8 kilograms per

38. Reddy, *Rise of Market Culture*, pp. 100–101.
39. Ibid., p. 93.
40. Ibid., p. 103.

spindle per year of average weight calico yarn.[41] The Deschamps mill produced close to 12 kilograms per spindle per year of the same weight yarn. Actual reports of mill owners varied greatly in the 1834 ministerial inquiry into the textile trades. Nicolas Koechlin of Mulhouse reported that his mills achieved a productivity equivalent to 12.5 kilograms per spindle per year. Other Alsatian mill owners were not so optimistic about their capacity. The Chamber of Commerce of Mulhouse stated that productivity for No. 30 yarn was closer to 10 kilograms per spindle per year. The firm Fouquet-Lemaitre et Crepel of Rouen estimated their own output at 13.9 kilograms per spindle per year. The Parisian firm of Sanson and Daviller, with a large mill in Gisor, claimed that their best spinners, working mules with 400 spindles, produced 11–12 kilograms of No. 30–33 yarn per day, the equivalent of 9 kilograms per spindle per year. My own estimates for the mills in the Choletais are extremely approximate and on the high side; still, it is evident from these reports that capitalist producers in the Mauges ran their mills with a degree of efficiency comparable to the most acclaimed cotton producers in France.

Aftermath: Survival of Small-Scale Production

Until the 1840s, textile production in the Choletais kept abreast of changes in the cotton industry nationally. Technological backwardness dates from the 1850s, with the decision of manufacturers to withdraw from cloth production. This decision did not, however, lead to the collapse of all forms of manufacturing in the region. In effect, the decision gave new life to the putting-out system. It enabled handloom weavers, putters-out, and other intermediaries a chance to survive on the margins of the national textile markets. In the next decade the numbers of fabricants and handloom weavers grew substantially. By 1859 estimates of the number of handlooms in operation reached as high as 45,000. Most reports, however, listed about

41. According to a technical manual published in Mulhouse in 1839, *Traité élémentaire de la filature du coton* by Oger, the ideal output for power-assisted mule jennies at recommended machine speeds and ideal labor intensity was 16.6 kilograms per spindle per year for No. 30 yarn (a common calico grade). Of course, no machine could achieve this rate because the calculation required that the mule be running nonstop, thirteen hours a day, six days a week, all year (based on 300 workdays). Another technical manual published in Paris in 1843 (*Nouveau manuel complet du filateur*, by C. E. Julien and E. Lorentz) estimated that No. 30 yarn could be more realistically spun at 7.1 kilograms per spindle per year. The latter calculation took into acount the actual experience in operating mills, incuding down time. See Reddy, *Rise of Market Culture*, pp. 106–12.

35,000.[42] In addition, the fabrique diversified its products. The region no longer produced calicos and baffetas, which were the cottons used for printing, but handloom weavers continued to produce cotton kerchiefs and siamoises and added fustians, known locally as "les petits cotons de Nantes." These changes testified to the flexibility and adaptability of dispersed production. There was also a marked expansion of linen weaving. The region had never abandoned linen, although for the first half of the century it had been in abeyance.

Structurally, changes in the linen trade paralleled that of cotton. In the 1840s there was a brief and futile attempt to mechanize linen spinning. The local mill could not compete in price with English linen yarn, even with subventions from the state.[43] Cholet began to import linen yarns from England and Belgium in the early 1830s. Many farm women lost spinning as a source of income. Flax farmers in the Loire valley switched to hemp.[44] As in the cotton, an extra-local source of materials, in this case linen yarn, reinforced the feasibility of the putting-out system. Kerchiefs remained the mainstay of the linen weavers. A great variety of linen cloths used for clothing, sheets, and household goods were produced as well.

In this chapter I have been emphasizing the causal role of weavers' actions in pushing manufacturers to abandon their role in cloth production. This abandonment ultimately enabled the survival of small-scale production in the region. Through these struggles, weavers held onto their positions as the organizers of cloth production and in this sense successfully resisted further proletarianization. Although the development of the putting-out system had encroached on the entrepreneurial activities weavers had once enjoyed, they were able to put a stop to further losses.

By demanding a uniform tarif and claiming the right to negotiate rates collectively, weavers altered investment patterns by escalating the social cost of certain entrepreneurial strategies. Their collective action threatened the profitability of the putting-out system, which had operated in favor of fabricants even in an era of intense competition. Because weavers had forced increases in piece rates to a level

42. A.D. M-et-L 67M3: "État des principales industries excercées dans l'arrondissement de Cholet," 1859.

43. See A.D. M-et-L 67M2 for an exchange of confidential letters between the mayor of Cholet and the prefect of Maine-et-Loire on developing a linen spinning mill in Cholet: Letter from mayor of Cholet to subprefect in Beaupréau, 9 July 1839; Letters from mayor of Cholet to prefect of Maine-et-Loire, 13 and 30 October 1839.

44. Oscar Leclerc-Thouin, *L'agriculture de l'Ouest de la France* (Paris: Bouchard-Huzard, 1843), pp. 296, 317.

that left almost no profit for the putters-out, the latter had to take action or go bankrupt. Spinning mill owners like Richard, who had the capital and had already invested in production, could have introduced powerlooms at this point to try to bring down the cost of production. But such a strategy would have entailed radically transforming the social relations of production. It would have required a true proletarianization of weaving—whether achieved by recruiting handloom weavers to become powerloom tenders or by recruiting among groups not previously connected to textiles. Given the level of social tension in Cholet, indeed the constant anxiety over armed conflict, displacing handloom weavers was difficult to contemplate. In addition, investing more capital in production would mean exposing more property to destruction. The most significant effects of the decade of conflict on the long-term economic transformation of the Choletais were the limitations imposed on entrepreneurial choices. Since it was unwise to risk capital and there was no other effective way to bring down the cost of transformation, the industrial capitalists of the town withdrew from production. Industrial spinners who put out to weavers, like Richard, decided not to fight the battles and contented themselves with spinning and finishing.

Unlike the mill owners, most fabricants had few options but to continue in their trade. For them, mechanizing cloth production was not an option because they did not have the capital to invest in powerlooms and loom sheds. Their only choice was to continue in their struggle to force weavers to accept lower rates. Since they produced nothing, they had no other means of survival. Their solution was to continue the putting-out system and switch into different cotton products, some of which were less remunerative. But this also meant continuing and sustaining the same social relations of production in the competitive environment of national markets dominated by mechanized production. Fabricants and the handloom weavers were tied to system where conflicts of this sort became a normal part of the functioning of local cloth production.

The events in the 1840s illuminate the special problems industrial capitalists encounter when they try to transform an existing handicraft industry. As we have seen in this and the previous chapters, such transformation involves more than just amassing capital, building factories, purchasing machinery, and training workers. Mechanization requires transforming the social relations of production as well. These social changes can be daunting when both entrepreneurship and control over production are diffuse. Although we generally consider industrialization a social and economic process, rarely do historians of industrialization emphasize the primacy of social relations over economic and technical considerations. Yet the outcome of the decade of conflict in this region's cotton trade shows clearly that technical change can be introduced and implemented only where and when it is socially feasible. In the 1840s and 1850s, handloom weavers obstructed the further development of the factory system in the Choletais. Although industrialists and putters-out held the greater economic power, and individual cotton weavers were dependent, weavers' strength was rooted not in their position in production but in their social presence and the power of their numbers. In fact, the crucial difference between the Choletais and Normandy, between manufacturers' inability to relegate handloom weavers to the role of wage laborers and successful mechanization, was the concentration of handloom weaving around a single commercial center in Cholet and the dispersal of handloom weaving among many centers in Normandy. Weavers' ability to hold the economic and social core of the region hostage to their demands clearly had a major effect in the Choletais.

Comparing the Choletais with other textile regions suggests that it is easier and more effective to build a fully mechanized textile industry in regions *without* a history of textile production than in an area with a long history of dispersed manufacturing. There are many disadvantages to older manufacturing centers, factors impeding the rapid integration of all phases of industrial manufacturing. There are many more entrepreneurs to contend with. The capital stock is more fractured and the manufacturing process is most likely divided among many entrepreneurs. And, as in the case of the Choletais, in such areas industrialization cannot proceed without contending with a socially entrenched manufacturing population.

The comparative disadvantages of older manufacturing regions must be verified with detailed comparative research. The hypothesis that results from my study, however, is the opposite of that suggested by the proto-industrialization hypothesis, which posits that a prior experience with export-oriented handicraft production promoted and even constituted a preparatory stage to the factory system. The logic of my argument follows a different empirical typology. Many students of the French textile industry, such as Claude Fohlen and Maurice Lévy-Leboyer, contrast the different structures and specializations of relatively new textile regions such as Alsace (which Fohlen calls "les industries d'implantation") with the long-established textile regions of western France such as Brittany, the Maine, and Anjou (which Fohlen calls "les industries résiduelles").[45] Although neither author would explain the differences in the way I have proposed, they both point to the disadvantages of the dispersed capital base and higher labor cost of western France when compared to the east. Though not conclusive, these typologies suggest the plausibility of the idea that so-called proto-industrialization might in fact impede successful industrialization.[46]

45. Claude Fohlen, *Les industries textiles au temps du Second Empire* (Paris: Librairie Plon, 1956); Lévy-Leboyer, *Banques européennes.*
46. For a similar argument for Germany, see Ekhart Schremmer, "Proto-industrialization: A Step towards Industrialization?" *Journal of European Economic History* 10 (Winter 1981): 653–70.

6

Handloom Weavers in the
Age of Powerlooms:
The Failures of Mobilization

The plight of handloom weavers in the late nineteenth century was brought to national attention in two widely publicized strikes, one in Cholet in 1887 and the other in the Avesnes-les-Auberts in the Cambrésis in 1889.[1] The Choletais was one of the last textile regions in France with a large population of handloom weavers. At the beginning of the twentieth century, about a third of all linen handloom weavers in France lived in the arrondissement. The Cambrésis ranked second in its population of linen hand weavers.[2] To the French public, these weavers were a curiosity, the last survivors of a preindustrial past. Their strikes and struggle appeared to be a last resistance against mechanization before the final and inevitable demise of hand production.

Indeed, the halt in mechanization produced by weavers' tactics in the struggle to maintain piece rates proved to be only temporary. In this chapter I examine the decision by industrialists in the Choletais to reenter cloth production and its consequences for the self-identity of weavers and for the place of handloom weaving in segmented markets. In the 1860s, in the midst of the "cotton famine," industrialists began once again to mechanize cloth production, this time with the installation of powerlooms. On this occasion they were much more successful. The renewed attempts to mechanize weaving touched off a wave of labor unrest. Handloom weavers were at the center of the disputes, because they stood to lose the most with competition from powerlooms.

1. Michèle Perrot, *Les ouvriers en grève: France, 1871–1890* (Paris: Mouton, 1974), 1:358–61.
2. J. H. Clapham, *Economic Development of France and Germany, 1815–1914* (Cambridge: Cambridge University Press, 1968), p. 255.

In 1882 handloom weavers formed a coalition to fight against declining piece rates. After some initial success, however, the movement split over tactical problems raised by the inclusion of factory operatives in the union. The dispute highlighted fundamental questions. Where did handloom weavers fit in a world dominated by machine production? Were hand weavers wage workers, and did their future thus lie with the socialist movement? Or were they independent producers who should organize politically as producers? The failure of common mobilization in the 1880s attests to the difficulty weavers faced in finding a place and a distinct social identity within the dominant political categories of industrial society.

Despite the failure of a common mobilization, handloom weaving survived. In the decades between 1880 and the First World War, a new division of labor between powerlooms and handlooms emerged. After an initial decline, the number of handloom weavers actually stabilized. In the final section of the chapter, I use recent theories of technical dualism to explore how hand weaving continued to find a place in the machine-dominated textile trades.

The Politics of Mechanization

In the summer of 1864, Maison Richard frères installed sixty powerlooms in a newly purchased plant on rue de Pineau in Cholet.[3] These were the first powerlooms in the fabrique, although Richard frères was following the example of other cotton enterprises in western France. In 1863, with only half the spinning mills operating and most of the handloom weavers idled, several merchants in La Ferté Macé in the department of Orne installed the first powerlooms in the region. A year later, two more powerloom plants were added. In 1864 local merchants unveiled three powerloom plants at Flers, a minor center for cotton production in the department of Calvados, comparable in size and importance to the Choletais.[4] These ventures represented the actions of a small minority of merchants and mill owners in western France. Nevertheless, the moment was well chosen.

The declaration of war in America between the Union and the Confederacy had an important impact on the world textile industry. The blockade of southern ports not only deprived the American South of revenues to aid its war of secession, it shut off the most im-

---

3. Elie Chamard, *La Maison Richard Frères* (Cholet: L'imprimerie Vétélé, 1959), p. 32.
4. Claude Fohlen, *Les industries textiles au temps du Second Empire* (Paris: Librairie Plon, 1956), pp. 259–61.

portant supply of raw cotton to the international cotton industry. In the annals of textile history, the period between 1860 and 1865 is known as the "cotton famine." Shortages of raw cotton hit France in autumn 1861. For workers the winter of 1861/62 was especially difficult, as shortages temporarily idled production in both the major and minor centers of the cotton industry. Unemployment was widespread; among handloom weavers in the Choletais it was the worst in history. Industrial reports in the first quarter of 1861 listed 30,000–35,000 active handlooms, with an equal number of people making their living from handloom weaving. By the beginning of the third quarter, only 12,000 looms were in operation.[5] Other centers of handloom weaving experienced the same high levels of unemployment. In the Pays de Caux in Normandy, more than 21,000 of a total of 47,000 looms were idled. Many firms ceased to put out work, and rural handloom weavers were the first to feel the effects of shortages. Handloom weavers in Cholet continued to work, but with only about half the usual orders. All over France, merchant manufacturers appealed to the municipal and departmental authorities to aid the unemployed. Among the most popular relief schemes were public works programs. In Normandy and in the Choletais, many weavers repaired roads in exchange for food relief.[6]

Historical accounts of this cotton shortage have focused primarily on the crisis: the bankruptcies, the unemployment, and the hardship for textile workers. As Claude Fohlen's study of the French textile industry during the Second Empire points out, though, the cotton famine facilitated an important structural change in all branches of the industry. The cotton industry, along with the woolen and linen industries, became more centralized in production and finances. Mechanization increased in all branches of the industry.[7]

Fohlen has shown that, despite its name, the cotton famine was never accompanied by prolonged shortages of raw materials. Some of the largest firms had stocked large supplies in anticipation of the conflict, and by 1863 new supply routes and new suppliers were in place. For many firms, the crisis was financial, not material. Owing more to speculation than to the actual blockade, the price of raw cotton and spun cotton yarns soared beyond the financial capacity of most small producers. Surviving the financial stress of the cotton crisis de-

5. A. D. M-et-L 67M4: États des principales industries exercées dans l'arrondissement de Cholet, rapport du 1er trimestre et 3ième trimestre, 1861.
6. Fohlen, *Industries textiles,* pp. 265–76.
7. Ibid., chap. 2, "La crise cotonnière: Les réalités," pp. 284–314.

manded a solid credit organization. Firms that had concentrated the various phases of production under one management were favored. These conditions tended to benefit more centralized regions like Alsace and worked to the detriment of centers with more dispersed production like Normandy and much of western France. Within these less-centralized areas, the upheaval in the market favored the larger and more financially secure family firms like the Richards in Cholet and Barré-Ladonné in La Ferté Macé. These firms used their local advantages and the extensive unemployment to further streamline and concentrate production under their control.[8]

The American Civil War was also a boon for the French linen industry. The cotton famine revived the linen industry from its long slump. Since the beginning of the century, French linen producers had been threatened by competition from cottons in the world consumer markets. After the Free Trade Treaty in 1860, French manufacturers felt the additional pressure of English and Irish competition in the domestic markets. During the cotton famine, competition from English linen yarn and Irish and Scottish linens continued unabated, but the growing demand for linen, especially linen yarn, aided the expansion of production and promoted a greater degree of mechanization. As a result, the structure of the French linen industry became closer to that of the British Isles.[9]

The results of the new vitality were not equally distributed among all linen fabriques in France. Cholet drew some benefits, but the entire linen industry of Brittany languished as before. In contrast to western France, the linen centers of the Nord, Lille, Armentières, and Dunkerque prospered. Even before the cotton famine, the Nord was the most important linen center in France. Its spinning mills housed two-thirds of all spindles in the French linen trade. Between 1863 and 1866, the number of spindles in the linen industry of the Nord grew from 416,237 to 531,092. At the end of the period, three-quarters of the spinning capacity of the French linen industry was concentrated in the Nord. Weaving was secondary to the Nord's linen industry, yet the region had the highest concentration of linen powerlooms in France. In 1863 there were a total of 2,768 powerlooms distributed among the three important weaving centers of the Nord. by 1869,

8. Ibid., "Structures nouvelles," pp. 441–67.
9. Alfred Picard, *Le bilan d'un siècle (1801–1900)*, vol. 5 (Paris: Imprimerie nationale, 1906), pp. 327–36; see also the definitive work on this subject by Albert Aftalion, *La crise de l'industrie linière et la concurrence victorieuse de l'industrie cotonnière* (Paris: L. Larose, 1904), and Émile Levasseur, *Questions ouvrières et industrielles en France sous la Troisième République* (Paris: Arthur Rousseau, 1907), pp. 97–100.

6,135 powerlooms operated in Lille alone.[10] Although the entire French linen industry drew benefits from the cotton famine, the resulting changes further concentrated it in the northeast.

As a residual center of the textile industry, the Choletais felt fewer effects of the cotton famine on linen production than did the country as a whole. Yet this was an important turning point for the local textile industry in a different sense. During the period, industrialists and wholesale merchants returned to cloth production. Although mill owners like Richard frères suffered setbacks during the crisis, especially between 1861 and 1863, the brothers' decision to venture into mechanized weaving in 1864 was a well-calculated gamble. In October of the same year, Brémond, a linen producer, unveiled his own factory housing sixty powerlooms. Brémond's looms were initially powered by horses, but he installed a steam engine two years later.[11] For the next decade in the Choletais, the number of powerlooms remained at 120. The two firms hired a total of 150 men and women.[12]

In comparative terms, the extent of mechanization in the Choletais was negligible. The importance of the new powerloom factories, one for linen and one for cotton, was local, not national. Although we can analyze the decisions to introduce powerlooms in terms of technical feasibility, market advantages, or the capital reserves of individual firms, these considerations were subsumed within another set of conflicts: the struggle between industrial entrepreneurs, petty merchants, and small-scale producers to secure their own economic futures. This is what I have called "the politics of mechanization." To understand why industrialists mechanized weaving in the mid-1860s, we need to assess how the cotton famine changed the power relations among these three groups.

The extensive unemployment of the 1860s created the opportunity for introducing machinery. It is significant that Maison Richard frères was one of the principal firms involved in the conflicts of the 1840s. Because of the intensity of conflicts and the constant threats of violence, the Richard family, with other prominent merchant-manufacturers and mill owners, withdrew from weaving and left the organization of that aspect of textile production to the rural fabricants. The social and political atmosphere of the 1840s and the strength of the weavers' resistance discouraged further attempts to extend industrial control over all phases of cloth production. But the

10. Fohlen *Industries textiles*, p. 320.
11. Elie Chamard, *Vingt siècles d'histoire de Cholet* (Cholet: Farré et fils, 1970), p. 224.
12. A.N. F12 4516B: Situations industrielles, Maine-et-Loire, 1869–1887.

cotton famine inverted the situation of the 1840s. Because of the high price of cotton and its general scarcity, small-scale producers, at the end of the supply chain, were most vulnerable to the possibility of losing access to raw materials. In a situation in which market conditions had effectively immobilized the opposition, the Richard brothers installed their powerlooms. Mechanizing when unemployment is high may seem strange economically, but it made perfect sense within the broader politics of production in the region.

The Richard family had been preparing to expand its operations for some time. In 1857 the brothers acquired the mill and adjoining buildings of the Cesbron-Descrance family when the widow retired from manufacturing after the death of Charles Cesbron-Descrance, deputy for the Choletais in Paris for two decades. In 1859, Richard updated the plant and installed a new steam engine. The new plant began operation in 1860. In conception and design, the plant on rue de Pineau replicated the Richard plant on rue Devau, combining spinning, bleaching, and finishing under one roof. After 1864 the rue de Pineau factory included weaving as well, with the introduction of powerlooms. Brémond's weaving factory, in contrast, was linked to his bleach works, which he had acquired in 1829. His entire holdings in the textile trade consisted of a dye works, a bleach works, and a loom shop. Whereas Richard expanded from a base upstream in the production process—mill-spun yarn—Brémond extended his control over the process from the finishing end. Both represented typical patterns for integrating production.[13]

In the 1860s and the early 1870s, mechanized weaving in the Choletais was not a serious threat to handloom weavers. The pace of mechanization was slow. The number of powerlooms in Cholet remained at 120 for nearly a decade despite an auspicious beginning. Only in 1876 did Jean-Elie Pellaumail install his own factory with 100 powerlooms, and in the next year Pellaumail added another 60 powerlooms.[14] Of the early industrialists, Pellaumail expanded production most aggressively. Within two years he more than doubled the volume of cloth produced by machines in the region. In 1878 industrial statistics covering the arrondissement reported 280 powerlooms in operation and approximately 13,000–14,000 people employed in weaving on 10,000 handlooms.[15]

13. Chamard, *La Maison Richard Frères*, pp. 30–34, and *Histoire de Cholet*, p. 224.
14. Chamard, *Histoire de Cholet*, p. 224.
15. A.N. F12 4516B: Situations industrielles, Maine-et-Loire, arrondissement de Cholet, 1er, 2ième, 3ième, 4ième trimestres, 1878.

The sluggishness of Cholet's linen industry in the 1870s paralleled the national situation. The French linen industry had reached the peak of its nineteenth-century prosperity during the cotton famine. As the cotton industry recovered with a new vigor, the linen industry once again faced difficulties. Most of the contemporary concern centered on the spinning branch. The number of spindles in the French linen industry reached its zenith of 705,000 in 1867; thereafter the number declined precipitously, to 480,000 in 1878.[16] French mills could not rival the capacity and capabilities of the British mills. For the higher counts of linen yarn used for the finer cloths, French manufacturers relied primarily on imports.[17] But not all the gains made during the cotton crisis were lost. Mechanized linen weaving continued to gain ground slowly. In Cholet, as nationally, the number of powerlooms grew steadily. In all of France in 1873 there were a total of 17,000 powerlooms and approximately 60,000 handlooms. In 1885 the number of powerlooms had risen to 18,000 and the number of handlooms had decreased dramatically to 22,800. The decline in the number of spindles had stabilized, leaving about 460,000 nationally.[18]

The difficulties of the linen industry should not be viewed apart from the general deflation in prices and the recurrent problem with overproduction in the first two decades of the Third Republic. Quarterly industrial reports for Maine-et-Loire from the years between 1869 and 1886 allow us to chart the performance of the textile sectors during the worst years of the "Great Depression." In 1880 and 1881, for the first time the prefect attributed the slump in the sale of handloom products to the surplus created by powerlooms.[19] The average daily income of handloom weavers, which had remained stable at around 1.50 francs to a high of 3.0 francs for almost thirty years, began to drop. The surplus created by machine production meant that in slow seasons handloom weavers were unemployed instead of producing for reserve stock. Even in peak seasons some handlooms could be idled. We must, however, qualify the prefect's assessment that powerlooms had created the surplus. Powerlooms only displaced handloom production at a ratio of 1 of 4; that is, one powerloom did the work of four handlooms. The powerlooms in the region, numbering less than 300, could displace at most only 1,200 handlooms. It is

16. Fohlen, *Industries textiles*, p. 319; Levasseur, *Questions*, p. 98.
17. Picard, *Bilan d'un siècle*, pp. 187–92, 203.
18. Levasseur, *Questions*, p. 98.
19. A.N. F12 4516B: Situations industrielles, Maine-et-Loire, arrondissement de Cholet, rapports trimestrielles, 1880 and 1881.

more likely that the deterioration in the position of handloom weavers resulted from a combination of declining prices, shrinking demand, and the resulting pressure on piece rates, and not from the higher productivity of powerlooms alone.

Mobilization

The reaction of handloom weavers to these new insecurities and to the drop in their income was once again to mobilize. During the summer of 1882, militant handloom weavers in Cholet formed the Association for Handloom Weavers of the Industrial Zone of Cholet. Their aim was to set fixed, uniform piece rates for all woven products in the region. They found an unexpected ally in this goal: in November of the same year, their association came to an agreement with the manufacturers' association (the Syndicat des patrons) on a fixed schedule of piece rates (a tarif) to take effect the first of the year.[20]

Four decades earlier, handloom weavers in the same town had mobilized around the same set of demands but had met a very different reaction. The protests of the 1840s and the accompanying threats of violence led mill owners to withdraw from cloth production; this time the tarif system was maintained with their active support. Although the industrialists claimed that they were concerned with the plight of the handloom weavers, this was not an alliance motivated by altruism. Industrialists supported handloom weavers in a battle against the small middlemen—the same fabricants to whom they had abandoned the task of organizing cloth production several decades before. This alliance made for strange comrades. It was a coalition of producers, but a highly artificial one, bringing together industrial producers with large mills and small-scale producers who labored in basement workshops. The union was inherently temporary, stitched together by a common interest in high and stable prices.

For handloom weavers, the tarif question was a matter of basic survival. Their standard of living was tied closely to the price of cloth. For industrialists, maintaining high prices and preventing price cutting was a matter of survival as well. The high cost of machinery and the relatively low productivity of linen powerlooms in relation to handlooms made high and predictable prices a critical concern if in-

---

20. Maurice Poperen, *Un siècle des luttes chez les tisserands des Mauges* (Angers: Imprimerie Coopérative Angevine, 1974), pp. 41–42.

dustrialists were to recoup their investments.[21] The battle against fabricants, who withdrew profits from the system and represented another source of unpredictability, was part of the struggle for control over cloth production instigated by industrialists trying to reenter cloth production.

Fabricants, too, were fighting for survival. Because they were middlemen who did not invest in the cost of production but who speculated on the difference between the price paid for production and the price of cloth sold to wholesalers, low piece rates worked to their advantage. For them, driving down the price paid weavers for cloth was an effective strategy in the fight against the industrialists who were trying to squeeze them out of the production process.

The mixed alliances in this three-way struggle testify to the complexities of mechanization in this region. On one hand, small-scale hand producers and large-scale industrial producers allied against merchant middlemen. On the other, the livelihoods of both middlemen and small-scale producers were threatened by industrial production.

With the power of the industrial manufacturers behind the coalition to maintain cloth prices, the weavers' mobilization flourished. With the full endorsement of the manufacturers, in the winter of 1883/84 weavers defeated an attempt mounted by the fabricants to renege on the deal struck a year earlier.[22] Emerging victorious out of the conflict, the Association for Handloom Weavers expanded its membership effortlessly by recruiting rural weavers into their organization. The association began with 200 members in the summer of 1882. By February 1884 the membership had risen to 2,500 (about a quarter of all handloom weavers in the region), divided among more than thirty chapters.[23] The tireless efforts of militant handloom

21. Powerlooms used for linens were more expensive and cumbersome than machines used for cottons and woolens. Because of the brittleness of the fiber, shuttles could not travel as fast or lay close as many times per minute as in the weaving of more elastic fibers like cotton and wool. In addition, because the fiber snapped easily, in linen weaving there was more down time when the worker was obliged to repair the web. For these reasons, weaving linen by machine was only four times faster than handweaving. This is significantly less efficient than machine work in cottons, where powerlooms realized a tenfold advantage over handlooms. Finally, whereas one worker often tended two powerlooms in a cotton factory, each operative tended a single powerloom in linen factories. For further details, see Aftalion, *Crise de l'industrie linière.*

22. A.D. M-et-L 71M1: Letter from subprefect of Cholet to the prefect of Maine-et-Loire, 30 August 1883.

23. Poperen, *Siècle des luttes,* pp. 41–43.

weavers who spent each Sunday traveling from bourg to bourg recruiting rural weavers had paid off.[24]

In fact, the most divisive issue in the early life of the organization developed over membership. Should the association open its ranks to weavers in the powerloom shops or should it remain strictly in the hands of handloom weavers? At their January 1885 general assembly, association leaders encouraged the members to look back over their first years with pride. Membership had steadily risen, and finances were in good order. It was time, a contingent argued, to extend their good fortunes to their confrères in the powerloom shops. After some debate and despite vehement opposition, the proposal was approved. Thereafter the association was renamed the "Chambre syndicale des ouvriers tisserands et parties similaires du rayon industriel de Cholet." As the Chambre syndicale, the group was open to all textile workers in the Choletais. This dramatic move changed the shape of political alliances in the region.[25]

The mobilization of industrial workers by artisans fits a common pattern. The past generation of research in French labor history has emphasized that working-class militancy and class consciousness developed out of the discontent and mobilization of skilled "artisanal" workers.[26] In addition, numerous important studies have traced the roots of French socialism to the cooperative and mutualist traditions of artisans.[27] This pattern of mobilization has led historians to blur the distinctions between skilled worker and artisan, at the cost of ignoring fundamental differences in training, property relations, modes of payment, and work conditions that make the alliances between the two groups fragile.[28] Scholars who analytically conflate artisans with skilled workers assume as a norm a greater degree of capitalist

24. François Simon, *Petite histoire des tisserands de la région de Cholet* (Angers: Imprimerie Anjou, 1946), pp. 109, 111.

25. Poperen, *Siècle des luttes*, pp. 44–46.

26. For examples, see Michael P. Hanagan, *The Logic of Solidarity: Artisans and Industrial Workers in Three French Towns, 1871–1914* (Urbana: University of Illinois Press, 1980), and Joan Wallach Scott, *The Glassworkers of Carmaux: French Craftsmen and Political Action in a Nineteenth-Century City* (Cambridge: Harvard University Press, 1974).

27. See Bernard H. Moss, *The Origins of the French Labor Movement, 1830–1914: The Socialism of Skilled Workers* (Berkeley: University of California Press, 1976), and William H. Sewell, Jr., *Work and Revolution in France: The Language of Labor from the Old Regime to 1848* (Cambridge: Cambridge University Press, 1980).

28. See Michael P. Hanagan, "Artisan and Skilled Worker: The Problem of Definition," *International Labor and Working Class History* 12 (November 1977): 28–31; see also Hanagan, *Logic of Solidarity*, pp. 14–15, and Moss, *Origins of the French Labor Movement*, pp. 8–25.

control than was actually achieved in many trades. In other words, they take for granted the proletarianization of small producers.

In the Choletais, it is more accurate to describe the handloom weaver as a dependent subcontractor or, as I have preferred to call him, a dependent producer.[29] When a handloom weaver received a commission, the fabricant, or an industrial capitalist acting as a fabricant, provided the raw materials and specified the quality and quantity of the final product.[30] The weaver provided the productive equipment, the skills required to produce the cloth, and the labor force consisting of himself and his family. Although he was dependent on the fabricant for supplies and markets, the weaver organized the actual production of the cloth and supplied the labor and skills. The mode of payment reflected this situation. A prix-de-façon was not a wage. It is literally the "cost of transformation."[31] The payment remunerated the weaver for his capital investment (however negligible the cost of handlooms), his knowledge, and the joint production of the hand-weaving household, because it was understood that the labor of other household members was subsumed in the price of transformation.[32]

By contrast, when an industrial capitalist hired labor, he employed workers to tend machines. Usually it was the machine that actually produced the product and the worker became skilled at its operation. For the time he or she labored, the worker received a wage. This payment was an individual wage, paid to the individual who was hired and fired. Nothing in the wage form itself took

29. The structural position of handloom weavers in the Choletais in the nineteenth century is similar to the position of the typical silk master weaver in Lyon in the 1830s. For a comparison, see Robert J. Bezucha, *The Lyon Uprising of 1834: Social and Political Conflict in the Early July Monarchy* (Cambridge: Harvard University Press, 1974), pp. 25–47.

30. Specifically, this means that the fabricant puts out a warp beam already wound with warp yarn and provides the heddles needed to produce the particular cloth. In most circumstances the weaver buys from the fabricant or another supplier the weft threads needed.

31. For a more extensive discussion of the social practices and work routines implied in the term "prix-de-façon," see Michael Sonenscher, *The Hatters of Eighteenth-Century France* (Berkeley: University of California Press, 1987), especially pp. 3–4, 68–74. Also consult Sonenscher, *Work and Wages: Natural Law, Politics, and the Eighteenth-Century French Trades* (Cambridge: Cambridge University Press, 1989).

32. See John Rule, "The Property in Skill in the Period of Manufacture," in *The Historical Meaning of Work*, ed. Patrick Joyce (Cambridge: Cambridge University Press, 1987), pp. 99–118, and Wally Seccombe, "Patriarchy Stabilized: The Construction of the Male Breadwinner Wage Norm in Nineteenth-Century Britain," *Social History* 11 (January 1986): 53–76, especially the discussion on p. 59 on the assumptions of male artisan househeadship.

account of the family circumstances of the worker.[33] Moreover, the employer owned all the productive equipment and organized production.

These distinctions in property relations and modes of payment may appear subtle, but they were manifested in significant differences in actual work conditions. Handloom weavers did not share the grievances of industrial workers. Issues like a 10-hour day, safety regulations, work rules, regulation of down time, and the problem of sick leaves did not affect handloom weavers, whose primary interest was the price of cloth. Handloom weavers also suffered from unemployment, sicknesses, and old age, but they solved their problems (however ineffectively) with mutual aid societies. Their disputes over work rules, safety, and illness were regulated within the household.

The wish to include industrial workers in the association of handloom weavers was motivated by more than just expedience. Among the leaders of the Chambre syndicale were handloom weavers who were influenced by socialist ideals. They perceived that any solution to the problems of handloom weavers in the modern world lay with working-class politics. For them, the fundamental division was between workers and bosses: those who lived by their labor against those who lived by the labor of others. They considered this divide deeper than whatever other differences existed between impoverished petty commodity producers and industrial workers. Their faith in the common interest of those who worked with their hands led them to underestimate how deeply other handloom weavers felt they were different from industrial workers. For the moment the underlying differences, smoothed over by good will and political fervor, did not surface. But, when tested under fire in a series of disputes between

33. For a more extensive discussion of the difference between individuated wage payments and modes of payment that assume a family economy, see Seccombe, "Patriarchy Stabilized." In labor disputes during the nineteenth century, however, both male and female workers urged that employers must consider family responsibility as well as family status as part of wage negotiations and apprenticeships. Unfortunately, when male workers put forth this argument, they used it to exclude female workers. For examples of this phenomenon, see William M. Reddy, "Family and Factory: French Linen Weavers in the Belle Epoque," *Journal of Social History* 8 (Winter 1975): 102–12, Joan W. Scott, "Men and Women in the Parisian Garment Trades: Discussions of Family and Work in the 1830s and 1840s," *The Power of the Past*, ed. Pat Thane and Geoffrey Crossick (Cambridge: Cambridge University Press, 1985), pp. 67–93, Barbara Taylor, *Eve and the New Jerusalem* (London: Virago Press, 1983), Sonya O. Rose, "Gender Antagonism and the Class Conflict: Exclusionary Strategies of Male Trade Unionists in Nineteenth-Century Britain," *Social History* 13 (1988): 163–84, and Michèle Barret and M. McIntosh, "The 'Family Wage': Some Problems for Socialists and Feminists," *Capital and Class* 11 (1980): 51–72.

handweavers and fabricants that escalated into general strikes, the coalition ultimately fell apart.[34]

Initially, the very fact of the coalition between industrial workers and handloom weavers was sufficient to force concessions from both fabricants and industrialists. The first showdown came in the form of minor incidents on the geographic fringes of the manufacturing district, in the commune of Les Épesses in Vendée, the neighboring department. Local handloom weavers struck against local fabricants for cutting the piece rate. This incident, the subprefect noted, would have passed by unnoticed except that several fabricants in the Choletais, long disgruntled about the agreed tarif, followed the example and cut piece rates. The fabricants resigned from the Syndicat des patrons to signal their intent. Two days later, 1,500 textile workers, both handloom weavers and powerloom tenders, responded to the rallying call from the Chambre syndicale.[35]

On the designated day for the rally and strike vote (Sunday, 23 May), the two sides were still at loggerheads. Moreover, the Syndicat des patrons was in complete disarray. Industrialists in Cholet continued to support the existing piece rates but they were unable to hold the smaller fabricants in line. Negotiations continued in secret even as six thousand angry men and women from all branches of the textile trades gathered in the center of town. In the last moments before the strike vote was called, union leaders rushed before the crowd to announce that an agreement had finally been reached. The piece rates established in 1883 would be honored once again.[36]

With this news, the crowd broke out in cheers. Enjoying the euphoria of victory, many weavers vowed to demonstrate before the houses of the recalcitrant patrons. Several days later, Morin, the fabricant responsible for waging the campaign to lower piece rates, closed up shop. He was later brought before the Conseil des prud'hommes for breach of contract.[37] With the success of the Chambre syndicale came new members, and some languishing rural chapters were roused out of their torpor. The credibility of the union was at its peak.[38] The coa-

---

34. A similar tension can be found in the alliance of glassworkers and miners in Joan Scott's analysis of socialist mobilization in *The Glassworkers of Carmaux.*

35. A.D. M-et-L 71M1: Letter from subprefect of Cholet to prefect of Maine-et-Loire, 16 April 1886, A.N. F124659: Letter from prefect of Maine-et-Loire to minister of commerce and industries, 21 April 1886.

36. A.N. F12 4659: Letter from prefect of Maine-et-Loire to minister of commerce and industries, 24 May 1886.

37. Ibid.

38. Poperen, *Siècle des luttes,* p. 50.

lition of handloom weavers and powerloom operatives had nearly brought the region's textile trades to a standstill. The Chambre syndicale had won the day by averting the strike and winning concessions for weavers.

A curious turn of events after the May victory, however, foreshadowed the growing discord between the leaders of the Chambre syndicale and many handloom weavers in the rank and file. By December 1886, except for the largest manufacturers, few fabricants were abiding by the tarif. When linen fabricants proposed a reduction of 10–15 centimes per dozen kerchiefs, handloom weavers initially voted down the measure. Nevertheless, the prefect noted in his report to the minister of commerce and industry that handloom weavers seemed disposed to accept this light reduction (amounting to a 40–60 centime loss to their weekly earnings) if the fabricants would agree to abide by the new tarif and not drive prices even lower. The agreement specified indemnities in case of violations.[39]

The decision to accept reductions in exchange for formal recognition of negotiated prices was controversial and did not reflect the unanimous decision of all members, much less the opinion of the Chambre syndicale's directing council. The first meeting of the general assembly in January 1887 was turbulent. Pelluaud, one of the delegates who rose to prominence in the May negotiations, was censured severely by his comrades in the council. The secretary of the assembly, Bonin, issued this critique: "By advocating a tarif which imposes a loss on several articles, Pelluaud has played the bosses' game. This behavior is unworthy of a union leader; willingly or not, the man in whom we have placed our trust has become the accomplice of those who starve us."[40]

Certainly, the anger of the leadership was understandable. The actions of the handloom weavers involved compromised the entire movement. There had been no need to concede when the Chambre syndicale had proven itself to be strong. In this period, we witness a new insistence on the language of class solidarity. The leaders of the Chambre syndicale increasingly portrayed both handloom weavers and powerloom tenders as workers with a common enemy and common demands. In the April general meeting in 1887, the union declared its common principles with the Congrès fédéral de Lyon. The president of the Chambre syndicale, Jules Allard, urged, "Let us unify

---

39. A.N. F12 4659: Letter from prefect of Maine-et-Loire to the minister of commerce and industries, 11 December 1886.
40. Poperen, *Siècle des luttes,* pp. 51–52.

and federate; it is the only way to escape our exploitation."[41] Bonin pushed vehemently for joining the Parti ouvrier.[42] This was not the first time the leadership of the Chambre syndicale had broached the idea of political engagement. In September 1886, fresh from the May victory, the directing council considered this issue. Unable to arrive at a unanimous decision, they put the question before the general assembly in October, but again it was not resolved.[43] Such political affiliation disquieted many members, especially among certain rural chapters. When the issue was revived in April 1887, the same misgivings overtook the crowd. The question was tabled again, as the meeting adjourned over these disagreements. In a subsequent meeting, however, affiliation with the Parti ouvrier was formalized, probably by fiat. The Chambre syndicale chose Pierre Chupin as their representative to the Congrès de Charleville (of the Fédérations des travailleurs socialistes de France) held in October 1887.[44] The discord over political engagement augured the conflicts to come.

In late August 1887, as the Chambre syndicale was busily negotiating a new tarif on behalf of handloom weavers (the same tarif it had denounced eight months earlier), the tension brewing within the coalition finally came to a head. On 23 August, 63 dévideuses in Pellaumail's factory walked off their jobs protesting an arbitrary reduction in wages. They had lost no less than 60 centimes from their daily wage of 1.75 francs. The next day, 203 male powerloom weavers walked out in support of the women.[45] The Chambre syndicale tried to negotiate the workers' return, but Pellaumail's partner Bergère would negotiate only after the strikers returned to their jobs and agreed to work under the new pay rates for five to six weeks. The

41. Ibid., p. 52.

42. The reference to the Parti ouvrier is ambiguous. Leaders of the Chambre syndicale were drawn into socialist politics through the federalist and collectivist notions of Paul Brousse. Most likely "Parti ouvrier" refers to the Fédérations des travailleurs socialistes de France. At the Congrès de Lyon, the politics of Brousse had won out over that of Jules Guesde; see Georges LeFranc, *Le mouvement socialiste sous la Troisième République* (Paris: Payot, 1963), pp. 29–31. Moreover, in the strike reports in 1888 the subprefect mentioned the presence of Victor Dalle in Cholet; see A.D. M-et-L 71M2: Letter from subprefect of Cholet to prefect of Maine-et-Loire, 29 October 1888. Dalle, a follower of Brousse, was a popular propagandist among the organized artisanal trades. On Brousse and his followers, see Claude Willard, *Le mouvement socialiste en France (1893–1905): Les Guesdistes* (Paris: Éditions sociales, 1965), pp. 395–38, 402, 404; for a discussion of the types of artisanal workers and small-scale producers attracted to socialist politics, consult pp. 315–16, 362–66.

43. Poperen, *Siècle des luttes*, p. 47.

44. Ibid., p. 52. See also the entry under Pierre Chupin in *Dictionnaire biographique du mouvement ouvrier français* (Paris: Les Éditions ouvrières, 1973), 11:3.208.

45. A.N. F12 4659: Letter from prefect of Maine-et-Loire to the minister of interior, 25 August 1887.

strikers categorically refused. The strike quickly spread to the factories of Richard, Godineau, and Brémond. Within a few days, five thousand handloom weavers joined the strike of the industrial workers. All linen production in the region was at a standstill.

The industrial workers had six demands: a 10-hour day with rate adjustments to maintain the same daily pay; suppression of fines and penalties; revision and simplification of the piece rates; obligatory posting of the rate schedule; guaranteed reemployment after illnesses; and no firing of members of shop committees without warning. The handloom weavers demanded the reimplementation of the 1883 rate schedule.[46]

The two sets of strike demands were fundamentally unconnected; they exposed the vastly different work conditions and relation to the product and to the means of production which separated industrial workers from handloom weavers. The demands of the former reflected a pent-up anger and expressed dissatisfaction with work rules and shop floor discipline; these grievances reflected factory conditions, challenging the absolute authority of the employer to set work rules and piece rates arbitrarily. Handloom weavers were concerned only with setting the price of the product; working conditions were a matter of parental authority and familial dispute. The demands of handloom weavers reflected their initial reasons for association, to band together to set prices in order to guarantee their own livelihood.

The espoused solidarity between the two groups was thus not easily converted into shared economic goals. In September 1887 the common interest of the two groups was put to the test. Just before the busy season, rural fabricants wanted to negotiate. This offer posed an almost insurmountable problem for the Chambre syndicale. First of all, not all fabricants agreed. Only 39 of more than a hundred wanted to negotiate. Fabricants in the Vendée, the source of the dispute in 1886, adamantly opposed any contract. Many handloom weavers were inclined to settle, but this contract would leave out the industrial workers. So, while one group of handloom weavers, including the directing council, denounced the contract as a ploy to divide textile workers, another group wanted to sign the rate agreement because handloom weavers had attained their goal. The former group pushed for prolonging the strike and demanded that the 1883 agreement be extended to cotton workers as well. This dispute among

46. Ibid.; A.N. F12 4659: Telegram from prefect of Maine-et-Loire to the minister of commerce and industries, 24 August 1887.

handloom weavers provoked a secessionist movement.[47] The general strike, which had begun in late August with an impressive show of solidarity, was rapidly losing its force by late September.

The strike was finally settled by late October 1887. Industrial workers, along with the handloom weavers who remained loyal to the Chambre syndicale, remained on strike for a total of nine weeks.[48] The strike was resolved largely through the mediation of the subprefect. After much persuasion, Pellaumail agreed to rescind the pay cuts and reinstate the dévideuses.[49] Industrial workers returned to work with restored wages but apparently gained none of their other demands. The end of the strike did not, however, terminate hostilities. Production in the factory resumed in an atmosphere poisoned by animosity and mistrust. Pellaumail was more determined than ever to rid himself of the contentious workers in his plant. In the years to come, the Pellaumail plant was plagued by dismissals and walkouts as workers and bosses tested the limits of each others' strength.[50]

The most devastating effect of the strike was the split in the movement of handloom weavers. In December 1887, handloom weavers who had led the secession movement in the commune of La Tes-

47. A.D. M-et-L 71M2: Letter from subprefect of Cholet to prefect of Maine-et-Loire, 29 October, 1888. Poperen, *Siècle des luttes*, pp. 54–55.

48. A.N. C7318: Chambre des députés, "Enquête sur l'industrie textile en France 1903," Régions non visitées par la commission: Maine-et-Loire, Réponse de la Bourse du travail, 1904.

49. Poperen, *Siècle des luttes*, p. 56.

50. For example, after the strike in 1887, work relations in Pellaumail's factory, which initially provoked the strike, were far from harmonious. In February 1888, the Pellaumail factory erupted again over discipline and work rules. The incident began when Pellaumail denied his workers permission to attend the funeral of a fellow worker. At the hour of the ceremony, a member of the factory council, Biton, encouraged his fellow workers to attend the funeral anyway. On their return, Biton was immediately fired for inciting disobedience. Rumors of the dismissal had circulated, no doubt, even before Biton returned to the shop floor to report his fate. At the moment of his return, on a signal given by one worker, all looms in Pellaumail's factory stopped. Two hundred and sixty workers walked out.

The walkout lasted two weeks. Immediately after the first display of unity, most workers regretted their emotional actions and asked the subprefect to intervene on their behalf. But the walkout served Pellaumail's purposes. He used this action to rid himself of the militants. In addition, his actions enjoyed the active support of the Syndicat des patrons. Only the intervention of the subprefect brought the two sides closer to a compromise. After several meetings with the subprefect, the workers' delegation agreed to a rehiring, on the condition that Biton and the worker who signaled the walkout be the only "victims" of the strike. While many workers objected that this resolution granted Pellaumail his main objectives, there was in fact little room to maneuver. Most workers were restored to their old jobs without a loss in pay. Biton and several other weavers as well as several skein winders who were probably the most militant in the walkout in 1887 were left off of Pellaumail's pay roster. The Biton affair was settled when, through the help of the mayor, the unemployed workers found work in Turpault's factory. See A.N. F12 4659: Letter from prefect of Maine-et-Loire to the minister of commerce and industries, 14 March 1888.

soualle back in September formed the Syndicat "le Prévoyant" des tisserands à la main de La Tessoualle.[51] By 1888 there were five other rural chapters affiliated with this movement. In the same year a new umbrella association exclusively for handloom weavers was formed in Cholet under the name "Union des syndicats profession-nels des ouvriers tisserands and similaires de Cholet," commonly re-ferred to as the Union des syndicats de prévoyance. In its bylaws, the Syndicats de prévoyance declared that its sole interest was in main-taining and defending piece rates for handloom products. It under-scored the desire to separate the issues concerning handloom production from those of mechanized production and, most of all, from all political affiliation.[52]

The Social and Political Identity of Small Producers in an Industrial World

The split in the weavers' movement was not surprising. From the beginning, there had been disagreements over politics and strategies. Particularly controversial was the push among some members to af-filiate with the Parti ouvrier.[53] The Chambre syndicale was socialist and anticlerical. Although the Syndicats de prévoyance claimed to stay away from all politics, some of the rural chapters, like the Syn-dicat Saint-Vincent-de-Paul des ouvriers tisserands à la main of the commune of Le-May-sur-Evre, maintained religious affiliations. Moreover, some of the movement's leaders, like Elie Catron of La Tes-soualle, had strong ties to conservative clerical politicians such as Jules Baron.[54] The Chambre syndicale called the new union the "yel-low" union and referred to itself as the "red" union. These political distinctions, though appropriate to contemporaries in the heat of bat-tle, do not help us understand the most important differences be-tween the two groups. This was not essentially a conflict between catholicism and socialism. What is important was how each group understood the situation and future of handloom weavers as depen-dent producers, which in turn affected each of their strategies for col-

51. A.N. F22 86: Syndicats 1914 et dessous, Maine-et-Loire, Syndicat "le prévoyant" des tisserands à la main de la Tessoualle; see also Poperen, *Siècle des luttes*, pp. 52, 54.
52. A.N. F22 85: Syndicats 1914 et dessous, Maine-et-Loire, Union des syndicats profes-sionnels des ouvriers tisserands et similaires de Cholet.
53. Poperen, *Siècle des luttes*, pp. 47, 52.
54. A.D. M-et-L 40M37: Confidential reports of the subprefect of Cholet to prefect of Maine-et-Loire, 30 September and 6 November 1888.

lective action. The variety of solutions pursued indicates the difficult and often contradictory position of the small dependent producer in an economy increasingly dominated by mechanized industries and capitalist relations of production.

By refusing to ally with industrial workers, the members of the Syndicats de prévoyance held themselves up as small-scale producers. As owners of the means of production and proprietors of the ability to make cloth, they felt fundamentally different from wage workers. As producers, handloom weavers reasoned correctly that the source of their difficulties was their dependence on suppliers and their limited access to markets. They thus considered the middleman, the fabricant, to be their primary enemy. This calculus, which did not take mechanization into account, may appear anachronistic for the late nineteenth century, but it was in fact reasonable for handloom weavers to expect a tacit market-sharing agreement with mechanized producers, giving them a niche in a segmented product market.

The strategy of the weavers in the Syndicats de prévoyance followed the same logic as that of their handloom weaver fathers in the 1840s. During the July Monarchy, small producers all over France fought against the encroachment of merchant control by demanding a uniform tarif in their trade.[55] The tarif had significance beyond the actual level of remuneration. It created a pattern of cooperation between small producers as a means for organizing their profession. Most important, setting common prices avoided damaging internal competition within the trade. As long as handloom weavers in the Choletais saw themselves primarily as small producers, the strategy developed in the 1840s could apply in the 1880s, because the logic of their relation to merchant capital had not changed. By using their collective strength to force through higher prices, small producers were able to cut the profit margin of the middlemen. Potentially, this was a winning strategy: as weavers saw in May 1886, after the successful renegotiation of the 1883 tarif, many fabricants were forced out of business because of the higher prices.

Attempts to circumvent the middlemen take on added importance when we consider the actions of another group of handloom weavers.

55. For an overview of strike activities in this period, see Jean-Pierre Aguet, *Les grèves sous la Monarchie de Juillet: Contribution à l'étude du mouvement ouvrier français* (Geneva, 1954). On the significance of the tarif issue, see Bezucha, *The Lyon Uprising of 1834*, Sewell, *Work and Revolution in France*, and William M. Reddy, *The Rise of Market Culture: The Textile Trades and French Society, 1750–1900* (Cambridge: Cambridge University Press, 1984).

In 1870 a small group, about three hundred in total, formed the So-ciété anonyme l'espérance des tisserands unis, a producers' coopera-tive organized to pool capital for the purposes of obtaining credit, purchasing supplies, and marketing cloth.[56] In forming this coopera-tive, these handloom weavers reunited the roles of entrepreneur and producer. Only handloom weavers under the age of 50 and who worked alone or with the aid of family members were eligible for membership. Any member who began to hire out labor or became in-volved in other commercial ventures was automatically barred.

Members of the Société purchased shares at 50 francs a piece. From its beginning in 1870 with 333 members and a capital fund of 36,400 francs, the association's membership grew slowly, but its capital as-sets increased significantly to 80,000 francs in 1875, 130,000 francs in 1877, and 180,000 francs in 1882, when the Société had 425 mem-bers. The Société was governed by an administrative council of eleven members elected from among the shareholders. This council had extensive power to purchase, sell, and enter into contracts, as well as powers over the capital funds and mutual aid funds of the So-ciété. The organization specified the rules under which members were to receive work and set a uniform tarif of prices, which were not below market prices. Returns from cloth sales were allocated among benefits paid to shareholders, the capital funds and mutual aid funds, and the capital equipment of the Société.

According to its original association papers, the Société l'espérance was constituted for thirty years. From the little evidence we have for its three decades of existence, the producers' association produced good returns for its members and enjoyed a fairly long lifespan for a producers' cooperative. Because this cooperative did not attract much police attention, we know little about it beyond its existence and or-ganization rules; its internal politics and day-to-day organization es-cape us.[57] Yet its existence at least demonstrates the concreteness of one viable option for small-scale producers. Moreover, many hand-loom weavers were sympathetic to the notion of producers' coopera-tives. At the initial formation of the Chambre syndicale, for example,

56. A.D. M-et-L 40 M 36: Syndicats professionnels, Livrets de la Société anonyme l'espér-ance des tisserands unis de Cholet et des environs; 40 M 37: Syndicats professionnels, État des sociétés coopératives, 1882–1893.
57. For a more detailed discussion on the daily functioning of producers' cooperatives and their successes and failures, see Bernard Schnapper, "Les sociétés ouvrières de production pendant la Seconde République: L'exemple girondin," *Revue d'histoire économique et so-ciale* 43 (1965): 162–91. Also consult André Gueslin, *L'invention de l'économie sociale: Le XIXe siècle* (Paris: Économica, 1987), pp. 253–70.

delegates from Saint-Macaire raised the possibility of establishing a producers' cooperative, which was met with wide approval.[58]

Like the Syndicats de prévoyance, the Société l'espérance organized within the diverse and heterogeneous traditions of producers' associations.[59] Although the aim of these cooperatives was to shelter their participants from the anarchy of market competition, and in some cases to turn workers into proprietors, this goal did not necessarily entail revolutionary means.[60] Especially after the political repressions during the July Monarchy and in the Second Republic, many producers' associations during the Second Empire sought an acceptable accommodation rather than a complete overthrow of the capitalist system. Moreover, during the Third Republic Opportunist leaders actively encouraged the nonrevolutionary association movement with political patronage and public contracts. Officials helped producers' associations obtain low-interest loans, for example. There was also talk of forming a national credit bank for associations. The central advocate for these reforms was Joseph Barbaret, the Radical journalist who entered the Ministry of Interior in 1880. Barbaret, as labor editor of a popular daily, had opposed strikes and favored syndical associations as the means to gradually abolish the wage system.[61] The strong clerical influence in the Syndicats de prévoyance would have placed this association at odds with Opportunist republicans. Yet its

58. Simon, *Petite histoire*, p. 111. Handloom weavers in the Cambrésis experimented with producers' cooperatives. See the discussion on the Société coopérative de fabrication la "Fraternelle" during the 12 October 1904 hearing on the deposition of the Syndicat patronal de la région d'Avesnes-les-Auberts et de Saint-Hilaire, published in the *Procès verbaux de la commission . . . l'industrie textile et la condition des ouvriers tisseurs*, 5:214. See also Scott, *Glassworkers of Carmaux*, on the cooperative glass factories formed by skilled glassworkers in the aftermath of the 1895 strike.

59. The idea behind producers' cooperatives can be clearly traced to Philippe Buchez, Étienne Cabet, and other "Utopian" socialists of the 1830s and 1840s. On Buchez, see Armand Cuvillier, *P.-J.-B. Buchez et les origines du socialisme chrétien* (Paris: Presses universitaires de France, 1948), and François-André Isambert, *Politique, religion et science de l'homme chez Philippe Buchez (1796–1865)* (Paris: Cujas, 1967). On Cabet, see Christopher H. Johnson, *Utopian Communism in France: Cabet and the Icarians, 1839–1851* (Ithaca: Cornell University Press, 1974). See also Moss, *Origins of the French Labor Movement*, chap. 2.

60. The debates between Louis Blanc and Pierre-Joseph Proudhon over property and collective ownership indicated the diverse conceptions of alternatives. Why Proudhon opposed collective ownership, however, has been the source of continuing controversy; see K. Steven Vincent, *Pierre-Joseph Proudhon and the Rise of French Republican Socialism* (New York: Oxford University Press, 1984), It is important to recognize that Proudhon was probably the most systematic thinker during the nineteenth century to articulate an alternative to capitalist society based on cooperation among independent small-scale producer/property owners. See Pierre Ansart, *Naissance de l'anarchisme: Esquisse d'une explication sociologique du proudhonisme* (Paris: Presses universitaires de France, 1970).

61. Moss, *Origins of the French Labor Movement*, chaps. 2 and 3.

goals and method of mobilization were representative of one active wing of the associational movement. Perhaps due to differences on the question of property—the Société l'espérance favored collective ownership and the Syndicats de prévoyance remained staunchly an association of independent, small-scale property owners—the Société was politically more sympathetic to the Chambre syndicale.[62] Nevertheless, as different as the two organizations were, they both mobilized handloom weavers as small-scale producers.

By contrast, the strategy of the Chambre syndicale was formed around the common plight of all those who labored with their hands, whether on handlooms or tending machines. Even so, the radical handloom weavers of the Chambre syndicale came out of the same associational tradition as the Syndicats de prévoyance, but from the more radical collectivist wing. The movement of Chambre syndicale leaders from cooperative to revolutionary socialism traced a path many radical artisans traveled during the 1870s and 1880s. Earlier, many leading figures among French cooperative socialists had been influenced, through the First International, by Bakunin-style revolutionary collectivism. Their activities as propagandists radicalized an important segment of artisans in the association movement who were becoming increasingly frustrated and disillusioned by the slow pace of change under Opportunist leadership.[63]

Compared to the position of the Syndicats de prévoyance, however, the class analysis of the Chambre syndicale was more internally contradictory. By asserting that there was a common solution for hand workers and machine workers, the Chambre syndicale was in fact claiming the victory of capitalist production over the small-scale producer. It tried to organize handloom weavers as if they were de facto wage workers who worked at home. This assessment did not fit well with the handloom weavers' actual structural position or with their self-perception. At best, the pronouncement was premature.

Even if the language of class struggle only rhetorically smoothed over the very different conditions faced by artisans and industrial workers, the vision of socialism as the alliance of the exploited was a powerful one. We witnessed its organizing potential in the region in 1885 and 1886. Clearly, local industrialists feared this alliance the most. Although the secession movement was motivated in part by the intensity of craft identity, we should not underestimate the

---

62. On overlapping membership between the Chambre syndicale and the Société l'espérance, see Simon, *Petite histoire*, p. 102.
63. Moss, *Origins of the French Labor Movement*, chaps. 4 and 5.

divisive meddling and punitive actions that both fabricants and industrialists engaged in trying to divide handloom weavers and industrial workers.

Ironically, it was probably only in coalition with industrial workers that handloom weavers could have challenged and driven out the fabricants and thus improved their position as small producers. Handloom weavers needed the collective bargaining power gained through a general strike. But the failure of common mobilization was due to the strong craft and artisan identity of handloom weavers. In their refusal to make industrial workers their political allies and to build organizational links to other national political movements as the Chambre syndicale had done, the Syndicats de prévoyance limited its choices of action.

The Syndicats de prévoyance relied almost exclusively on arbitration in its disputes with fabricants. In 1887 and 1888, the subprefect was instrumental in settling conflicts over piece rates, after a decade in which this official had progressively taken on the role of mediator. The 1892 law creating arbitration boards composed of both workers and patrons formalized what had already evolved into practice.[64] And though workers, particularly handloom weavers, placed great importance on state recognition of arbitration as a crucial step in enforcing the rate schedule, the disputes of the 1890s still centered on the tarif and violation of agreements and price cutting.[65]

The splits within the socialist movement in Cholet indicate that the tension between small producers and industrial workers was never fully resolved. In the 1890s, after the Allemanist departure from the Fédération des travailleurs socialiste de France, an industrial worker, Biton (a vocal militant fired from Pellaumail's factory after leading a workout in 1888)[66] led the Allemanist faction in Cholet. The Broussist movement floundered after 1890. Many socialist handloom weavers like Guérin and Pierre Chupin, who continued to be active in the Chambre syndicale and in the Bourse du travail established in 1891, were increasingly described in police documents as "independent socialists." Throughout the 1890s, most socialists in Cholet had become progressively alienated by Biton's "dogmatic"

64. On the law setting up arbitration committees, see Levasseur, *Questions,* pp. 670, 711, 712.

65. A.N. C7318: Enquête textile 1904, Réponse de l'Union des syndicats professionnels d'ouvriers tisserands et similaires du rayon industrielle de Cholet (the Syndicats de prévoyance), and Réponse de la Bourse du travail de Cholet et de la Chambre syndicale des ouvriers tisserands et parties similaires du rayon industriel de Cholet.

66. See note 50.

politics.[67] By the end of the decade, Chupin had publicly broken with Biton and many socialists in Cholet, most notably Guérin and De-Serre of the Bourse du travail, envisaged creating an alternative group uniting various "independent socialists."[68]

The movement was to bring "petty bourgeois" elements—small boutiquiers, commercants, and even small rentiers—into a republican-radical-socialist coalition. Such a amalgam would clearly emphasize social reform over violent revolution.[69] In 1899, Georges Turpault, a prominent cloth manufacturer well known for his republican sympathies, together with other leading republican bourgeois citizens of Cholet, proposed an expanded coalition for republican-socialists to bring together the liberal elements of Cholet's bourgeoisie with those socialists alienated by Allemanist politics. Guérin and DeSerre were once again active in this movement to gain local electoral power.[70] Interesting for us, the socialism of many militant handloom weavers retained a strong awareness of the economic difficulties of small producers and sought to view these problems as a point of common oppression shared by other small producers, entrepreneurs, and property owners, all equally threatened by industrial capitalism. This coalition apparently had some political effect. Socialists in Cholet often voted republican in national elections in this overwhelmingly conservative political stronghold.

In essence, the full range of political and organizational experiments in which weavers engaged—producers' cooperatives, socialist politics, small producers' associations—were attempts to resolve the contradictions inherent in the position of small producers in a society increasingly dominated by large-scale production.[71] We can see

67. A.D. M-et-L 4M6/43: Rapport du Commissariat spécial sur le socialisme à Cholet, Angers, 3 August 1898.

68. A.D. M-et-L 4M6/43: Rapport du Commissariat spécial de police, Angers, 21 April 1896.

69. A.D. M-et-L 4M6/43: Rapport du Commissariat spécial sur le socialisme à Cholet, Angers, 3 August 1898. For further discussions on the relationship between socialists and small producers and merchants, see Madeleine Rebérioux, "Les socialistes français et le petit commerce au tournant du siècle," and Eugen Sinner, "La politique de la social-democratie allemande vis-à-vis l'artisanat à la fin du XIXe siècle," *Le mouvement social* 114 (January–March 1981): 57–70, 105–23.

70. A.D. M-et-L 4M6/43: Rapport du Commissariat special: Création d'un comité republicain (socialiste) à Cholet, Angers, 9 April 1899.

71. For an interesting comparison of the economic position and political organizations of the "petite bourgeoisie," "mittelstand," or "lower-middle class" in various European countries, see the special edition of *Le mouvement social* 114 (January–March 1981), titled "Petite entreprise et politique." See also David Blackbourn, "The Mittelstand in German Society and Politics, 1871–1914," *Social History* 4 (January 1977): 409–33, and Geoffrey Crossick, *The Lower Middleclass in Britain, 1870–1916* (London: Croom Helm, 1977).

that the difficulties scholars have had in defining artisanry reflect
real ambiguities in the structural position of small producers. As
Steven M. Zdatny points out, the question of definition was at the
center of political and ideological battles waged among artisans, between artisans and other groups, and between artisans and the
state.[72] The controversy derived from the indeterminacy of artisanal
status: artisans are skilled workers, proprietors, and entrepreneurs
rolled into one.

The problem of definition is further compounded by the fluid
boundaries of the artisanat. As Zdatny shows, in one lifetime individuals could move from skilled worker to independent entrepreneur
and back to skilled worker again. This mobility among roles is not
only characteristic of artisans in an industrial society; as I emphasized in Chapter 3, in the age before industrial capitalism there was a
similar fluidity between producers and entrepreneurs, particularly in
the countryside. The problem for merchants was how to freeze the
identity of handloom weavers as producers and force them to relin-
quish entrepreneurship.

The self-perception of artisans depended on which aspect of their
identity they emphasized. This emphasis, which determined the social and political solutions they adopted, was often a source of contention within the community. One might ask, at this juncture,
whether there was more at stake here than nostalgic yearnings for a
simpler past, absent the changes brought by machines and large-scale
capital? Were there any real options for handloom weavers once textile production was mechanized? Even if the Chambre syndicale had
succeeded in holding together the coalition, and handloom weavers
consistently won observance of the tarif, were they not just hanging
on, waiting for their inevitable extinction?

Modern historians are often unintentionally cruel in our assessment of such people as handloom weavers. The arrogance of hind-
sight makes us quick to judge certain actions as nostalgic, utopian, or
economically irrational. This attitude blinds us to the types of experimentation in which weavers tried to find a satisfactory accommodation, if not a solution. Above all, this involved making sense of the
world in which they lived and exploring the possibilities for change
that would also provide continuity. The course of action weavers
took depended on how they viewed their future, on whether they be-

72. Steven M. Zdatny, "The Artisanat in France: An Economic Portrait, 1900–1956,"
French Historical Studies 13 (Spring 1984): 415–40; see also *The Politics of Survival: Artisans in 20th-Century France* (New York: Oxford University Press, 1990).

lieved handloom weaving was doomed. Moreover, their actions reflected an assessment of which aspects of their lives they wanted to preserve, and which aspects they wanted to change.

We tend to look askance at such experimentation because we assume that handloom weaving, and small production generally, was doomed by mechanization. Yet the simple truth is that handloom weaving did not disappear. In fact, most handloom weavers active in the 1880s finished their lives at their looms.

The Survival of Handloom Weaving

By the early twentieth century, mechanized production dominated local production. We are fortunate that in 1903 the Chambre des députés ordered a study of conditions in the French textile industry, resulting in an enquête containing a wealth of information on markets, production techniques, and labor organization. The responses from Maine-et-Loire were unanimous in stating that handloom weaving had given way to mechanized weaving. Yet the enquête indicated a sizable hand-weaving population in the region. In fact, many handloom weavers told the inquiring commission that there was more work than ever.[73] In 1904 there were 2,000 workers in mechanized weaving, 7,000–8,000 handloom weavers on the same number of handlooms, 500 bleach workers, and 200 dye workers.[74] In 1878 there had been 280 powerlooms in the Choletais with a total of just 360 workers, and 10,000 handlooms employing 13,000–14,000 men, women, and children.[75]

Although the broad picture is one of an increase in powerlooms and a decline in handloom weaving, mechanized production had not replaced handloom production. In fact, the number of handlooms in operation had remained steady since the 1880s. In 1887 and 1888, approximately 10,000 people made their living from 7,000–8,000 handlooms.[76] If powerlooms were directly competing with handlooms, then handloom weaving would have disappeared. In linens,

73. A.N. C7318: Enquête textile 1904, depositions of the Bourse du travail and Chambre syndicale of Cholet, the Union des syndicats professionnels (the Syndicat de prévoyance), and the justice of the peace of Cholet.
74. A.N. C7318: Enquête textile 1904, Réponse de l'Union des syndicats professionnels d'ouvriers tisserands.
75. A.N. F12 4516B: Situation industrielle, Maine-et-Loire, arrondissement de Cholet, rapports de l'année 1878.
76. Ibid., rapports des années 1886, 1887.

one powerloom matched the productivity of four handlooms, so 2,000 powerlooms would have displaced the entire handloom population. During the two decades of rapid expansion of mechanized production, though, the number of handlooms fell by only 2,000, or the equivalent in productivity of 500 powerlooms. Moreover, the figures for Cholet mirrored the pattern for the country as a whole. In 1874 there were an estimated 60,000 handlooms involved in linen production, before a dramatic decline to approximately 23,000 in 1885. An estimate fourteen years later, in 1899, reported approximately 20,000 handloom weavers in the French linen industry.[77]

Beneath the stability in numbers, however, the structure of the linen industry had changed dramatically. In the Choletais, as elsewhere, mechanized producers had forced through profound changes since the 1880s, which resulted in a new division of labor and product markets between hand work and mechanized production.

When powerloom weaving was introduced, it competed directly against handloom weaving. Rather than abandon handloom weaving, however, many weavers found refuge in market niches unsuited to machine production. As economist Albert Aftalion astutely noted in his study of mechanization in the nineteenth century, machines dominate production by producing median grades at cheap prices, turning this grade into a mass market product.[78] In the Choletais, for example, powerlooms produced the medium counts of linen used for clothing, trousers and shirts, and sheets. The coarse grades of linen used for sacks and dishcloths, napkins, and tablecloths were produced on handlooms, as were the finest grades of linen, known as *linon* and *batiste*, used for luxury products and the fine and medium grades of linen kerchiefs.

The reasons for this division of production were both economic and technical. The resale value of the lowest grades was too low in relation to the cost of machinery to make it cost efficient to produce coarse linens in factories. The skill demanded by fine grades of cloth, on the other hand, could not be reproduced mechanically. Powerloom production dominated only the range of products for which machines were best suited. The fast, tireless, and regular action of machines was ideal for the types of cloths that could be produced with few changes in pattern, using a grade and count of yarn that could endure the greater stress of rapid machine movement.[79]

77. Aftalion, *Crise de l'industrie linière*, p. 27.

78. Albert Aftalion, *Le développement de la fabrique et le travail à domicile dans les industries de l'habillement* (Paris: L. Larose et L. Tenin, 1906), pp. 106–9.

79. Aftalion, *Crise de l'industrie linière*, pp. 27–28; Picard, *Bilan d'un siècle*, pp. 333–34.

The dominance of machine-made products in the middle range of the product market thus pushed handwork into retreat. Handloom weavers found refuge in the coarsest grades, which were not profitable enough to mechanize, and in the finer grades machines were not sophisticated enough to produce. Many depositions from the 1904 enquête attest to this development. The Bourse du travail of Cholet reported that weavers who twenty years earlier had made their living weaving a cloth called "Sainte-Marie," used for making trousers, had been displaced by machines. These weavers now produced only kerchiefs. The justice of the peace of Cholet concurred, reporting that, after two decades of competition from mechanized weaving, rural weavers who used to produce a great variety of cloths could produce only kerchiefs.[80]

The depositions in the 1904 enquête further confirmed this shift, indicating that handloom weavers did not have difficulties finding work. Rather, handloom weavers complained uniformly of the declining quality of materials. The justice of the peace understood the trap ensnaring handloom weavers: "We make more and more products of inferior quality. They sell easily because of their low price. [But] the result is diminishing benefits." The Syndicats de prévoyance described the same phenomenon more fully: "Over the past twenty years great changes have occurred in production. The fine-quality articles have almost completely disappeared, replaced by low-priced articles. This has resulted in an increase in production. Gaining less from making these goods, the workers find themselves obliged to produce more, which only further increases the production." The Bourse du travail explained the situation in this way: "The patrons will try to show, no doubt, that the prices listed on the rate schedules have risen in the past twenty years. Unfortunately this is not the case, because even if prices have risen, salaries have fallen. . . . if the cost of making kerchiefs has increased, the material is finer and of lower quality, [so it takes] more passes to complete the same length of cloth than it did twenty years ago. [This] results in a reduction in salaries by at least 25 percent."[81]

These complaints reveal another area of advantage for hand production over machine production. Low-quality yarns, too brittle and uneven for machine work, could be transformed into good-quality cloth under the watchful eyes and skilled hands of the handloom

80. Aftalion, *Développement de la fabrique*, pp. 106–9, 132–36; A.N. C7318: Enquête textile 1904, Réponse de la Bourse du travail de Cholet.

81. A.N. C7318: Enquête textile 1904, Réponse du juge de paix de Cholet; Réponse de l'Union des syndicats professionnels d'ouvriers tisserands; Réponse de la Bourse du travail.

weaver. Such work reduced the productivity of handloom weavers, not to mention the insult to their skill and pride. Still, it permitted handloom production to compete effectively against machine production. Such a strategy, however, meant a loss in total earnings for handloom weavers, because producing good cloth from poor materials was time consuming.

Finally, industrialists tended to use capital equipment to meet only the constant component of demand.[82] Subcontracting was a cost-effective way to meet the seasonal variations in demand, the rush orders, and the small orders with unusual specifications and limited applications for bulk manufacture. In these cases, the subcontracts went to handloom producers.[83] Although this insurance for industrial producers against fluctuating demand carved out another specialization for handloom weaving, the effect was also a reduction in yearly income. A weaver might realize a good piece rate for the special orders, but the work was irregular.

Thus machine production and the factory system did not eliminate hand work and dispersed production. Using machines in the most cost-effective way meant preserving a sphere for small-scale producers. But machines circumscribed the range of production in which hand work could continue. So handloom weaving survived, and by the early twentieth century had even reached a stable state, but the livelihood of handloom weavers was clearly dependent on and structured by the mechanized sector.

This livelihood was increasingly an impoverished one. Daily income for handloom weavers varied widely throughout the region because of the range of cloths produced and the variety of ways handloom weaving could be adapted to complement powerloom production. In 1904 the Union des syndicats de prévoyance reported that, on average, handloom weavers earned as little as 1.5 francs a day. The Bourse du travail reported in its deposition that some handloom weavers in Cholet earned as little as 75–90 centimes a day. Incomes for rural weavers were slightly higher: the Bourse du travail estimated that rural weavers on average earned 1.0–1.25 francs per day. This estimate was corroborated by the report of the Chambre syndicale of Saint-Léger-sous-Cholet, which noted that, whereas a good strong weaver could net as much as 2 francs a day, average daily

82. As discussed in Chapter 2. See also Michael J. Piore, "Dualism as a Response to Flux and Uncertainty," in *Dualism and Discontinuities in Industrial Societies,* ed. Suzanne Berger and Piore (Cambridge: Cambridge University Press, 1980).
83. Aftalion, *Développement de la fabrique,* pp. 144–49.

incomes fell between 1.0 and 1.25 francs. The justice of the peace of Beaupréau reported a higher average daily income for the hand-loom weavers of his canton. Listing the maximum at 2.50 francs a day, or a yearly income of 750 francs, and the minimum at half that, he estimated that the average income was closer to 2 francs a day, or 600 francs a year.[84]

The wide range in incomes prevents a simple estimate of the per-centage changes since the 1880s. But clearly the range had shifted to a lower scale. The industrial report on Maine-et-Loire in 1880 listed the daily income range for handloom weavers as 1.75–2.50 francs. In 1883 the range was 1.25–3.0 francs, and that in 1885 was 1.5–3.0 francs.[85] The top of the scale did not decline dramatically over the next twenty years, by no more than 50 centimes; the bottom of the scale fell from 1.75 francs to 75–90 centimes. Most of the depositions agreed that piece rates and incomes had declined by a third over the last two decades of the nineteenth century.

The deteriorating standard of living for handloom weavers was one consequence of their inability to find workable alternatives. The fail-ure of socialist mobilization and of producers' cooperatives and asso-ciations to define better solutions meant that the future of handloom weaving, and the relation between hand labor and machine labor, was increasingly under the control of industrial capitalists. Thus, al-though handloom weaving survived by finding new niches in the product market, the economic life of small producers was defined by the risk-averting strategies of industrial capitalists.

This result reveals how far handloom weavers had come from their experiments of the 1880s and also fully exposes the contradictions implicit in attempts to define small producers as either wage workers or independent entrepreneurs. The common cause handloom weavers made with industrial works, though initially successful in defending piece-rates for handloom weavers, was later fraught with difficulties arising from fundamental differences in the structural positions of the two groups. As factory operatives fought their battles against ar-bitrary factory discipline and work rules and for their right to orga-nize, handloom weavers wanted mainly to negotiate and establish uniform piece rates. These different priorities worked against a sim-

---

84. A.N. C7318: Enquête textile 1904, Réponse de l'Union des syndicats professionnels d'ouvriers tisserands; Réponse de la Bourse du travail; Réponse de la Chambre syndicale des ouvriers tisserands de Saint-Léger-sous-Cholet; Réponse de justice de paix de canton de Beaupréau.
85. A.N. F12 4516B: Situation industrielle, Maine-et-Loire, arrondissement de Cholet, rapports des années 1880, 1883, 1885.

ple unity. The split in 1887 marked the end of a short florescence when textile workers, both small producers and factory operatives, were a united and powerful force in local affairs. The basic grievances remained alive in the next decades, and both factory operatives and handloom weavers won concessions and small victories, but the workers' and small producers' movement had lost its initial vitality. As Pierre Chupin cynically wrote about the movement in Cholet, "il y a beaucoup de pâte, mais pas de levain" ("there's a lot of dough, but not enough leavening).[86]

86. A.D. M-et-L 4M6/43: Rapport du Commissariat spécial de police, Angers, 21 April, 1896, lettre de Pierre Chupin à ses camarades d'Angers.

7

New Domestic Industries: The Sweated Trades

In the second half of the nineteenth century, a new confidence animated French urban culture. Although the problems of urban squalor and mass in-migration that emerged earlier in the century continued, urban renovation physically and mentally removed the overt reminders of their presence.[1] The urban bourgeoisie settled down to enjoy the material comforts of industrial and commercial growth. The increase in wealth, however, was not confined to the upper echelons of society. Throughout the century, increases in real wages and a rising standard of living created new groups of consumers, but again concentrated primarily in cities.[2] Under the banner of the "democratization of luxury," retailers and manufacturers sought to replicate with mass-produced goods the diversity and styles previously accessible only to an upper class clientele.

Business historians have documented the transformation of retail practices underlying these changes.[3] Cultural historians have discussed the new definitions of bourgeois identity and self-understanding, which became expressed increasingly through consumption.[4] In

1. See David H. Pinkney, *Napoleon III and the Rebuilding of Paris* (Princeton: Princeton University Press, 1958).

2. See Jean Fourastié, *Le grand espoir du XXième siècle, progrès technique, progrès économique, progrès social* (Paris: Presses universitaires de France, 1949), esp. pp. 46–47, 124–25, 198; also Fourastié, *Machinisme et bien-être* (Paris: Editions de Minuit, 1951).

3. Michael B. Miller, *The Bon Marché: Bourgeois Culture and the Department Store, 1869–1920* (Princeton: Princeton University Press, 1981); see also Alfred Chandler, *The Visible Hand: The Managerial Revolution in American Business* (Cambridge: Harvard University Press, 1977).

4. Rosalind H. Williams, *Dream Worlds: Mass Consumption in Late Nineteenth Century France* (Berkeley: University of California Press, 1982). See also, Rémy G. Saisselin, *The Bourgeois and the Bibelot* (New Brunswick: Rutgers University Press, 1984). For a study of

this chapter, I am primarily interested in what this new consumer culture and the new retail practices that accompanied it meant for production. In the last decades of the nineteenth century, new products and new specializations revitalized rural outwork in the Choletais. In addition to fine kerchiefs and coarse linens, many weaving communes began to produce finished goods for urban consumer markets, including shoes, undergarments, and household linens. This development was extremely important in the economic evolution of the region. The shoe and needle trades of the late nineteenth century became the basis for the light industries in the twentieth century. These new engagements however, did not, bring prosperity. Instead, just as in weaving, the new manufacturing concentrated in the sweated end of product markets.[5]

Theories of technical dualism try to explain the variety of ways to organize manufacturing in an industrial society by appealing to the structure of product markets or to the logic of production techniques.[6] These explanations address the problem at the level of general tendencies in capitalist production. This chapter has a very different goal. Using theories of technical dualism as a backdrop, I seek to specify those local conditions that encouraged the adoption of the sweated alternative as opposed to other forms of mass production. In particular, I argue that conditions in the labor market were significant factors in entrepreneurs' choices between different production strategies in the Choletais.[7] My first task is to explore the economics of outwork. I begin by examining in detail the specific organization of production and the position of local producers in na-

---

the role of female sensibilities in shaping production priorities, and particularly the role of bourgeois women as consumers, see Whitney Walton, " 'To Triumph before Feminine Taste': Bourgeois Women's Consumption and Hand Methods of Production in Mid-Nineteenth-Century Paris," *Business History Review* 60 (Winter 1986): 541–63.

5. For a comprehensive bibliography on the sweated trades at the end of the nineteenth and early twentieth centuries, consult Paul Boyaval, *La lutte contre le sweating-system* (Paris: Taffin-Lefort, 1911); the bibliography cites the literature on England, France, Belgium, Switzerland, the United States, Germany, Austria, Australia, and New Zealand.

6. On the economic logic of sweating, see Duncan Bythell, *The Sweated Trades: Outwork in the Nineteenth Century* (London: Batsford Academic, 1978); see also James A. Schmiechen, *Sweated Industries and Sweated Labor: The London Clothing Trades, 1860–1914* (Urbana: University of Illinois Press, 1984).

7. Paul Gemähling, *Travailleurs au rabais: La lutte syndicale contre le sous-concurrence ouvrier* (Paris: Bloud et cie, 1910). See also Jill Rubery and Frank Wilkinson, "Outwork and Segmented Labor Markets," in *The Dynamics of Labor Market Segmentation*, ed. Frank Wilkinson (New York: Academic Press, 1981), pp. 115–32, and Christine Craig, Jill Rubery, Roger Tarling, and Frank Wilkinson, *Labor Market Structure, Industrial Organization, and Low Pay* (Cambridge: Cambridge University Press, 1982).

tional markets. For both the needle trades and shoe manufacturing, I show that cheap labor is the key to understanding the local choice of technology. Understanding why labor was cheap is the subject of Chapter 9, where I explain the dynamics of labor market stratification by focusing on social processes within weaving households.

Dependence on cheap labor locked local entrepreneurs into strategies, both social and economic, aimed at keeping down labor costs. In the final section of this chapter I explore how entrepreneurs interpreted their own actions. Small-scale entrepreneurs subscribed to and perpetuated a myth of continuity in small-scale production which was instrumental in establishing the uniqueness of the region's economy and identity in relation to the rest of industrial France. This interpretation veiled the actual power relations between bosses and workers in the sweated trades, by obfuscating the differences between the social relations of production in handloom weaving and those in shoe manufacturing and needle trades. Exploring the social basis of this ideology reveals the economic vulnerability of this group of entrepreneurs. Their slim margin of survival rested on sets of social relations symbolized through notions of tradition and continuity which, for very different reasons, were also shared by handloom weavers.

The Economics of Outwork I: Homework and the Needle Trades

The needle trades in the Choletais developed as the finishing branch of the textile industry. Sometime in the last decades of the nineteenth century, possibly in the 1880s, the most important industrial textile producers such as Brémond, Pellaumail, and Turpault began to sell finished products directly to urban retailers rather than send their cloth to wholesale merchants. Cholet's trademark became associated with a new specialization, household linens. In addition to plain and decorated linen kerchiefs, Cholet's manufacturers sold a tremendous variety of sheets, pillow cases, tablecloths, and napkins adorned with open-work embroidery (*broderie à jour*).

The finishing trade hired a large number of female homeworkers in Cholet and in the countryside. It is difficult to assess how many women were brought into this new branch of the textile industry, because the French census did not pay particular attention to homeworkers until the census of 1896. Even in this census, we cannot easily assess the number of women who worked in household linens because the diversity of their occupational titles tended to amalgamate these workers with workers in other needle trades. To give a general indication of the level of employment in the region's finishing trade, the population census of 1896 reported 5,065 of these *lingères* in Maine-et-Loire. In 1901 the number had risen slightly to 5,143 and after the First World War the number had grown to 10,000–12,000 women working at home.[8]

The new specialization was another aspect of industrialists' efforts to consolidate their control of the local textile industry. They stood at the center of this new network: their factories produced the linen and linen-cotton blends used in the finishing trades; they subcontracted the cutting, sewing, and embroidering to middlemen; and they sold the finished products to retailers in bulk. Industrialists used their access to materials and to markets to lock out their small-scale competitors. By further closing off alternatives, they subordinated the rural fabricants and handloom weavers to contractual work.

The subcontracting network was complex and competitive. Many of the subcontractors who organized the finishing operation, subdivided the tasks, and organized the outworkers were rural fabricants in the linen trade. They added finishing to their kerchief commerce. Other subcontractors were carters (*voituriers*) who transported the semifinished and finished goods. These carters were often intermediaries who further subcontracted to female grocers, small storekeepers, and innkeepers living in the bourgs of rural communes. These women, in turn, put out among their neighbors and customers. There were many routes in subcontracting. Someone with five thousand francs, a rudimentary familiarity with the work process, and access to workers could set himself or herself up as a subcontractor. However, the ease of entry also meant a high failure rate. Subcontractors tended to underbid each other, producing thin profit margins.[9]

Locally, Cholet's shift toward finished consumer goods was part of the power struggles among different groups of producers and mer-

8. Ministère du commerce, Office du travail, Résultats statistiques du recensement des industries et professions [le dénombrement général de la population du 29 mars 1896] (Paris: Imprimerie nationale, 1901). Statistique générale, *Résultats statistiques du recensement de la population effectué le 24 mars 1901*. vol. 3 (Paris: Imprimerie nationale, 1906); Chambre de commerce de Cholet, *Monographie géographique et économique de l'arrondissement* (n.d., ca. 1924), p. 31.

9. Ministère du commerce, Office du travail, *Enquête sur le travail à domicile dans l'industrie de la lingerie*. 5 vols. (Paris: Imprimerie nationale, 1908–1911), 5:19–27 (hereafter *Enquête sur le travail à domicile, lingerie*).

chants in the local industry. Nationally, building a finishing industry on the basis of an established textile industry was not an isolated phenomenon. Other textile regions made similar changes. Significantly, Cholet's longtime competitors in the north, the linen producers of the Cambrésis, took the same route.[10] The household linens of the Choletais also faced competition from the east, in the embroidered sheets and other decorated woven housewares of the Vosges.[11] The expansion of needlework and outwork was thus not unique to the Choletais.

In the broadest sense, these textile-producing regions responded to changing consumer demands, but consumer desires were themselves shaped by a revolution in retail methods. At the center of the revolution was the department store. The quintessence of consumer culture, the *grands magasins* of Paris can be traced directly to the *magasins de nouveauté* of the 1830s and 1840s. These dry goods stores invented new merchandising techniques based on selling at low prices for high turnover. They bought in bulk at discount prices and sold for cash only. Taking a lower profit on each item, these stores expected to gain primarily from the volume of sales and a quick turnover in stock. They relied on a plentiful flow of cash to finance their operations. Many Parisian department stores of the 1850s, like the Bon Marché, the Printemps, and the Bazaars de Hotel de Ville, adopted this basic principle on a grander scale and streamlined their operations for efficiency. These retail giants dominated not only both sides of the Seine but much of French manufacturing as well.

High-volume buying and rapid turnover required tight control over the flow of supplies. By necessity, the retailers tried to extend their control over production. Department stores bypassed the established wholesale networks, preferring to deal directly with manufacturers through their own representatives in the field. Often it was the department stores that obliged suppliers to provide finished goods.[12] In addition, department stores often bought from small firms, taking advantage of the fact that, as the firm's most important customers, department stores were able to dictate the terms of the supply and the design. Department stores also used this leverage to demand lower rates. Their ultimate goal in all these price-cutting strategies was to

10. Chambre des députés, session 1904, *Procès-verbaux de la commission chargée de procéder à une enquête sur l'état de l'industrie textile et la condition des ouvriers tisseurs* (Paris: Imprimerie de la Chambre des députés, 1906), 5:212, 217.
11. *Enquête sur le travail à domicile, lingerie*, 2:695.
12. Ibid., 5:18.

enhance the competitiveness of their stores by passing on the savings to their customers.

At the retail end, department stores were designed for the pleasures of consumption. To the marvel of their customers, the store decor created a world of endless variety, a "fantasy land of colors, sensations and dreams," all available for purchase at bargain prices. Browsing and buying became public events. White sales at the Bon Marché were famous affairs. Michael Miller describes them: "On these occasions the entire store was adorned in white: white sheets, white towels, white curtains, white flowers ad infinitum, all forming a single blanc motif that covered even stairways and balconies. Gone were the days when solid and stiffly starched family sheets passed from one generation to the next. The new varieties of *linge de maison* (household linen) symbolized the abundance in the lifestyle of Belle Epoque bourgeois and petty bourgeois households.[13]

The varieties and subspecialities offered to customers in the lingerie departments of these large stores stretched the limits of imagination. First of all there were men's shirts: white shirts and colored shirts in cottons, in linens, in flannel, in plain and fancy weaves; men's drawers made of linen, silks, and flannel; vests, shirt fronts, collars, and cuffs. Then there was the branch of the trade specialized for women and children. Lingerie for women incorporated an endless variety of articles: chemises de jour and chemises de nuit, camisoles, slips, dressing gowns, collars, sleeves, cuffs, pillow cases, sheets, napkins, and so on. For children, there was an equally sophisticated array of garments and infant layettes.[14]

With its many subbranches, the lingerie trade was among the most complex of the needle trades. Specialties differed from one region to the next. Paris and its suburbs constituted the largest center in France and also the most diverse. Parisian production covered the entire range, from shirts to baby layettes, from the coarsest grades to the finest. The center of France, including the departments of the Cher, Indre-et-Loire, and Loire-et-Cher, specialized in men's shirts and undergarments for women and children. In the east, the departments of the Vosges and Meurthe-et-Moselle, the lingerie trade for household linens and for women's and children's undergarments grew out of the region's famed embroidery trades. Here the addition of finished gar-

13. Miller, *Bon Marché*, pp. 178–89.
14. Alfred Picard, *Le bilan d'un siècle (1801–1900)*, vol. 5 (Paris: Imprimerie nationale, 1906), pp. 426–29.

ment work was seen as the solution to a crisis of hand embroidery that followed the introduction of embroidery machines.[15]

The lingerie trade in France employed a significant proportion of the female working population. According to the census of 1896, 1,234,916 women worked in the trade, of whom nearly 56 percent (688,098 workers) worked at home. The number of women employed in the lingerie trade represented about 57 percent of all women employed in industry. Nationally, female lingerie workers were three times more numerous than women employed in textiles.[16]

The Organization of Production

To many contemporary observers, the actual organization of production in the lingerie trade appeared to defy easy description. Although reform movements aimed at eliminating abusive work conditions in the needle trades had characterized the trade as dominated by homework and hand labor, a significant portion of production was located in factories where the work was done with the aid of machines. Furthermore, there was not a simple division between mechanized production in factories and hand labor at home. Because the general purpose sewing machine was highly portable (the adaptation of electric motors, as well as small kerosene and petroleum motors, made these machines even faster without altering their flexibility), many women worked on the latest-model machines at home. Alternatively, we can find many cases where women in factories stitched only by hand. Given these variations, it was difficult to discern the underlying principles behind the choice of technology and location of work.[17]

15. *Enquête sur le travail à domicile, lingerie,* 5:17.

16. The total active female population in 1896 was 6,382,658, of whom 2,750,364 were employed in agriculture and 2,178,894 in industry. Ministère du commerce, Office du travail, *Résultats statistiques.*

17. For a history of the invention and marketing of the sewing machine, see Ruth Brandon, *A Capitalist Romance: Singer and the Sewing Machine* (Philadelphia: Lippincott, 1977). The important transformation of artisanal needle trades took place before Isaac Singer introduced his machine to the European public in the Great Exhibition of 1851. The greater technical efficiency of the sewing machine only translated into higher profits within the appropriate social relations of production. As indicated in Christopher H. Johnson's study of the Parisian tailoring trades, "Economic Change and Artisan Discontent: The Tailors' History, 1800–1848," in *Revolution and Reaction: 1848 and the Second French Republic,* ed. Roger Price (London: Croom Helm, 1975), pp. 87–114, the changes pushed through by merchant clothiers early in the nineteenth century—extensive subdivision of labor and taking the task of coordinating production away from master tailors—were far more corrosive of

Asking manufacturers to generalize about their choices only confused the matter, as the French Office du travail discovered when it conducted a national survey between 1905 and 1908 on the conditions of the lingerie trade. When investigators asked manufacturers in various regions whether they preferred to group workers into factories or put out to homeworkers, they were of mixed opinions and often gave contradictory reasons.

Those who favored workshops and factories argued that the pace of production was more rapid and regular when work was centralized. Entrepreneurs had greater control over quality as well, it was claimed: they could supervise the work more closely, ensuring that mistakes were repaired and guarding against waste. With centralized production, there were fewer problems with uncertain delivery dates and irregular and faulty work. Partisans of workshops and factories also argued that centralized production was better for workers. They earned more money, worked shorter days, and labored under more hygienic conditions.[18]

Manufacturers who favored outwork argued that it was more economical for them. Overhead costs were significantly lower. Capital was not immobilized in equipment and materials, and during the slack season the entrepreneurs did not waste their investments in idled plants. They could more easily reduce work to a minimum than if they had regularly employed workers. These manufacturers claimed that the quality of work done at home was not necessarily inferior and often was superior. In addition, outwork gave entrepreneurs more flexibility. They did not have to follow state legislation on work hours and work conditions. Moreover, because workers were dispersed, there were fewer strikes and no unions to challenge their authority. For women, they argued, homework provided

the artisanal organization of the garment industry than was the introduction of machine work. In fact, the latter was possible only after the proletarianization of the trade. For the effects of these processes on women workers in the Parisian garment trades, see Joan W. Scott, "Men and Women in the Parisian Garment Trades: Discussions of Family and Work in the 1830s and 1840s," in *The Power of the Past,* ed. Pat Thane and Geoffrey Crossick (Cambridge: Cambridge University Press, 1985), pp. 67–93. For a similar discussion of the garment industry in London, see Schmiechen, *Sweated Industries and Sweated Labor.* For a discussion on similar trends in Germany, see Karin Hausen, "Technical Progress and Women's Labour in the Nineteenth Century: The Social History of the Sewing Machine," in *The Social History of Politics: Critical Perspectives in West German Historical Writing since 1945,* ed. Georg Iggers (New York: St. Martin's Press, 1986), pp. 259–81.

18. *Enquête sur le travail à domicile, lingerie,* 5:58–60.

a way to combine work and home life; hence, it was more moral than factory work.[19]

Economist Albert Aftalion argued, from preliminary findings of the Office du travail survey, that production arrangements were influenced by the nature of fashion markets. The logic of factory production, he reasoned, did not always match the demands of a fashion industry. To adopt the factory system effectively, the demand for a particular style or for a particular decorative design must be great enough to justify a long-run series. Product-specific machines could be operated profitably only if the mounting and specifications did not change and machines were not often idled. For these reasons men's clothing, especially army clothes and work clothes, for which style changes were less frequent and demand was more constant and predictable, became and remained one of the few branches of the cloth-finishing industry to be located in factories. In other areas of the industry, the demand for variety and seasonal changes in materials and styles often went against the logic and economic advantages of factory-based mass-production strategies. The extreme seasonality of the industry and the constant changes in fashion tended to favor smaller workshops and homework.[20]

Given these efficiency arguments for matching production strategy to product markets, one might expect preferences for work organization to have been divided along specialties. But this proved not to be the case. The results of the survey clearly indicated that, taking the nation as a whole, French entrepreneurs used homework and shopwork in almost equal proportions regardless of product specialty. Tallying the advantages and disadvantages of each, investigators were surprised to learn that the most important factor governing the choice between homework and shopwork seemed to be location: "The geographic situation of the establishments—the conditions which include the particular industrial and social situation—exerts more influence on whether homework or factory work is preferable than the type of articles made."[21] The importance of regional varia-

19. Ibid.

20. Albert Aftalion, *Le développement de la fabrique et le travail à domicile dans les industries de l'habillement* (Paris: L. Larose et L. Tenin, 1906), esp. pp. 65–96, 144–56. For a recent version of the same argument, see Michael J. Piore, "Dualism as a Response to Flux and Uncertainty," and "Technological Foundations of Dualism and Discontinuity," in *Dualism and Discontinuities in Industrialized Societies,* ed. Suzanne Berger and Piore (Cambridge: Cambridge University Press, 1980).

21. *Enquête sur le travail à domicile, lingerie,* 5:60–62.

tions tell us that entrepreneurs had to pay attention not only to the nature of product markets but also to differences in the conditions of local labor markets.

For example, in the department of Cher, one of the most important centers for the lingerie trade, manufacturers told investigators that they increasingly resorted to factories and small workshops because competition from other industries and from agriculture made it difficult to recruit homeworkers. At Bourges, many women homeworkers left the trade to work for higher wages in an establishment making army clothes. At Aubigny, a men's shirt factory competed against lingerie, and at Vierzon a porcelain factory was the chief competitor. The situation was the same in the department of Indre. At Villedieu (Indre), the construction of a shirt factory by Parisians and the development of a porcelain works attracted workers away from the lingerie trade. Facing these difficulties, local entrepreneurs searched the countryside for homeworkers but found the rural situation equally unsatisfactory. As one of them explained,

> all the finishing work is done in the countryside [and] that is the inconvenience. The workers work only when they have nothing better to do. They do their lingerie work between All Saints Day and May, most often when watching over their goats. In summer they work in the fields; they work in the harvest and gather grapes, which lasts a long time because there are so many large vineyards. Between the rush season and slow season in manufacturing, which depends on many factors, from time to time we are blocked by the mismatch between our need for workers and times when we have enough labor.

Many rural entrepreneurs complained that it was difficult to push farm women to work sufficient hours. They sewed only when they had nothing more pressing to do. Between the seasonal demands of fieldwork and harvest and the daily demands of the farmyard animals and dairying, many women would do needlework for only an hour a day, and that was not enough for the needs of the industry.[22]

Similar difficulties explain why the industrial northeast never became an important center for the lingerie trade. In the town of Saint-Quentin, for example, too many competing industries hired female workers. In the surrounding countryside, entrepreneurs complained that the work rhythm was too irregular. Women abandoned needlework for farmwork. Beet cultivation, especially, took female labor

22. Ibid., 5:39–43.

away from needlework. In one center, Villers-Outreaux in the department of the Nord, most of the year there was a sufficient female population for the lingerie trade, but the situation was untenable because during the harvest season most families migrated to the Soissonais.[23]

Indeed, finding appropriate workers was much more problematic than many urban merchants, and historians of the sweated trades, might have imagined. Many manufacturers thought married women provided an ideal labor force. They thought that women wanted homework because it allowed them to combine and balance reproductive activities with wage earning. The nature of hand work and piece work was such that women could work when they liked. They were not obliged to meet the regimen of machines and an established workday. They could allow the necessities of day-to-day family life to interrupt their labor and turn their empty hours into cash. Manufacturers argued that, since many women worked for supplemental incomes, "une salaire d'appoint" or "pin money," they would be relatively indifferent to low wages. The fact that all women were presumed to know how to sew, thus requiring no training at the entrepreneur's expense, added to the vision that women with domestic responsibilities were the ideal homeworkers.

But there was not an inexhaustible reservoir of female workers ready to be tapped. Reality did not mesh with such wishful thinking. The volatile character of fashion markets may well have encouraged entrepreneurs toward dispersed production, in order to minimize investments in capital and product-specific machinery and to emphasize flexibility in the production process. We should not, however, minimize the tremendous problems incurred by dispersing production. The geographic successes and failures of the French lingerie trade suggest several often overlooked aspects of labor relations peculiar to outwork.

First, even though the fashion trades were highly seasonal and the conditions of retail markets favored outwork and even part-time workers, business succeeded only when the entrepreneur controlled the work season and the slack seasons and could reasonable regulate hours and productivity. In other words, workers had to be flexible according to the needs of the entrepreneur and not according to their own needs. This distinction is crucial because it gives a different meaning to the "matching" of labor demand and labor supply. The usual analysis of homework presents it as an adaptive strategy for un-

23. Ibid., 5:46–47.

stable markets but underemphasizes that homework is an entrepreneurial strategy for minimizing risks by passing on their consequences to workers. Recognizing this fact highlights the power imbalances in the social relations of production necessary for this strategy to be viable economically. Thus, when workers had many choices or could impose their own priorities onto the work routine, as could women in agricultural households, manufacturers who had the capital resources felt that centralized production was preferable to homework. Manufacturers closer to the edge of survival, and unable to afford the capital investment this production strategy demanded, probably had to abandon the trade.

Second, although gathering workers together introduces problems of collective action, homework is not free of disciplinary problems. For dispersed production to function effectively, entrepreneurs must hold even greater disciplinary power than factory foremen, because homeworkers must be regulated without direct supervision. Here we must be careful not to exaggerate the power of the entrepreneur. This power to enforce sweated conditions did not necessarily derive from the relations of production. More often, entrepreneurs were benefiting from other, more intimate forms of discipline.

The Choletais

The entrepreneurs and subcontractors of the Choletais favored homework. The obstacles blocking the successful organization of outwork in the fashion trades in other regions did not impinge on the fabricants of the Choletais. This was one of the few centers nationally where the entrepreneurs did not complain of labor shortages.[24] The workforce was available year round and could be depended on to work at their trades as a primary occupation. Local fabricants did not have to adjust to changes in the labor supply with the demands of agriculture. They enjoyed a high degree of control over a decentralized production process.

By their own testimony, many entrepreneurs began with workshops and small factories for finishing work but soon abandoned them in favor of outwork. Putting-out did create problems for distributing and collecting the work, and some merchants complained that

24. Ibid., 5:43, 127.

the quality of work suffered. For example, one fabricant noted that he could not produce the finer decorations that required detailed supervision. But the benefits of outwork clearly outweighed the difficulties. As another fabricant explained, "production is more intense at home." One fabricant claimed that workers preferred to work at home. His assistant elaborated on this theme: "In the factory, workers can earn 25–30 francs [a month], [but] at home they can earn almost 60 francs." This difference in pay, a representative of a competing firm confided to the investigators, could be attributed to the fact that homework was not regulated by protective legislation.[25]

Although in principle homeworkers could work as much or as little as they wanted or needed, most homeworkers in the region worked 11–13 hours a day. This is longer than workers covered by factory regulations, which allowed 10 hours a day. Workers in the Choletais worked the longest average workdays of all the lingères surveyed in the national inquiry.[26] No disciplinarian obliged these workers to put in such long hours; their low piece rates did. By necessity they disciplined themselves. Most homeworkers prolonged the workday in order to earn a decent daily income.

Piece rates were extremely low in the Choletais, and, as everywhere, lingerie work was highly specialized. Tasks in the finishing trade were extensively subdivided. One piece often passed through five, six, seven, and even eight workers. Finishing pillow cases, for example, was subdivided into the following tasks, with a different specialized worker performing each task: drawing threads paid 90 centimes per dozen; basting and quilting paid about 70 centimes per dozen; making button holes by machine paid 40 centimes per dozen; and sewing buttons by hand paid 10 centimes for every six dozen buttons. For a final finishing, the pillow cases were distributed for embroidery—yet another special subbranch of the finishing trades, with its own elaborate divisions and pay scale. A similar division of tasks and piece rates existed for sheets. Napkins paid 34–40 centimes a dozen, but it often required a worker 12–14 hours to realize that dozen. Hemming hand towels and dish towels by hand required almost 10 hours of labor to finish a dozen. This task, however, paid only 35 centimes per dozen. Finishing handkerchiefs paid 40–60 centimes per dozen depending on the style. On a good day, working by hand,

25. Ibid., 2:693–96.
26. Ibid., 5:80–84.

one worker reported that she could finish eighteen kerchiefs. Others reported a productivity of two dozen kerchiefs a day.[27]

After 12–14 hour workdays, typically needlewomen could earn as little as 10, 15, or 20 francs a month, depending on their specialty. Rarely, a woman earned 80 francs a month. These rates could support a family; in fact, many of the daily wages could not even support a single earner. On average, each of the twelve workers interviewed by investigators contributed about a third of the household resources. Individually, yearly wages and the contributions differed dramatically, from 8 percent to as high as 53 percent.[28] Clearly, this was part-time pay for full-time work. Women did not fill empty hours after housework and family duties with a little stitching. Sewing invaded family life. Stray threads littered the floors. Patterns, finished pieces, material, scissors, and pins covered the family table. Children helped with this work, and sometimes even husbands lent a hand.

Some needlewomen made a good living at home and were content. These were usually women who used sewing machines. The cost of the machines was often beyond the means of the average worker. Some fabricants rented machines to their workers at one franc per month but obliged their workers to accept only the fabricant's commissions. More typically, workers had many complaints. Besides low wages, many complained of eye strain and back problems. The most bitter were the *tireuses:* pulling stray threads and working on the imperfections of the cloth was a thankless and lowly paid job. One of the investigators noted with concern that some of these young women, with their blistery and swollen eyes, looked prematurely old.[29]

Despite the many complaints, however, fabricants had no difficulties finding workers. Unlike the center or the north of France, where fabricants complained of labor shortages, labor was abundant in the Choletais and the labor force was willing to accept the conditions. The success of outwork in this region bespeaks the power relations between entrepreneurs and workers. Clearly, fabricants were powerful enough to impose the kinds of conditions just described. Their power derived from the limited opportunities for female employment and the urgency that must have motivated these lingères to work such long hours for such low returns.

27. Ibid., 2:696–97, 700–715.
28. Ibid.
29. Ibid., 2:691–94.

The Economics of Outwork II: Homework and the Shoe Trade

Compared with other shoe-producing regions, the organization of shoe production in the Choletais was unusual. Outwork in shoe manufacturing expanded in the Choletais when most important centers of shoe production in France began to centralize manufacturing and to use specialized powered machinery. Between the 1870s and the First World War, major shoe producers on the Continent and in Great Britain were forced to reorganize production in order to increase output and refine their products. Whereas in the 1870s and 1880s outwork had been the basic organization for the mass production of shoes, by the early twentieth century the number of outworkers had declined dramatically at the national level.[30] The Choletais moved against this current. Local entrepreneurs seemed to favor the production strategies discarded by others.

Competition from the United States drove European producers to rethink their production strategies. Although it was not until the late 1890s that American-made shoes began to inundate European domestic markets, American producers had already successfully entered many of Europe's, especially Great Britain's, overseas markets. In this competition, European mass-produced footwear did not compare well to American footwear. Importers complained that British mass-produced shoes were ill fitting, clumsy in design and construction, and shoddily finished. In the same product range, American mass-produced footwear was cheaper, fit better (because Americans standardized half-sizes) and was more durable and more uniform in quality. American mass-produced shoes also rivaled French shoes aimed at a higher-quality market. It was not that the American producers could replicate the quality of finer hand-stitched shoes, but that the quality of the mass-produced shoe could approach hand-stitched shoes and was preferred by some consumers because it was cheaper. To compete, major European manufacturers began to emulate the American system.[31]

The popularity of American boots and shoes at home and abroad attested to the success attained by centralizing, mechanizing, and imposing uniform standards. Two important inventions patented and

30. Aftalion, *Développement de la fabrique*, pp. 51–61.
31. Ibid., pp. 61–64; P. Head, "Boots and Shoes," in *The Development of British Industry and Foreign Competition, 1875–1914*, ed. Derek H. Aldcroft (London: Allen and Unwin, 1968), pp. 158–85.

distributed by Americans, the McKay sewing machine and the Goodyear welt stitcher, gave American producers their advantage. Mechanizing shoe production had begun with the adaptation of the sewing
machines for leather. There were several models of machines for
stitching uppers in operation in the 1850s, but it was the machines
produced by McKay and Goodyear in the 1860s and 1870s that transformed the output and quality of mass-produced shoes.[32]

In 1858, Lyman R. Blake, a shoemaker in Massachusetts, invented
a machine to sew the soles of the shoes to the uppers. This machine
was subsequently improved by Robert Mathias and later manufactured and distributed by Gordon McKay. The machine was first used
in Lynn, Massachusetts, in the early 1860s. It was said that the
McKay machine, more than any other, transformed modern shoe production. It lightened the construction of the shoe by making it possible to build shoes with thread instead of pegs and nails.[33]

The basic principle behind the Goodyear welt machine was developed in 1862 by August Destouy, a New York mechanic. Destouy invented a machine with a curved needle to stitch turned shoes. The
machine was later improved by mechanics employed by Charles
Goodyear, adapted to sew welts in the bottom of the shoe, and patented as the Goodyear welt machine in 1871 and 1875. This machine
reproduced the quality of hand-sewn shoes but worked 54 times
faster than sewing with awl and thread.[34]

When the French Office du travail conducted a study of homework
in the shoe industry in 1909, the majority of manufacturers interviewed preferred mechanized production to homework and hand labor. Yet, despite their preference, most manufacturers noted that
homework and hand labor were unlikely to disappear entirely, certainly not in the bespoke, luxury end of the market. In addition, dispersed production and hand work were likely to continue even in
the lower reaches of the market. Although homework was on the decline nationally, manufacturers predicted that it would expand and
prosper in some small villages and in nonindustrial regions because
rural workers often accepted lower wages. The lower cost of production in the countryside, in turn, threatened urban homework. Although many urban bootmakers and small manufacturers continued

32. Ruth T. Wilcox, *The Mode in Footwear* (New York: Scribner's 1948), p. 139; see also
B. E. Hazard, *The Organization of the Boot and Shoe Industry in Massachusetts before 1875*
(Cambridge: Harvard University Press, 1921).
33. Frederick J. Allen, *The Shoe Industry* (Boston: Vocation Bureau, 1916), p. 58.
34. Ibid., p. 59.

to put out work, market conditions were forcing many small manufacturers to move out of the cheaper end of the product market to produce higher-quality shoes or to centralize production into factories and workshops.[35]

The Choletais was one of the new locations where outwork was introduced late in the nineteenth century. Shoe production prospered in the Choletais because it aimed at a special segment of the product market. As one of the first generation of entrepreneurs admitted, the first products of the new manufacture were primitive and in poor taste. The first manufacturers used brightly colored canvases with gaudy designs, trying to imitate the espadrilles popular in that era. It was only in the 1890s that the Choletais established its own reputations for products known in the trade as "genre Choletais." Several local firms, notably in the communes of Le-May-sur-Evre and Villedieu-la-Blouère, produced finer grades of leather shoes, but these were the exceptions. The genre Choletais consisted primarily of *pantoufles* and *chaussons*—slippers and light shoes with soft soles, often without heels. The uppers were made from soft leathers, felt, velour, or canvas, and the soles were of leather or felt. These shoes found a ready market in the large urban areas of France. About half the annual production was sold to retailers and wholesalers in Paris. The other half went to the large industrial cities of the northeast: Lille, Armentières, Roubaix-Tourcoing. Their chief selling point was low price.[36]

Entrepreneurs in the Choletais kept prices low by minimizing the cost of materials, labor, and tools. The soft soles and uppers did not require costly materials, since felt, lambskin, and canvas were cheaper than well-tanned and thicker leathers such as calfskin or cowhide. In addition, the Choletais specialized in "turned shoes." The "turn" method was used in making fine shoes for women and children, as well as for light sports shoes and slippers. The shoe was made wrong side out and then turned right side out. After piecing and sewing together the lining and the uppers, the sole was fastened to the last (the shoe form). The uppers were drawn over the last, wrong side out, and then sewn to the sole through a channel cut at the edge of the sole. The resulting seam did not show in the finished shoe. The turned shoe could be made by machine, but was just as easily made

---

35. Office du travail, *Enquête sur le travail à domicile dans l'industrie de la chaussure* (Paris: Imprimerie nationale, 1914), pp. 544–46.

36. René Chéné, *Les débuts du commerce et de l'industrie de la chaussure dans la région de Cholet* (Maulévier, Maine-et-Loire: Hérault, 1980), pp. 63–67, 75–81, 114.

by hand.[37] Local entrepreneurs favored this style because of the possibility of hand work. By specializing in hand-sewn slippers and light shoes, they further reduced production costs by eliminating the need for costly machinery. Except for cutting and pattern and form making, the "turned shoe" was entirely executed by homeworkers. Homework represented another saving on the cost of running and maintaining workshops and factories. Finally and most important, it was the low cost of labor itself and the availability of homeworkers in the region that made the production of genre Choletais a feasible undertaking.

With the exception of several towns in the Pyrénées and in the Isère, as well as some factories in Nancy, this style of light shoe and slipper was almost exclusively produced in the Choletais. In effect, the Choletais entered a market vacated by other more established centers of shoe production like Fougères, Nîmes, Romans, and Limoges. These centers left the low-price end of the market because labor agitation and strikes had increased their labor costs. Manufacturers in these regions began to rely more on machinery and switched to more expensive shoes, creating an opportunity for an economically depressed manufacturing region like the Choletais.[38]

The Division of Labor and Composition of the Labor Force

For a more detailed view of the division of labor and the composition of the labor force, we are particularly indebted to the assiduous census taker of the 1911 population census of the commune of Villedieu-la-Blouère. Villedieu-la-Blouère is a typical commune located in the interior bocage and was active in the linen industry, shoe manufacture, and needle trades. The 1911 population census is particularly useful for studies of the organization of its shoe industry, because the census taker noted not only the general branch of industry when he recorded occupation but also the person's specialization, the place of employment, and whether the person worked at home. From this information we can reconstruct the general division of tasks in the industry, the sexual division of labor, and the composition of the labor force by sex and age.

37. Ibid., pp. 64–65. Allen, *Shoe Industry,* pp. 129, 315.
38. Chéné, *Débuts du commerce,* p. 46.

There were two shoe firms in the bourg of Villedieu in 1911. Maison Ménard-Raffegeau produced fashionable leather shoes ("les articles fantaisie"), and Maison Rousseau produced cheaper grades of light shoes (le genre choletais).[39] Most of the local merchant families prominent in the linen trade had a hand in the development of the shoe industry. Victor Ménard came from a family long established in Villedieu-la-Blouère. They were fabricants who dealt primarily in kerchiefs. René Raffegeau, Ménard's partner, was the son of a local baker who was active as a middleman in linen kerchiefs before venturing into the shoe trade. Philbert Thomas, at one time mayor of Villedieu-la-Blouère, and a fabricant de mouchoirs whose family had been merchant/putters-out in the linen trade since before the eighteenth century, was reputed to have started the first shoe firm in the commune. In 1902, Thomas went into the slipper business with a local shoemaker named Morinneau.[40] The exact shape of this partnership is unclear. It is possible that Thomas was involved with Maison Rousseau. In 1936 the firm was renamed Rousseau-Robert. Henri Robert of Rousseau-Robert was Thomas's son-in-law. After the First World War, Philbert's son Thomas began his own shoe firm, as did Morinneau's son. The origins of the four main shoe firms in the commune were thus linked to the fabricant families in linen production.

Shoe production in the first decades of the new manufacture combined homework with production in workshops according to the following subdivision of tasks.[41] Cutting was done exclusively in workshops under careful supervision. In this department, the leathers and cloths used to make the upper shoe and its lining were sorted and cut to preshaped patterns that set the style and basic shape of the final product. The same sets of operations were used to cut the soles. Only adult men (called *coupeurs*) were hired for this operation. In the next step, the cut pieces were put out to homeworkers to "close" the upper shoe. In this operation, female stitchers (*piqueuses*) sewed the outer pieces and lining together, mostly by hand and rarely on a sewing machine. Stitching was an exclusively female task. Next, the completed uppers were put out to another group of specialized workers, *monteurs* and *monteuses,* who attached the uppers to the sole. In Villedieu-la-Blouère, the "lasting" and "making" operations were performed by homeworkers, the majority of whom were women and

39. Ibid., p. 55.
40. Paul Bouyx, "Naissance de la chaussure dans le Choletais," *Bulletin de la Société des sciences, lettres et beaux-arts de Cholet,* 1948–49, p. 153.
41. Ibid., pp. 155–156; Chéné, *Débuts du commerce,* pp. 95–203.

occasionally adolescent boys. With the uppers and soles attached, the shoes were sent back to the workshop for heeling, cleaning, polishing, treeing, and boxing. These tasks, which finished the shoes and readied them for sale, were subdivided again by sex and age. Heeling and finishing the shoe were done by adult men; cleaning and polishing, lacing, and so on were done by young women (the only tasks performed by women in the factory); and treeing and boxing were assigned to adolescent boys.

Of the 129 shoeworkers in Villedieu-la-Blouère in 1911, 76 workers (60 percent) were female and 53 workers (40 percent) were male. Fifty-nine percent of the workers worked at home, and 88 percent of the homeworkers were women. The high percentage of female workers was unusual for the shoe industry. By comparison, 69 percent of shoeworkers in Lynn, Massachusetts, were male and 31 percent female; in Paris, 58 percent were male and 42 percent female.[42]

This difference in sex ratio was built on a more fundamental difference in the allocation of tasks between factory and outwork. The allocation of employees among departments within the factory was quite similar in Lynn and in Paris, but it differed substantially in the Choletais. In particular, tasks that were generally done in the factory elsewhere were put out in Villedieu-la-Blouère. In Villedieu-la-Blouère as elsewhere, stitching was primarily a female occupation. This group generally constituted about a third of the total workforce in shoe production. The crucial difference accounting for the much higher percentage of female workers in Villedieu-la-Blouère was in the bottoming operations—the making and lasting. Whereas in most shoe factories bottoming was exclusively an adult male domain, in Villedieu-la-Blouère these tasks were assigned primarily to women and distributed for homework. This difference was even more striking when we consider that men in the bottoming department in most factories were considered among the highest skilled and best paid workers in the factory. This department typically absorbed some of the most substantial investments in machinery, like the McKay sewer or the Goodyear welt sewer. Only after years of apprenticeship were these machines entrusted to a worker skilled in their operations.[43]

Even more than in the lingerie trade, where the dominance of female workers was typical of all regions in France, the recruitment of women and the sexual division of tasks in the shoe trade illustrate

42. Allen, *Shoe Industry*, p. 261; Aftalion, *Développement de la fabrique*, p. 57; Archives communales de Villedieu-la-Blouère, Liste nominative du recensement de la population de 1911.
43. Allen, *Shoe Industry*, pp. 135–253.

Table 7.1

Daily wages for shoeworkers, pre-1914

	Choletais (francs)	Fougères, Nîmes, Nancy, Limoges (francs)
Factory work		
Young women	1.50–1.75	2.50–3.50
Older women	1.75–1.50	3.50–4.50
Older men	2.50–4.00	4.50–7.00
Homework		
Women (all ages)	1.50–2.25	

Source: Chéné, *Débuts du commerce,* pp. 86–87.

dramatically how local labor markets influenced the organization of production. Shoe production in Villedieu-la-Blouère was organized around female homeworkers. Both the choice of women homeworkers and the tasks assigned to women made the local organization of production quite unique. The question remains, why? Were women workers more available than men? Did women make better workers?

Combining female labor and homework was an extension of the entrepreneurs' self-conscious formula for success: specialization in cheaper goods, with low overhead investments, using cheap labor. A look at the wage structure in local production as compared to other regions makes the "cheap labor strategy" more tangible (see Table 7.1) Whereas a factory in Nancy or Fougères would have 60 percent of its workers at daily wages between 4.50 and 7.0 francs, and 40 percent of its workers at daily wages between 2.50 and 4.50 francs, entrepreneurs in the Choletais paid out 2.50–4.00 francs a day to only 40 percent of their workers, while 50 percent earned between 1.50 and 2.25 francs a day and 10 percent earned 1.50–1.75 francs daily. This wage structure was the source of the savings on labor costs for local entrepreneurs, and it made sweating a viable strategy.

Labor costs were lower than in other regions. The most significant characteristic of low labor costs, however, was that the wages paid in the Choletais barely covered the subsistence needs of the worker and could not be stretched to support the subsistence needs of a household. Typically a female worker provided between 12 and 29 percent of the total household expenses, and male shoeworkers provided 51–88 percent of household expenses. Few shoeworkers were the sole support for their families.[44]

44. Office du travail, *Enquête sur le travail à domicile, chaussure,* p. 184.

It is important to note that, at these wage levels, female labor was not cheaper than most male labor in the region. The daily incomes of handloom weavers had descended to the level of most homeworkers, so at least in theory entrepreneurs could have recruited men for the same wages. Particularly since men already produced at home, it should have been just as easy to recruit men as women. Certainly we can put forward hypotheses about why entrepreneurs recruited women rather than men. Perhaps they thought women were more docile and would not strike, or that women did not expect their wages to feed their families and thus would more easily accept low wages. But the scholarship in women's history has shown explanations that resort to stereotypes of feminine dispositions to be more myth than reality.[45] The evidence (see Chapter 9) suggests that initially entrepreneurs in the shoe industry expected to hire men rather than women. It was the particularities of the local labor supply that provided the new manufacturing with an abundance of female labor. The internal logic of this supply reflected the dynamics of familial relationships and household production.[46]

For both the lingerie and shoe trades, then, the ability of entrepreneurs to make homework a viable production strategy ultimately rested on the conditions of the local labor market. Moreover, entrepreneurs in the Choletais did not disguise the fact that their strategy was based on cheap labor. Nor did they feel compelled to apologize. One shoe manufacturer puts it plainly: "[With] labor being relatively cheap in the region and the general expenses decidedly not very high, it was possible for industrialists to establish excessively low prices which assures the sale of [our] shoes.[47] Neither did they explore the broader implications of their reliance on keeping labor costs low. They chose instead to emphasize their own uniqueness. Well aware of their rather anomalous situation, the most articulate entrepreneurs stressed that dispersed production was peculiar to their regional mentality. In fact, it is around the shoe industry that we find the first articulation of a regional identity centered on small-scale production and home-based manufacturing. The social world of these rural entrepreneurs spawned the notion that the region's manufacturing his-

45. For an overview assessing such arguments, see Kate Purcell, "Militancy and Acquiescence among Women Workers," in *Fit Work for Women*, ed. Sandra Burman (New York: St. Martin's Press, 1979).

46. Jane Humphries and Jill Rubery adopt a similar approach in "The Reconstitution of the Supply Side of the Labour Market: The Relative Autonomy of Social Reproduction," *Cambridge Journal of Economics* 8 (December 1984): 331–46.

47. Chéné, *Débuts du Commerce*, p. 46.

tory represented a more harmonious and traditional alternative to industrial society.

The Myth of Continuity in Small-Scale Production

According to local lore, the inspiration for shoe manufacturing in the region originated with outsiders. Although the early history of the industry is vividly remembered, it is not well documented.[48] It seems that just after the Franco-Prussian War several Parisian merchants came to the region in search of a suitable location and workforce to set up shoe factories. They hoped to open workshops in several villages in order to train workers. Little is known about why their venture failed. Around the same time, a former prison director and a native of the western Pyrénées named Adam came to Cholet to set up a shoe factory. Adam brought his partner, a man named Cloud; a slipper maker named Roche; and a factory foreman from the Nord named Golbert. Adam hoped to make use of the expertise of his partners and his own experience in directing the work of prisoners making *savates* (a light heelless shoe) to build a successful business. But this venture also failed. Again, we do not know the reasons. When the partnership dissolved, Adam left the region.

Paul Bouyx, longtime president of the Chamber of Commerce of Cholet and one of the chroniclers of the local industry, remarked that these new enterprises usually failed unless the business was taken over by local people. Certainly anecdotes bear out this observation, especially when we consider the misadventures of Monsieur Cloud. Several years after the dissolution of his partnership with Adam, Cloud found a new associate, a tailor from Le-May-sur-Evre named Bureau-Beaufréton. Around 1875 they established a small shoe workshop at Chalonnes-sur-Loire. Within two years, Cloud had left the business and Bureau-Beaufréton carried on alone. But soon after Cloud's departure, Bureau-Beaufréton, who had little luck in Chalonnes, disbanded and returned to tailoring in Le-May-sur-Evre. Meanwhile, Cloud had started his third shoe factory in Châtillon-sur-Evre, south of Cholet, in the department of Deux-Sèvres. There, too, Cloud stayed only a short time. Eventually, in 1884, the factory was

48. The history in this section is based on Chéné, *Débuts du commerce,* pp. 41–46, and Bouyx, *Naissance de la chaussure,* pp. 149–54.

sold to a local tanner named Demaleon, who attached the workshop to his own tanning works and turned Cloud's original factory into a successful operation making shoes and clogs.

Around 1877 or 1878, Cloud reformed his partnership with Roche. Together with Golbert, the former factory foreman, and several shoe-workers he went to Saint-Macaire-en-Mauges to set up a shoe factory. This enterprise also failed within a few months, but the activity attracted the attention of a local cloth merchant named Doisy. Seeing that there was probably a small fortune to be made in light shoes, Doisy purchased the materials from Roche and Cloud and began his own enterprise. After selling their materials, Roche and Cloud left the region permanently, taking with them the shoeworkers they had brought. Golbert stayed on in Saint-Macaire and later worked as Doisy's foreman.

Doisy's apprenticeship in the slipper trade was marked by several business upsets and losses. After a year or two, however, he was hiring 30–40 people to make hand-sewn slippers with leather soles called *cousus chaussons*. By 1885 he employed 50–70 workers, depending on the season and the orders. The number of workers grew to 100 in 1890, to 250 in the next decade, and numbered 400 in 1910. In the first thirteen or fourteen years of business, all the work was done by hand and on the basis of outwork. In 1892, Doisy introduced several machines but continued to rely on outworkers. At his death in 1914, Doisy had amassed a considerable fortune. He had bought land and built several workshops attached to his large private residence. The productive capacity of his enterprise reached 3,500 pairs of slippers a day. Doisy, a cloth merchant created, at Saint-Macaire-en-Mauges the first successful shoe business in the Choletais.

The second center of shoe production in the Choletais was the commune Le-May-sur-Evre. Like Saint-Macaire-en-Mauges, Le-May-sur-Evre had an important weaving population and many fabricants. In 1887 a baker named Constant Chasseloup, and a weaver, Michel Boisteau, started to produce slippers. Chasseloup stayed only eleven months in the partnership; thereafter Boisteau continued alone. Boisteau had been a weaver since his youth and knew very little about the shoe trade. This was typical of many of the first shoe entrepreneurs in the region. He began slowly with a few workers. Within a few years, however, he took on new partners and expanded production into the neighboring communes of La Tessoualle and Trémentines.

The decade from 1895 to 1905 marked the first spurt in the growth of the shoe industry in the Choletais. In 1895 there were only two established centers of shoe production in the region: Saint-Macaire-en-Mauges and Le-May-sur-Evre. In 1899 there were fifteen fabriques in the Choletais. By 1905 the number of companies had risen to forty. This shoe industry was almost exclusively a village or bourg affair. Most of the entrepreneurs, like Doisy, Chasseloup, and Boisteau, came from the group of artisans and petty merchants who made up part of the bourg elite. Many of the entrepreneurs were involved in the linen trade. Others were grocers, shoemakers, carters, and inn-keepers. All these men were longtime residents of their communes. Noticeably absent among the investors in the first shoe enterprises were the wealthy industrialists in Cholet or the even wealthier landed owners of the Choletais. This was in industry of small-time artisans and petty merchants struggling to survive in the country-side. These enterprises were so small that in the early years of the shoe industry they often escaped the attention of reports on local manufacturing and the employment census.

Local parish priests played an important role as well. Doisy was said to have been aided financially and morally by his brother, who in 1882 became the curé of Le-May-sur-Evre. We do not whether the curé helped to establish Chasseloup and Boisteau in the shoe trade in his parish, but often it was the curé of a commune who fostered the new manufacturing. Abbé Vincent, the curé of Saint-André-de-la-Marche, was one such entrepreneurial parish priest.

In 1899, abbé Vincent had heard of the successes of the shoe industry in Saint-Macaire-en-Mauges. Thinking that this industry might employ the many destitute handloom weavers in his commune, the abbé set out to bring shoe manufacturing to Saint-André. After raising five thousand francs, he succeeded in finding a Monsieur Morinière who agreed to undertake the business and to direct production and sales. The shoe manufacture began in 1901 with four workers. Within six months, the initial capital had been used for materials, tools, and some rudimentary machines, with nothing left for operating expenses. Determined to see the venture work, the abbé sold some of his personal family property, which brought another four thousand francs to the enterprise. This time the business succeeded. When the abbé died in 1911, he had lived long enough to see his idea take root and prosper. The firm Morinière-Ripoche hired 200 workers in Saint-André-de-la-Marche.

Why were local entrepreneurs more successful than outsiders with more capital and more experience? Those who came to the Choletais had far greater familiarity with shoe production and knowledge of the markets, whereas local entrepreneurs had much to learn. Not only did they have to learn how to make shoes and slippers; they needed to establish the right connections to suppliers, wholesalers, and retailers. What advantages, then, did local entrepreneurs have? René Chéné, a shoe manufacturer in the early twentieth century and also a nephew of abbé Vincent, explained that the need to develop a new industry originated with the mechanization of cloth production: "Because weaving could no longer employ all the labor . . . the economic problem for the region was how to find work for the workers while keeping them in our countryside. . . . The handloom weavers generally did not want to enter the few factories in Cholet. . . . At length, shoes were chosen primarily because this industry permitted homework. . . . In effect, the workers wanted above all a job that they could do at home."

The implication of Chéné's remarks is that the local entrepreneurs were successful because they were morally committed. Locals understood and shared the same condition of life; strangers did not. Indigenous entrepreneurs were committed to the society. They knew the needs of the workforce and understood how to organize them effectively. For Chéné, as for abbé Vincent and later for Paul Bouyx, developing a shoe industry in their native region was an act of preservation. The transition from linens to shoes was not simply a change of product. In their view, the shoe industry saved a way of life threatened by the crisis or rural weaving—a way of life threatened by industrialization.

By creating new employment, the shoe industry offered the manufacturing population an alternative to emigration. It provided rural society in the Choletais a means to retain its population. Beyond offering jobs, as Chéné noted, manufacturing was particularly suited to succeed the hand weaving of linen because the organization of production chosen by the entrepreneurs was the same. Shoe manufacturing was suitable because it was organized around homework. The shoe industry, entrepreneurs argued, aided both fabricants and handloom weavers. Handloom weavers resisting factory work could find a new source of income by working at home. Fabricants who were bring squeezed out of the textile trades by large industrialists had new products to sell. Indeed, this interpretation of the rise of shoe manufacturing drew a direct connection between the new homework and the household production of independent producers. The new homework preserved the very social relations of production threatened by industrialization, by reproducing family-based production in a new product line. It lifted the decision to produce shoes out of the realm of economic expediency and merged the pursuit of economic opportunities with moral decisions about how to maintain the fabric of local society.

Certainly, this was a compelling interpretation, and one that fits a contemporary interpretation of the importance of small-scale production as an alternative to industrial society offered by Frédéric LePlay, Albert De Mun, and their followers and by more recent theorists. No doubt, these issues were the foremost considerations for the curés who encouraged the new manufacturers.[49]

The critical point in this moral argument is the assertion that the new type of dispersed production and the household production of independent producers were essentially the same because of the importance of familial relationships. The argument assumes that the new outwork was not different from the older household production, because in both cases production took place at home. This point, however, is also where the argument is most vulnerable. In fact, very few handloom weavers took up shoemaking. They refused shoe manufacturing just as they refused to enter the factory; there was little continuity between the social organization of handloom weaving and that of the new shoe industry.[50] Similarly, the home-based production of handloom weavers differed radically from homework in the needle trades. When we examine the social origins of this labor force, it becomes evident that, far from providing continuity and a solution to the crisis of rural weaving, the new sweated trades lived off the impoverishment of weavers. In the growth of the shoe industry, as well as the cloth-finishing trades, we witness the final vanquishing of small-scale producers—not in the proletarianization of handloom weavers but in the proletarianization of their wives, sons, and daughters. This was the reality of a production strategy based on cheap labor.

The argument that shoe production helped to preserve the fabric of local society, however, is not entirely false, at least not from the point of view of shoe entrepreneurs. Despite its harsh realities, one still

49. Pierre Guillaum Frédéric LePlay, *La réforme sociale en France,* 2 vols. (Paris: Denta, 1867); LePlay's followers published two important journals: *La réforme sociale* and *La science sociale d'après la méthode de LePlay.* LePlay's student's monographs were published under the title *Les ouvriers de deux mondes.* See Catherine Bodard Silver, *Frédéric LePlay on Family, Work, and Social Change* (Chicago: University of Chicago Press, 1982). See also E. F. Schumacher, *Small Is Beautiful* (London: Blond and Briggs, 1973).

50. See Chapter 9. For a clear explanation of the two types of dispersed manufacturing, see Valentine Paulin, "Homework in France: Its Origins, Evolution, and Future," *International Labor Review* 37 (February 1938): 192–225.

must recognize that shoe production was important to the economic survival of the area as a manufacturing region. The new trades did offer work to the local population. That the transition from linens to shoes was possible only with the participation of local entrepreneurs is also undoubtedly true. Thus the question of why local entrepreneurs succeeded when others failed remains important in explaining this transition.

It is likely that a Parisian merchant, or business venturers like Adam or Cloud, expected a higher return on their investment than local businessmen did. Perhaps only local entrepreneurs with deep roots in the community, who shared the fate of that community and who also felt the uncertainty of their own future, would put in the effort required despite the low returns. In other words, it may have been the vulnerability of this group of rural entrepreneurs—the fact that they themselves had few other options—that pushed them toward the sweated trades.

Within rural society, these entrepreneurs ranked near the bottom in terms of wealth. In a typical village in the bocage, the wealthiest were the absentee (aristocratic and bourgeois) landlords who owned tracts of land upward of 100 hectares. This land was subdivided into sizable family farms, which were leased out to tenant farmers. Rural entrepreneurs owned very little land. Their holdings were almost exclusively garden plots, houses, meadows, and an occasional tract of arable land close to the bourg. Rural entrepreneurs drew their income almost exclusively from commerce.[51]

Yet, although those in this group were decidedly poor, they were also among the stable population of the village, along with the weaving population and a handful of peasant proprietors. In contrast, tenant farmers, by far the most prosperous resident population in any commune, tended to be much more mobile; it is often not possible to trace tenant farmer families beyond several censuses, but it is easy to trace the manufacturing population, generation after generation. Thus we often find that these rural entrepreneurs, like the fabricants in the linen trade, served as mayors and other communal political officials. From this group also issued many village curés. Rural entrepreneurs also maintained ties through marriage with their counter-

51. For example, from the États sections of the cadaster of Villedieu-la-Blouère (A.D. M-et-L Serie P: États sections du Cadastre, Villedieu-la-Blouère, 1913) only four entrepreneurs in the linen and shoe trades were listed as property owners in the commune. Only one holding was sizeable (18 hectares). Other holdings varied between 5 and 7 hectares. Other fabricants, whom I could identify by name but whose occupations were not listed in the cadaster, typically owned less than one hectare of land.

parts in other communes. Through these networks of family ties and political and ecclesiastical offices, this group constituted an influential rural village elite reaching from bourg to bourg across the region.

The only economic resource this village elite could claim, however, was their access to local labor—to the increasingly impoverished and underemployed rural manufacturing population. Their position in commerce rested on their ability to remain middlemen between merchants operating in larger markets and this rural labor force. When the linen industry mechanized locally, the livelihood of this group was threatened. The ability to change product markets and enter a new field, finished consumer goods, was a testament to the ingeniousness of this group of petty entrepreneurs, as well as to their desperation. Without the consumer good industry, both rural entrepreneurs and the workforce would likely have had to migrate elsewhere to search for new sources of livelihood. In this sense, the shoe entrepreneurs' claim to be preserving the rural community was accurate, if only from their own perspective. Looking more closely at social relations, however, we can see that the new sweated trades helped entrepreneurs to safeguard their position in rural society. Only in this sense did older social relations remain the same.

The Future of the Sweated Trades

Although shoe producers in the Choletais found a niche in the national market much like that for the region's kerchiefs and cheap grades of linen, they remained vulnerable to competition from mechanized production and to cutthroat underbidding from other shoe fabricants. The division of the market between factory-based mass production and dispersed mass production was neither fixed nor constant. Factory-produced shoes clearly dominated the mass market for shoes. Machines produced for the most constant segment of demand, the segment of the market with the most regular return. Dispersed production in the cheap end of the scale lived off the leftovers, where the returns on investments were either too low or too insecure. Over time, factory production tended to increase its share of the market. In addition, improvement in technology tended to reduce the cost of machine-made shoes at the same time these advancements increased output. Thus industrial shoe production challenged dispersed shoe producers, both at the luxury end and at the cheap end. As the cost of medium-grade factory-made shoes fell, consumers often substituted

them for cheap handmade shoes. To stay competitive, some shoe fabricants were forced to lower their prices by cutting costs. By now, the
sweating scenario should be familiar. All the ways to cut costs also
reduced the incomes of hand workers. Because dispersed labor-
intensive producers could not increase productivity in the same way
as producers using machines, the only ways to compete were to cut
piece rates or to use poorer grades of materials. This latter method
had the same effect as reducing piece rates, because inferior materials
demand more time and care in their transformation.[52]

Conditions in the needle trades and in shoe manufacturing did not
improve over the first several decades of their existence. Workers consistently complained to the investigating commission of the Office
du travail that piece rates were declining. In the lingerie trade especially, workers reported a continuous drop in rates. One worker who
finished kerchiefs by hand showed her paybook as evidence. Between
1902 and 1907, rates had declined by 5 centimes a dozen for certain
grades and 10 centimes a dozen for others. Another worker in the sub-
specialty reported that kerchiefs that had paid 90 centimes per dozen
just two years before now paid only 55 centimes per dozen.[53] Generally, shoeworkers were more content with their wages than needlewomen. Some workers actually noted that there had been increases
in piece rates, but others quickly added that the increase had been absorbed by the rising cost of the materials the worker had to purchase
from the fabricant. Most male workers reported that piece rates remained stable, but that the quality of the materials had declined,
thus rendering their work more difficult and reducing their overall
productivity. By contrast, many female homeworkers complained of
declining piece rates. Three rural stitchers pointed out that certain
articles that had paid 3 francs a dozen just three years before pres-
ently paid only 1.60 francs a dozen.[54]

Local entrepreneurs, however, also paid a price for resorting to outwork and sweating. Unquestionably, there were clear disadvantages
to outwork. Capitalist industrialization held advantages for the entrepreneur. When given a choice, most manufacturers were right to
prefer centralized and machine-aided production, because the factory
system strengthened their position in the product market. Local entrepreneurs favored homework and hand labor because they had little
capital. In the short run, their production strategy gave them a point

52. Aftalion, *Développement de la fabrique,* pp. 51–61.
53. *Enquête sur le travail à domicile, lingerie,* 2:700–715.
54. *Enquête sur le travail à domicile, chaussure,* p. 185.

of entry, but in the long run such strategies were not necessarily beneficial to the region's economy, nor did they necessarily promote the long-term economic survival of the rural entrepreneur. For the most part, local producers were locked in at the insecure end of the product market. They experienced the special disadvantages of producing coarse grades of mass market goods.[55]

The ideal strategy for entrepreneurs, of course, was to accumulate enough capital from profits from outwork and gain enough experience in the trade to break out of the cheap end of the market into centralized and mechanized production. There were such success stories, but in most cases, because these entrepreneurs entered at the cheap end of the product market where returns on investments were lower, it was more difficult for them to accumulate enough to break out. Moreover, because they began in a weak position within a very competitive market, they remained susceptible to swings in the market. Just to survive, they had to adapt constantly to its vicissitudes.[56] Given the structure of competition in consumer goods, the combined forces of competition among entrepreneurs and from machine-made goods, and constant efforts by retailers to drive down prices, prices and profits tended to decline over time. For all these reasons, outwork tended to replicate its own marginality. The overall structure of the industry promoted sweating more than it encouraged industrialization.

55. Aftalion, *Développement de la fabrique,* pp. 106–36.
56. Ibid., pp. 132–36.

8

The Agricultural Labor Market

City dwellers often assume that all rural workers supplement their manufacturing incomes with seasonal agricultural labor. Many historians of rural development have made similar assumptions about economic opportunity in the countryside. Students of proto-industrialization, for example, base much of their central hypothesis on the seasonal complementarity of agriculture and manufacturing. Given what we know about conditions of manufacturing in the Mauges in the late nineteenth century, we might even hope that this was the case, because it would mean that shoe workers, lingerie workers, and handloom weavers lived a better life than their piece rates and wages indicate. However, such a happy symbiotic relationship between rural industries and agriculture did not develop in the Mauges. When weavers and their family members were most desperate for additional income, such resources were not available to them.

Contrary to the persistent images of rural changelessness (see Chapter 1), the agricultural economy of the Mauges in the nineteenth century was undergoing changes at least as fundamental as the manufacturing economy. In both sectors, rural producers responded quickly to shifts in urban consumer tastes. In the second half of the century, the Mauges was transformed from one of the poorest rye-based agricultural regions in France to one of the richest areas for livestock farming, with specialization in beef cattle. The agricultural revolution began in the 1830s when long-established routines were toppled with the introduction of lime. Liming made it possible for farmers both to intensify grain production and to respond to the increasing demand among urban dwellers for meat.

The new agricultural routines doubled the demand for labor, potentially opening up opportunities for weavers to earn supplemental wages. Throughout much of the nineteenth century, various industrial surveys reported that handloom weavers were engaged in agricultural work during the "belle saison." Yet we have surprisingly little information about how weavers fit into the agricultural economy. For example, none of the reports indicate which farm tasks weavers and their families performed, or what portion of their yearly income came from farmwork. When numbers are cited in these reports, they are suspiciously vague and rounded to the nearest thousand. In fact, this chapter demonstrates that farmers met the increase in demand for labor by introducing labor-saving machinery, intensifying the work done by family members, and hiring specialized farmworkers on annual contracts. Farmers complained about the cost of agricultural labor. But the tasks for which they considered weavers suitable were the most menial and least remunerative, paying no more than the average daily wage in weaving.

In the absence of more direct information, I reconstruct the changing technical demands of commercial livestock farming and then examine the new social organization of farming that resulted. In studying how individual family farms adapted to the work routines necessary to commercialize beef production, it is possible to approximate the nature of the demand for labor under the new agricultural regime. In this way, we can better determine where weavers, shoeworkers, and garment workers fit among other workers in the agricultural labor market. This is a lengthy process, yet one that is necessary for understanding the rural labor market. In particular, understanding the bargaining power of weavers and other rural manufacturing workers will enhance our appreciation of power relations in the sweated trades.

The results of this investigation into the agricultural economy underscore the general argument of the second half of this book that the availability of cheap labor for the sweated trades must be explained in terms of power relations and struggles within the manufacturing sector. We can thus reject one seemingly obvious possibility: that the sweated trades flourished because workers, needing only supplemental incomes, willingly accepted low wages and seasonal work.

The Changing Structure of Demand

The most important stimulus for change in French agriculture in the nineteenth century came from changes in the pattern of final demand for agricultural products. Throughout the century, markets for agricultural goods expanded along with urban population growth. At the same time, rising per capita income boosted the demand for luxury foods. Before mid-century, growth in incomes had already affected the composition of agricultural output. As incomes rose, consumers shifted away from nutritionally inferior grains such as rye to more nutritious grains like wheat. As incomes climbed, more people added meat to their diets. By the early years of the Second Empire, the demand for meats was growing at a faster rate than the demand for subsistence crops such as cereals and potatoes.[1]

The market for meat was highly stratified and differed greatly between urban and rural markets. City dwellers consumed, on the average, three times more meat than rural people. The two groups ate different kinds of meat as well. City inhabitants ate three times more beef, twice as much lamb, and a little less pork than people in the countryside. An agricultural inquiry in 1882 reported that towns with populations over 10,000 (26 percent of the population) consumed 51 percent of the total output in meat. The Paris market alone absorbed 14 percent of the total output in meat. So, although meat consumption more than doubled between 1840 and 1880, most of this increase came from urban markets. This distribution of demand meant that beef production and beef prices grew at a rapid pace, while pork production and prices remained stable.[2]

Records on prices and output reveal more precisely the changing relationship between the demand for cereals and vegetables and the demand for meat. From these records we can begin to chart the changes in habits and lifestyle in an industrializing and urbanizing society and establish some of the economic incentives these changes created for French food producers to alter agricultural practices.

In the first half of the century, the production of animals and vegetables grew at approximately the same rate. From 1825 through 1855, vegetable production, which consisted primarily of small grains, grew at an average rate of about 13 percent per decade. Meat and other animal products grew at a slightly higher rate of 15 percent. Until around 1855, the relative prices of these two groups of

1. Jean-Claude Toutain, "Le produit de l'agriculture française de 1700 à 1958," *Institut de Science Économique Appliquée, Cahiers de L'I.N.S.E.A. Histoire quantitative de l'économie française*, series AF, no. 2 (Paris: I.N.S.E.A., 1961), table 82 (p. 16), table 110 (pp. 128–29), table 138 (pp. 188–89); see also George W. Grantham, "Technical and Organization Change in French Agriculture between 1840 and 1880: An Economic Interpretation," Ph.D. dissertation, Yale University, 1972, table I-3 (p. 16).

2. Ministère de l'agriculture, *Statistique agricole de la France: Résultats généraux de l'enquête décennale de 1882* (Nancy: Berger-Lévrault, 1887), pp. 264–66 (hereafter *Enquête décennale 1882*).

agricultural products were stable. But after 1855, meat prices rose at a distinctly faster rate than those for cereals. The balance between vegetable and animal products was further upset after 1865 when the growth in wheat production slowed to 2 percent for the decade. Wheat prices peaked in the decade between 1865 and 1874 but then fell below 1815 prices during the next two decades. After two decades of rapid increase in meat prices in 1855–1864 and 1875–1884, meat prices remained at about twice the 1815 level and declined only modestly between 1885 and 1904. Economic historian George Grantham has argued that this prolonged and irreversible change in the price of meat relative to the price of cereal induced French farmers to introduce new farming techniques and overturned the long-established balance between arable farming and livestock husbandry.[3]

In the early nineteenth century, the arable sector and the livestock sector on most French farms were held in such a tight balance that it was difficult to change the mix of final products quickly. On each farm, animals provided not only meat and dairy products but also fertilizer (manure) and draft power for arable farming. The arable sector of the farm produced food for human consumption. But, in addition, part of the arable land had to be devoted to fodder to maintain the stock of animals. The interdependence between the arable and livestock sectors meant that farms could not easily expand cereal production, because the need for additional draft services and manure would require a larger stock of farm animals. More animals meant more arable land needed for fodder, thus conflicting directly with the additional land needed for grain. Similarly, the farm could not produce more meat without reducing the stock of draft animals and the supply of manure. Such reductions would endanger future output in cereal and livestock.[4] These problems constrained most French farms early in the century, but the equilibrium between arable and livestock sectors particularly typified the agricultural practices in the West of France. This tight balance was the first major hurdle commercial livestock farming had to overcome.

Traditional Agriculture in the West

Subsistence agriculture in the West of France was closely bound to the limitations of topography and soil conditions. The terrain was

3. Grantham, *Technical and Organizational Change*, pp. 7–12.
4. Ibid., pp. 35–38.

rocky and hilly and the topsoil consisted of damp clays and sand layered on a schist and granite bedrock.[5] Historical geographer Pierre Flâtres writes that western France once supported a "veritable moorland civilization involving communal pasture for livestock, gathering stable litter and kindling materials, and a periodic clearing of land for cultivation."[6] Between the fifteenth and sixteenth centuries, the reassertion of aristocratic claims on land destroyed many peasant villages. Systematic land clearing and the subdivision of common land into tenant farms may have begun in the seventeenth century and continued throughout the eighteenth. By the nineteenth century, much of the moorland was held by individuals. Communal grazing, along with communal rights to stable litter and kindling, gradually disappeared in this enclosure movement.

The agricultural patterns of "moorland civilization" continued on tenant farms (which continued to be called *métairies* locally). The rhythm of planting and fallow on these farms was characterized by one historian as only a "temporary" working of the land. The practice of long fallow (called *jachère morte* or *jachère nue*) especially typified arable farming in the West. Crop rotation was designed to avoid depleting the already infertile soil and to ensure an abundance of rough grazing land and pasture.

Tenant farms in the bocage country south of the Loire were large single farmsteads, with isolated farmhouses and dependent buildings surrounded by fields bordered by hedges. On a typical farm with 50 hectares of arable land, in any year two-thirds of the land was left uncultivated. From the remaining third the farm household eked out its living with plantings of rye, cabbage, and a little wheat. The uncultivated portion was divided between land left in long fallow and land *en guéret*, that is, plowed fallow land.

Land in long fallow was left uncultivated for five or six consecutive years. During this time, when broom, gorse, couch grass, bracken, and thistle covered the land, it was used for pasture. The year before planting, this growth was burned and the ashes turned under as fertilizer. This process, called *écoubage*, replenished the soil of needed potassium, nitrates, and phosphates. The fallow land, now land en guéret, was plowed several times to clean out unwanted roots and

5. Ministère de l'agriculture, *Enquête sur la situation et les besoins de l'agriculture*, 2d series, 2d district: *Maine-et-Loire* (Paris: Imprimerie imperiale, 1867), pp. 233–36 (hereafter *Enquête agricole 1866*); Richard H. Andrews, *Les paysans des Mauges au XVIIIe siècle* (Tours: Arrault, 1935), pp. 83–84.

6. Pierre Flâtres, "Historical Geography of Western France," in *Themes in the Historical Geography of France*, Hugh D. Clout (New York: Academic Press, 1977), p. 327.

weeds to prepare the soil for planting. The turned-under ashes sufficed for the first crop of wheat. In a three-year rotation, rye followed
wheat, and oats and cabbages were planted after rye. This rotation
yielded only three harvests every eight to nine years. Even though
productivity may appear low, the long periods of fallow were necessary to prevent soil depletion and to maintain yields.[7]

Livestock was important in arable agriculture in the region. The
heavy clay soil made it impossible to cultivate without a draft team.
Although grazing on fallow land provided scant nourishment for the
draft stock, foraging sustained these animals enough for them to
serve their work function. Farmers in the region also sold cattle for
meat to raise cash for rent and taxes. After Toussaint (All Saints'
Day), farmers selected four draft animals on a large farm or two draft
animals on a smaller farm to fatten on straw and cabbage in the winter months and sell for slaughter in early spring. Still, the quantity
and quality of fodder severely limited the cash value of this beef. Animals fed primarily on straw, broom, and bracken were stunted by
lack of nutrients. Meat production was a last-ditch effort to gain additional returns from oxen exhausted from fieldwork.

In 1768 a report from the district of Cholet noted that, in order to
break even on the cost of fattening, each tenant farmer had to sell cattle at one-third to one-half above the price of young calves. According
to a similar report from Nantes, a pair of cattle to be fattened could
cost 400 livres. After seven to eight months of stable life, sometimes
up to a year, the same pair could sell for 500–600 livres, and sometimes for as much as 700 livres. But few cattle were actually sold at
the higher prices. For every pair that sold for 600–700 livres (that is,
at a price at which the métayer realized a good profit), there were a
hundred pairs that sold for under 500 livres.[8] In other words, farmers
in the eighteen century barely broke even on the average, and even
lost money, in fattening and selling their cattle for beef.

Livestock husbandry in the mid-eighteenth century and well into
the first decades of the nineteenth century was secondary to the primary task of growing enough cereal to sustain the farm household.
Because of the low productivity of the soil and the necessity for long
periods of fallow, few resources could be diverted from staple crops to

7. "Jachère," *La grande encyclopédie*, 1886 ed., 20:1155–56; A.D. M-et-L 7M42: Enquête
sur le labourage, 1811; Oscar Leclerc-Thouin, *L'agriculture de l'Ouest de la France* (Paris:
Bouchard-Huzard, 1843), p. 206; Andrews, *Paysans des Mauges*, pp. 87–88, 102–3; *Enquête
agricole 1866*, p. 227.
8. Andrews, *Paysans des Mauges*, pp. 124–35; A.D. M-et-L 7M42: Enquête sur le labourage.

improve the quality of fodder crops. Consequently, the financial success of livestock farming was held back by subsistence agriculture. This state of affairs may have inspired the Angevin proverb: "L'homme et le boeuf ne sont jamais bien ensemble."[9]

The Agricultural Revolution in Maine-et-Loire

The traditional system of agriculture survived in western France as long as the chemical composition of the soil could not be altered. Long periods of fallow were essential to maintain yields because repeated planting depleted the soil of its calcium content, rendering the soil more acidic. An acidic environment not only lowered yield but ultimately destroyed the physical condition of the soil, leading to tillage and drainage problems and ultimately to soil erosion. The basic problem was how to introduce the much needed calcium. Liming, which began in the 1830s, providing the ideal solution. By supplying calcium, lime reduced soil acidity. More intensive cultivation, with clover and other leguminous annual forage crops in place of fallow in the crop rotation, was now possible.[10]

Annual forage plants like clover, lucerne, vetch, and sainfoin are nitrogen-accumulating crops. They promote the growth of microorganisms in their root systems which absorb atmospheric nitrogen. Such annual forage thus replenishes the soil with nitrogen, achieving the same result as leaving the land in fallow. In addition, forage crops provide nutrients for nitrogen-accumulating crops like wheat. Wheat grown in nitrogen-rich soil matures faster and is more resistant to disease and frost.

Before the introduction of lime, rye was planted before wheat in the crop rotation in order to provide nitrates for wheat, but clover has many advantages over rye. First, it "cleans out" the soil in much the same way as fallow plowing. Its tight root system suffocates weeds and prevents deep-rooted weeds from becoming established. Second, clover provides fodder rich in calcium and phosphates.[11] Not only does the livestock sector benefit from additional food, but the nutrients derived from fodder grown in limed fields improve the stature

9. Roughly translated, the proverb says "men and cattle can't eat off of the same land." Ministère de l'agriculture, *Statistique agricole de la France: Résultats généraux de l'enquête décennale de 1862* (Strasbourg: Berger-Lévrault, 1868) (hereafter *Enquête décennale 1862*).

10. F. Nicolle, *Les progrès culturaux dans le canton de Cholet depuis cent ans* (Angers: La Chèse et cie, 1898), pp. 6–8; Grantham, *Technical and Organizational Change*, pp. 56–62.

11. "Jachère," *La grande encyclopédie*; Nicolle, *Progrès culturaux*, p. 8; Grantham, *Technical and Organizational Change*, p. 57.

and weight animals attain at maturity. These new crops thus increased the cash returns from animal husbandry.

Comparing the land in fallow and that allocated to cereals and fodder from French national agricultural surveys in 1840 and 1852 confirms the important impact of lime on agricultural production in Maine-et-Loire.[12] In 1840, 176,440 hectares of the arable land of Maine-et-Loire were left in fallow. This figure represented almost 40 percent of the arable land, which nearly equaled the land planted in grains. This balance reconfirms the close connection between fallow and grain yields in traditional agriculture. By 1852 the agricultural survey reported 97,694 hectares in fallow. In absolute area, fallow was reduced by 45 percent (78,746 hectares) over these twelve years. Only 21 percent of the arable land was left in fallow. Between 1840 and 1852, the most significant change in land allocation was the increase in the area planted in wheat. Wheat production expanded by 63,016 hectares, representing a 64 percent increase in twelve years. In 1840 wheat occupied 23 percent of the arable land. By 1852 its share had grown to 36 percent. The output in wheat grew from 1,486,921 to 2,660,087 hectoliters. In addition, the yield per hectare improved from 12.67 to 16.23 hectoliters per hectare. The increase in wheat was accompanied by a decline in rye and *méteil* (a mixture of wheat and rye), which had been the basic subsistence crops. About 11 percent of the region's arable land was planted in rye in 1840. By 1852 its share had fallen to 4 percent. Together, there were 37,709 hectares in the department previously planted in rye and méteil that were subsequently planted with wheat. The remaining 25,307 hectares of new wheat fields must have been land taken out of fallow.

The trend toward wheat production was consistent with the structure of demand nationally. All over France, wheat was favored over darker, less nutritious grains. Gradually, wheat displaced most other grains for human consumption. In Maine-et-Loire, however, despite the rapid progress of wheat culture, the cereal sector as a whole did not expand rapidly. The total share of arable land used for cereals for human consumption increased from 37 to 41 percent. The shift from rye and méteil to wheat was the most significant change within this sector. But only one-third of the land taken out of fallow was planted in wheat. The rest of the newly cultivated fallow fields were used for fodder crops.

12. The following analysis is based on Ministère de l'agriculture, *Statistique générale de la France*, 1st series, vol. 6: *Agriculture* (Paris: Imprimerie royale, 1841), and *Statistique de la France: Statistique agricole. Enquête décennale de 1852*, 2d series, vol. 12 (Paris: Imprimerie impériale, 1860) (hereafter *Enquête décennale 1840* and *Enquête décennale 1852*).

Between 1840 and 1852, the cultivation of nitrogen-accumulating fodder crops like clover, lucerne, alfalfa, vetch, and sainfoin expanded by 60 percent: 16,939 additional hectares were sown in green forage. Sown meadows, which had occupied 6 percent of the arable land in 1840, increased to 10 percent in 1852. These crops reduced soil acidity, preparing the soil for other fodder crops that do not tolerate acidic environment, such as beets, rutabagas, and carrots. Fodder beets were first introduced in Maine-et-Loire in 1831. The 1840 survey indicates 961 hectares planted with fodder beets. By 1852 this crop occupied 2,215 hectares. The expansion of such root crops, along with the cultivation of cabbages, provided the essential winter fodder when farm animals could no longer graze. In addition, an abundant supply of winter greens and roots was needed to fatten cattle for slaughter. Other sources for fodder grew as well: natural meadows expanded by 18,104 hectares, and oat production grew by 12,267 hectares.

The expanding capacity to produce fodder increased the size of the animal stock arable farming could support. In 1840 there were a total of 207,965 head of cattle in Maine-et-Loire. By 1852 the cattle stock had increased by 22 percent to a total of 254,055 head. Within this group, calves and yearlings increased their numbers by 68 percent, cows by 22 percent, and steers by 18 percent. Not only did additional fodder permit larger herds, the animals were better nourished. Liveweights improved considerably between 1840 and 1852. The average weight grew from 297 to 358 kilograms for draft oxen and 509 kilograms for beef cattle. The average liveweight of cows grew from 217 to 258 kilograms and for calves sold for slaughter from 32 to 47 kilograms. The total value of the cattle stock grew from 20,329,149 francs in 1840 to 35,754,270 francs in 1852, an increase of 76 percent.

Commercial livestock farming meant more than selling surplus; commercialization transformed every aspect of farming. The new priorities set by animal husbandry mandated new crop rotations and a new organization of farm routines. With the suppression of fallow and a new emphasis on fodder crops, most farms introduced a three-field triennial rotation. In the first planting, the field was sown with wheat and clover, followed by winter oats, vetch, and clover, then in the third year by cabbage and root crops. On a typical 50-hectare tenant farm with 10 hectares of meadows and 40 hectares of arable land, a little more than half the arable land was devoted to feeding animals in addition to the 10 hectares of natural meadows for grazing. The other half of the arable land was devoted to grain to feed the farm household. The goal of each farm was to be self-sufficient in grain and in fodder and to produce cash income by selling cattle for beef. Breeding and fattening cattle was no longer a by-product of the subsistence sector. Commercial livestock farming clearly had its own financial and production objectives.

The Changing Demand for Labor and the New Fodder Crops

The new, mid-century crop rotation methods introduced a new set of problems which themselves threatened the feasibility of commercial livestock farming. It is evident from contemporary accounts that the new cropping regimes were achieved only with a tremendous investment of additional labor. Not only did farmers cultivate a greater proportion of the arable land because less land lay fallow, but they also expanded the culture of labor-intensive crops. Specifically, the winter fodder (beets, turnips, and cabbages) essential in those months when cattle could not graze require the most backbreaking labor. Table 8.1 compares the labor input for all crops planted in Maine-et-Loire using a standard measure of workdays per hectare. In every phase of cultivation, from preparing the soil for planting to harvest, weeded row crops such as potatoes, fodder beets, cabbages, and turnips required the most work of all the field crops for human or animal consumption.

To illustrate the actual changes in the demand for labor, I have constructed two contrasting examples, one using the land allocation of a 50-hectare farm worked by a successful livestock farmer in the late 1860s, the other using what we know about the prevailing crop rotations of the early nineteenth century. As can be seen from Table 8.2, the labor required to raise the crops on similar sized farms more than doubled with the transition from subsistence to commercial livestock farming. This comparison is designed to reveal the extent of changes in the total labor input resulting from changes in the crop rotation alone, discounting any changes in agricultural techniques such as the introduction of labor-saving technology. As we see shortly, farmers incorporated labor-saving devices in order to cope with this dramatic increase in the demand for labor. This was certainly a formidable challenge, one which, if left unsolved, threatened to undermine the possibility of commercial agriculture in the region.

Before I examine how farmers coped with this substantial increase in the demand for labor, let us understand more precisely what

Table 8.1

Labor input for selected field crops, Maine-et-Loire, 1852

Crop	Labor cost (francs)	Workdays/ha
Wheat	44.16	30
Méteil	38.86	26
Rye	40.91	27
Oats	27.08	18
Potatoes	44.91	28
Beets	65.80	45
Weeded row crops	130.60	89
Sown meadows	29.50	20

Source: *Enquête décenniale 1852.*
Note: Where available, the direct estimates of labor input per hectare are listed in this table. Where direct estimates are not available, I use the total cost of production provided in the published census returns, subtracting the cost of seeds and fertilizer to arrive at a total labor cost. I then divide the estimated total cost for labor by the daily wage of male adult day laborers as reported in the same agricultural survey. These estimates are riddled with difficulties. For example I do not try to account for rent and machinery costs, because the direct estimates calculated in the manuscript sources to the 1852 survey do not seem to include land or machinery costs. For a technical discussion of calculations, see Grantham, *Technical and Organizational Change*, app. 3.

Table 8.2

Annual Labor inputs

Land allocation	Workdays/ha	Total workdays
Subsistence farming		
13 hectares rye	27	351
3 hectares cabbage/turnips	89	267
13 hectares fallow plowing	12	156
11 hectares fallow (pasture)		
Total labor input for arable farming		774
Commercial livestock farming		
13 hectares wheat	30	390
13 hectares clover	20	260
8 hectares oats	18	144
7 hectares fallow plowing	12	84
6 hectares cabbages/turnips	89	534
6 hectares beets	45	270
Total labor input for arable farming		1,682

Note: Presumes a 50-hectare farm with 10 hectares of meadowland and 40 hectares of arable land.

specific new tasks this overall increase in labor represented. From the perspective of cultivators, the real problem was not how to meet the total increase in demand for labor but rather how to satisfy the new seasonal variations in tasks and changes in the intensity of work throughout the year.

On subsistence farm, more than half the total yearly labor time is concentrated in the period from July to November. Except for harrowing and hoeing fields, and cultivating small plots of fodder crops, most of the labor is absorbed in the grain harvest, threshing, fall plowing, and sowing. As farms introduced root fodders, sown meadows, and extensive cabbage cultivation, the demand for labor became more evenly distributed throughout the year, but at a higher constant work level. The new fodder crops created a completely new period of peak demand in March and a second new peak in June and intensified and prolonged the period of peak demand for summer work, which traditionally fell between Saint-Jean's Day (June 24) and Saint-Martin's Day (November 11).[13]

Root vegetables and cabbages require deeper seedbeds than most other field crops. In early spring, to prepare for planting, either the fields were plowed several times with a draft team or the soil was turned by hand. Just before planting the seedlings, the fields were tilled yet again, manured, and then harrowed by plow or by hand. For planting seedlings, most farms used a team of three people. In one swing the worker dug the soil with one hand, set the plant with the other hand, and with a third motion heaped the soil around the base of the plant. Working at a regular rhythm, experienced workers could plant 0.2 hectare in a full day's labor. The team required almost one and half days for planting one hectare of roots or cabbages.[14]

Once planted, these crops still required frequent tending—mostly thinning, weeding, and fertilizing. Over the growing season crops received two or three hoeings to keep the topsoil loose and free from weeds. This operation could be accomplished by hand hoeing or by harrowing with draft animals.[15] Since weed infestation significantly reduced yields, the progress of the fields during the growing season needed regular surveillance.

---

13. For an analysis of similar changes in England, see C. Peter Timmer, "The Turnip, the New Husbandry, and the English Agricultural Revolution," *Quarterly Journal of Economics* 83 (August 1969): 375–95.

14. Leclerc-Thouin, *L'agriculture de l'Ouest*, pp. 338–39, 350–59, 428–33; Jeanne-Marie Delord, *La famille rurale dans l'économie du Limousin (1769–1939)* (Limoges: Ch. Paulhac, 1940), pp. 22–26.

15. Grantham, *Technical and Organizational Change*, pp. 130–32.

Finally, the root harvest was the most tedious of all operations. Roots were most often dug out by hand, cleaned, and then carted away and stored. For potatoes, beets, and turnips it was possible to plow the rows before harvesting to loosen the soil. But even then, the roots were still pulled out by hand, and cleaning and carting was still substantial and backbreaking fieldwork. The estimated time needed for the root harvest varied widely, from a high of 40 man-days per hectare harvesting by hand to a low of 4 woman-days, 4 child-days, and 4 man-days per hectare using work teams and a plow in combination.[16]

Extending sown meadows into once fallow fields increased the demand for labor to mow, turn, and stack the hay. The substitution of green forage for fallow did not significantly change the total labor requirements per hectare of arable land. Sown meadows did not require additional plowing or much weeding, particularly because farmers sowed clover in the same fields as wheat. But the expansion of sown meadows contributed to the summer bulge in the demand for labor and thus accentuated the seasonal harvest labor shortages between June and September.[17]

If the new farm routines had merely extended the growing season, then the solution to the labor shortages might have been for the existing farm workforce to work longer. But in addition to prolonging the work seasons, the various tasks often conflicted with or intensified the already existing work schedule for cereal culture. The greatest stress on the labor supply of the farm was the periodic conflict between the demands of cereal culture and that of fodder culture. In early spring, plow teams worked double-duty to prepare the cereal beds for spring cereals and for the especially heavy plowing for the roots and cabbages. From June to mid-August, planting root fodders and cabbages conflicted with the labor needed for haymaking and the grain harvest. This period was particularly busy because the expansion of sown meadows added to the labor demand for haymaking. In October and early November, root harvesting interfered with threshing and grain storage.

Changes in the demand for labor were thus more complex than a general undifferentiated increase. Satisfying the various components of this demand was certainly not a simple task. At important turning points, like the decade between 1840 and 1850, farmers thought that the prospect for agricultural progress was clouded by labor shortages.

16. Ibid., pp. 323–24.
17. Ibid., pp. 132–33.

What were the alternatives and strategies available to farmers who wished to take advantage of the growing urban market for beef? They could increase the total labor time available, by either working the existing labor force harder or recruiting more workers; they could use labor-saving implements; or they could reduce the extent of arable land to accommodate the increase in work intensity. In the Choletais, the solutions farmers found combined all these possibilities.

Declining Farm Size and Commercial Agriculture

One of the immediate consequences of improvements in farming techniques in Maine-et-Loire was the dismantling of the largest tenant farms. Until the mid-nineteenth century the distribution of farm size followed particular geographic patterns, which differentiàted the open-field country from the bocage. North of the Loire river, the arrondissements of Segré and Baugé were territories of large estates. Closer to the fertile Loire valley, farm size dropped considerably under 20 hectares. Ten to twelve hectares was the average farm size around Angers. In the arrondissement of Beaupréau (Cholet) south of the Loire river, we come again to the region of large farms. The average in this arrondissement was between 30 and 40 hectares, although farms in the heart of the bocage, in the canton of Champtoceaux, for example, often surpassed 50 hectares while in the canton of Chemillé, closer to the Loire valley, the average was just under 20.[18]

Traditionally in the bocage, farm size was inversely related to the proportion of arable land under cultivation: the small farms in the fertile Loire valley often had more land under cultivation than large farms in the interior of the region. The infertility of the soil in the inner bocage forced farmers to practice long fallow. The introduction of lime in the 1830s thus affected farm routines in the interior more than in the Loire valley, and it was in the interior cantons that farm size declined most precipitously. By the late 1840s, many of the largest tenant farms had been divided into smaller farms. The report of the cantonal commission of Beaupréau to the enquête of 1848 noted that, due to the great advances in agriculture in the previous two

18. Leclerc-Thouin, *L'agriculture de l'Ouest*, pp. 70–72; A.D. M-et-L 7M42: Enquête sur le labourage.

decades, many of the large tenant farms of 50 hectares and more had been subdivided into smaller units of 25–30 hectares.[19]

Subdividing large tenant farms was one strategy for meeting the increased demand for labor. The results were positive. A 50-hectare farm that formerly maintained one household now provided livelihood for two households. The land was better cultivated and the farmers were more prosperous. By 1862, 92 percent of all farms in the arrondissement of Cholet (called Beaupréau until 1859, when the administrative seat was changed) were under 40 hectares. Nearly half (47 percent) were between 10 and 30 hectares, distributed about evenly between farms of 10–20 hectares and farms of 20–30 hectares. Farms between 30 and 40 hectares represented only 12 percent of all farms 40 hectares and smaller. Farms under 10 hectares constituted about a third of all farms. This distribution represented a change even from the early 1840s, when the largest cluster of farms fell between 30 and 40 hectares. Twenty years later the most important cluster fell between 20 and 30 hectares.[20] By the late nineteenth century, the optimal size of tenant farms were considered to be 20 hectares.[21]

The reduction in the size of tenant farms did not, however, affect the distribution of land ownership. The declining size of tenant farms did not in any way signify the division of the larger estates in the region.[22] The arrondissement of Cholet remained an area dominated

19. A.N. C958: Assemblée constituante, Enquête sur le travail agricole et industriel, 1848, Maine-et-Loire, Commission cantonale de Beaupréau.

20. For the arrondissement of Cholet in 1862, 92 percent of all farms were 40 hectares or less: 23 percent of all farms were between 10 and 20 hectares; 24 percent were between 20 and 30 hectares; 12 percent between 30 and 40 hectares; 15 percent between 5 and 10 hectares; and 18 percent under 5 hectares. Within the arrondissement, farms in the interior bocage were larger than in the Loire valley. In the canton of Saint-Florent-le-Vieil, for example, 58 percent of all farms were under 10 hectares and 31 percent under 5 hectares; in comparison, in the canton of Beaupréau 38 percent of all farms were between 20 and 30 hectares and only 10 percent were under 5 hectares, and in Monfaucon 31 percent of the farms were between 20 and 30 hectares and 16 percent under 5 hectares. A.N. F11 2706: Enquête agricole décennale de 1862, arrondissement de Cholet, Maine-et-Loire.

21. Jean Renard, "Problème agraire du Nord-Est de la Vendée," NOROIS 55 (July–September 1967): 379–97. See also Ministère de l'agriculture, La petite propriété rurale en France: Enquêtes monographiques (1908–1909) (Paris: Imprimerie nationale, 1909).

22. See André Siegfried, "Le régime et la division de la propriété dans le Maine et l'Anjou," Le musée social, mémoires et documents, supplement, July 1911, pp. 197–215, esp. pp. 208–12. In the arrondissement of Cholet, large estates (greater than 100 hectares) constituted 45 percent of all property holdings. Estates of 500, 600, and 1,000 hectares were not unusual. During the nineteenth century, although farm sizes declined, the size of landholdings did not. In some communes, the number of largest land owners and the number of small holders increased. In Villedieu-la-Blouère, for example, in 1835 28 percent of the land in the commune was held in estates of 100 hectares and larger, and in 1913 these estates constituted 37 percent of the land in the commune. The land occupied by medium-size holdings, between 30 and 50 hectares, declined from 20 percent in 1835 to 2 percent in 1913. Holdings between

by large-scale landowners. Although the largest holdings had been divided, the number of bourgeois landowners who possessed two or three medium-size tenant farms actually increased over the nineteenth century.

These declines in farm size run counter to the general expectation that commercialization of agriculture causes farm sizes to increase since large farms represent a more efficient use of resources. In this case, carving up larger holdings into 25–30-hectare tenancies benefited both cultivators and landowners. Scaling down the tenant farms solved a problem for each individual farm by alleviating a potential shortage of labor that would have stunted the expansion of livestock farming. As a result, more tenancies became available. The splitting of many large farms also meant more income for landowners. Although the rent increases were initially marginal, in the second half of the century the "prix de fermage" increased considerably, matching and in some cases surpassing the increase in returns from commercialized farming.

Labor-Saving Devices

Introducing new tools to increase the productivity of each worker was another way to meet the increase in demand for labor.[23] Mechanical technology and metallurgy made steady progress during the nineteenth century. Because better materials were available, and techniques for joining parts had improved, by the middle of the nineteenth century farm machinery could reproduce such motions as cutting, turning, sawing, and rotary beating. Between 1850 and 1900, the number of specialized implements for tilling increased and mechanical devices for harvesting and threshing became available.

Farmers in the Choletais, however, adopted labor-saving machinery only selectively. The machinery available had but limited application for reducing the workload of labor-intensive crops like root fodders. Farmers introduced new techniques only when the innovations re-

---

50 and 100 hectares, which held 22 percent of the land in 1835, held only 8 percent of the land in 1913. At the same time, the average size of a working farm declined from 50 hectares to 20–30 hectares of arable and pasture lands. A.D. M-et-L serie P:État section de cadastre, Villedieu-la-Blouère, 1er matrice 1835, 2me matrice 1913.

23. This section based primarily on Grantham, *Technical and Organizational Change*, pp. 142–70; Leclerc-Thouin, *L'agriculture de l'Ouest*, pp. 271–76; and *Enquête agricole 1866*, pp. 248–49, 666.

duced the conflicting demands for labor in the peak seasons. The labor-saving devices that made the furthest inroads were those that reduced the time and labor required for harvesting and threshing. The goal was to integrate the cultivation of winter fodder without disrupting the needs of cereal culture. Mechanical reapers made their appearance in French grain fields in the 1860s, but technical problems with these machines, their inability to work on land plowed into ridges and furrows (as fields were plowed in the region), and their expense all discouraged their adoption even on the largest farms until the 1880s. In the nineteenth century, the most important labor-saving devices for reaping were based on human power rather than mechanical or animal power.

To economize on the labor required for reaping, by the 1860s farmers in western France had largely substituted reaping hooks and scythes for sickles. Both the scythe and the reaping hook greatly reduced the number of days needed for reaping and the number of workers required. With scythes it took only 2 man-days to reap one hectare of grain, as against an average of 10 man-days (and a minimum estimate of 7–8 man-days) to sickle the same hectare of grain. Reaping hooks required a maximum of 8 man-days and a minimum of 5–6 man-days per hectare of grain. Although significantly slower than the scythe, the *volant*, or reaping hook, cut the grain at ground level, thus saving the labor of scything the stubble left by the arc of the scythe.

Despite their speed, both implements had their distinct disadvantages. Unlike the sickle, which detached the beards of grain by a short sawing motion, both the scythe and reaping hook cut the grain with a vigorous chopping motion. Chopping was more rapid than sawing, but the motion tended to spill grain. Both the scythe and reaping hook actually reduced grain yields. In addition, unless care was taken to restrict the arc, the vigorous sweep of the scythe tended to scatter the sheaves so that more labor was needed to gather and bind. Sickling, on the other hand, left a cleaner sheaf and thus facilitated binding and threshing. Overall, the scythe greatly reduced reaping time but increased the time required for gathering and binding. The disadvantages of the scythe and reaping hook would have outweighed the gains had farmers not felt pressure to shorten the harvest season because of the need to reallocate labor to fodder crops. These conditions favored the scythe and reaping hook over the sickle.

Shortening the harvest only partially solved the problem of how to release labor for autumn plowing and harvesting root crops. The equally pressing demand on labor for the period after the harvest was the time needed to thresh grain. Of all the large machinery available to agriculture between 1850 and 1900, only threshing machines made significant headway. Between 1852 and 1892, the number of threshing machines in Maine-et-Loire grew almost fourfold, from 1,220 to 4,496.[24] The greatest increase corresponded to the period of most intense increases in cereal production, between 1852 and 1862. In this decade the number grew from 1,220 to 4,100.[25] The majority of these machines were powered by draft animals, with a small minority powered by steam engines. The mechanical threshers surpassed older methods of threshing by 10 to 15 times. The oldest method was known as *chaubage,* in which the cut sheaves were dashed against a hard object or the ground. This method produced only about one and a half hectoliters of grain for a day's labor and was used only when preserving the straw for thatch was important. Striking the sheaves with the tip of a flail was the preferred method in the early nineteenth century. This method brought two to three hectoliters of grain for a day's work. At an average yield of 14–15 hectoliters per hectare, the amount of time required for threshing could consume many weeks after the harvest itself.[26]

By the 1840s, threshing with wooden and stone rollers had been introduced to Maine-et-Loire but did not enjoy widespread usage. Treading and rolling were considerably more labor saving. Some agronomists estimated the daily yield per man-day at 8–9 hectoliters. This method approached the rate of mechanical threshers, estimated at between 15 and 24 hectoliters per man-day depending on the region and the machine.

Improvements in harvest implements and threshing techniques worked in tandem. The reaping hook and scythe reduced the period of the grain harvest, so that the winnowing could be moved forward in the season. Wooden and stone rollers, as well as threshing machines, reduced the time required to separate the grain from the hull. Under the new work regimen, the tasks of cereal culture ended by early September. Labor was then available for root harvest and fall plowing. It is important to remember that labor-saving technology freed labor for tasks (in root fodder and row crops) for which there were no labor-saving devices. Thus, for those who labored in the fields, the reallocation of their labor time through labor-saving devices meant an intensification of work, not more leisure.

24. *Enquête décennale 1852;* Ministère de l'agriculture, *Statistique agricole de la France. Résultats généraux de l'enquête décennale de 1892* (Nancy: Imprimerie nationale 1897) (hereafter *Enquête décennale 1892*).
25. *Enquête décennale 1852; Enquête décennale 1862.*
26. Ministère de l'agriculture, *Statistique de la France: Agriculture,* 1st series, vol. 6 (Paris: Imprimerie royale, 1841).

The Changing Role of Women's Work

Reducing farm sizes and adopting labor-saving devices were not alternative strategies; they were complementary ways to permit the family farm to adapt commercial farming to the available labor supply. The success of these innovations in turn rested on important changes in the allocation of labor within farm households. Without these changes, commercial farming would not have been feasible.

Commercial livestock farming established a new family economy based exclusively on agriculture. Under the new market orientation, the intensity of farmwork increased for all family members, but the internal allocation of tasks most dramatically affected women's work.[27] With the growing demand for fieldworkers, farm households initially drew on the labor of female family members. From the 1830s to the 1840s, the labor of wives and daughters shifted from handicraft production to full-time agricultural work. Female labor was central to the agricultural development of the region.

Before the turn to commercial farming, subsistence farms in the bocage had combined handicraft and agricultural activities. These two types of production represented, not seasonal variations in activities, but the different spheres of male and female labor. Men had taken primary responsibility for the arable and livestock sectors of the farm, women were spinners. Except for the grain harvest, women did not participate in arable agriculture. In addition to spinning, women looked after the reproductive needs of the household. This included cooking and laundry, raising small animals and pigs, dairying, and tending gardens. This pattern was significantly different on farms in the plains and valleys of Anjou, where farm women took on a much more active role in fieldwork. On the small farms of these areas, women often sowed grain, led draft teams, and even occasionally took the plow. In the bocage, by contrast, particularly on the large métairies in the interior, female servants often took over much of the female agricultural work in dairying and gardening, while daughters and wives spun.[28]

Spinning gave women in subsistence farm households a cash income not associated with agriculture. Spinners in the bocage did not

27. These observations are confirmed by Martine Segalen's study of farm women in France, *Love and Power in the Peasant Family: Rural France in the Nineteenth Century,* trans. Sarah Mathews (London: Blackwell, 1983); see also Daniel Faucher, "Aspects sociologiques du travail agricole," *Études rurales* 13–14 (April–September 1964): 125–31.

28. Leclerc-Thouin, *L'agriculture de l'Ouest,* pp. 111–13, 117.

grow the flax they spun. Some spinners were independent entrepreneurs, who purchased the scutched fibers and resold the yarn. Others depended on merchants and middlemen. In the interior of the bocage, rural spinning continued until the 1830s. The spinning wheel and other hand techniques were the predominant methods to spin linen before the perfection of mill-spinning techniques. Unlike hand-spun cotton yarn, which died out in the countryside in the first decade of the nineteenth century, linen continued to be spun by hand because of the difficulties of spinning the fiber mechanically.

In the 1830s and early 1840s, the local market for hand-spun linen collapsed. The dramatic decline was the result of imported spun linen from Belgium, and to a lesser extent of the beginning of mill spinning in the region.[29] The resulting crisis in female employment is one of the great unrecorded events of the era. There are no records that estimate the number of rural spinners in the region, and the number of spinners left unemployed as a result is equally unrecorded. Our only evidence of the presence of female spinners in the rural economy and the loss of this employment comes from communal population censuses.

A profile of the changing division of labor in farm households in the commune of Villedieu-la-Blouère illustrates these changes. The developments in the commune were typical of the economic changes in the canton of Beaupréau in the interior of the bocage. In 1836, the year of the earliest extant manuscript census listing the occupations of each member of the household in a household-by-household survey of the population, we find a total of 185 households and 901 inhabitants. With its 55 farming households and 41 households headed by day laborers, Villedieu-la-Blouère was primarily an agricultural community. Most nonagricultural households were engaged in trades connected to agriculture except for the eighteen weaving households and the one resident fabricant.[30] The commune had not been an important manufacturing center during the eighteenth century, nor had it turned to cotton in the early nineteenth century. Weavers and spinners in Villedieu-la-Blouère specialized in linen products.

In 1836 there were 182 spinners, 42 percent of the female population in the commune. In age range and marital status, spinners came from almost all the social strata in the local rural society. Of the 182

29. Ibid., p. 317; A.D. M-et-L 67M2: Responses to questions from the minister of commerce and manufacture, prepared by the subprefect of Beaupréau, 23 August 1831.
30. Archives communales de Villedieu-la-Blouère, Liste nominative du recensement de la population, 1836.

spinners, 30 lived in all-female households, where often the spinner herself was the head of the household. Thirty-three spinners came from the households of agricultural day laborers, 10 from weaving households, and 29 from other artisanal households. The largest grouping of spinners, numbering 80, lived in farm households. This proportion reflected the importance of farmers in the commune's population. Ten years later, in the census of 1846, the number of spinners had declined by 80 percent. There were only 37 spinners living in the commune, of whom 10 lived in all-female households. Seven lived in the households of day laborers, eight in the households of servants, three in weaving households, and six among other rural artisanal households. Only three spinners lived in agricultural households. Proportionately, the decline in the number of spinners in agricultural households was the most significant. In 1836, 40 percent of the spinners came from farm households, whereas by 1846 only 8 percent did so. Considering that the number of agricultural households increased by 54 percent, from 55 to 85 households, spinning was an even less significant part of the activities of farm households than these figures suggest. This change in the work patterns of farm women must be understood within the framework of concurrent changes in arable farming.

The availability of female labor was an important factor in the adaptation of family farms to commercial agriculture. Female labor was quickly absorbed into agricultural work. As Table 8.3 makes clear, the labor of female family members accounted for the increase in the total labor available for farming. This table shows the structure of farm households in Villedieu-la-Blouère in 1836 and 1846 at distinct phases of the family reproductive cycle; it compares, in standard labor units (S.L.U.), the division of labor between agriculture and manufacturing.[31]

In 1836 most farm households divided their activities between agriculture and spinning. The amount of labor devoted to each activity differed across the life cycle. In the earliest phases of the life of a nu-

---

31. Standard labor units in agriculture are calculated on the basis of the full-time work effort of an adult male in good health and in the prime of his working life. The amount of labor available to a household over the family life cycle is based on the following calculations, taken from James Lehning. *The Peasants of Marhles* (Chapel Hill: University of North Carolina Press, 1980), chap. 9, esp. pp. 131–32, 197–98, nn. 4–6. Males: 8–13 (0.3 S.L.U.), 14–16 (0.5), 17–18 (0.8), 19–59 (1.0), 60–64 (0.8), 65–69 (0.5), 70+ (0.3); Females: 8–13 (0.3), 14–16 (0.5), 17–64 (0.8), 65–69 (0.5), 70+ (0.3); Women of child-bearing age: with one child under 8 (0.5), with all children under 8 (0.3), with children under and over 8 (0.5). These calculations assume a sexual division of labor in productive and reproductive activities.

Table 8.3

Division of labor in agricultural households, Villedieu-la-Blouère

	Age of male head of household				
	25–34	35–44	45–54	55–64	65+
1836					
Average household size	8.0	7.8	7.1	7.9	6.0
S.L.U. agriculture	2.8	3.8	3.4	4.0	4.0
S.L.U. manufacturing	0.3	0.5	1.0	1.6	1.0
S.L.U. servants	1.8	1.7	1.0	0.6	1.3
1846					
Average household size	7.8	6.7	7.6	6.6	9.3
S.L.U. agriculture	4.6	3.9	4.2	5.0	4.6
S.L.U. manufacturing	0	0	0	0	0
S.L.U. servants	1.9	1.6	0.9	0.7	0.9

Source: Archives communales de Villedieu-la-Blouère, listes nominatives de recensement de la population, 1836, 1846.

clear family, the period of the greatest shortage in adult labor, farmers hired domestic servants to secure the necessary labor for agriculture. We see in Table 8.3 that domestic servants constituted a primary source of agriculture labor. Most farms hired two servants, one adult male and one female. As children aged and assumed a greater share of the farmwork, the number of servants decreased, but most households continued to hire a female servant even when the labor of family members was most abundant. As the parents aged and children married and left their parents' house, the farm household again relied on hiring domestic servants. Spinning as a female productive activity gained greater importance in the later phases of the family cycle, suggesting that for married women spinning might have been balanced against child rearing. As children aged, farm wives devoted more time to spinning. In addition, daughters in their early teens also spun. Thus, in a household of 7–8 people in the middle range of the family reproductive cycle, three adults and one child worked in agriculture, and one adult and one child in spinning. The number of workers in manufacturing increased as mothers and daughters, and sometimes daughters-in-law, found more time to spin.

In 1846, the average agricultural workforce on each farm over the course of the life cycle ranged from 3.9 to 5.1 S.L.U., that is, approximately four to five fulltime male adult workers. In 1836 the agricultural workforce on the average ranged from 2.8 to 4.6 S.L.U., or approximately three to four and a half male adult workers. There was thus an increase in the average number of workers used in agricultural work. The average number of servants did not change appreciably at any point in the life cycle. The additional agricultural workforce in each household came primarily from manufacturing (spinning), as Table 8.3 documents.

Although we cannot show a strict arithmetic relationship between the increase in the agricultural workforce and the changes in female work patterns, the conjuncture of several trends strongly suggests this conclusion. Consider, for example, the growing intensity of agricultural work as represented by the changes in the ratio of land to labor in the commune: for 1836 we can estimate a ratio of one S.L.U. to 4.7 hectares of arable agricultural land; for 1846, with the influx of female labor into agriculture, we estimate one S.L.U. for every 2.9 hectares of agricultural land.[32]

Men's Work and Skill Hierarchies

In contrast to the basic reorientation of female productive labor, commercial livestock farming did not fundamentally alter the responsibilities of men. Cattle and beef production, which together represented the major capital investment as well as the primary cash product, belonged to the male domain. Men continued to work the plows and draft teams, and they performed the central tasks during the grain harvest and haymaking.

The new work routines of commercial livestock farming further emphasized the existing skill hierarchies based on gender and age. More labor was required on both ends of the spectrum, increasing the demand for skilled far labor (highly prized jobs like plowing, sowing, reaping, and selling cattle) as well as for unskilled fieldhands (for tedious gathering and binding sheaves, weeding, digging, cleaning, and hauling roots and tubers.)[33] The differences between "skilled" and "unskilled" were closely linked to gender. Scythes, plows, and mechanical threshers, the farm implements representing the many

32. To attain these estimates, I divided the total amount of arable land in Villedieu-la-Blouère as reported in the cadastral survey of 1835 (871 hectares 50 ares) by the total S.L.U.s available to agriculture calculated from the list nominative of the population censuses of 1836 and 1846. These totals were 186.8 and 305 respectively. These estimates, of course, are very rough measures of labor inputs in agriculture. In the absence of more precise measures, however, they are the best guesses available. A.D. M-et-L série P cadastre: Villedieu-la-Blouère, 1er matrice, 1835.

33. For a discussion of skill hierarchies in farm tasks, see Ann Kussmaul, *Servants in Husbandry in Early Modern England* (Cambridge: Cambridge University Press, 1981), pp. 34–35; see also Delord, *Famille rurale*, pp. 25–27.

changes in agricultural routines which enabled family farms to specialize in commercial livestock farming, also signify the differential effects of these changes on men and women. Let us look at these specific implements, and in particular at how the hierarchy implicit in the gendered division of labor affected the demand for wage laborers.

Reaping hooks and long-handled scythes were used by adult male workteams. Since women, old men, and adolescent boys had worked the harvest with sickles, the displacement of sickles meant their displacement as harvest workers. The new reapers reduced the time to mow a field, but they created more labor for gathering and binding sheaves. These latter tasks were given over to fieldhands. Threshing grain used to involve the entire household, as everyone worked well into the winter months releasing the kernels by flailing or beating the sheaves. Wooden and stone rollers and threshing machines now accomplished this task quickly, but threshing became more closely tied to the adult sphere of the division of labor. The labor freed from threshing was diverted to different tasks. Again, there was an important segregation of activities. Adult males and adolescent boys plowed fields and sowed winter wheat. To the extent that they participated in the root harvest, it was to plow the land to loosen the soil around each plant. Such work facilitated the initial digging, but the onerous aspect of the actual harvest, the uprooting, cleaning, and carting, was left for fieldworkers.[34]

Women shouldered much of the burden of the labor-intensive field crops. Root vegetables and cabbages, in particular, required careful tending. In growing fodder, women worked in the fields for the first time. Hand spades, hoes, and rakes were the "female" agricultural tools. In early spring, men plowed the seedbeds. Women then prepared the beds for planting with hand spades. To ensure high yields, workers thinned and weeded root crops and cabbages, often by hand, several times in spring and early summer. These tasks fell to adult women, children, and elderly men and women. The most arduous aspects of the root harvest were also the responsibility of women.[35]

Women shared responsibility for the success of the farm enterprise. Their work and cooperation were essential. Yet the fieldwork wives, younger children, and old folks performed did not command re-

34. Leclerc-Thouin, *L'agriculture de l'Ouest*, pp. 163–70; Grantham, *Technical and Organizational Change*, pp. 144–67.

35. Delord, *Famille rurale*, pp. 25, 27; Leclerc-Thouin, *L'agriculture de l'Ouest*, pp. 111–13; Grantham, *Technical and Organizational Change*, pp. 318–26, 332–35; see also Segalen, *Love and Power*, and Faucher, "Aspects sociologiques."

sources. Herein lies the difference. Fodder was an intermediary product. The end product with cash value was beef, and raising and
selling cattle was an adult male reserve. This difference characterized
the female condition in agricultural families. Their labor was essential, but it did not allow them direct control over the most important
products of the farm economy.[36]

Wage Workers and the Family Farm

The new division of labor on the commercial family farm affected
farmers' recruitment of wage labor as servants and day workers, returning us to the question of the availability of agricultural work for

36. The types of resources farm women could claim as agricultural workers and food
provisioners on the family farm differed greatly from the material resources to which
women had access as spinners. As spinners their labor earned a wage. In farmwork there
was no monetary remuneration for their labor, except for their earnings on the market.
The striking difference, however, was the changing balance between "male resources" and
"female resources."
In the subsistence economy, both men and women had access to cash incomes, women
from spinning and men from selling cattle. Surprisingly, the revenues were comparable. In
the mid-eighteen century, a farmer could make 100 livres profit from selling a pair of oxen at
500 livres. A prosperous farmer usually fattened four head of cattle a year, realizing a profit
of 200 livres. In the same period, a spinner could earn 8–9 sous a day. If a woman spun the
maximum number of days, except during the harvest, she could earn 150–200 livres a year.
Compared to the daily wages of agricultural workers at 20 sous, or the daily income of weavers at 30 to 35 sous, the daily income of spinners was barely a subsistence income. It took the
combined income of three spinners to feed a household of two adults and three children on
a meager diet of bread and soup. But as a supplemental income, a spinner's annual wage was
enough to pay rent on the family farm, which varied from 100 to about 150 livres. A hard-
working spinner could thus be an attractive marriage partner. Her resources could pay rent
on a new tenancy, provision a new household, or buy looms or cattle. Commercial livestock
farming, in contrast, did not offer women resources independent of the family farm enterprise. In addition, the growing capital investment and returns from raising cattle tipped the
balance of resources toward men.
Women did have access to cash incomes. With the growing market for farmyard products,
this domain became an important part of women's work. The farmyard remained the independent reserve of farm wives. Women sold milk, butter, eggs, chicken, geese, and rabbits at
local markets. Although we cannot discount the market value of these products, the cash
products controlled by men were monetarily far more important than those controlled by
women. For example, in 1882 in Maine-et-Loire, beef production was worth 7.8 million
francs, while farmyard animals produced only of 1.9 million francs, *Enquête décennale
1882.* The most valuable product women controlled was milk. An average milk cow produced 13 hectoliters of milk per year. At 19 francs a hectoliter, on the average, the cash returns from the milk of two cows equaled the returns on the sale of one steer. But a 50-hectare
métairie in the bocage typically maintained at most three milk cows, while it sold six to
eight heads of fattened cattle a year. Here again we observe the imbalance between male and
female cash products.

handloom weavers.[37] The demand for agricultural labor must be understood in terms of the social hierarchies of rural society as well as the hierarchies within farm families. Such social factors determined who was deemed fit for which jobs.

Wage workers in the countryside were divided into three groups. Farm servants, called *domestique de ferme* or *servant(e)*, were hired on a yearly basis. Typically, their contracts began and ended on Saint-Jean's Day (June 24). Summer servants were hired for the *métive*, the period between Saint-Jean's Day and Saint-Martin's Day (November 11). These workers, known as *métiviers*, were hired for haymaking, for the harvest, and at times for fall plowing. Day workers, called *journaliers* or *journalières*, were hired by the day or by the task for odd jobs. Each group of agricultural wage workers performed distinctly different types of farm tasks and were recruited from different tiers of rural society.

For domestiques, service was considered a family life cycle phenomenon, from the perspective of both servant and employer. Generally, farm service was not considered an adult occupation, but a status and an occupation of youth. Farm servants were mostly the sons and daughters of farmers. Socially, farm servants entered households whose social status was not appreciably different from their own. Servants worked closely with the master and mistress of the farm; they were lodged with the family and often shared meals with the family at a common table. Thus, ideally, service was a stage of life in the progression from child living with parents to married adult living with spouse and children. Wages from service very often served as the means of saving to set up a household or to pay a leasehold at marriage.[38] In Villedieu-la-Blouère as elsewhere, the majority of the servants employed in subsistence households and commercial farm households were single and between the ages of 13 and 25 (see Table 8.4). But Table 8.4 also shows many mature men and women (age 35 or older) working as live-in servants. The lives of these servants reflect one harsh reality of property relations in farm families which frequently undermined the ideal. Although the West of France was generally a region of partible inheritance, in practice the division

37. This section is reconstructed primarily from Leclerc-Thouin, *L'agriculture de l'Ouest,* pp. 95–118; *Enquête agricole 1866,* pp. 247, 665, 694; and Ministère de l'agriculture, *Enquête sur les salaires agricoles* (Paris: Imprimerie nationale, 1912), pp. 251–52.

38. Delord, *Famille rurale,* pp. 73–75; Kussmaul, *Servants in Husbandry,* pp. 24–27, 31, 76–85.

Table 8.4

Servants in farm households, Villedieu-la-Blouère

	\<15	15–24	25–34	35–44	45–54	55–64	65+
			Distribution of age (percent)				
Males							
1836	0	74	16	7	3	0	0
1846	12	47	19	14	2	3	3
1881	5	34	36	11	11	3	0
Females							
1836	12	53	23	9	3	0	0
1846	19	57	14	5	0	5	0
1881	0	70	24	6	0	0	0

	Males	Females	N
	Distribution by sex (percent)		
1836	53	47	72
1846	58	42	100
1881	69	31	55

Source: Archives communales de Villedieu-la-Blouère, listes nominatives de recensement de la population, 1836, 1846, 1881.

of the patrimony tended to be unequal. Usually, there was only one designated heir to the father's leasehold or to the family farm. Many farm children did not receive adequate settlement from their parents. Thus many found themselves without the means to set up their own household. These children of farmers had to remain in service or, as many did when they grew older, become day workers living among the land-poor and landless artisans of the bourg.[39]

From the perspective of the employer, hiring servants was part of the life cycle of the nuclear family. The number of servants in the household was inversely related to the number of adults and adolescent children living in the household. In Table 8.3 I approximated household composition by the age of the head of household. Generally the number of servants decreased as the age of the head increased, indicating that young children replaced servants as they grew old enough to take on farmwork.

The tasks live-in servants performed were based on their gender, age, and "apprentice" status. Young women generally aided the mistress of the farm with running the dairy, caring for pigs and other

39. See Martine Segalen, " 'Avoir sa part': Sibling Relations in Partible Inheritance Brittany," in *Interest and Emotion: Essays on the Study of Family and Kinship,* ed. Hans Medick and David Warren Sabean (Cambridge: Cambridge University Press, 1984), pp. 129–44.

farmyard animals, gardening, cooking, and performing such field-work as weeding, carting, and some ancillary tasks during the harvest. Male servants worked under the supervision of their masters. They were assigned the same tasks as the masters' sons. Draft animals and cattle fattened for slaughter were not entrusted to young servants. Young adolescent boys cleaned the stables and stalls, replaced the straw, and occasionally milked cows. They fed the livestock, carted turnips, harvested fodder greens, and led the plow and draft team. Older servants plowed fields and aided in the care and sale of cattle. Of all farm jobs, plowing carried the most prestige. Other tasks, such as leading the grain harvest and caring for and selling livestock, conferred status as well. At the top of the order of tasks, of course, was the supervisory role of the master of the farm, the head of the production unit. Only sons and male servants would eventually ascend to this position.[40]

The commercialization of agriculture affected male and female servants differently. Specifically, commercial livestock farming increased the demand for male servants. More workers were needed to tend livestock. Farms needed workers to take on the additional work in plowing, and for the scythe and reaping hook rather than the sickle. The increase in demand for male labor was manifested in the commercializing farms in Villedieu-la-Blouère. As is evident in Table 8.4, after the introduction of labor-saving instruments in the 1860s, the profile of the servant population changed. Between 1836 and 1846, the number of servants and the proportion of men to women remained relatively constant. By 1881 the number of servants had declined. Farm families were able to make do with fewer servants. Significantly, the proportion of women in the servant population declined dramatically from 1836 to 1881. In age profile and marital status, male farm servants remained basically unchanged.

Wage differences between male and female servants also reflect the increased demand for male workers. In the earlier phases of commercial agriculture, wages rose quickly for both male and female servants. Although male wages were always higher than female wages, between the 1840s and 1860s wages for both sexes more than doubled. On the average, male wages rose from 100–150 francs a year to as much as 400 francs a year, and female wages rose from 60–90 francs to as much as 250 francs. These wages were the money wages paid in addition to room and board and laundry. After the 1860s, fe-

40. Kussmaul, *Servants in Husbandry*, pp. 31–35.

male wages stabilized at around 250 francs and did not increase over the next decades, while male servant wages continued to rise. In the 1880s farmers complained of the rapid increase in wages in the previous twenty-five years.[41] Farm wages rose faster in the bocage than in other regions. An inquiry on agricultural workers in 1912 indicated that an adult agricultural worker could earn as much as 600 francs a year, and on average between 400 and 500 francs, whereas female wages remained much lower, between 200 and 300 francs. Only in exceptional cases did female servants earn 350–400 francs a year.

Métiviers also had their distinct social patterns. In the Choletais, they were migrant workers. Wine growers from the Saumurois migrated seasonally for harvest work. They returned to their vines only at the time of the grape harvest. Workers from Brittany also migrated for the métive. Local sources are less precise about the occupation of these Breton workers. Some sources suggest that they were smallholders and agricultural workers. Others suggest that these workers were actually linen weavers migrating from Loire-Atlantique and Ile-et-Vilaine.[42] Whatever the source of their other income, métiviers earned most of their annual income during the summer months. In addition to their wages, they also were fed and housed on the farms, which amounted to an additional savings on living costs for a third of the year. A summer wage, combined with a small plot of land and a cow, was sufficient for the livelihood of a worker and his family.

This migration pattern did not change significantly during the nineteenth century. Changes in harvest technology, however, increased the reliance on adult men for the métive. Whereas early in the century many farms hired an additional boy and girl as summer servants, this was apparently no longer the practice by the end of the century. The wages of métiviers reflected the importance of their labor to the farm economy. In the 1840s they earned between 100 and 120 francs. During the second half of the century, their wages nearly tripled, following the same patterns as the male servants. In the early twentieth century, the métivier earned between 250 and 350 francs in the period between June 24 and November 11.

Of the three groups of agricultural wage workers, day workers saw the least employment expansion from commercial agriculture. As

41. A.D. M-et-L 67M11: "Enquête sur la crise industrielle, commerciale, et agricole, Situation de l'agriculture, 1884."

42. Henry Cormeau, *Terroirs Mauges: Miette d'une vie provinciale* (Paris: Georges Crès, 1912), pp. 283–88.

early as the 1840s, agronomists were noting that farmers tended to employ day workers only as a last resort, preferring seasonal or year-round workers as a more secure source of adequate labor for the essential farm tasks. With the changing work routines, the demand for métiviers and year-round servants grew throughout the century at the expense of employment possibilities for day workers.

In Villedieu-la-Blouère, the number of day workers declined. In 1836 there were 52 day workers living in the commune—43 men and 9 women. In 1846 the population grew slightly to 65. The increase may have reflected the loss of spinning incomes, because it was primarily women who joined this workforce. In the latter half of the nineteenth century, the number of day workers was reduced by half, to 26 in 1881 and 27 in 1911.[43]

In 1912 a survey of agricultural wages reported that day workers constituted only 17 percent of the population of agricultural workers in Maine-et-Loire. Métiviers and year-round servants together made up 75 percent of agricultural workers. Like surveys in the nineteenth century, this report noted that farmers hired as few day workers as possible, and when they did it was by the hour rather than by the task. It is not surprising then, that wages for day workers were stagnant compared to the wages for métiviers and domestiques de ferme. Wages for servants and métiviers increased by 300 percent between the 1840s and the first decade of the twentieth century, whereas wages for male day workers increased by only 25 percent between 1840 and 1852 and another 20 percent between 1852 and 1912.

Did weavers become agricultural wage earners? Where did they fit in this rural labor market? Writing in the early 1840s, agronomist Oscar Leclerc-Thouin remarked that a growing number of weavers were pushed by their deteriorating economic circumstances to seek out fieldwork. Unfortunately, despite the complaints of labor shortages throughout the second half of the nineteenth century, there were few opportunities for weavers. If we examine the seasonal variation in the number of looms active during the summer season, we see that only a small minority of weavers found summer fieldwork. The decennial agricultural survey of 1852 listed only 1,400 workers in the arrondissement of Cholet who were seasonally employed as weavers. During the summer quarters, the number of active looms in the in-

43. Archives communales de Villedieu-la-Blouère, Listes nominatives du recensement de la population de Villedieu-la-Blouère, 1836, 1846, 1881, 1911.

dustrial reports declined by only 2,200. This figure, admittedly just an estimate, represents only about 6 percent of the weaving population.[44]

That few weavers were seasonal agricultural workers should not be surprising. Country people considered sedentary professionals like weaving to be incompatible with farmwork.[45] Farmers, particularly those hiring for summer fieldwork, prized strong workers endowed with great endurance and speed. Mowing meadows and reaping grain were arduous tasks that also required experience. Leclerc-Thouin had much sympathy for the weavers who worked in the fields. They were caricatured as puny artisans clumsily trying to keep pace with the robust farmers and farmhands. In the enquête of 1848, the cantonal commission from Champtoceaux lamented that, in spite of the potential the weaving population represented as a reserve of agricultural workers, they were fit for few tasks besides terracing and maintaining ditches.[46] Members of the cantonal commission explained that weavers were weakened by their impoverished diets and suffered from ailments due to long hours bent over a loom in humid basements. They were thus much disdained as farmworkers. Never hired for tasks that required experience, agility, or speed, they were considered ideal for the root harvest and as extra hands for stacking, binding, and weeding.

When weavers found agricultural work, they worked as journaliers and not as métiviers. Certainly they had little hope of acquiring the more lucrative agricultural jobs. Although wages rose quickly for certain types of agricultural laborers, the kind of work available for weavers did not pay appreciably more than their daily income from weaving. Thus weavers could not improve their income from agricultural work.

The reality of the weaver's existence was harsher than we might have imagined. Although commercial agriculture brought greater prosperity to land owners, tenant farmers, and male farm servants, it did not significantly improve the lot of the landless and land-poor rural proletariat in the region. No doubt agricultural work provided some part of a weaver's household income. Digging turnips for several days during the harvest and repairing ditches and irrigation drains in the winter months were odd jobs that supplemented the household budget and hence aided survival. But these jobs were

44. *Enquête décennale 1852.*
45. Paul Sébillot, "Les tisserands," in *Légendes et curiosités des métiers* (Paris: Flammarion, 1895).
46. A.N. C958: Enquête 1848, Commission cantonale de Champtoceaux.

available only intermittently. They were not the crucial farm tasks farmers could not leave to chance. For the important jobs like plowing, planting, and harvest activities, farmers guaranteed their labor supply by hiring year-round servants, using the labor of family members, or, in the case of the métive, relying on long-established seasonal migration patterns.

The promise of a complementary symbiosis between the needs of agriculture and the needs of rural artisans which many local officials had hoped for in the middle of the nineteenth century was not fulfilled. Clearly, the commercialization of agriculture did not create new opportunities for weavers. The changes created neither regular seasonal employment nor the possibility that weavers and other rural artisans could switch into the more lucrative sector of the rural economy. Any explanation for the continued survival of handloom weavers in the countryside does not lie in the agricultural economy.

As we have seen, the central problem of labor organization for commercial farmers was how to accommodate the higher demand for labor on a year-round basis, and how to accommodate the peak demands when the needs of fodder culture added to the already pressing work schedule of the grain harvest. The broad patterns of behavior reveal that the solutions favored the priority of maintaining the kin-based, family-run farm. Rather than hiring more workers, farmers adjusted the size of the arable land to the labor supply available. Labor-saving technology redistributed the demand for labor by leveling out as much as possible the labor input throughout the year. Further, the internal allocation of tasks and recruitment of workers reflected the embedded cultural notions of work—notions of male tasks and female tasks, skill, and prestige. Consistent with these notions, the new work routines emphasized male skilled work. Not only did women feel the impact of these changes, but these definitions extended to all forms of labor allocation. Commercial livestock farming on family farms emphasized male servants and male harvest workers. There was work available for women, and also tasks allotted to weavers and other day laborers, but these were the least remunerative fieldwork. Commercial livestock farming brought prosperity to the agricultural West, but the distribution of benefits was unequal. Commercial agriculture in the bocage reinforced the inequalities of rural society, rendering hierarchies of skill and social status even more rigid than before. The poorest weavers and rural proletarians remained in their place at the bottom of rural society.

9

What Price Dignity?
The Transformation of the Weaving
Family Economy and
the Creation of Cheap Labor

In the bourg of the village of X, an old, poor weaver sat bent over his loom. "Tic-tac," "tic-tac," "tic-tac" went the shuttle as the weaver pushed it through the weft. Exhausted by his long labor, he cursed the old wooden loom that could not produce enough to feed his family. Suddenly, the devil appeared. "Bring that cursed loom and throw it in the flames of the inferno," the devil ordered. With little choice, the weaver obeyed and carried his trusty loom on his back and followed the devil to hell. Standing before the flames, the devil ordered the weaver to throw in his old loom. Next, he threw in his shuttle. The old weaver stood and watched the heddles, the warp beam, and the reeds as they went up in flames. Finally, the devil said in triumph, throw in the passerole,[1] and then I will have your soul. Now the weaver began to chuckle. In secret, he had left the passerole back on earth. Thus outsmarting the devil's plan, the weaver was allowed to return to his family. The next morning, his neighbors heard the regular "tic-tac," "tic-tac" of the shuttle, the sounds of the weaver back at work.[2]

This story, called "The Passerole," comes to us from François Simon, a school teacher, socialist, and historian of the Mauges, his native region. Like the old weaver in the story who beat the devil, handloom weavers in this region could be said to have beaten the

---

1. A passerole is the weight tied to the warp beam of a handloom. This weight keeps the warp yarn straight and maintains the tension in the cloth as it is woven. This weight is essential to the quality of the weave—hence to the quality of the product.

2. François Simon, *Petite histoire des tisserands de la région de Cholet* (Angers: Imprimerie Anjou, 1946). I have reconstructed this version of the story from memory. It is not a verbatim reproduction of Simon's printed version, which unfortunately I did not transcribe.

odds. Writing in the first decades of the twentieth century, Simon notes that "several old hand weavers, seized by the love of liberty and pride for their independence and ancestral virtues, have eluded the discipline of the powerloom imposed for the bosses. They have installed one or two looms in their own shops and work at their own pace. They are their own masters."[3] As a socialist who believed strongly in enlightenment notions of human progress, Simon respected mechanical innovations. Yet, as the son of a handloom weaver, whose elder brothers and uncles had also been weavers, his history of the textile industry in the Choletais articulates a sense of sympathy and admiration that grows out of familiarity with the hard work and poverty endemic to the weaving life.

As we have already seen, Simon's portrayal is accurate. Handloom weavers won their survival through long and difficult struggles. The story of class struggle in this region was the history of weavers' resistance to industrialization. There is another part of this story, however, as yet untold. Handloom weavers may have outwitted the devil in maintaining their craft, but what about the broader consequences of their determination to remain at their looms? What was the social basis of the weavers' survival? Who bore the costs of the struggle, and why? What were the consequences for the regional labor market and economy?

By the end of the nineteenth century, weavers and members of weaving households were forced to make difficult and often contradictory decisions. This period thus presents us a strategic opportunity to study the organization and dynamics of these family economies. These crises exposed assumptions that had operated previously but remained submerged, so we gain retrospective insight into the workings of the family economy in earlier, more prosperous, times. In addition, and more critical for our understanding of the pattern of regional economic development, we see the relationship between the breakdown of the family production unit under pressure from outside forces and the restructuring of the local labor market. Thus, my ultimate goal in this chapter is to expose the causal link between the crisis in handloom weaving and the emergence of a pool of cheap female labor for the new, sweated outwork industries. The resulting analysis shows not only how families adapt to changes in the broader economy but also how dynamics within families can actually shape the future of economic development in a region.

3. Ibid., p. 82.

The Weaving Family

Throughout my analysis thus far, I have in effect treated weavers as if they were individual producers. Yet the very reality of weavers' daily existence, and their very ability to resist, belies this image of the weaver as a solitary producer. By self-definition, weaving was a collective family enterprise, engaged in by the weaver and his family. There is, of course, an unstated androcentric bias in this discussion of weaving families. But this bias existed in the culture itself. The subsuming of many individual identities and interests within the singular identity of the male weaver and head of household is the key to the analysis ahead. My task is to make plain the reality of these assumptions and their implications.

A hierarchical organization of status and tasks in weaving underscores the importance of work in defining relationships between parents and children. As in farming and other artisanal trades in which the unpaid labor of family members is critical for the survival of the enterprise, the disciplining of bodies and habits was the first lesson children had to learn from their weaver parents. To understand the significance of discipline, we must remember that handloom weaving is physical labor. A weaver's productivity and likelihood depended on speed and endurance. The patience required for sedentary yet tiring work, the conscientiousness needed to count threads, to keep edges square and cloth taut, were qualities drilled into the body, inculcated in children by example and constant correction.

Young children learned early on that the people who loved them depended on their labor. While some children chafed and rebelled at attempts to rein in their spunk and youthful enthusiasm, many others thought that returning their parents' love meant never disappointing their expectations. In her memoirs, Mémé Santerre, born Marie-Catherine Gardez to a weaving family in the Cambrésis in the north of France, provides us with an example of a dutiful daughter.[4] Being the youngest child, Marie-Catherine enjoyed the luxury of a few years of schooling, but the needs of her family soon called her away from the classroom. Awakened every morning at 4 A.M. by her parents, she and her older sisters would shiver at their kerchief looms, waiting for their mother to call them at 10 o'clock for their

---

4. Serge Grafteaux, *Mémé Santerre: A French Woman of the People*, trans. Louise A. Tilly and Kathryn L. Tilly (New York: Schocken Books, 1985); see also Louise A. Tilly, "Linen Was Their Life: Family Survival Strategies and Parent-Child Relations in Nineteenth-Century France," in *Interest and Emotion: Essays on the Study of Family and Kinship,* ed. Hans Medick and David Warren Sabean (New York: Cambridge University Press, 1984).

mid-morning reward—a warming bowl of chicory "coffee." As an old woman, Mémé Santerre recalled clearly her first day at the loom, when wooden "skates" had to be tied to her legs because she was too small to reach the pedals that moved the sheds. With equal vividness, she described her father's tenderness at the end of the day when he carried her to bed after she had fallen asleep at her loom. When the girls tired or their attention wandered during their long workday, her father sang to amuse and encourage his little workers. Decades later, Mémé Santerre still heard her father's rich voice echoing in the cellar as she struggled to keep her loom in pace with the song. In this world, a parent's loving concern could never be fully divorced from control. Singing songs and devising games initiated children to work rhythms. It was part of the process of internalizing standards. Thus a weaver's child who proudly brought his or her bolt of kerchiefs to the local factor and ran home to contribute the money to the family purse took pride in his or her work. Such pride, however, was inseparable from the sense of obligation to others.

Given the significance of work in cultivating a sense of belonging, and the dominance of family obligation in creating what Dorinne Kondo has called "disciplined selves," it is not surprising that weavers reacted to declining piece rates by recounting their toll on family life.[5] Yet developing a critical eye for how the notion of "family" is constructed is central the analysis to come.

The Crisis in Handloom Weaving

In 1904, during a government inquiry on the conditions of the French textile industry, a deposition from the members of Chambre syndicale of Saint-Léger-sous-Cholet exposed the inadequacy of weaving incomes. Earning on average, 1.25 francs a day, and at best 2 francs, weavers argued that these rates could not sustain a family: "In order that a father of a family can survive with two or three children and his wife, he must be able to earn three francs a day just to pay his suppliers regularly. And we must tell you that even working 12 hours a day [we cannot earn this amount]. We get so little in return [for our labor]."[6]

Compared to other workers in the region, the situation of handloom weavers was difficult indeed. In a survey of the local shoe in-

5. Dorinne K. Kondo, *Crafting Selves: Power, Gender, and Discourses of Identity in a Japanese Workplace* (Chicago: University of Chicago Press, 1990).

6. A.N. C7318: Enquête textile 1904, Réponse de la Chambre syndicale des ouvriers tisserands de Saint-Léger-sous-Cholet.

dustry conducted between 1909 and 1911 that included household budgets, a male shoeworker earning 983 francs a year could barely support his wife and three young children.[7] Even with aid from the city of Cholet (a modest 38 francs a year), the family still could not meet its expenses, which amounted to just a little above 1,150 francs a year. For weavers in Saint-Léger-sous-Cholet, who earned between 375 and 600 francs a year, 900 francs (or 3 francs a day) represented the good life, one that was no longer attainable. Indeed, many weavers earned even less. Some averaged as low as 75 centimes a day, yielding an annual wage of 225 francs, barely enough to purchase bread to feed the shoeworker in the survey and his young family. Comparing such incomes to the cost of living, a member of the Bourse du travail asked passionately,

> How can a father of a family with two children live honorably after deducting from an average annual salary, 115 francs for rent, 70 francs for fuel, 200 francs for bread? . . . Even for the highest paid handloom weaver, what is left to maintain the household of four people? There's no use to mention stew [*fricot*], 'cause it's only made of potatoes and dry beans and greens filched from neighboring fields. . . . For the poorest paid in the countryside, three-fourths of the first necessities of life are pilfered from farmers by moonlight. Seeing such great misery, the farmers dare not complain. Who has the right? It is sad to report, but it's exactly the truth. How can it be otherwise with such vile rates?[8]

Certainly, stealing cabbages and turnips was a desperate solution to the crisis, but one that effectively dramatized the weavers' plight. If we take weavers at their word, and there is sufficient evidence to corroborate their reports on wages and cost of living, we are led to wonder how, indeed, weaving families survived. In Chapter 6 I argued that handloom weavers' militant defense of the tarif was a struggle against becoming wage workers. But, surely as these testimonies assert, defending piece rates was also a fight for the physical survival of weaving families. The two problems, of course, are linked. Yet, as we saw, despite the failure of mobilization and weavers' inability to maintain rates, handloom weaving continued in the region. In light of the persistence of handloom weaving, how should we interpret the depositions given in 1904? Is it that rates were adequate before but

7. Office du travail, *Enquête sur le travail à domicile dans l'industrie de la chaussure* (Paris: Imprimerie nationale, 1914), p. 188.
8. A.N. C7318: Enquête textile, 1904, Réponse de la Bourse du travail de Cholet.

had now fallen below a physiological limit? If staying at their looms meant that children must go hungry, how did weavers justify their choice? To answer these questions, we need to look more carefully at the lives of weavers and their families during this period.

The Changing Profile of Handloom Weaving

In the last decades of the nineteenth century, the lives of handloom weavers changed significantly.[9] We can trace these transformations by following several weavers over this period. For example, according to the population census of Villedieu-la-Blouère conducted in 1881, Jean Pineau, a 30-year-old handloom weaver, lived with his wife, Marie, and two young sons, Louis and Jean. Marie aided Jean in his work. The couple would have expected that, when Louis and little Jean reached early adolescence, they too would weave. Three decades later, we find the family listed in the population census of 1911. Young Jean and Louis have both married and live in their own households as handloom weavers. Louis's wife aids him in weaving, and Jean's wife takes in embroidery work in addition to helping her husband. She is listed as an embroiderer by the census taker. Jean Pineau the father, now widowed, lives with three sons born after the 1881 census. He continues to weave but not all the sons living under his roof practice his trade. Henri, 29, and Joseph, 23, are weavers, but the youngest, Georges, has become a shoeworker. Although Jean and Louis both followed in their father's profession, they are not themselves heads of household production units, households in which all adults perform some part of the weaving production process. This experience is typical of their generation.

François Sécher was 18 in 1881. He lived with his widowed mother and five siblings. François, his mother, and older brothers were listed in the 1881 census as weavers. His sisters also worked within the family production unit. In 1911, François has married and continues the trade he practiced as an adolescent. We do not know how many children François and his wife Julie had in total. In 1911 only a 15-year-old daughter lives with François and Julie. The daughter is a shoeworker. François's brother Henri also continues to weave. Henri Sécher is the head of a weaving household production unit consisting

9. The following household information comes from the manuscripts to 1881 and 1911 censuses of Villedieu-la-Blouère. The households described in the text are actual households; however, I have changed the names of their members.

of himself and his 26-year-old nephew. Handloom weavers who apprenticed under their fathers and older brothers in the last decades of the nineteenth century still practiced their trade in the early twentieth century, but they could no longer replicate the family work patterns of their youth.

Frédéric Dubois grew up in weaving household. In 1911 he is widowed and lives with his four children. Unlike his father's household, where the children participated in weaving, in Frédéric's household only he weaves. His two older daughters are shoeworkers. His sons are too young to work. When they reach adolescence, they are more likely to become shoeworkers than weavers.

Jean Lallemand also grew up in a weaving family. In 1881 he lived with his parents, brother, and two sisters. His father was a weaver and his mother kept a small grocery business. All the children worked in weaving. In 1911, Jean unmarried lives with his siblings and their widowed mother. The two brothers continue to weave, but the two sisters have become embroiderers.

The number of weaving households did not decline significantly in Villedieu-la-Blouère 1881 and 1911. The population census of 1881 recorded 130 weaving households, whereas in 1911 the census taker listed 114 handloom weavers as heads of household. This mirrors the relative constancy in the number of handloom weavers we observed at the regional level. The general characteristics of weavers as a group, however, had changed, as their individual stories should lead us to expect. On the whole, the population of handloom weavers had aged. The average age of heads of weaving households increased from 49 in 1881 to 55 in 1911. The aging of handloom weavers is even more pronounced when we consider that in 1846, in Villedieu-la-Blouère, the average age of the male head of household was 40.1. This aging was accompanied by a decline in average household size, from 3.4 to 3.1.

Underlying these aggregate shifts is the fact that the ability of households to adequately feed and provide for their members differed from one stage of the family life cycle to another. These differences were greatly exacerbated in a period of declining piece rates. In general, but especially under these circumstances, it was easier for households with older children to adopt an effective strategy. With more producers, they could increase the pool of resources without straining the physiological limits of labor resources within the household. In addition, the resources brought in by each producer did not have to stretch as far to cover nonproductive members, particularly children too young to work.

Table 9.1

Distribution of weaving households by family life cycle, Villedieu-la-Blouère (percentage)

	Age of head of household					
	<25	25–34	35–44	45–54	55–64	65+
1846 N = 38	7.7	25.6	35.9	12.8	12.8	5.1
1881 N = 130	0.0	12.9	30.5	19.1	26.7	10.7
1911 N = 114	0.0	8.8	11.4	20.2	33.3	26.3

Source: Archives communales de Villedieu-la-Blouère, listes nominatives du recensement de la population, 1846, 1881, 1911.

A second look at the household budgets of shoe workers is instructive on this point. Not only did families with many wage earners live better than those with few, but some even enjoyed a surplus. For example, the total household income for a family of seven with six wage earners (which included a widower father and five children between the ages of 14 and 21) was 3,301 francs. This sum exceeded their expenditures on food, clothing, rent, and heat by 1,591 francs. Under these circumstances, it did not matter that the contribution of the father was only 655 francs. The wages of adolescent children more than made up the difference. Even without the 840 francs brought in by the oldest son, an 18-year-old, the subsistence of the household was easily met because the number of people who brought in resources substantially outnumbered those who were too young or too infirm to work for money. In this family, only one child, an 8-year-old, did not earn wages. Thus, even if all wages were low, the cumulative effort of many wage earners ensured a margin for survival. Another shoeworker family of seven was able to save more than 400 francs a year even though both husband and wife earned only about 500 francs each. The contribution of two sons, who together made 1,188 francs a year, and a daughter who added 200 francs to the family purse, enabled the family to live adequately while supporting two daughters, age 12 and 8, who did not yet work.[10]

The contribution of older children to the well-being of households heightens our understanding of the problem for younger households. Table 9.1 shows the distribution of weaving households by family life cycle over several historical phases of textile production. The growing difficulties young males faced in sustaining their households through weaving is reflected in the decline in number of young weaving households. Over the nearly six decades represented in the table,

10. *Enquête sur le travail à domicile dans l'industrie de la chaussure*, pp. 187–89.

Table 9.2

Percentage of household production units among weaving households, Villedieu-la-Blouère

	Age of head of household				
	25–34	35–44	45–54	55–64	65+
1881 *N* = 130	94	100	88	97	100
1911 *N* = 114	63	50	38	50	50

Source: Archives communales de Villedieu-la-Blouère, listes nominatives du recensement de la population, 1881, 1911.

the proportion of weaving households in the early phases of the family life cycle declined sharply. Equally striking is the increase in older households. Particularly in the decades between 1881 and 1911, when piece rates declined most rapidly, the relative proportion of weaving households remained most stable when the household had access to the labor of grown children, that is, during the 45–54 and 55–64 phases. The decline in the proportion of younger households was substantial in this period, as was the rising proportion of households in the oldest category.

Even if older weaving households were not threatened in the same way as younger households, the internal organization of weaving itself was changing, as typified by the experiences of François Sécher, Frédéric Dubois, and Jean Pineau. In 1881, 93 percent of weaving households were family production units—that is, every working member of the household held some occupation connected to cloth production, either as weavers or in an auxiliary task. Three percent of weaving households consisted of older weavers living alone. In the remaining 4 percent of households headed by weavers, other members of the household were employed in different trades. Thirty years later, only 44 percent of the 114 weavers were heads of family production units. In 46 percent of the households headed by weavers, children, and less frequently wives, were employed in another occupation, up from 5 percent in 1881. The number of elderly weavers living alone increased to 10 percent of all weaving households.

Not only did the absolute number of household production units decline between 1881 and 1911, but, as Table 9.2 demonstrates, the decline in the number of family production units was most pronounced when adult children were old enough to work but were not yet ready to form their own families through marriage (when the head of household was between 45 and 54 years old). Put in slightly

Table 9.3
Average size of weaving households, Villedieu-la-Blouère

	Age of head of household				
	25–34	35–44	45–54	55–64	65+
1881 N = 126	3.2	4.4	4.5	3.4	3.2
1911 N = 103	2.9	4.2	3.8	3.2	2.8

Source: Archives communales de Villedieu-la-Blouère, listes nominatives du recensement de la population, 1881, 1911.
Note: Includes only households containing more than one person.

different terms, at this stage in the family life cycle the opportunities for devoting the labor of some family members to wage earning were greatest without abandoning weaving altogether. It was possible to incorporate wages into the family's subsistence and maintain the household head as a weaver. Older weaving households appear more successful in maintaining a family production unit, but this result is a function of older children having already left the parental household. As we see from Table 9.3, households in the 55–64 years and 65+ years categories were generally smaller than younger households.

The three phenomena discussed here—the greater capacity for older households to meet the subsistence needs of their members, the gradual disappearance of young weaving families, and the demise of family production units—are related. Resource-pooling strategies that enabled families to survive in an era of declining rates undermined the continuation of the family production unit. Such strategies were not feasible for families with young children, so fathers with young families had to leave the trade. To the extent that handloom weaving was a viable occupation, it survived mainly as the occupation of the head of the household, who was able to stay in weaving only because other members of the household made up for the diminishing returns from weaving. The casualty of thirty years of economic hardship was weaving as a family enterprise.

Survival Strategies and Visions of Family

The developments reviewed in the previous section contrast sharply with weavers' own characterization of the crisis in 1904. The members of the Bourse du travail and the Chambre syndicale argued that declining rates threatened the survival of their families. Yet, as we have just seen, except for young families in which children were too young to work, weaving families could live adequately if everyone in the household pooled their resources. Given the fact that families did survive, how should we interpret the words of handloom weavers? Clearly, we must be attuned to other meanings implied in the question "How can a father of a family live honorably?" When the weavers of Saint-Léger-sous-Cholet spoke of survival, whose survival did they mean? To clarify what was at stake in this discussion of survival, I contrast two analytical models that family historians and theorists of petty commodity production have used to generalize about small producers' and other poor peoples' struggles to survive poverty. Although the two models address overlapping concerns, their conceptions of the problem are fundamentally different.

The first model, developed by Soviet economist A. V. Chayanov and later adopted by theorists of petty commodity production, focuses on strategies followed by peasants and other small producers to ensure the survival of the production unit. Small producers using family labor have a special competitive advantage in doing this, embodied in the principle of "self-exploitation." According to Chayanov, family enterprises are unlike capitalist enterprises in that there is no separate accounting for wages. Their familial organization is the source of their ability to survive adversity. When prices for the goods produced declined or when the production unit is threatened in other ways, family members tend to work harder and consume less to preserve the competitiveness of their enterprise. This phenomenon has been called the "backward bending supply curve": for family enterprises, when the returns to labor go down, the supply of labor increases rather than decreases.[11]

A second model for conceptualizing family survival strategies was developed by Louise Tilly and Joan Scott and subsequently elaborated by Tilly.[12] This model emphasizes the collective survival of household members rather than the continued existence of the pro-

11. For an English translation of the works of A. V. Chayanov, see Daniel Thorner, Basile Kerbaly, and R. E. F. Smith, eds., *A. V. Chayanov on the Theory of Peasant Economy* (Homewood, Ill.: Richard D. Irwin, published for the American Economics Association, 1966). See also Harriet Friedmann, "Household Production and National Economy: Concepts for the Analysis of Agrarian Formations," *Journal of Peasant Studies* 7 (January 1980): 158–84.

12. Louise A. Tilly and Joan W. Scott, *Women, Work, and Family* (New York: Holt, Rinehart and Winston, 1978). For a critique of Tilly and Scott and their notion of family interest, see Patricia Hilden, "Family History vs. Women in History: A Critique of Tilly and Scott," *International Labor and Working Class History* 16 (Fall 1979): 1–11. See also Scott's reply in the same issue on pp. 12–17. Louise Tilly clarified her model of family strategies in "After Family Strategies, What?" *Historical Methods* 20 (Summer 1987): 123–25.

duction unit. According to Tilly and Scott, family economies are governed by the need to bring into balance the necessities of subsistence for household members, on the one hand, and the number of people laboring in the family, on the other. Tilly and Scott focus on how the allocation of labor varies over the life cycle as families attempt to meet the challenges produced by the changing ratio of consumers to producers.

Although demographic composition and family life cycle are also central concerns in Chayanov's model, these two models of family behavior posit two different goals: the survival of the production unit and the survival of household members. Ideally, these goals were compatible—at least handloom weavers of the Mauges thought that they ought to be. But when the family production unit cannot generate enough resources to sustain family members, the two goals do not imply the same course of action or even the same range of possible strategies. In the Tilly and Scott model, maximizing resources does not preclude breaking apart the production unit itself if necessity indicates that greater resources are available by its sacrifice. Households governed by a Chayanovian logic, in contrast, go to great lengths to avoid dismantling the production unit.

Looking at the composition of households headed by weavers in the census of 1911, one might argue that both conceptions of survival strategies were in play. The behavior of wives and children suggests that the physical sustenance of family members was paramount, even if it meant leaving weaving itself. In this sense, to save the family as a unit of consumption, their actions help to destroy it as a unit of production. From the perspective of weaver-fathers, the problem was more complex and contradictory. When the weavers of Saint-Léger-sous-Cholet said, "In order that a father of a family can survive with two or three children and his wife . . . ," they subsumed the survival of children and wife within the survival of the weaver in his trade. The word order in this sentence is significant. It poses the problem as the survival of fathers and then considers the welfare of children and wives as dependent on attaining the first goal. We can find a more explicit expression of this presumption in the stirring words with which members of the Chambre syndicale concluded their testimony:

What does the honest and diligent worker want? It is to live by the work of his profession, to raise his family honestly, to give to our beloved France soldiers robust in body and spirit, and mothers who possess the moral energy to raise their children. It is greed that grows in society and perhap [in all] humanity, all society should be based on the three grand words of human thought, Duty in all things, Justice, and Reason. For us, the cost of labor must be raised to where the worker has a proportional part of the boss's profits because they contribute to the wealth of the latter.[13]

It is important to note here that the handloom weavers of Saint-Léger-sous-Cholet placed profession first. They did not indicate that their first duty was to family, and consequently that they would take any work to support their families. For many handloom weavers, the struggle to maintain and raise piece rates was a battle for justice. In their view, a just society would give to the weaver his fair share, a share that would allow him to carry on his profession *and* adequately fulfill his duty to his family. The perception of the crisis in weaving thus revealed an order of priorities that subsumed family interest into the individual professional identity of the father, who could not conceive of family interest independent of that identity. In this sense, the ability of adult male weavers to continue weaving came to stand for the survival of the production unit. The strategies employed by household members to meet their collective subsistence were regarded as means to attain that goal.

The Contradictions of Weaving as a Masculine Identity

In their indictments of declining piece rates, male weavers presented themselves simultaneously as weavers and as fathers. Indeed, they made little distinction between the two roles. Defining family interest around the prerogatives of the father revealed that for weavers masculinity, skill, and househeadship were indivisibly entwined.[14] Traditionally, within weaving households, one distinguished between male and female tasks. Male heads of household

13. A.N. C7318: Enquête textile 1904, Réponse de la Chambre syndicale des ouvriers tisserands de Saint-Léger-sous-Cholet.
14. Joan W. Scott, "Work Identities for Men and Women: The Politics of Work and Family in the Parisian Garment Trades in 1848," in *Gender and the Politics of History* (New York: Columbia University Press, 1988). See also note 20. For a similar analysis, consult Keith McClelland, "Masculinity and the 'Representative Artisan' in Britain, 1850–80," in *Manful Assertions: Masculinities in Britain since 1800*, ed. Michael Roper and John Tosh (London: Routledge, 1991).

were "weavers" or "master weavers," younger males were "apprentice weavers" or simply "weavers." Female members were identified by ancillary tasks in cloth making, such as mounting the warp and skein winding—"ourdisseuse" and "dévideuse." Embedded in this division was a notion of male skills linked to craftsmanship—that is, knowledge and adeptness at making cloth—and a notion of female activities linked to helping and aiding the main productive activities of the household but not directly responsible for the quality and production of the product.

It mattered little that in day-to-day production work roles were flexible.[15] Occupational titles did not necessarily govern or limit the kinds of tasks people performed. Rather, it is more useful to conceive of occupational titles, in this case, as signifying relationships. Although "ourdisseuse" or "dévideuse" denote specific activities, the names actually specified the relationship of those who bore these titles to those who were named "tisserand" (weaver). It was *tissage* that gave the household its social identity, not *ourdissage* or *dévidage*. The notion of male craftsmanship or skill in cloth making integrated members of the household into the production process through a clear authority structure. This underlying logic subdivided tasks by gender and generation, affirming the power of men over women, of older men over younger men.

The equation between masculinity and skill was not unique to the male handloom weavers of the Choletais. Sally Alexander and Barbara Taylor have observed that Chartist tailors and bootmakers in nineteenth-century England made the same claims about their activities, especially when they wished to exclude women from their trades.[16] The frequency of this pattern led John Rule to conclude that

15. According to François Simon, although preparing the yarn for weaving was primarily women's work, both men and women wove; see *Départment de Maine-et-Loire, Commune de la Romagne* (Angers: A. Bruel, 1927), p. 58. Mémé Santerre wove as a young girl and observed the same flexibility of activities in her father's house; see Grafteaux, *Mémé Santerre*.

16. Sally Alexander, "Women, Class, and Sexual Differences in the 1830s and 1840s: Some Reflections on the Writing of Feminist History," *History Workshop Journal* 17 (Spring 1984): 125–49; Barbara Taylor, " 'The Men Are as Bad as Their Masters': Socialism, Feminism, and Sexual Antagonism in the London Tailoring Trade in the 1830s," in *Sex and Class in Women's History*, ed. Judith I. Newton, Mary P. Ryan, and Judith R. Walkowitz (London: Routledge and Kegan Paul, 1983), pp. 187–200. There is an extensive literature documenting the association between masculinity and skill. For examples, see Anne Philips and Barbara Taylor, "Sex and Skill: Notes towards a Feminist Economics," *Feminist Review* 6 (1980): 79–88, Cynthia Cockburn, *Brothers: Male Dominance and Technological Change* (London: Pluto Press, 1983), Sonya Rose, "Gender Antagonism and Class Conflict: Exclusionary Strategies of Male Trade Unionists in Nineteenth-Century Britain," *Social History* 13 (1988):

most artisans believed that they held "property" in their skills, but that this property was thought to inhere in men exclusively.[17] Extending the analogy further, skill is not just any possession; I liken it to patrimony. Like patrimonial property it does not signal simple individual ownership. Patrimony centers kin relations around the patriarch and orders the relationships of individual family members to each other.[18]

This arrangement rested on a conception of moral order. Like all such constructs, they described the "ought" in the system rather than the "is." The belief did not ensure the actual authority of fathers as heads of household, nor did it describe how compliance and cooperation were actually achieved. Nor was it a matter of personal gain that fathers should assume responsibility for the family enterprise. Certainly not all fathers lived up to or even welcomed this responsibility. As suggested in the language of handloom weavers in Saint-Léger-sous-Cholet, however, the patriarchal sense of self was very real in the moral self-perception of handloom weavers. The weaver was a man of honor who lived up to his duty to family and obligations to country. How could an enlightened world deny a hard-working man the simple rewards of his labor?

The intensity of these feelings help us understand why handloom weavers refused better-paying jobs in shoe manufacture even when they were offered. This refusal both puzzled and angered shoe entrepreneurs. As we recall, the first shoe manufacturers in the Mauges claimed that the development of the shoe industry in their native region served an important social purpose: rescuing male handloom weavers threatened by the loss of economic viability. Beyond offering jobs, shoe manufacturing was particularly suited to succeed the hand weaving of linen because it too was organized around homework. The transition from linen to shoes was supposed to occur without social dislocation.

Yet shoe entrepreneur René Chéné was both disturbed and surprised to discover that, despite new opportunities and better wages, weavers

191–208, and Ava Baron, "Contested Terrain Revisited: Technology and Gender Definitions of Work in the Printing Industry, 1850–1920," in *Women, Work, and Technology,* ed. Barbara Drygulski Wright et al. (Ann Arbor: University of Michigan Press, 1987), pp. 58–83.

17. John Rule, "The Property in Skill in the Period of Manufacture," in *The Historical Meaning of Work,* ed. Patrick Joyce (Cambridge: Cambridge University Press, 1987), pp. 99–118. See also Wally Seccombe, "Patriarchy Stabilized: The Construction of the Male Breadwinner Wage Norm in Nineteenth-Century Britain," *Social History* 11 (January 1986): 53–76.

18. Pierre Bourdieu, "Marriage Strategies as Social Reproduction," in *Family and Society,* ed. Robert Forster and Orest Ranum (Baltimore: Johns Hopkins University Press, 1976), pp. 117–44.

left their looms with great reluctance. Many tried three or four times to take on work in the shoe trade but returned each time to weaving. Having no other explanation, Chéné attributed this behavior to habit and a regional suspicion of new ways.[19] With few other options, Chéné and other shoe entrepreneurs hired women instead.

Given what we know about these handloom weavers—and remembering that, for some, even political alliance with factory workers was a difficult compromise—their reluctance to become shoeworkers should not be surprising. Homework in shoe manufacture and the lingerie trade had little in common with handloom weaving. These former trades used proletarianized labor. Workers performed simple, partial, repetitive tasks in an elaborate division of labor designed and controlled by the entrepreneur. In contrast, handloom weavers organized the processes of transformation from yarn to cloth. Although handloom weavers were dependent on merchants for supplies and markets, they had not always been so. This memory of other times, as well as the reality that weavers continued to coordinate the production process in cloth making, reinforced the sense of difference. The entrepreneurs' analogy would have been more apt had they compared handloom weavers to subcontractors in the shoe and lingerie trades, and homeworkers in these trades to the individuals weavers engaged to perform various tasks in weaving. Thus it makes sense that established handloom weavers would resist earning wages at home as they resisted factory work, seeing both as part of the broader threat of proletarianization.

Despite the refusal of handloom weavers, the connection between the crisis in weaving and the new sweated trades was intimate, in a double sense. Although weavers themselves refused these jobs, their children did not. When we link the new workers in the shoe and lingerie trades to their household of origin, it is evident that weaving households provided a disproportionate number of recruits.

Looking again at Villedieu-la-Blouère, of the fifty-three men working in the shoe industry listed in the population census of 1911, the majority (60 percent) were heads of their own household. Forty percent were dependent members of households. Of these twenty-one dependent workers, nine were sons of weavers living at home, four were sons of shoeworkers, and none were the sons of cultivators. Of the 70 percent of shoeworkers working in 1911 whom I successfully traced back to the 1881 census, nearly all (90 percent) came originally from weaving households. Of the seventy-six women employed in

19. René Chéné, *Les débuts du commerce et de l'industrie de la chaussure dans la région de Cholet* (Maulévier, Maine-et-Loire: Hérault, 1980), p. 45.

the shoe trade, 40 percent came from weaving households, 24 percent came from the households of shoeworkers, and 8 percent came from farming households. The remaining 22 percent were from the households of day workers, service artisans, and small shopkeepers. We find comparable patterns in the needle trades, where seventy-eight women were employed as lingères, couturières, and brodeuses in 1911. Of these workers, 27 percent came from weaving households, 15 percent from shoemaking households, and only 4 percent from cultivator households.

The disproportionate representation of weaving households among sweated workers can be summarized as follows. Cultivators represented about 32 percent of the population of Villedieu-la-Blouère, but only 6 percent of the female workers in the new sweated trades came from these households. No male sweated workers came from agricultural households. If we count weaving households and shoeworkers' households (themselves largely headed by children of weavers) together, these households provided 52 percent of the female labor force and 100 percent of the smaller male labor force in the new sweated shoe and lingerie trades. This result is not due to the greater number of weaving households, which constituted about the same proportion of the population as agricultural households. Thus weaving households supplied the crucial labor to sustain the new manufacturing. Without this labor force, shoe and lingerie entrepreneurs would have had to rely on the households of service artisans and farmers to meet their labor needs. As I discussed in Chapters 7 and 8, this labor force was too unreliable, because of the demands of commercial agriculture, to satisfy the requirements of sweated industries.

This pattern raises perplexing questions about the nature of weaving identities and the structure of weaving households. Why did the weavers' resistance to proletarianization not apply to other members of their households? Was the entry of household members into sweated work a signal of the breakdown of the household's collective identity as a production unit, or was it consistent with that logic?

The Different Fates of Weavers' Sons and Daughters

When we examine what children in weaving households in Villedieu-la-Blouère were actually doing, we see an important difference in the relation of sons and daughters to the family production

Table 9.4

Occupations of weavers' children, Villedieu-la-Blouère, 1911

Occupation	Sons		Daughters	
	Mean age	N	Mean age	N
Weaver	24.3	23	30.8	6
Shoeworker	22.1	9	21.5	23
Needleworker	0.0	0	24.3	10
Other wage work	0.0	0	17.0	1
No occupation	8.3	22	8.2	29
All	17.4	54	17.1	69

Source: Archives communales de Villedieu-la-Blouère, listes nominatives du recensement de la population, 1911.

unit (Table 9.4). Sons (23) were far more likely to devote themselves to weaving than were daughters (6). Daughters concentrated mostly in wage work in the shoe and needle trades, whereas only a few weavers' sons were shoeworkers. The differences in the occupations of daughters and sons explains why the sex ratios in weaving households that remained family production units tended to favor males, as Table 9.5 indicates: sons who stayed stayed as weavers, not as wage earners.

These patterns suggest that weaver-fathers conceived of the contributions of sons and daughters in terms of different strategies and goals. Preserving and continuing the production unit was given primacy when these men considered the occupation and future of sons. In contrast, weaver-fathers conceived of their daughters' work and contributions primarily in relation to the collective survival of household members. Returning to the distinction between the Chayanov model and the Tilly and Scott model, weaving families seem to

Table 9.5

Mean ratio males to females over 12 in weaving households, Villedieu-la-Blouère, 1911

	Age of head of household				
	25–34	35–44	45–54	55–64	65+
Not in family production unit	0.50	0.43	0.37	0.53	0.51
Family production unit	0.50	0.57	0.68	0.57	0.50

Source: Archives communales de Villedieu-la-Blouère, listes nominatives du recensement de la population, 1911.
Note: For households containing more than one person.

have adopted a mixed strategy, depending on the gender of the household member whose labor was at issue.

A preference for sons to continue in weaving is consistent with notions of male identity in weaving households. Craft continuity between father and son is but an extension of the inextricable entwining of masculine identity with househeadship and craftsmanship. Just as it would have been a sign of defeat for the head of the household to enter another profession, sons, in a sense, carried the burden of the father's struggle. The identification of the skills and social identity of the household with patrimony assumes a new significance here: integral to the value of patrimonial property is that it is passed on, as a concrete symbol of the success of the father. That daughters became proletarianized workers laboring at home and in factories is also consistent with the constitution of gender identities in weaving households. Women were conceived of as helpers and secondary producers in the process of cloth making. Although certainly many wives and daughters were adept weavers, their occupational classification as "dévideuse" or "ourdisseuse" signified a marginal position in relation to the core identity of the household.

These were not gender identities of a predictable sort. Women in weaving households were not defined by their reproductive activities, although they clearly performed them. Instead, they were defined as producers, but secondary producers whose specific activities were not crucial to family identity.[20] The discussion of the participation of women during the formation of the Chambre syndicale is indicative of male weavers' attitude toward women's labor. In one of the initial meetings, local handloom weavers gathered to hear the speech of an organizer from Angers. His speech urging a ban on female wage work and blaming women for low male wages was not well received by local handloom weavers, who insisted that their organization should include the wives and daughters of weavers. Yet, though male weavers recognized women as producers, female members of the Chambre syndicale were not given the right to vote at meetings. This was also the case for the Syndicats de prévoyance. Women were present but silenced. So, women's contributions were recognized as pro-

20. Joan W. Scott has found that skilled Parisian tailors in the 1830s and 1840s held similar conceptions about maleness and femaleness in relation to family identity. As in the Choletais, these arguments about the nature of gender identities became salient in a period of profound transformation in the basic social relations of production in the garment industry. See Scott, "Men and Women in the Parisian Garment Trades: Discussions of Family and Work in the 1830s and 1840s," in *The Power of the Past,* ed. Pat Thane and Geoffrey Crossick (Cambridge: Cambridge University Press, 1985), pp. 67–93.

Table 9.6

Average number of sons and daughters in weaving households, Villedieu-la-Blouère, 1911

	Age of head of household				
	25–34	35–44	45–54	55–64	65+
Sons	0.4	0.8	0.5	0.6	0.3
Daughters	0.5	1.1	1.1	0.5	0.5

Source: Archives communales de Villedieu-la-Blouère, listes nominatives du recensement de la population, 1911.
Note: For households containing more than one person.

ductive labor, but women were still viewed as dependents, subordinated to their husbands and fathers who articulated the opinions of the household.

This is not the whole story, however. We must still consider the success of households in pursuing even this modified attempt to maintain a family production unit. To do so, I turn next to an examination of the relative ability of families to hold their sons and daughters in the household. As Table 9.6 indicates, fewer sons than daughters stayed, and in the critical 45–54 phase daughters strongly outnumbered sons. Even when we consider only households that remained family production units, the higher concentration of males revealed in Table 9.5 is deceptive, because it masks the generally smaller size of these households. As Table 9.7 indicates, there were in

Table 9.7

Size and composition of weaving households, Villedieu-la-Blouère, 1911

	Age of head of household				
	25–34	35–44	45–54	55–64	65+
Not a family production unit	N = 3	N = 9	N = 10	N = 18	N = 12
Average size	3.0	4.0	4.1	3.6	3.4
daughters/household	0.3	1.0	1.4	0.9	0.9
sons/household	0.6	0.5	0.4	0.9	0.5
Family production unit	N = 5	N = 9	N = 6	N = 18	N = 12
Average size	2.8	4.3	3.3	2.7	2.2
daughters/household	0.6	1.1	0.5	0.1	0
sons/household	0.2	1.0	0.6	0.3	0.2

Source: Archives communales de Villedieu-la-Blouère, listes nominatives du recensement de la population, 1911.
Note: For households containing more than one person.

Table 9.8
Distribution of male heads of household in shoemaking, Villedieu-la-Blouère, 1911

	Age of head of household					
	<25	25–34	35–44	45–54	55–64	65 +
Number	0	12	12	7	3	0
Percentage	0	35.3	35.3	20.6	8.8	0

Source: Archives communales de Villedieu-la-Blouère, Liste nominative du recensement de la population, 1911.

fact very few sons in these households. As the parents grew older, the number of sons steadily declined.

If the average size of family production units were the same as the size of households with mixed occupations, one might suspect that the distinction between these two types of household was purely the result of the distribution of sons and daughters. As evidenced in Table 9.7, however, in older phases of the family life cycle (phases 45–54, 55–64, 65 +), households with mixed occupations were consistently larger (by approximately one person). The presence of daughters in these households was relatively constant (on the average, between 0.9 and 1.4 daughters, depending on the phase) and did not diminish appreciably as parents aged. We expect those households where all members wove to have had more sons than daughters; in fact, the number of sons was negligible and declined with the age of the parents. Thus older weaving households were actually divided between elderly couples aided by working daughters and elderly couples living alone. This may account for the fact that the sex ratio of males to females in the two kinds of household becomes more similar as households grow older (see Table 9.5).

The demographic profile of older weaving families suggests that sons were leaving the parental household to constitute their own. This pattern is further corroborated by Table 9.8, which examines the age of male heads of household in the shoemaking trades. The strong preponderance of younger households reflects the economic choices of weavers' sons who were able to set up their own households. As I pointed out earlier, about 90 percent of young male shoeworkers can be traced back to weaving households. That sons of weavers had a more difficult time taking up weaving as head of their own household is testified to by the small number of young weaving households in the 1911 census (Table 9.1). Many of their fathers, however, continued as weavers in the bourg. The small number of older households headed by shoeworkers also reflects the newness of the shoe industry, as well as the fact that relatively few older adult males entered the shoe industry. The small number of older male shoeworkers did not come from weaving households but were formerly independent shoe-workers in the local bespoke trade.

Whereas sons went off to constitute their own households, daughters stayed longer and were more consistently present in older households. In households where sons and daughters were both present (the 45–54 phase), the mean age of the oldest daughter was 18, whereas the mean age of the oldest son was 14.3, suggesting that parents were holding onto their daughters longer than their sons. Older households relied on daughters' income to aid the parents' survival. Ironically, because daughters were peripheral to the social identity of weaving households, weaving families relied more heavily on them to help support elderly parents.

The different treatment of sons and daughters indicates that weavers' strategy for the survival of the production unit had not changed from earlier, more prosperous, eras. The peripheral position of women in the social identity of the household justified their being "sacrificed" first in efforts to save the family production unit. It seems likely that daughters' wage work would have been considered a temporary measure to see the family through hard times, with the expectation that they would return to the family production unit once the family weathered the difficulties. Yet, as conditions deteriorated, the temporary passage into wage work became a permanent condition. The very actions designed to save the production unit now became the instrument of its demise.[21] For sons, the decline in the economic viability of weaving produced an opposite reaction. Sons in the traditional structure of the weaving family occupied a different position than daughters: future weavers developing skills, rather than ancillary parts of the production process. Unable to promise a future in handloom weaving, weaving households lost their claims on sons' presence and labor. Certainly, it served the material interest of fathers to hold onto sons, but the very notion of manhood weavers defended stipulated that under these material circumstances sons must break away.

Undergirded by these contradictions, small-scale production enjoyed a remarkable degree of staying power. In retrospect, the resis-

21. Harriet Friedmann points out a similar contradiction in strategies for families in the American Plains, in "World Market, State, and Family Farm: Social Basis of Household Production in the Era of Wage Labor," *Comparative Studies of Society and History* 20 (October 1978): 545–86.

244 The Weaver's Knot

tance of handloom weavers may seem to have been doomed to fail, but the fact that many of these weavers who were in the prime of life in the 1880s finished their days as handloom weavers thirty or forty years later should indicate the tenacity of their grip on this identity and their notion of craft and skill. Their ability to stay rather than migrate, to remain handloom weavers and not to search out new jobs, was, however, predicated emotionally and materially on the acceptance of the same set of associated meanings by the women in the households. The final link in the chain rested on the ties that bound these women as family members. The struggle against proletarianization was a victory only for the "père de famille." Wives and daughters were called on to maintain the fiction.

It is evident that women in weaving families lived under the dual pressures of capitalist and patriarchal demands, although they would certainly not use this vocabulary. The two systems, however, did not act as one. The precapitalist handicraft economy was organized by particular sets of patriarchal principles. Capitalists did not simply take over these principles, as some feminist theorists have argued.[22] In fact, this was not possible, because patriarchal authority was inseparable from the market-based autonomy of small-scale producers, their knowledge of manufacturing processes (what we would call skill), and the sexual division of labor that allowed the household to function as a production unit. To proletarianize artisans was to attack precisely those aspects of artisanal production in which patriarchal authority was embedded. Thus the artisanal struggle against capitalist relations of production was at the same time a struggle for the notion of the father's prerogatives.

Interpreting the Power of Fathers and the Sacrifice of Daughters

The emotional and economic complexities of the situation of daughters in weaving families came from the unspoken demands on them to fill in the gaps—the shortfalls in money and ideology. Young women in these families were under tremendous pressure to sacrifice

22. For an overview of this debate, see the essays in Lydia Sargent, ed., *Women and Revolution: A Discussion of the Unhappy Marriage of Marxism and Feminism* (Boston: Southend Press, 1981). My own position is closest to that of Ann Ferguson and Nancy Folbre, who emphasize the tensions and contradictions between patriarchy and capitalism in their contributions to this collection.

for the good of the whole. The overwhelming difference between sons and daughters in this situation makes it tempting for us to explain behavior in terms of gender socialization. Certainly, the notion that feminine moral character is defined by sacrifice is a familiar and much abused image of womanhood. I cannot fully explore here the vast cultural apparatus deployed around such images, but they are readily available whenever one looks for them. For example, the local memory of the Vendée counterrevolution, the central historical myth of the region's identity, is suffused with images of women who gave up their comfort and their lives to support the fight against republican forces.[23] Yet women did not necessarily have to believe in the positive value of sacrifice for them to stay longer in their parental households. In fact, the causal connections may be reversed. In contrast to their brothers, who could legitimately break free within the ideology espoused by fathers, the daughters' inability resembled sacrifice. This difference, once articulated in gendered terms, may have encouraged women to associate sacrifice with femininity.[24]

How, then, did these women assess their situation? The reality is that we may never know. At a first glance, the problem appears to be the silence of women on this subject in the available records. On further consideration, however, this silence goes beyond the technical problems of historical documentation. It is also a problem of forbid-

---

23. See Roger Dupuy, "Les femmes et la Contre-Révolution dans l'Ouest," *Bulletin d'histoire économique et sociale de la Révolution française,* 1979, pp. 61–70, and Émile Gabory, *Les femmes dans la tempête: Les vendéennes* (Paris: Perrin, 1934). For a sample of the numerous memoires written by women who were active in the counterrevolution, see Renée Bordereau, *Mémoires de Renée Bordereau, dite l'angevin* (Denée, Maine-et-Loire: Éditions Ivan Davy, 1983), La Comtesse de la Bouère, *La guerre de la Vendée, 1793–1796: Mémoires inédits* (Paris: Plon-Nourrit, 1907), and Marquise de la Rochejaquelein, *Mémoires de la Marquise de la Rochejaquelein, 1772–1857* (Paris: Mercure de France, 1984).

24. It is important to keep in mind that although the daughters' oppression seems overdetermined in this case, different economic circumstances could have put the sons in the position to sacrifice for fathers and the patrimony. As Susan Carol Rogers describes for the village of Sainte-Foy in southwestern France, since the Second World War inheriting sons have been more tied to the parental household than noninheriting children. In the 1960s and 70s an unprecedented number of women left Saint-Foy because technological advances in agriculture lessened the demand for female labor. This outmigration produced a generation of bachelor farmers who own lucrative holdings but do not have the social means to continue the family farm. The heir may be wealthy in land and local prospects but, in an increasingly mobile and commercialized society, he is also less equipped in terms of education and other forms of transportable wealth to make a life away from the farm. See Rogers, *Shaping Modern Times in Rural France: The Transformation and Reproduction of an Aveyronnais Community* (Princeton: Princeton University Press, 1991). For similar patterns among peasants in the Béarn, see Pierre Bourdieu, "Marriage Strategies as Strategies of Social Reproduction." Also consult Bourdieu's earlier article, "Célibat et condition paysanne," *Études rurales* 5/6 (1962): 32–135.

den speech. Especially within families, there are realms of experience and social understanding which are "experienced" but not officially acknowledged, felt but never fully articulated.[25] As scholars we must not be so naive as to believe that we can easily recover the submerged experiences of women, as if such "authentic" voices were only cloaked by obscuring ideology.[26] Such methods assume that oppressive structures are only constraints external to the subject rather than constituents of subjectivity. In other words, we may never be able to differentiate "free" consent from coerced submission, since we know only what can be consciously expressed and not what remains inchoate or repressed.

Turning to "oppressing structures" raises a new set of problems. How should we understand the power of fathers? We need some explanation of the nature of fathers' authority and power in order to understand how fathers framed the choices for daughters, but do we need a theory of patriarchy to accomplish this task? At present, feminist scholars tend to shy away from such a theory, and rightly so. Although the notion of patriarchy was initially useful in asserting the systemic nature of male dominance, the notion becomes too imprecise as a guide to concrete analysis when it is used ahistorically to refer to all forms of male dominance.[27] The turn in feminist scholarship toward gender analysis was taken originally to avoid the pitfalls of building feminist theory on such a theory of patriarchy.[28] Yet even the most vocal critics of "patriarchy" recognize the need for feminists to analyze the multiple and changing ideologies, institutions, and daily practices through which men as men exercise power and authority over women. The debate does not center on whether patriarchy exists. The problem confronting feminist scholars is that

25. For further discussion of this form of silencing, see Hermann Rebel, "Cultural Hegemony and Class Experience: A Critical Reading of Recent Ethnological-Historical Approaches" (Part One), *American Ethnologist* 16 (1989): 117–36. See also Joan W. Scott, "The Evidence of Experience," *Critical Inquiry* 17 (Summer 1991): 773–97.

26. Marilyn Strathern cautions feminist scholars against this assumption in "Self-Interest and the Social Good: Some Implications of Hagen Gender Imagery," in *Sexual Meanings,* ed. Sherry B. Ortner and Harriet Whitehead (Cambridge: Cambridge University Press, 1981), p. 167.

27. For an overview of this discussion, see Sheila Rowbotham, "The Trouble with 'Patriarchy,' " and Sally Alexander and Barbara Taylor, "In Defense of 'Patriarchy,' " in *People's History and Socialist Theory,* ed. Raphael Samuel (London: Routledge and Kegan Paul, 1981), pp. 364–72. See also Michael Roper and John Tosh, "Introduction: Historians and the Politics of Masculinity," in *Manful Assertions: Masculinities in Britain since 1800,* ed. Roper and Tosh (London: Routledge, 1991).

28. See Gayle Rubin, "The Traffic in Women: Notes on the 'Political Economy' of Sex," in *Towards an Anthropology of Women,* ed. Rayna Reiter (New York: Monthly Review Press, 1975), pp. 157–210.

the sources of male priviledge and dominance seem to evade generalization, that is, from one situation to another and one moment in time to another, the contours of male power may change radically. Even when one can readily identify the various sources of male power, both official and unofficial, ideologies and laws do not work by themselves. We still need to ask, how does a potential resource turn into an actual advantage in particular social interactions?[29] The mistake, perhaps, lies in our understanding of what theory must accomplish. Demanding a generative logic for male power which must hold true across time and space seems self-defeating when the exercise of power is so contextual.

The logic by which handloom weavers maintained a measure of control within their families can be understood within the framework introduced in Chapter 2 under the rubric "the logic of sweating." In this logic, power is not a hard nugget, a reality that can be stored in structures such as "patriarchy" and called on when needed. Instead, it is the result of struggles over position and access to resources, in which success is achieved through holding open one's own options while shutting down those of others. The terrain of struggle is multiple, as this book suggests, ranging from markets for cloth to the language of moral obligation. In all these contexts, however, identity becomes simply another word for the range of possible actions open to actors. In other words, the struggle to preserve an identity is indistinguishable from the positioning to frame the choices of others.

The positioning of daughters to sacrifice reveals an important dimension of how the notion of "family interest," as defined by fathers, operated as a hegemonic ideology.[30] The ability of fathers to define

29. David Warren Sabean makes a similar point in his analysis of "Herrschaft" in *Power in the Blood: Popular Culture and Village Discourse in Early Modern Germany* (New York: Cambridge University Press, 1984).

30. This analysis differs from current feminist assessments of family history. Feminist scholars have long argued against family historians who use the notion of "family interest" to explain how families act. Arguing that such scholarship usually studies only the interests and actions of the families' most powerful member, thus obscuring the lives of the less powerful and leaving unexamined the power relations within families, feminist scholars have persuasively stated the need to disaggregate "the family" into many overlapping structures of activities and institutions through which individuals identified by sex and generation experience family life in radically different ways. For this critique of family history, see Rayna Rapp, Ellen Ross, and Renate Bridenthal, "Examining Family History," in *Sex and Class in Women's History*, ed. Judith L. Newton, Mary P. Ryan, and Judith R. Walkowitz (London: Routledge and Kegan Paul, 1983), pp. 232–58, and Barrie Thorne, "Feminist Rethinking of the Family: An Overview," in *Rethinking the Family: Some Feminist Questions*, ed. Thorne with Marilyn Yalom (New York: Longman, 1982), pp. 1–24. For an assessment of the relationship between family history and women's history, see Louise A. Tilly, "Women's History

the collective interest of the household does not necessarily rest on brute force or greater economic strength. Instead, hegemonic ideologies present particular visions of the world and of social relationships as the natural and seemingly uncontestable moral order. These ideologies operate at the cognitive level. They attempt to structure peoples' perception and evaluation of social reality, and hence their possible courses of action. Hegemonic ideologies enforce compliance, not through explicit coercion, but by suppressing alternative interpretations of the same social situation which might lead to other actions. For households to be solidary behind the survival of handloom weaving meant repressing other possible goals, and specifically suppressing the articulation of conflicting individual interests in such a way that alternative definitions of common goals were not expressed. It is not that hegemonic ideologies have total control, or that there is no possibility of opposition. But opposition must command matching ideological force and legitimacy. As I briefly suggested in referring to the memory of the Vendée, for women in the Choletais the anger and resentment that might have led to an alternative vision of family interest, and to a new division of responsibilities and sacrifices, could claim little moral legitimacy on which to base another course of action.[31]

The power of weaver-fathers, however, must be understood in a more complex way, as an ability to bind daughters to the household

---

and Family History: Fruitful Collaboration of Missed Connection?" *Journal of Family History* 12 (1987): 303–15.

Although demystifying unitary notions of family interest is important, many feminist scholars have moved too quickly to take individual women as the starting point of analysis—as if "family interest" were merely a masking ideology, a veil drawn across family relations which once torn would reveal their true individual constituents. These scholars thus underestimate the power notions of family interest have to order the daily reality of family life. The mistake is in assuming that, since the content of "family interest" is problematic, not natural, it must have no real content at all. On this debate, see Leslie Page Moch et al., "Family Strategy: A Dialogue," *Historical Methods* 20 (Summer 1987): 115–18, especially the contribution of Nancy Folbre, "Family Strategy, Feminist Strategy." For other illuminating discussions, see Folbre, "Hearts and Spades: Paradigms of Household Economics," *World Development* 14 (1986): 245–55, and Folbre and Heidi Hartmann, "The Rhetoric of Self-Interest: Ideology and Gender in Economic Theory," in *The Consequences of Economic Rhetoric*, ed. Arjo Klamer, Donald N. McCloskey, and Robert M. Solow (Cambridge: Cambridge University Press, 1988), pp. 184–203.

31. This analysis of hegemony relies on the concepts of Antonio Gramsci, see *Selections from the Prison Notebooks* (London: Lawrence and Wishart, 1976). For an insightful analysis of Gramsci's notion of consent and ideology, see Joseph V. Femia, *Gramsci's Political Thought* (Oxford: Oxford University Press, 1981). On the broader applications of the notion of cultural hegemony, see T. J. Jackson Lears, "The Concept of Cultural Hegemony: Problems and Possibilities," *American Historical Review* 90 (June 1985): 567–93.

coupled with a failure to do the same with sons. The patrimony that bound sons when handloom weaving was viable became, in the late nineteenth century, an absence that broke the ties linking sons to their fathers. The eroding economic position of weaving did not alter the relation between fathers and daughters, however. If anything, it strengthened the claims of fathers on daughters. Ultimately, the power fathers held over daughters was the fathers' dependence. Unlike their brothers, weavers' daughters could not refuse the demands of family interest and still remain ethical. Thus fathers did not need to act purposely to shape daughters' behavior. Rather, fathers were beneficiaries of the inability of daughters to find new ways to define their relation to family. In this way, the daughters' position constituted a resource in the struggle waged by fathers.

In the early twentieth century, women from weaving families stood at the juncture of entrepreneurs' search for cheap labor and male weavers' struggle for craft identity and independence. They stood at the point where the demand for labor and the supply of labor converged. Holding these disparate strands, these women bore the costs passed on by others and absorbed the consequences of other people's priorities.

10

Conclusions

"Ah, we were poor in those days," Madame P. reminisced without a trace of nostalgia. "And we worked hard, too!"

"The people of this region are no shirkers, no they're not," Monsieur B. joined in, pointing his fork at me for emphasis. "Take the people of my region, for example," Madame P.'s lodger mused, "... the people of the Midi are slow. Now the people around here, they know what hard work is. You hire a Maugeois for a good day's labor, he's there ten minutes before to check the machinery."

"And what do we get for it?" Madame P. interjected. "Poverty, that's what. Poverty and ignorance. If you ask me," she said, leaning against the door of the kitchen, "we're all too quick to go to work. We ought to emphasize education. Sure, we have little unemployment in this area. But is that something to boast about? These parents can't wait for their children to get jobs, bring in extra income. The children, too, they want to earn money—their own freedom, they say. But they have no skills. They'll stay cheap labor. Now, my daughter, she stayed in school. We made sacrifices—we sacrifice for our families. She has a job in Paris now."

"We're going soon to see her . . ." said Madame P., her voice trailing off into the kitchen. "But things are not so bad these days, as before," she said as she came back with dessert. "We were awfully poor until the revolution of '36.[1] We were . . . we were . . . under-

---

1. The "revolution of '36" refers to the years of the Popular Front. Many other recently published memoirs of working people also recall that the Popular Front marked a distinct change for the better. Foremost, they talk of paid vacations, and secondarily, the expansion of social security. For examples, see Bonnie G. Smith, *Confessions of a Concierge: Madame Lucie's History of Twentieth-Century France* (New Haven: Yale University Press, 1985), and Serge Grafteaux, *Mémé Santerre: A French Woman of the People,* trans. Louis A. Tilly and Kathryn L. Tilly (New York: Schocken Books, 1985).

developed." She emphasized each syllable of the word. "Things are much better now."

Madame P., a friendly woman in her late fifties, runs a small restaurant and hotel in one of the communes in the Choletais. The commune is typical of the interior bocage. The population is evenly divided between those employed in agriculture and in manufacturing. The commune has several small workshops making expensive baby clothes and several defunct small shoe factories. Historically the commune had a large population of handloom weavers. Shoe manufacturing was introduced in the early twentieth century, along with an extensive putting-out industry for finishing sheets and other household linens. In her youth, Madame P. was a finisher in a shoe factory by day. At night, she told me, she and her siblings sat around a single lamp and stitched uppers with their mother. Her mother kept the inn, which Madame P. took over. Her mother took in homework to make ends meet.

"I have worked hard all my life," she said, looking at her hands. Time has not dulled her memory of poverty. Nor is the past so remote. Madame P.'s life is typical of most working people of the Choletais with deep roots in the region. Her life, her work, and the lives of her neighbors and friends are marked by what they have endured. The words "poverty" and "hard work" resonate as she speaks them. They capture for her the essence of her past and of her region.

"Backwardness" or "underdeveloped" are other people's words to describe why Madame P. and other Maugeois generations before her have not shared in the promised prosperity of modern industrial society. Scholars using these concepts have tended to characterize the economic and social development of the Mauges as a series of missed opportunities and to evaluate the lives of its inhabitants by the goods they do not possess. Within these frameworks, people are often viewed as if they were inert—as vehicles through which larger social processes are played out and as victims who suffer their fates without comprehension of the larger whole. Social history provides a powerful corrective. One of its premises is the possibility, indeed the imperative, of connecting large-scale social processes with the struggles of day-to-day existence. But social history is more than a "people's history"; it endeavors to accomplish more than documenting how "big" events affect "little" people.[2] Put most simply, more than re-

---

2. For a more thorough discussion of these distinctions, consult the essays in *People's History and Socialist Theory,* ed. Raphael Samuel (London: Routledge and Kegan Paul, 1981). See also Philip Abrams, *Historical Sociology* (Ithaca: Cornell University Press, 1982).

constituting the human drama behind world historical events, social historians try to see people as actors.[3]

Focusing on social action recasts how we think about social processes, respecifying how change occurs and bringing different types of reasoning to bear on questions of causation. It is important to remember that, although we can always point to concrete examples of mechanization, and although there have been great transformations over time, the processes that constitute the concept "industrialization" are abstractions whose coherence is more real to historians than to those who experience them. From the vantage point of merchants, petty producers, industrialists, and workers, industrialization was not a single event but a series of alternatives and choices whose results were unknown to them. For historians who do not recognize the limitations of these abstractions and who search for explanations only at the level of the systemic logic of the abstracted whole (i.e., the logic of markets and technical efficiency), there exists the danger of misunderstanding the general phenomenon and misspecifying the workings of the particulars. Although we can account for the distinctive (although not unique) survival and transformation of decentralized small-scale manufacturing by specifying its location within broader labor and product markets, we must keep in mind that market niches and specializations do not exist waiting for producers to fill them. Rather, specialized roles within a broader whole are themselves results of struggles for secure positions in markets.

---

3. Such a view of social action does not rely on a unitary or fixed notion of identity in order to define agency and motivation. In fact, shifting circumstances and the multiplicity of social ties make action inseparable from identity formation, a project that is necessarily tendentious but yet always incomplete. Thus handloom weavers may want continuity, but achieving that stability requires constant movement. Their continual search for new positions and innovative alliances impinges on the possibilities of others for constituting identities and social relationships. Unlike many social historians who worry that poststructuralist theories invite political paralysis, I believe that the destabilizing effect of this inquiry (as articulated particularly in feminist theory) has heightened rather than diminished attention to social action. These perspectives have expanded the realm of the political by taking a more encompassing view of the terrains of struggle and negotiation. For an overview of the debate among social historians, see Bryan D. Palmer, *Descent into Discourse: The Reification of Language and the Writing of Social History* (Philadelphia: Temple University Press, 1990), and Lenard R. Berlanstein, ed., *Rethinking Labor History: Essays in Discourse and Class Analysis* (Urbana: University of Illinois Press, 1993). For a perspective closest to my own views, see Mariana Valverde's two articles "As If Subjects Existed: Analyzing Social Discourse," *Canadian Review of Sociology and Anthropology* 28 (May 1991): 173–87, and "Poststructuralist Gender Historians: Are We Those Names?" *Labour/le travail* 25 (Spring 1990): 227–36.

Through these conflicts we witness the process and progress of capitalist class formation in the region: the creation of industrial capitalists from groups of merchant capitalists who neither owned productive capital nor controlled the labor process, and the transformation of independent small-scale producers into dependent producers and wage workers who provided only labor. I have argued that the actual evolution of productive arrangements—combinations of machinery and scale of production, location of work, type of workers employed, and the tasks these workers performed—were the results of struggles to establish and enforce these social arrangements. And the lessons from this case can be generalized. Social formations are not mandated by technical necessity, as many machine-centered accounts of industrialization imply. Nor are the efforts of those who resist change without effect. Rather, it is in the struggle to lock in particular social relationships, those specifying property rights, discipline, and control, that productive arrangements begin to take shape. The introduction of labor-saving machines is but one moment in the "politics of production." In the Choletais, as elsewhere, class was a process of becoming, not an endpoint.

Individual testimonies like these offered by Madame P. add an important dimension to our understanding of social relations of production in the Pays des Mauges. Such confidences are rare. In this book, I have had to be content with the types of sources available to me. I have retrieved from archival sources the actions these people took on their own behalf. Relying on a historian's reconstruction of social relationships between groups within communities, and between and within families, I have tried to understand motivations, aspirations, and hopes.

Turning to personal memories to document the past can, however, be disappointing. Madame P. has only vague memories of the handloom weavers in her commune. Their houses are used only for storage now, she explained. But their work lives on in the old linen dishcloths, still bleached and untattered, that line her shelves. When she remembers them, they are not the heroic weavers who struggled to maintain their status as independent producers, they are the old men she and her sisters used to peer down at through the cellar windows. She remembers them as she remembers herself as a young worker: hard working and extremely poor.

It is not Madame P.'s recounting of past events that is crucial to our understanding. Her memory, in fact, cannot serve as a document of the past.[4] Moreover, in her retelling the past is outside human volition and control. Sadly, the struggles of the past are not remembered; they are lost to popular memory. Rather, what is essential is Madame P.'s cogent intelligence about her own situation and her analysis of the dynamics of skill and the processes that cheapen labor. She remembers her relationship to local merchants and what the priest taught her about how to act toward local elites. She knows the importance of family ties, the sacrifices exacted in their name, and the explanations given for those sacrifices. Her analysis is implicit in how she tells her story, from the experience of her youth to the strategies she adapted for herself and her family in her mature years. It is not the material reality of that life I seek to recreate in recounting this conversation with Madame P. but the implicit social knowledge of the multiple layers of power relations in which people conduct their social and productive lives.

Ultimately, this element is both most necessary and most absent in our understanding of sweated work and what this path of development meant for the region. Through my analysis of the logic of sweating I have tried to capture her insights. Her stories help us explain why sweated work is predicated on a discipline that cannot be effectively imposed by entrepreneurs, why other disciplinary forces, most notably the moral sanction of family and women's internalized sense of place in their community, kept them sewing fourteen hours a day. It is in this respect that Madame P.'s understanding of social relationships brings into focus the connections between the most intimate emotional lives of families and the process of industrialization.

At a broader level, the logic of sweating is the key to grasping power relations in this region. For example, it describes well the actions of textile industrialists after they succeeded in mechanizing weaving. To ensure the safety of their investments, industrialists carved out and reserved for their plants the constant element of the market demand, pushing handloom weavers to rely on the insecure and fluctuating component of demand and to specialize in those segments of the product market in which the returns were too low for mechanization to be profitable. The viability of a risk-averting

---

4. See Popular Memory Group, "Popular Memory: Theory, Politics, Method," in *Making Histories: Studies in History-Writing and Politics* (London: Hutchinson, 1982), and Michel Bozon and Anne-Marie Thiesse, "The Collapse of Memory: The Case of Farm Workers (Vexin, pays de France)," *History and Anthropology* 2 (1986): 237–59.

strategy for the center meant forcing those on the periphery to absorb the uncertainties.[5]

The same economic logic operated in the shoe and lingerie trades. Local middlemen found themselves in the position of small producers in relation to other manufactureres and retailers. Within the national ready-to-wear consumer goods industry, the Choletais specialized in the most seasonal, cheap segments of the product market. Local fabricants, squeezed into a vulnerable position and struggling to survive, forced workers to absorb the cost of their insecurity by pushing down wage rates, intensifying the workday in the busy seasons, and withdrawing all orders in the off-seasons.

These economic strategies are not different in kind from the notion of family interest that both allowed and impelled handloom weavers to push their daughters into sweated work to give themselves a margin of security. In this sense, my analysis of patriarchal power and identity is similar to my conception of power and identity throughout this book. Within such a system, in which those on top use their margin of advantage to press on those below, there is a bottom that must absorb the pressure from above.

Historians can integrate the histories of such regions as the Mauges into a new, more inclusive understanding of capitalist development. But we cannot erase the pain of those who have been marginalized by the process even as they participated in it. Long-term impoverishment leaves scars. Looking at the hurt is not only a question of developing empathy. Coming to terms with the injuries of class reminds us that the creation of capitalist relations of production is a process of dispossession.

I imagine that as a young woman Madame P. felt caught between the demands of others and a dimly articulated sense that things could be different. Without the latter, she would not have fought so hard for a different future for her daughter. Yet keeping alive those vague dreams of another life required that she nurse a sense of grievance. She lived, I suspect, with the ambivalence of wanting to both be loyal to those who loved her and reject the validity of their claims.[6]

5. For a parallel analysis of the formative role of workers' struggles against employer domination of the work process, see Alain Cottereau, "The Distinctiveness of Working-Class Cultures in France, 1848–1900," in *Working-Class Formation*, ed. Ira Katznelson and Aristide R. Zolberg (Princeton: Princeton University Press, 1986).

6. For a brilliant analysis of overt demands and implicit expectations in the relationship between mothers and daughters in working-class families, see Carolyn Kay Steedman, *Landscape for a Good Woman: A Story of Two Lives* (New Brunswick: Rutgers University Press, 1987).

For weavers' daughters, the dominant political ideas so crucial to the weavers' mobilization, notions that linked the value of skill to the dignity of the producers, articulated a proprietary relation to the production process they did not share. Because the self-understanding of the community of handloom weavers equated solidarity with family interest (as defined by male heads of household), women could not mobilize in accord with their actual class position. In this region, where the history of class formation centered on the resistance of small producers to proletarian status, self-identification as a wage worker meant assuming a status rejected by others. In this respect, women are the emblematic proletarians, even if they were not the only wage workers.

By titling this book *The Weaver's Knot* I hope to capture the criss-crossing binds of family and class solidarity in which the people of the Mauges struggled to make a livable life in the midst of contingencies. In seeing them as actors, we must not innocently believe that by acting they necessarily attained what they intended, or wanted what they achieved. Indeed, for handloom weavers, winning their goals was at best an ambivalent victory. For them, the weaver's knot was a double-bind.

Bibliography

Archival Sources

Archives départementales de Maine-et-Loire [A.D. M-et-L]

Serie C: Provincial administration before 1790
C16   Manufactures: Toiles à voiles. Bureau de Cholet, Bureau de Vihiers, Bureau de Beauforts, 1748–87.
C321   Statistique des paroisses: District de Beaupréau, 1788.
C323   Statistique des paroisses: Canton de Cholet, 1788.

Serie L: Administration, revolutionary period, 1790–1800
1L546   Tableau de la fabrique de Bureau de marques de Vihiers, 1790.
5L9   Industries et commerce, 1791–An III (1795)

Serie M: General administration and economy
1M   Situation politique et morale, An XIV (1806)
7M42   Agriculture, Enquête sur le labourage, 1811.
66M1   Statistique commerciale—faillites 1820–42.
66M3   Prêts du gouvernement—Michel Cesbron, 1809–21.
67M2   Renseignements généraux sur le commerce et l'industrie dans le département de Maine-et-Loire, 1831–42.
67M3   Renseignements généraux sur le commerce et l'industrie . . . , 1849–61.
67M4   Renseignements généraux sur le commerce et l'industrie . . . , 1861–96.
67M5   Renseignements généraux sur le commerce et l'industrie . . . , 1806–15.
67M9   Enquête et rapports sur l'état de l'agriculture, du commerce et de l'industrie dans le département de Maine-et-Loire par la Société industrielle d'Angers et la Société d'agriculture, sciences et arts d'Angers, 1835.
67M10   Enquête sur les conditions de travail en France, 1872
67M11   Enquête sur la crise industrielle, commerciale, et agricole. Situation de l'agriculture, 1884.

67M12   Enquête sur l'industrie textile, réponses aux questionnaires de la commission d'enquête, 1903–4.
67M13   Enquête sur la situation du commerce en France, 1912–13.
70M3   Durée du travail dans les manufactures, travail des enfants, 1841–1937.
70M4   Travail des adultes, rapports annuels, enquêtes, procès-verbaux, et inspection du travail, 1889–1913.
71M1   Grèves et coalitions d'ouvriers, les ouvriers tisserands de Cholet, 1833–86.
71M2   Grèves et coalitions d'ouvriers, les ouvriers tisserands de Cholet, 1888–91.
71M7   Grèves et coalitions d'ouvriers, les ouvriers tisserands de Cholet, 1904.
Serie P: Finances, cadaster, postal services
    Cadastre, Villedieu-la-Blouère, 1er matrice, 1835.
    Cadastre, Villedieu-la-Blouère, 2e matrice, 1913.

Archives nationales [A.N.]
Serie BB18: Ministry of Justice, correspondences of the criminal division
BB18 1396   Grève à Cholet, 1840
BB18 1423   Grève à Cholet, 1844
BB18 1445   Grève à Cholet, 1846
Serie C: Parliamentary archives
C958   Assemblée constituante, Enquête sur le travail agricole et industriel, 1848, arrondissement de Beaupréau, Maine-et-Loire.
C7318   Chambre des députés, Enquête sur l'industrie textile en France, 1903–4, régions non-visitées: Maine-et-Loire.
Serie F11:
F11 2706   Enquêtes agricoles décennales, 1862.
F11 2718   Enquêtes agricoles décennales, 1882.
Serie F12: Commerce and industry
F12 4516B   Situation industrielle de Maine-et-Loire, 1866–88.
F12 4659   Grèves et coalitions, 1853–89.
Serie F22: Work and social security
F22 85   Syndicats 1914 et dessous, Maine-et-Loire.
F22 86   Syndicats 1914 et dessous, Maine-et-Loire.

Archives municipales de Cholet

Serie J: Military affairs
JA   Garde Nationale, 1840–49

Archives communales de Villedieu-la-Blouère

Listes nominatives du recensement de la population, les années 1836, 1846, 1881, 1911.

Printed Government Documents

Chambre des députés. *Procès-verbaux de la commission chargée de procéder à une enquête sur l'état de l'industrie textile et la condition des ouvriers tis-seurs.* 5 vols. Paris: Imprimerie de la Chambre des députés, 1906.

Ministère de l'agriculture. *Enquête sur la situation et les besoins de l'agriculture, 2d series, 2d district: Maine-et-Loire.* Paris: Imprimerie impériale, 1867.

———. *Statistique de la France: Agriculture,* 1st series, vol. 6. Paris: Imprimerie royale, 1841.

———. *Statistique de la France: Statistique agricole. Enquête décennale de 1852,* 2d series, vol. 12. Paris: Imprimerie impériale, 1860.

———. *Statistique agricole de la France: Résultats généraux de l'enquête décennale de 1862.* Strasbourg: Berger-Lévrault, 1868.

———. *Statistique agricole de la France: Résultats généraux de l'enquête décennale de 1882.* Nancy: Berger-Lévrault, 1887.

———. *Statistique agricole de la France: Résultats généraux de l'enquête décennale de 1892.* Nancy: Imprimerie nationale, 1897.

———. Direction de l'agriculture, Office de renseignements agricoles. *La petite propriété rurale en France: Enquêtes monographiques (1908–1909).* Paris: Imprimerie nationale, 1909.

———. Office de renseignements agricoles. *Enquête sur les salaires agricoles.* Paris: Imprimerie nationale, 1912.

Ministère du commerce, Office du travail. *Enquête sur le travail à domicile dans l'industrie de la chaussure.* Paris: Imprimerie nationale, 1914.

———. *Enquête sur le travail à domicile dans l'industrie de la lingerie.* Paris: Imprimerie nationale, 1908–14.

———. *Résultats statistiques du recensement des industries et professions [le dé-nombrement général de la population du 29 mars 1896].* Paris: Imprimerie nationale, 1901.

Statistique générale. *Résultats statistiques du recensement de la population effectué le 24 mars 1901,* vol. 3. Paris: Imprimerie nationale, 1906.

Secondary Sources

Abrams, Philip. *Historical Sociology.* Ithaca: Cornell University Press, 1982.

Aftalion, Albert. *La crise de l'industrie linière et la concurrence victorieuse de l'industrie cotonnière.* Paris: L. Larose, 1904.

———. *Le développement de la fabrique et le travail à domicile dans les indus-tries de l'habillement.* Paris: L. Larose et L. Tenin, 1906.

Alexander, Sally. "Women, Class, and Sexual Differences in the 1830s and 1840s: Some Reflections on Writing Feminist History." *History Workshop Journal* 17 (Spring 1984): 125–49.

Alexander, Sally, and Barbara Taylor. "In Defense of 'Patriarchy.' " In *People's His-tory and Socialist Theory,* ed. Raphael Samuels. London: Routledge and Kegan Paul, 1981.

Allen, Frederick, J. *The Shoe Industry.* Boston: Vocation Bureau, 1916.

Amin, Ash. "Flexible Specialization and Small Firms in Italy: Myths and Reali-ties." *Antipodes* 21 (1989): 13–34.

Andrews, Richard, H. *Les paysans des Mauges au XVIIIe siècle.* Tours: Arrault, 1935.

Ansart, Pierre. *Naissance de l'anarchisme: Esquisse d'une explication sociologique du proudhonisme.* Paris: Presses universitaires de France, 1970.

Ashton, T. H. and C. H. E. Philipon, eds. *The Brenner Debates.* Cambridge: Cambridge University Press, 1985.

Baron, Ava. "Contested Terrain Revisited: Technology and Gender Definitions of Work in the Printing Industry, 1850–1920." In *Women, Work, and Technology,* ed. Barbara Drygulski Wright et al. Ann Arbor: University of Michigan Press, 1987.

Barrett, Michèle, and M. McIntosh. "The 'Family Wage': Some Problems for Socialists and Feminists." *Capital and Class* 11 (Summer 1980): 51–72.

Berg, Maxine. *The Machinery Question and the Making of Political Economy, 1815–1848.* Cambridge: Cambridge University Press, 1980.

Berg, Maxine, and Pat Hudson. "Rehabilitating the Industrial Revolution." *Economic History Review* 45 (1992): 24–50.

Berg, Maxine, Pat Hudson, and Michael Sonenscher, eds. *Manufacture in Town and Country before the Factory.* New York: Cambridge University Press, 1983.

Bergeron, Louis. *L'épisode napoléonien: Aspects intérieurs 1799–1815.* Paris: Éditions du Seuil, 1972.

Berlanstein, Lenard, ed. *Rethinking Labor History: Essays in Discourse and Class Analysis.* Urbana: University of Illinois Press, 1993.

Bezucha, Robert J. *The Lyon Uprising of 1834: Social and Political Conflict in the Early July Monarchy.* Cambridge: Harvard University Press, 1974.

Blackbourn, David. "The Mittelstand in German Society and Politics, 1871–1914." *Social History* 4 (January 1977): 409–33.

Bois, Paul. *Paysans de l'Ouest* (Le Mans: Imprimerie M. Vilaire, 1960).

Bossenga, Gail. *The Politics of Privilege: Old Regime and Revolution in Lille.* New York: Cambridge University Press, 1991.

————. "Protecting Merchants: Guilds and Commercial Capitalism in Eighteenth-Century France." *French Historical Studies* 15 (Fall 1988): 693–703.

————. "La Révolution française et les corporations: Trois exemples lillois." *Annales: Économies, sociétés, civilisations* 43 (March-April 1988): 405–26.

Bourdieu, Pierre. "Célibat et condition paysanne." *Études rurales* 5/6 (1962): 32–135.

————. "Marriage Strategies as Strategies of Social Reproduction." In *Family and Society,* ed. Robert Forster and Orest Ranum. Baltimore: Johns Hopkins University Press, 1976.

————. *Outline for a Theory of Practice,* trans. Richard Nice. Cambridge: Cambridge University Press, 1977.

Bouyx, Paul. "Naissance de la chaussure dans de Choletais." *Bulletin de la Société des sciences, lettres et beaux-arts de Cholet,* 1948–49.

Boyaval, Paul. *La lutte contre le sweating-système.* Paris: Taffin-Lefort, 1911.

Bozzoli, Belinda. "Marxism, Feminism, and South African Studies." *Journal of South African Studies* 9 (April 1983): 139–71.

Brandon, Ruth. *A Capitalist Romance: Singer and the Sewing Machine.* Philadelphia: Lippincott, 1977.

Braun, Rudolf. "Early Industrialization and Demographic Change in the Canton of Zurich." In *Historical Studies of Changing Fertility,* ed. Charles Tilly. Princeton: Princeton University Press, 1978.

———. "The Impact of Cottage Industry on an Agricultural Population." In *The Rise of Capitalism*, ed. David S. Landes. New York: Macmillan, 1966.

———. *Industrialisierung und Volksleben*. Zurich: Rentsch, 1960.

———. "The Rise of a Rural Class of Industrial Entrepreneurs." *Cahiers d'histoire mondiale* 10 (1967): 551–66.

Brenner, Robert. "Agrarian Class Structure and Economic Development in Pre-Industrial Europe." *Past and Present*. 70 (February 1976): 30–75.

———. "The Origins of Capitalist Development: A Critique of Neo-Smithian Marxism." *New Left Review* 104 (July–August 1977): 25–92.

Bull, Anna Cento. "Proto-industrialization, Small-Scale Capital Accumulation, and Diffused Entrepreneurship: The Case of the Brianza in Lombardy." *Social History* 14 (May 1989): 177–200.

Butel, Paul. *Les négociants bordelaises: L'Europe et les îles au XVIIIe siècle*. Paris: Aubier, 1974.

Bythell, Duncan. *The Handloom Weavers: A Study in the English Cotton Industry during the Industrial Revolution*. Cambridge: Cambridge University Press, 1969.

———. *The Sweated Trades: Outwork in the Nineteenth Century*. London: Batsford Academic, 1978.

Cameron, Rondo E. *France and the Economic Development of Europe, 1800–1914*. Princeton: Princeton University Press, 1967.

———. "France, 1800–1867." In *Banking in the Early Stages of Industrialization*, ed. Rondo Cameron et al. New York: Oxford University Press, 1967.

Cardoso, Fernando Henrique. "The Consumption of Dependency Theory in the United States." *Latin American Research Review* 12 (1977): 7–24.

Chamard, Elie. *La Maison Richard Frères*. Cholet: L'imprimerie Vetélé, 1959.

———. *Vingt siècles de l'histoire de Cholet*. Cholet: Farré et fils, 1970.

Chambre de commerce de Cholet. *Monographie géographique et économique de l'arrondissement*. Cholet: n.d. [ca. 1924].

Chapman, Stanley D. *The Early Factory Masters: The Transition to the Factory System in the Midlands Textile Trades*. Newton Abbot, Devon: David and Charles, 1967.

Chapman, Stanley D., and Serge Chassagne. *European Textile Printers in the Eighteenth Century: A Study of Peel and Oberkampf*. London: Heineman, 1981.

Chassagne, Serge. "La diffusion rurale de l'industrie cotonnière en France (1750–1850)." *Revue du Nord* 61 (January–March 1979): 97–114.

Châtelain, Abel. "Évolution des densités de population en Anjou (1806–1936)." *Revue de géographie de Lyon* 31 (1956): 43–60.

Chéné, René. *Les débuts du commerce et de l'industrie de la chaussure dans la région de Cholet*. Maulévier, Maine-et-Loire: Hérault, 1980.

Clapham, J. H. *Economic Development of France and Germany, 1815–1914*. 4th ed. Cambridge: Cambridge University Press, 1968.

Clough, Shepard B. *France: A History of National Economics, 1789–1939*. New York: Octogon Books, 1939.

———. "Retardative Factors in French Economic Development in the Nineteenth and Twentieth Centuries." *Journal of Economic History* 6, supplement (1946): 91–102.

Coleman, D. C. "Proto-industrialization: A Concept Too Many." *Economic History Review*, 2d series, 36 (August 1983): 435–48.

Cormeau, Henry. *Terroirs Mauges: Miette d'une vie provinciale.* Paris: Georges Crès, 1912.

Cottereau, Alain. "The Distinctiveness of Working-Class Cultures in France, 1848–1900." In *Working-Class Formation: Nineteenth Century Patterns in Western Europe and the United States,* ed. Ira Katznelson and Aristide R. Zolberg. Princeton: Princeton University Press, 1986.

Crafts, N. F. R. *British Economic Growth during the Industrial Revolution.* Oxford: Oxford University Press, 1985.

———. "Economic Growth in France and Britain, 1830–1910: A Review of the Evidence." *Journal of Economic History* 44 (March 1984): 49–67.

Crossick, Geoffrey. *The Lower Middleclass in Britain, 1870–1916.* London: Croom Helm, 1977.

Crouzet, François. "Essai de construction d'un indice annuel de la production industrielle française au XIXe siècle." *Annales: Économies, sociétés, civilisations* 25(1970): 56–99.

———. "French Economic Growth Reconsidered." *History* 59 (1974): 167–79.

———. *De la superiorité de l'Angleterre sur la France: L'économie et l'imaginaire, XVIIIe–XXe siècle.* Paris: Perrin, 1985.

———. "Wars, Blockades, and Economic Change in Europe, 1792–1815." *Journal of Economic History* 24 (December 1964): 567–88.

Cuvillier, Armand. *P.-J.-B. Buchez et les origines du socialisme chrétien.* Paris: Presses universitaires de France, 1948.

Daumas, Maurice. *Histoire générale des techniques.* Paris: Presses universitaires de France, 1962.

Dauphin, Victor. "Le textile dans les Mauges avant 1789." *Bulletin de la Société des sciences, lettres, et beaux-arts de Cholet et de sa région,* 1954.

De Brant, Jacques, Peter Mandi, and Dudley Seers, eds. *European Studies in Development: New Trends in European Development.* New York: St. Martin's Press, 1980.

Delord, Jeanne-Marie. *La famille rurale dans l'économie du Limousin (1769–1939).* Limoges: Ch. Paulhac, 1940.

Demangeon, Albert. *Géographie économique et humaine de la France.* Paris: A. Colin, 1948.

Desert, Gabriel. "Aspects agricoles de la crise: La région de Caen." *Bibliothèque de la Révolution de 1848,* Vol. 19: *Aspects de la crise et de la dépression de l'économie française au milieu du XIXe siècle, 1846–1851,* 1956, pp. 37–64.

———. *Une société rurale au XIXe siècle: Les paysans du Calvados.* New York: Arno Press, 1977.

Dornic, François. *L'industrie textile dans le Maine et ses débouchés internationaux.* Le Mans: Édition Pierre-Bellon, 1955.

Dubois, E., and A. Julin. *Les moteurs électriques dans les industries à domicile.* Brussels, 1902.

Faucher, Daniel. "Aspects sociologiques du travail agricole." *Études rurales* 13–14 (April–September 1964): 125–31.

Flâtres, Pierre. "Historical Geography of Western France." In *Themes in the Historical Geography of France,* ed. Hugh D. Clout. New York: Academic Press, 1977.

Fohlen, Claude. "The Industrial Revolution in France, 1700–1914." In *The Emergence of Industrial Societies,* vol. 4, pt.1 of The Fontana Economic History of Europe, ed. Carlo M. Cippolla London: Fontana, 1973, pp. 7–75.

———. *Les industries textiles au temps du Second Empire.* Paris: Librairie Plon, 1956.

Folbre, Nancy. "Hearts and Spades: Paradigms of Household Economics." *World Development* 14 (1986): 245–55.

Folbre, Nancy, and Heidi Hartmann. "The Rhetoric of Self-Interest: Ideology and Gender in Economic Theory." In *The Consequences of Economic Rhetoric,* ed. Arjo Klamer, Donald N. McCloskey, and Robert M. Solow. Cambridge: Cambridge University Press, 1988.

Forster, Robert. "Obstacles to Agricultural Growth in 18th Century France." *American Historical Review* 75 (1970): 1600–1615.

Fourastié, Jean. *Le grand espoir du XXe siècle, progrès technique, progrès économique, progrès social.* Paris: Presses universitaires de France, 1949.

———. *Machinisme et bien-être.* Paris: Éditions de Minuit, 1951.

Frank, André Gunder. *Capitalism and Underdevelopment in Latin America: Historical Studies of Chile and Brazil.* New York: Monthly Review Press, 1969.

Fridenson, Patrick, and André Straus. *Le capitalisme français XIXe–XXe siècle: Blocage et dynamisme d'une croissance.* Paris: Fayard, 1987.

Friedmann, Harriet. "Household Production and National Economy: Concepts for the Analysis of Agrarian Formations." *Journal of Peasant Studies* 7 (January 1980): 158–84.

———. "Patriarchal Commodity Production." *Social Analysis* 20 (December 1986): 47–55.

———. "World Market, State, and Family Farm: Social Basis of Household Production in the Era of Wage Labor." *Comparative Studies of Society and History* 20 (October 1978): 545–86.

Gellusseau, Auguste-Amaury. *Histoire de Cholet et de son industrie,* Vol. 2. Cholet: Édition Fillion, 1862.

Gemähling, Paul. *Travailleurs au rabais: La lutte syndicale contre le sous-concurrence ouvrier.* Paris: Bloud et cie, 1910.

Grafteaux, Serge. *Mémé Santerre: A French Woman of the People,* trans. Louise A. Tilly and Kathryn L. Tilly. New York: Schocken Books, 1985.

Grantham, George W. "Technical and Organizational Change in French Agriculture between 1840 and 1880: An Economic Interpretation." Ph.D. dissertation, Yale University, 1972.

Gueslin, André. *L'invention de l'économie sociale: Le XIXe siècle.* Paris: Économica, 1987.

Guignet, Philippe. *Mines, manufactures, et ouvriers du Valenciennois au XVIIIe siècle.* New York: Arno Press, 1977.

Gullickson, Gay L. "Agriculture and Cottage Industry: Redefining the Causes of Proto-Industrialization." *Journal of Economic History* 43 (December 1983): 831–50.

———. "Proto-Industrialization, Demographic Behavior, and the Sexual Division of Labor in Auffay, France, 1750–1850." *Peasant Studies* 9 (Winter 1982): 106–18.

———. "The Sexual Division of Labor in Cottage Industry and Agriculture in the Pays de Caux, Auffay, 1750–1850." *French Historical Studies* 12 (Fall 1981): 177–99.

———. *The Spinners and Weavers of Auffay: Rural Industry and the Sexual Division of Labor in a French Village, 1750–1850.* Cambridge: Cambridge University Press, 1986.

Halperin-Donghi, Tulio. "Dependency Theory and Latin American Historiography." *Latin American Research Review* 17 (1982): 115–30.

Hanagan, Michael P. "Artisan and Skilled Worker: The Problem of Definition." *International Labor and Working-Class History* 12 (November 1977): 28–31.

——. *The Logic of Solidarity: Artisans and Industrial Workers in Three French Towns, 1871–1914.* Urbana: University of Illinois Press, 1980.

Hartmann, Heidi. "Capitalism, Patriarchy, and Job Segregation by Sex." *Signs* 1 (Spring 1976): 137–69.

Hausen, Karin. "Technical Progress and Women's Labour in the Nineteenth Century: The Social History of the Sewing Machine." In *The Social History of Politics: Critical Perspectives in West German Historical Writing since 1945,* ed. Georg Iggers. New York: St. Martin's Press, 1986.

Hazard, B. E. *The Organization of the Boot and Shoe Industry in Massachusetts before 1875.* Cambridge: Harvard University Press, 1921.

Head, P. "Boots and Shoes." In *The Development of British Industry and Foreign Competition, 1875–1914,* ed. Derek H. Alcroft. London: Allen and Unwin, 1968.

Heywood, Colin. "The Role of the Peasantry in French Industrialization, 1815–1880." *Economic History Review* 34 (August 1981): 359–76.

Hilden, Patricia. "Family History vs. Women in History: A Critique of Tilly and Scott." *International Labor and Working Class History* 16 (Fall 1979): 1–11.

Hills, R. L. "Hargreaves, Arkwright, and Crompton: Why Three Inventors?" *Textile History* 10 (1979): 114–26.

Hilton, Rodney, ed. *The Transition from Feudalism to Capitalism.* London: New Left Books, 1976.

Hudson, Pat. "Proto-industrialization: The Case of the West Riding Wool Textile Industry in the 18th and Early 19th centuries." *History Workshop Journal* 12 (Autumn 1981): 34–61.

Hudson, Pat, ed. *Regions and Industries: A Perspective on the Industrial Revolution in Britain.* Cambridge: Cambridge University Press, 1989.

Humphries, Jane, and Jill Rubery. "The Reconstitution of the Supply Side of the Labour Market: The Relative Autonomy of Social Reproduction." *Cambridge Journal of Economics* 8 (December 1984): 331–46.

Jeulin, Paul. *L'évolution du port de Nantes, organisation et trafic depuis les origines.* Paris: Presses universitaires de France, 1929.

Johnson, Christopher H. "Economic Change and Artisan Discontent: The Tailors' History, 1800–1848." In *Revolution and Reaction: 1848 and the Second French Republic,* ed. Roger Price. London: Croom Helm, 1975.

——. "Proto-industrialization and De-industrialization in Languedoc: Lodève and Its Region, 1700–1870." Paper presented at the "Proto-industrialization: Theory and Reality" conference, Bad Homburg, 1981.

——. *Utopian Communism in France: Cabet and the Icarians, 1839–1851.* Ithaca: Cornell University Press, 1974.

Jones, Eric L. "The Agricultural Origins of Industry." *Past and Present* 40 (1968): 58–71.

Kaplan, Steven A. *Provisioning Paris: Merchants and Millers in the Grain and Flour Trade during the Eighteenth Century.* Ithaca: Cornell University Press, 1984.

Katznelson, Ira. "Working-Class Formation: Constructing Cases and Comparisons." In *Working-Class Formation: Nineteenth Century Patterns in Western Europe and the United States*, ed. Katznelson and Aristide R. Zolberg. Princeton: Princeton University Press, 1986.

Kemp, Tom. *Economic Forces in French History*. London: Dobson, 1971.

———. "Structural Factors in the Retardation of French Economic Growth," *Kyklos* 15 (1962): 325–50.

Kisch, Herbert. "From Monopoly to Laissez-faire: The Early Growth of the Wupper Valley Textile Trades." *Journal of European Economic History* 1 (1972): 298–407.

———. *Prussian Mercantilism and the Rise of the Krefeld Silk Industry: Variations on an Eighteenth-Century Theme*. Philadelphia: Transactions of the American Philosophical Society 58, 1968.

———. "The Textile Industries in Silesia and the Rhineland: A Comparative Study in Industrialization." *Journal of Economic History* 19 (1959): 541–63.

Kitching, Gavin. *Development and Underdevelopment in Historical Perspective: Populism, Nationalism, and Industrialization*. London: Methuen, 1982.

Kondo, Dorinne K. *Crafting Selves: Power, Gender, and Discourses of Identity in a Japanese Workplace*. Chicago: University of Chicago Press, 1990.

Kriedte, Peter, Hans Medick, and Jurgen Schlumbohm. *Industrialization before Industrialization*, trans. Beate Schempp. New York: Cambridge University Press, 1981.

Kropotkin, Peter. *Fields, Factories, and Workshops*. New York: Putnam and Sons, 1913.

Kuhn, Annette, and Annmarie Wolpe, eds. *Feminism and Materialism*. London: Routledge and Kegan Paul, 1978.

Kussmaul, Ann. *Servants in Husbandry in Early Modern England*. Cambridge: Cambridge University Press, 1981.

Landes, David S. "French Business and the Businessman: A Social and Cultural Analysis." In *Modern France: Problems of the Third and Fourth Republics*, ed. E. M. Earle. New York: Russel and Russel, 1951.

———. "French Entrepreneurship and Industrial Growth in the Nineteenth Century." *Journal of Economic History* 9 (1949): 45–61.

———. "New Model Entrepreneurship in France and Problems of Historical Explanation." *Explorations in Economic History* 1 (1963): 56–75.

———. *The Unbound Prometheus: Technological Change and Industrial Development in Western Europe from 1750 to the Present*. Cambridge: Cambridge University Press, 1970.

———. "What Do Bosses Really Do?" *Journal of Economic History* 46 (September 1986): 585–623.

Le Bas, Christian. *Histoire sociale des faits économiques: La France au XIXe siècle*. Lyon: Presses universitaires de Lyon, 1984.

Leclerc-Thouin, Oscar. *L'agriculture de l'Ouest de la France*. Paris: Bouchard-Huzard, 1843.

Lehning, James. *The Peasants of Marhles*. Chapel Hill: University of North Carolina Press, 1980.

Lemière, Edmond. *Bibliographie de la contre-révolution dans les provinces de l'Ouest ou des guerres de la Vendée et de la chouannerie*. Nantes: Librairie Nantaise, 1976.

LePlay, Pierre Guillaume Frédéric. *La réforme sociale en France.* Paris: Denta, 1867.

Levasseur, Émile. *Questions ouvrières et industrielles en France sous la Troisième République.* Paris: Arthur Rousseau, 1907.

Levine, David. *Family Formation in the Age of Nascent Capitalism.* New York: Academic Press, 1977.

Lévy-Leboyer, Maurice. *Les banques européennes et l'industrialisation internationale dans la première moitié du XIXe siècle.* Paris: Presses universitaires de France, 1964.

———. "La croissance économique en France au XIXe siècle," *Annales: Économies, sociétés, civilisations* 23 (1968): 788–807.

———. "La décélération de l'économie française dans la seconde moitié du siècle." *Revue d'histoire économique et sociale* 49 (1971): 485–507.

———. "Les processus d'industrialisation: Le cas de l'Angleterre et de la France." *Revue historique* 239 (1968): 281–98.

Lévy-Leboyer, Maurice, and François Bourguignon. *The French Economy in the Nineteenth Century: An Essay in Econometric Analysis,* trans. Jesse Bryant and Virginie Pérotin. Cambridge: Cambridge University Press, 1990.

Lindenlaub, Dieter. *Richtungskaempfe im Verein für Sozialpolitik.* Wiesbaden: F. Stein, 1967.

McClelland, Keith. "Masculinity and the 'Representative Artisan' in Britain, 1850–80." In *Manful Assertions: Masculinities in Britain since 1800,* ed. Michael Roper and John Tosh. London: Routledge, 1991.

McPhee, Peter. "A Reconsideration of the 'Peasantry' of Nineteenth-Century France." *Peasant Studies* 9 (Fall 1981): 5–25.

Marchegay, Paul. *Archives de l'Anjou: Recueil de documents et mémoires inédits sur cette province.* Angers: Charles Labussière, 1843.

Marczewski, Jean. "The Take-off and French Experience." In *The Economics of Take-off into Sustained Growth,* ed. W. W. Rostow. London: Macmillan, 1963.

Marglin, Stephen A. "What Do Bosses Do? The Origins and Functions of Hierarchy in Capitalist Production." In *The Division of Labor: The Labor Process and Class Struggle in Modern Capitalism,* ed. André Gorz. London: Harvester Press, 1978.

Martin, Gaston. *Nantes au XVIIIe siècle: L'ère des négriers 1714–1774.* Paris: L. Durance, 1928.

Martin, Jean-Clément. *La Vendée de la mémoire (1800–1980).* Paris: Seuil, 1989.

———. "La Vendée, région-mémoire." In *Les lieux de mémoire: La République,* ed. Pierre Nora. Paris: Gallimard, 1984.

Medick, Hans. "Privilegiertes Handelskapital und Kleine Industrie." *Archiv für Sozialgeschichte* 23 (1983): 587–607.

———. "The Proto-industrial Family Economy: The Structural Function of Household and Family during the Transition from Peasant Society to Industrial Capitalism." *Social History* 3 (October 1976): 291–315.

———. "Village Spinning Bees: Sexual Culture and Free Time among Rural Youth in Early Modern Germany." In *Interest and Emotion: Essays on the Study of Family and Kinship,* ed. Hans Medick and David Warren Sabean. Cambridge: Cambridge University Press, 1984.

Mendels, Franklin F. "Agriculture and Peasant Industry in Eighteenth-Century Flanders." In *European Peasants and Their Markets,* ed. William N. Parker and Eric L. Jones. Princeton: Princeton University Press, 1975.

———. "General Report, Eighth International Economic History Congress, Section A.2: Proto-industrialization: Theory and Reality," Budapest, August, 1982.

———. *Industrialization and Population Pressure in Eighteenth-Century Flanders*. New York: Arno Press, 1981.

———. "Proto-industrialization: The First Phase in the Industrialization Process," *Journal of Economic History* 32 (1972): 241–61.

———. "Seasons and Regions in Agriculture and Industry during the Process of Industrialization." In *Region und Industrialisierung*, ed. Sidney Pollard. Göttingen: Vandenhoeck and Ruprecht, 1980.

Merle, Louis. *Le métairie et l'évolution de la gâtine poitevine de la fin du moyen âge à la Révolution*. Paris: S.E.V.P.E.N., 1958.

Meyer, Jean. *L'armement nantais dans la deuxième moitié du XVIIIe siècle*. Paris: S.E.V.P.E.N., 1969.

———. "Le commerce négrier nantais (1774–1792)." *Annales: Économies, sociétés, civilisations* 15 (January–February 1960): 120–29.

Miller, Michael. B. *The Bon Marché: Bourgeois Culture and the Department Store, 1869–1920*. Princeton: Princeton University Press, 1981.

Millet de la Turtaudière, P. A. *Indicateur de Maine-et-Loire*. Angers: Cosnier et Lachèse, 1865.

Minguet, Guy. *Naissance de l'Anjou industriel: Entreprise et société locales à Angers et dans le Choletais*. Paris: Éditions L'Harmattan, 1985.

Moch, Leslie Page, et al. "Family Strategy: A Dialogue." *Historical Methods* 20 (Summer 1987): 115–18.

Mokyr, Joel. "Has the Industrial Revolution Been Crowded Out? Some Reflections on Crafts and Williamson." *Explorations in Economic History* 24 (1987): 293–319.

Moss, Bernard H. *The Origins of the French Labor Movement, 1830–1914: The Socialism of Skilled Workers*. Berkeley: University of California Press, 1976.

Nicolle, F. *Les progrès culturaux dans le canton de Cholet depuis cent ans*. Angers: La Chèse et cie, 1898.

O'Brien, Patrick, and Caglar Keyder. *Economic Growth in Britain and France, 1780–1940: Two Paths to the Twentieth Century*. London: Allen and Unwin, 1978.

Palmer, Bryan D. *Descent into Discourse: The Reification of Language and the Writing of Social History*. Philadelphia: Temple University Press, 1990.

Parker, Harold T. *The Bureau of Commerce in 1781 and Its Policies with Respect to French Industry*. Durham, N.C.: Carolina Academic Press, 1979.

Paulin, Valentine. "Homework in France: Its Origins, Evolution, and Future." *International Labor Review* 37 (February 1938): 192–225.

Perrot, Michelle. "Aspects industriels de la crise: Les régions textiles du Calvados." In *Bibliothèque de la Révolution de 1848*, Vol. 19: *Aspects de la crise et de la dépression de l'économie française au milieu du XIXe siècle, 1845–1851*, 1956, pp. 164–99.

———. *Les ouvriers en grève: France, 1871–1890*. Paris: Mouton, 1974.

Petitfrère, Claude. *Les Vendéens d'Anjou: Analyse des structures militaires, sociales, et mentales*. Paris: Bibliothèque nationale, 1981.

Philips, Anne, and Barbara Taylor, "Sex and Skill: Notes towards a Feminist Economics." *Feminist Review* 6 (1980): 79–88.

Picard, Alfred. *Le bilan d'un siècle (1801–1900)*, vol. 5. Paris: Imprimerie nationale, 1906.

Pinchbeck, Ivy. *Women Workers and the Industrial Revolution.* London: Virago Press, 1981.

Pinkney, David. H. *Napoleon III and the Rebuilding of Paris.* Princeton: Princeton University Press, 1958.

Piore, Michael J. "Dualism as a Response to Flux and Uncertainty." In *Dualism and Discontinuities in Industrialized Societies,* ed. Suzanne Berger and Michael J. Piore. Cambridge: Cambridge University Press, 1980.

———. "Technological Foundations of Dualism and Discontinuity." In *Dualism and Discontinuities in Industrialized Societies,* ed. Suzanne Berger and Michael J. Piore. Cambridge: Cambridge University Press, 1980.

Piore, Michael J., and Charles F. Sabel. *The Second Industrial Divide: Possibilities for Prosperity.* New York: Basic Books, 1984.

Poperen, Maurice. *Un siècle de luttes chez les tisserands des Mauges.* Angers: Imprimerie coopérative angevine, 1974.

Purcell, Kate. "Militance and Acquiescence among Women Workers." In *Fit Work for Women,* ed. Sandra Burman. New York: St. Martin's Press, 1979.

Quataert, Jean H. "A New View of Industrialization: 'Protoindustry' or the Role of Small-Scale, Labor-Intensive Manufacturing in the Capitalist Environment." *International Labor and Working-Class History* 33 (Spring 1988): 3–22.

Rapp, Rayna, Ellen Ross, and Renate Bridenthal. "Examining Family History." In *Sex and Class in Women's History,* ed. Judith L. Newton, Mary P. Ryan, and Judith R. Walkowitz. London: Routledge and Kegan Paul, 1983, pp. 232–58.

Rebel, Hermann. "Cultural Hegemony and Class Experience: A Critical Reading of Recent Ethnological-Historical Approaches (Part One)." *American Ethnologist* 16 (1989): 117–36.

Rebérioux, Madeleine. "Les socialistes français et le petit commerce au tournant du siècle." *Le mouvement social* 114 (January–March 1981): 57–70.

Reddy, William M. "Family and Factory: French Linen Weavers in the Belle Epoque." *Journal of Social History* 8 (Winter 1975): 102–12.

———. *The Rise of Market Culture: The Textile Trades and French Society, 1750–1900.* Cambridge: Cambridge University Press, 1984.

Reid, Donald. *The Miners of Decazeville: A Genealogy of Deindustrialization.* Cambridge: Harvard University Press, 1985.

Renard, Jean. "Problème agraire du Nord-Est de la Vendée." *NOROIS* 55 (July–September 1967): 373–97.

Renard, Louis. "Les maisons d'habitations des tisserands." *Bulletin de la Société de sciences, lettres, et beaux-arts de Cholet,* 1890.

Richard, Louis. "Petite contribution à l'histoire du Bureau de marque de Cholet." *Bulletin de la Société des sciences, lettres, et beaux-arts de Cholet,* 1966, 1968, 1969.

Roehl, Richard. "French Industrialization: A Reconsideration" *Explorations in Economic History* 13 (1976): 233–81.

Rogers, Susan Carol. *Shaping Modern Times in Rural France: The Transformation and Reproduction of an Aveyronnais Community.* Princeton: Princeton University Press, 1991.

Rose, Sonya O. "Gender Antagonism and the Class Conflict: Exclusionary Strategies of Male Trade of Unionists in Nineteenth-Century Britain." *Social History* 13 (1988): 163–88.

————. *Limited Livelihoods: Gender and Class in Nineteenth-Century England.* Berkeley: University of California Press, 1992.

Rostow, Walt W. *The Stages of Economic Growth: A Non-Communist Manifesto.* Cambridge: Cambridge University Press, 1960.

Rowbotham, Sheila. "The Trouble with 'Patriarchy'." In *People's History and Socialist Theory*, ed. Raphael Samuel. London: Routledge and Kegan Paul, 1981.

Rubery, Jill. "Structured Labour Markets, Worker Organization, and Low Pay." *Cambridge Journal of Economics* 2 (1978): 17–36.

Rubery, Jill, and Frank Wilkinson. "Outwork and Segmented Labor Markets." In *The Dynamics of Labor Market Segmentation*, ed. Frank Wilkinson. New York: Academic Press, 1981.

Rubin, Gayle. "The Traffic in Women: Notes on the 'Political Economy' of Sex." In *Towards an Anthropology of Women*, ed. Rayna Reiter. New York: Monthly Review Press, 1975.

Rule, John. "The Property in Skill in the Period of Manufacturing." In *Historical Meaning of Work*, ed. Patrick Joyce. Cambridge: Cambridge University Press, 1987.

Sabean, David Warren. *Power in the Blood: Popular Culture and Village Discourse in Early Modern Germany.* New York: Cambridge University Press, 1984.

Sabel, Charles F. "Protoindustry and the Problem of Capitalism as a Concept: Response to Jean H. Quataert." *International Labor and Working-Class History* 33 (Spring 1988): 30–37.

————. *Work and Politics: Division of Labor in Industry.* Cambridge: Cambridge University Press, 1982.

Sabel, Charles F., and Jonathan Zeitlin. "Historical Alternatives to Mass Production." *Past and Present* 108 (August 1985): 133–76.

Samuel, Raphael, ed. *People's History and Socialist Theory.* London: Routledge and Kegan Paul, 1981.

————. "Workshop of the World: Steam Power and Hand Technology in Mid-Victorian Britain." *History Workshop* 3 (1977): 6–72.

Sargent, Lydia, ed. *Women and Revolution: A Discussion of the Unhappy Marriage of Marxism and Feminism.* Boston: Southend Press, 1981.

Schmiechen, James A. *Sweated Industries and Sweated Labor: The London Clothing Trades, 1860–1914.* Urbana: University of Illinois Press, 1984.

Schmoller, Gustav. *Zur Geschichte der deutschen Kleingewerbe im 19 Jahrhundert. Statistisches und Nationalukonomomische Untersuchengen.* Halle, 1870.

————. *Grundriss der Allgemeinen Volkwerschaftslehre.* Munich, 1919.

Schremmer, Ekhart. "Proto-industrialization: A Step towards Industrialization?" *Journal of European Economic History* 10 (Winter 1981): 653–70.

Schumacher, E. F. *Small Is Beautiful.* London: Blond and Briggs, 1973.

Scott, Joan W. "The Evidence of Experience." *Critical Inquiry* 17 (Summer 1991): 773–97.

————. *Gender and the Politics of History.* New York: Columbia University Press, 1988.

————. *The Glassworkers of Carmaux: French Craftsmen and Political Action in a Nineteenth Century City.* Cambridge: Harvard University Press, 1974.

———. "Men and Women in the Parisian Garment Trades: Discussions of Family and Work in the 1830s and 40s." In *The Power of the Past*, ed. Pat Thane and Geoffrey Crossick. Cambridge: Cambridge University Press, 1985.

Sébillot, Paul. "Les tisserands." In *Légendes et curiosités des métiers*. Paris: Flammarion, 1895.

Seccombe, Wally. "Marxism and Demography." *New Left Review* 13 (1983): 22–47.

———. "Patriarchy Stabilized: The Construction of the Male Breadwinner Wage Form in Nineteenth-Century Britain." *Social History* 11 (January 1986): 53–76.

Secher, Reynald. *Le génocide franco-français: La Vendée-Vengé*. Paris: Presses universitaires de France, 1986.

Sée, Henri. *Les classes rurales en Bretagne du XVIe siècle à la Révolution*. Paris: V. Girard et E. Brière, 1906.

———. "Le commerce des toiles du Bas-Maine." In *Mémoires et documents pour servir à l'histoire de France*. Paris: Hachette, 1926.

———. *L'évolution commerciale et industrielle de la France sous l'Ancien Régime*. Paris: Marcel Giard, 1925.

———. "Remarques sur le caractère de l'industrie rurale en France et les causes de son extension au XVIIIe siècle." *Revue historique* 142 (1923): 47–53.

Segalen, Martine. " 'Avoir sa part': Sibling Relations in Partible Inheritance Brittany." In *Interest and Emotion: Essays on the Study of Family and Kinship*, ed. Hans Medick and David Warren Sabean. New York: Cambridge University Press, 1984.

———. *Love and Power in the Peasant Family: Rural France in the Nineteenth Century*, trans. Sarah Mathews. London: Basil Blackwell, 1983.

Sewell, William H., Jr. "A Theory of Structure: Duality, Agency, and Transformation." *American Journal of Sociology* 98 (July 1992): 1–29.

———. *Work and Revolution in France: The Language of Labor from the Old Regime to 1848*. Cambridge: Cambridge University Press, 1980.

Siegfried, André. "Le régime et la division de la propriété dans le Maine et l'Anjou." *Le musée social, mémoires et documents*, supplement (July 1911): 197–215.

———. *Tableau politique de la France de l'Ouest sous la Troisième République*. Paris: A. Colin, 1913.

Silver, Catherine Bodard. *Frédéric LePlay on Family, Work, and Social Change*. Chicago: University of Chicago Press, 1982.

Simon, François. *Département de Maine-et-Loire, Commune de la Romagne*. Angers: A. Bruel, 1927.

———. *Petite histoire des tisserands de la région de Cholet*. Angers: Imprimerie Anjou, 1946.

Smith, Bonnie G. *Confessions of a Concierge: Madame Lucie's History of Twentieth-Century France*. New Haven: Yale University Press, 1985.

Sonenscher, Michael. *The Hatters of Eighteenth-Century France*. Berkeley: University of California Press, 1987.

———. *Work and Wages: Natural Law, Politics, and the Eighteenth-Century French Trades*. Cambridge: Cambridge University Press, 1989.

Steedman, Carolyn Kay. *Landscape for a Good Woman: A Story of Two Lives*. New Brunswick: Rutgers University Press, 1987.

Strathern, Marilyn. "Self-Interest and the Social Good: Some Implications of Hagen Gender Imagery." In *Sexual Meanings*, ed. Sherry B. Ortner and Harriet Whitehead. Cambridge: Cambridge University Press, 1981.

Tarlé, Evgenii. *L'industrie dans les campagnes en France à la fin de l'Ancien Régime*. Paris: Édouard Cornéley, 1910.

Taylor, Barbara. *Eve and the New Jerusalem*. London: Virago Press, 1983.

———. " 'The Men Are as Bad as Their Masters': Socialism, Feminism, and Sexual Antagonism in the London Tailoring Trade in the 1830s." In *Sex and Class in Women's History*, ed. Judith I. Newton, Mary P. Ryan, and Judith R. Walkowitz. London: Routledge and Kegan Paul, 1983.

Thabault, Roger. *Education and Change in a Village Community: Mazières-en-Gâtine, 1848–1914*, trans. Peter Tregear. New York: Schoken Books, 1971.

Thirsk, Joan. "Industries in the Countryside." In *Essays in the Economic and Social History of Tudor and Stuart England*, ed. F. J. Fisher. Cambridge: Cambridge University Press, 1961, pp. 70–88.

Thompson, E. P. "Patrician Society, Plebian Culture." *Journal of Social History*, 7 (1974): 382–405.

Thompson, Paul. *The Nature of Work: An Introduction to Debates on the Labor Process*. London: Macmillan, 1983.

Thorne, Barrie. "Feminist Rethinking of the Family: An Overview." In *Rethinking the Family: Some Feminist Questions*, ed. Thorne with Marilyn Yalom. New York: Longman, 1982.

Thorner, Daniel, Basile Kerbaly, and R. E. F. Smith, eds. *A. V. Chayanov on the Theory of Peasant Economy*. Homewood, Ill.: Richard D. Irwin, published for the American Economics Association, 1966.

Tilly, Charles. "The Demographic Origins of the European Proletariat." In *Proletarianization and Family History*, ed. David Levine, Orlando: Academic Press, 1984.

———. *The Vendée*. Cambridge: Harvard University Press, 1964.

Tilly, Charles, and Richard Tilly. "An Agenda for Economic History in the 1970's." *Journal of Economic History* 31 (1971): 184–98.

Tilly, Louise A. "Linen Was Their Life: Family Survival Strategies and Parent-Child Relations in Nineteenth-Century France." In *Interest and Emotion: Essays on the Study of Family and Kinship*, ed. Hans Medick and David Warren Sabean. New York: Cambridge University Press, 1990.

———. "Women's History and Family History: Fruitful Collaboration or Missed Connection?" *Journal of Family History* 12 (1987): 303–15.

Tilly, Louise A., and Joan W. Scott. *Women, Work, and Family*. New York: Holt, Rinehart and Winston, 1978.

Timmer, C. Peter. "The Turnip, the New Husbandry, and the English Agricultural Revolution." *Quarterly Journal of Economics* 83 (August 1969): 375–95.

Toutain, Jean-Claude. "Le produit de l'agriculture française de 1700 à 1958." *Institut de Science Économique Appliquée, Cahiers de l'I.N.S.E.A: Histoire quantitative de l'économie française*, series AF, no. 2. Paris: I.N.S.E.A., 1961.

———. "The Uneven Growth of Regional Incomes in France from 1840 to 1970." In *Disparities in Economic Development since the Industrial Revolution*, ed. Paul Bairoch and Maurice Lévy-Leboyer. London: Macmillan, 1981.

Valverde, Mariana. "As If Subjects Existed: Analyzing Social Discourse." *Canadian Review of Sociology and Anthropology* 28 (May 1991): 173–87.

———. "Poststructuralist Gender Historians: Are We Those Names?" *Labour/le travail* 25 (Spring 1990): 227–36.

Vardi, Liana. "The Abolition of Guilds during the French Revolution." *French Historical Studies* 15 (Fall 1988): 704–17.

Vergneau, G. "La mise en valeur du domaine de Bouzillé (commune de Mélay, Maine-et-Loire): Contribution à l'étude de la métairie dans le bocage vendéen." *Actes du 97e congrès national des sociétés savantes,* Nantes, 1972, pp. 153–68.

Vincent, K. Steven. *Pierre-Joseph Proudhon and the Rise of French Republican Socialism.* New York: Oxford University Press, 1984.

Wallerstein, Immanuel. *The Modern World System: Capitalist Agriculture and the Origins of the European World Economy in the Sixteenth Century.* New York: Academic Press, 1974.

———. *The Modern World System: Mercantilism and the Consolidation of the European World Economy, 1600–1750.* New York: Academic Press, 1980.

Walton, Whitney. " 'To Triumph before Feminine Taste': Bourgeois Women's Consumption and Hand Methods of Production in Mid-Nineteenth-Century Paris." *Business History Review* 60 (Winter 1986): 541–63.

Warden, A. J. *The Linen Trade: Ancient and Modern.* London: Longman, 1864.

Weber, Eugen. *Peasants into Frenchmen: The Modernization of Rural France, 1870–1914.* Stanford: Stanford University Press, 1976.

Wilcox, Ruth T. *The Mode in Footwear.* New York: Scribner's, 1948.

Willard, Claude. *Le mouvement socialiste en France (1893–1905): Les Guesdistes.* Paris: Éditions sociales, 1965.

Williams, Rosalind H. *Dream Worlds: Mass Consumption in Late Nineteenth-Century France.* Berkeley: University of California Press, 1982.

Young, Arthur. *Voyages en France en 1787, 1788, 1789,* trans. Henri Sée (French) Paris: A. Colin, 1932.

Zdatney, Steven M. "The Artisanat in France: An Economic Portrait, 1900–1956." *French Historical Studies* 13 (Spring 1984): 415–40.

———. *The Politics of Survival: Artisans in Twentieth-Century France.* New York: Oxford University Press, 1990.

Zeitlin, Jonathan. "Les voies multiples de l'industrialisation." *Le mouvement social* 133 (October–December 1985).

Index